57840

CW01083493

# INTELLECT AND CHARACTER IN
# VICTORIAN ENGLAND

In the Victorian period English universities were transformed beyond recognition, and the modern academic profession began to take shape. Mark Pattison was one of the foremost Oxford dons in this crucial period, and articulated a distinctive vision of the academic's vocation frequently at odds with those of his contemporaries. In the first serious study of Pattison as a thinker, Stuart Jones shows his importance in the cultural and intellectual life of the time: as a proponent of the German idea of the university, as a follower of Newman who became an agnostic and a thoroughly secular intellectual, and as a pioneer in the study of the history of ideas. Pattison is now remembered (misleadingly) as the supposed prototype for Mr Casaubon in George Eliot's *Middlemarch*, but this book retrieves his status as one of the most original and self-conscious of Victorian intellectuals.

H. S. JONES is Reader in Intellectual History at the University of Manchester. His previous publications include *The French State in Question* (Cambridge, 1993), an edition of Auguste Comte's Early Political Writings for the Cambridge Texts series (1998) and *Victorian Political Thought* (2000).

# INTELLECT AND CHARACTER
# IN VICTORIAN ENGLAND

*Mark Pattison and the Invention of the Don*

H. S. JONES

CAMBRIDGE
UNIVERSITY PRESS

CAMBRIDGE UNIVERSITY PRESS

Cambridge, New York, Melbourne, Madrid, Cape Town, Singapore, São Paulo

Cambridge University Press
The Edinburgh Building, Cambridge CB2 8RU, UK

Published in the United States of America by Cambridge University Press, New York

www.cambridge.org
Information on this title: www.cambridge.org/9780521876056

© H. S. Jones 2007

This book is in copyright. Subject to statutory exception
and to the provisions of relevant collective licensing agreements,
no reproduction of any part may take place without
the written permission of Cambridge University Press.

First published 2007

Printed in the United Kingdom at the University Press, Cambridge

*A catalogue record for this book is available from the British Library*

*Library of Congress Cataloguing in Publication data*
Jones, H. S. (H. Stuart)
Intellect and character in Victorian England : Mark Pattison and the invention of the don / H. S. Jones.
p.   cm.
Includes bibliographical references and index.
ISBN 13: 978-0-521-87605-6 (hardback)
ISBN 10: 0-521-87605-2 (hardback)
1. Pattison, Mark, 1813–1884.   2. Lincoln College (University of Oxford) – Presidents –
Biography.   3. College presidents – England – Biography.   I. Title.
LF624.P3J66   2007
378.1′′11
[B]     2007002296

ISBN 978-0-521-87605-6 hardback

Cambridge University Press has no responsibility for
the persistence or accuracy of URLs for external or
third-party internet websites referred to in this book,
and does not guarantee that any content on such
websites is, or will remain, accurate or appropriate.

# Contents

v

# *Acknowledgements*

I am grateful to Dr Mark Curthoys and the late Professor Colin Matthew, who, more than twelve years ago, commissioned me to write the article on Pattison for the *Oxford Dictionary of National Biography*. They also followed Sir Leslie Stephen's example and recognized Pattison's importance with a generous word limit. It was in working on that article that I first saw the need for a proper study of Pattison's thought, although I did not conceive the intention of writing such a work until much later.

The staff of many libraries have helped me in the course of my work. The book rests chiefly upon the huge collection (over 140 volumes) of Pattison's papers in the Bodleian Library, and I must therefore single out in particular the staff of Duke Humfrey's Library and the Modern Papers Room for their assistance. I am also indebted to Andrew Mussell, Archivist of Lincoln College, and Fiona Piddock, the Librarian, who were generous with their help. In Oxford I also drew on the resources of the libraries of All Souls and Balliol Colleges, and of Pusey House. Elsewhere I had valuable help from the staff of St Deiniol's Library, the John Rylands University Library of Manchester, Manchester Central Library and the Harry Ransom Humanities Research Center at the University of Texas at Austin.

The research and writing of the book was funded by the British Academy, the Arts and Humanities Research Board (now Council), and the University of Manchester. Mrs Anne Walters provided invaluable research assistance which enabled me to work through the Pattison papers in the Bodleian much more rapidly than would otherwise have been possible. The University of Manchester granted me the necessary research leave, and the Master and Fellows of St Catherine's College, Oxford elected me to a Visiting Fellowship for the Michaelmas Term 2003, which gave me a base from which to pursue my research and agreeable company while doing so.

Professor Jose Harris, Mr William Thomas and Professor Gregory Claeys wrote references in support of applications for funding. I am also grateful to Dr Brian Young and Dr Mark Curthoys for reading draft chapters. I have benefited in various ways from the advice and assistance of Professor Donald Sniegowski, Dr Peter Nockles, Dr Ruth Clayton Windscheffel, Dr Ruth Morello, Miss Pauline Adams and the late Revd Dr V. H. H. Green.

Cambridge University Press continues to be an invaluable patron of the history of ideas, and I am especially grateful to Richard Fisher for his advice and encouragement. Three anonymous referees provided exceptionally pertinent criticism and encouragement.

# Introduction. The invention of the don

'It may be said with deliberation, and without fear of contradiction from any competent authority, that in Mr Mark Pattison the University of Oxford has lost by far the most distinguished of her resident members.'[1] So wrote the *Saturday Review* in August 1884, on the death of the rector of Lincoln College. This was a strong assertion to make at a time when the University housed Benjamin Jowett, Max Müller and John Ruskin, but the spirit of the remark was echoed in other obituaries in the national press, and it captures the extraordinary reputation Pattison enjoyed at the end of his life. He occupies a shadowy presence in Victorian studies today, but his contemporaries would have been surprised to find that his intellectual distinction has been lost from view by historians. In his last decade he enjoyed nationwide renown for the exceptional qualities of his mind; and that renown reached continental Europe too. Even his antagonists recognized that they were dealing with a man of rare ability. Jowett, who was more aware than most of his personal deficiencies, could nevertheless call him a genius.[2]

Pattison lived through a formative period in the history of the modern university in England, and in his person he embodied many of the transformations that occurred in the half century he spent at Oxford. To re-trace his life and thought is therefore to explore through the eyes of a key figure the elements of that transition to the modern university: the secularization of intellectual life, the emergence of the professional academic, and the challenge posed by the emergent German idea of the university to the traditions of English university life. When Pattison arrived at Oxford as an undergraduate in 1832, the University's chief purpose was to provide a gentlemanly education for intending clergy. As many as a half of Oxford

---

[1] *Saturday Review*, 2 August 1884.
[2] Benjamin Jowett to unknown correspondent (either Lady Airlie or Lady Abercromby), 27 July 1884, and Jowett to Morier, 22 Oct. 1876, Jowett papers, Balliol College, Oxford, I F 2/40, and III M67.

undergraduates would go on to take holy orders, whereas law, the next most popular profession, claimed just one in twenty.[3] The college fellows were themselves mostly required to be in holy orders, and they thought of themselves as clergy rather than as academics in the modern sense.[4] They were not required to be resident; and those who were resident thought of this as a pleasant interlude in their lives until a college living fell vacant and they could therefore afford to marry – at which point they would be forced to resign their fellowships, which were held on condition of celibacy. There were a small number of professors – twenty or so – and they were allowed to marry, but these were not regarded as full-time posts requiring residence in Oxford. They might well be held in plurality with other offices, as Richard Whately, for example, combined the professorship of political economy with the archbishopric of Dublin. There was, in other words, no concept of an academic profession as a lifelong vocation: only about one college fellow in eight would spend his entire active career in Oxford or another university.[5] The religious and ecclesiastical character of the University was, moreover, reasserted by the Tractarian Movement which dominated Oxford's intellectual life, and Pattison's too, for a decade and a half after his matriculation. There was little notion that a university existed for the purposes of research or the advancement of knowledge. There was not even an academic division of labour, for all students who sought honours followed the same classically based curriculum, and all tutors taught all parts of that limited curriculum. The written examination was introduced for the first time in the revised Examination Statute of 1830. Pattison's cohort would be one of the first to experience what has become a *sine qua non* of the modern university.[6]

By the end of Pattison's life, young men who were elected fellows of colleges mostly expected to pursue academic careers. In the last two decades

---

[3] M. C. Curthoys, 'The careers of Oxford men', in M. G. Brock and M. C. Curthoys (eds.), *Nineteenth-Century Oxford*, Part 1 (Volume VI of *The History of the University of Oxford*) (Oxford: Oxford University Press, 1997), p. 503.

[4] In 1840, 60 per cent of fellows were in holy orders, and another 30 per cent were required to proceed to ordination if they wished to retain their fellowships. Lay fellows were chiefly concentrated in All Souls and Merton: M. C. Curthoys, 'The "unreformed" colleges', in Brock and Curthoys, *Nineteenth-Century Oxford*, Part 1, p. 180.

[5] A. J. Engel, *From Clergyman to Don: The Rise of an Academic Profession in Nineteenth-Century Oxford* (Oxford: Oxford University Press, 1983), p. 286.

[6] Written as well as oral exercises formed part of the examination process prior to this reform, but each candidate was examined separately. The first printed examination papers in Literae Humaniores were used in Easter term, 1831: M. C. Curthoys, 'The examination system', in Brock and Curthoys (eds.), *Nineteenth-Century Oxford*, Part 1, p. 347. See also Christopher Stray, 'From oral to written examinations: Cambridge, Oxford and Dublin, 1700–1914', *History of Universities* 20.2 (2005), 76–130.

of the century, a clear majority of those elected to college fellowships would go on to spend their entire professional lives in universities.[7] The ecclesiastical character of the University had largely been eroded: colleges were still required, under the terms of the Universities Tests Act of 1871, to provide religious instruction and daily chapel services, but religious tests were abolished and colleges statutes had been redrafted in the aftermath of the Oxford and Cambridge Universities Act of 1877 to reduce the number of clerical fellowships. Fewer than a third of dons elected in the wake of these reforms were in or proceeded to take holy orders.[8] The marginalization of religion in an increasingly secular University was symbolized by the foundation, in the year of Pattison's death, of 'Dr Pusey's Library' (later Pusey House), the aim of which was to serve as a focus for theological study and the Christian life within the University.[9] Fifty years before, Pusey and Newman would have assumed that these were integral dimensions of the work of a college, rather than a differentiated need to be met at the edges of the University's life. At the same time, academic specialization took root: in 1864 classical Greats lost its compulsory status, and in 1882 faculties were created (or re-created) and endowed with control of the honour schools within their subject areas.[10] The examination system, still experimental when Pattison was an undergraduate, would, in the course of his lifetime, not only transform Oxford but reshape civil society throughout the advanced nations. Oxford itself houses a giant monument to this system, for the University's largest single building project in the nineteenth century was the construction of the Examination Schools on the High Street, completed to the designs of T. G. Jackson between 1876 and 1882 at an eventual cost of over a hundred thousand pounds.[11] In the words of G. M. Young, England was marching 'through the gateway of the Competitive Examination ... out into the Waste Land of Experts, each knowing so much about so little that he can neither be contradicted nor is worth contradicting'.[12]

---

[7] Engel, *From Clergyman to Don*, p. 286.

[8] A. G. L. Haig, 'The church, the universities and learning in later Victorian England', *Historical Journal* 29 (1986), 187, correcting an incorrect figure given by Engel, *From Clergyman to Don*, p. 286.

[9] Peter Hinchliff, 'Religious issues, 1870–1914', in M. G. Brock and M. C. Curthoys (eds.), *Nineteenth-Century Oxford*, Part 2 (Volume VII of *The History of the University of Oxford*) (Oxford: Oxford University Press, 2000), p. 107.

[10] Curthoys, 'Examination system', pp. 352–3, 355.

[11] Peter Howell, Oxford architecture, 1800–1914', in Brock and Curthoys, *Nineteenth-Century Oxford*, Part 2, p. 749.

[12] G. M. Young, *Victorian England: Portrait of an Age* (London: Oxford University Press, 1936), p. 160.

This period of reform was decisively important in the history of European universities. Today we take the university's existence for granted. The western university as it took shape in its modern form in the course of the nineteenth century has been exported to the rest of the world too, because it was seen as an integral component of what a modern society should be.[13] Universities in former European colonies in Africa and Asia were moulded on the pattern of their European counterparts, borrowing a classification system invented in nineteenth-century Oxford and Cambridge and adopting forms of academic dress which trace their origins back to scholars' robes in medieval Europe. Yet things might have been very different. We can imagine different modes of professional training than full-time education beyond the age of eighteen, but even if we accept that model, why does it follow that the institutions entrusted with this 'higher' education should also assume the very different function of 'research' – the discovery of new knowledge? At the beginning of the nineteenth century no university conceived its central purpose in this way, and as demands for institutional provision for research grew in the nineteenth century, there were many who believed that this function did not properly belong with universities at all, but could be more effectively performed by specialized institutions such as academies. Had universities not developed in such a way as to appropriate the role of pushing back the frontiers of knowledge they would not today possess anything like the cultural centrality they do enjoy.

Indeed, an observer of European universities at the time of Pattison's birth in 1813 might reasonably have seen them as part of Europe's *ancien régime*, destined to be swept away by the revolutionary wave inspired by the enlightened and critical spirit of the previous century. For universities were privileged corporations – the Latin word 'universitas' signified a guild or corporation – of exactly the kind that was under attack in the age of Enlightenment and revolution. They also had a limited curriculum, mostly confined to law, theology and medicine, that was typically studied through time-honoured textual authorities, and this was precisely the kind of deference to hallowed authority that Enlightenment *philosophes* aimed to sweep away.[14] French universities were indeed dissolved by the National Convention in 1793, as embodiments of the 'spirit of corporation' that was

---

[13] Edward Shils and John Roberts, 'The diffusion of European models outside Europe', in Walter Rüegg (ed.), *Universities in the Nineteenth and Early Twentieth Centuries* (Volume III of *A History of the University in Europe*) (Cambridge: Cambridge University Press, 2004), p. 164.
[14] L. W. B. Brockliss, 'The European university in the age of revolution, 1789–1850', Brock and Curthoys (eds.), *Nineteenth-Century Oxford* Part I, pp. 84–9.

the enemy of the 'career open to talents', and they did not regain an autonomous institutional standing until the end of the nineteenth century.[15] Instead, at Talleyrand's instigation, the French Republic set about creating the network of professional schools which have remained a distinctive feature of the landscape of higher education in France. Reformers elsewhere, and not least in Germany, sought to follow France's lead. The Revolutionary and Napoleonic era saw the number of universities in Europe slashed from 143 to 83.[16] By the end of the eighteenth century, in the words of one historian, 'most European governments now viewed the university as a terminological anomaly'.[17]

That the European university survived, and in the end prospered, was essentially due to the distinctive German response to the French-inspired assault on the university. 'The institution ultimately survived on the Continent', Brockliss has written, 'because the Germans invented the research university'.[18] Challenged to justify the purpose of the university in the face of these attacks, German philosophers from Kant onwards asserted that the university must claim a higher dignity than mere professional training, which might indeed be more efficiently performed in specialist institutions. The Prussian government had declared in 1770 that 'the ultimate purpose of the universities is the instruction of youth. A professor of a university has fulfilled his office satisfactorily if he thoroughly teaches the youth what is known and discovered in his subject.'[19] By contrast the idealists maintained that the university's higher purpose lay in the pursuit of knowledge as something intrinsically desirable, and not for the practical benefits it offered. It would not be true to say that the new University of Berlin, founded at the instigation of Wilhelm von Humboldt in 1810, marked the triumph of the research ideal, for German universities remained chiefly focused on professional training. But the new university attracted scholars – such as Hegel in philosophy and Ranke in history – who did not regard themselves as mere teachers, but stood at the forefront of new work in their fields. This was the idea of the university which, more than any other, transformed the functioning of learning and higher education in nineteenth-century Europe.

[15] George Weisz, *The Emergence of Modern Universities in France, 1863–1914* (Princeton: Princeton University Press, 1983), especially pp. 134–61.
[16] Walter Rüegg, 'Themes', in Rüegg (ed.), *Universities in the Nineteenth and Early Twentieth Centuries*, p. 3.
[17] Brockliss, 'European university', p. 101.   [18] Brockliss, 'European university', p. 103.
[19] Brockliss, 'European university', p. 104.

The English universities – and there were only two – were not immune to the attacks directed at their counterparts on the continent. The English Enlightenment was moderate in comparison with its French analogue, but in eighteenth-century England too there was a battle of the ancients and the moderns, an identifiable antagonism between the polished intellectual world of metropolitan letters and the supposedly pedantic academic mind of Oxford and Cambridge: polite learning versus clerical antiquarianism. For Gibbon, the clerical dons of Oxford and Cambridge were men 'whose manners are remote from the present world, and whose eyes are dazzled by the light of philosophy'.[20] Something of this antagonism survived into the nineteenth century. Reformers such as the associates of the *Edinburgh Review* continued to see Oxford and Cambridge as an *ancien régime* right up to 1850, when the Whig prime minister Lord John Russell, a graduate of Edinburgh, set up a Royal Commission to enquire into the affairs of the University of Oxford. In the first half of the nineteenth century Oxford and Cambridge were socially privileged but would not generally have been regarded as the intellectual power-houses of the nation.

By the 1880s the standing of European universities had been transformed. Far from appearing to be anachronisms, they were increasingly regarded as central institutions of modern society. In England, Oxford and Cambridge had attained a position of intellectual ascendancy which they would continue to enjoy for most of the twentieth century.[21] We should not exaggerate the extent of the transformation: even by the end of the nineteenth century a sizeable minority of fellows of colleges were not engaged in educational work, and 'university teacher' did not become a census category until 1921.[22] Universities remained largely independent of the state: royal commissions instigated reform at Oxford and Cambridge, but in Pattison's lifetime there was no state funding for English universities.[23] Nevertheless, it is difficult to find, at least before the end of the twentieth century, a single period of fifty years in which English universities

---

[20] Quoted by T. W. Heyck, *The Transformation of Intellectual Life in Victorian England* (London: Croom Helm, 1982), p. 65.

[21] Stefan Collini, *Public Moralists: Political Thought and Intellectual Life in Britain 1850–1930* (Oxford: Oxford University Press, 1991), pp. 19, 22–3.

[22] Collini, *Public Moralists*, pp. 206–7.

[23] The only exception to this is the University of London, established as a state-supported institution in 1836. But it was simply an examining and not a teaching body: Sheldon Rothblatt and Martin Trow, 'Government policies and higher education: a comparison of Britain and the United States, 1630–1860', in Colin Crouch and Anthony Heath (eds.), *Social Research and Social Reform: Essays in Honour of A. H. Halsey* (Oxford: Clarendon 1992), pp. 194–5.

changed more fundamentally than they did in the half-century Pattison spent at Oxford.

These changes have been traced in detail by a number of historians since the study of the history of universities began to flourish in the 1960s. Arthur Engel and Sheldon Rothblatt have published detailed studies of the making of the academic profession with particular reference to Oxford and Cambridge respectively.[24] More recently, Michael Brock and Mark Curthoys have brought the eight-volume *History of the University of Oxford* to completion with two rich and authoritative volumes on nineteenth-century Oxford.[25] The European University Association has sponsored a collaborative four-volume *History of the University of Europe*, attracting contributions from a host of grandees. Historians today, following the 'cultural turn', ask a further set of questions about how the 'self-fashioning' of identities: how did the dons of this transitional period 'imagine' the academic profession as a lifelong calling? How did they 'perform' what was essentially a new social role? Pattison was crucial to this self-fashioning of the don. He seems to have conceived the idea of a life devoted to learning at a remarkably early stage, and, moreover, always saw the university as the proper environment in which to nurture such a life. In his posthumous *Memoirs* – which, for good or ill, shaped the way he has been remembered – he unambiguously represented his life as a life consecrated almost from the outset to the academic life.

Ask any group of half a dozen academics what the academic life means to them, and you will surely get seven or eight different answers.[26] There are the researchers, the teachers and the administrators, the public intellectuals and the pastoral tutors. There are the lone scholars, for whom the essence of the academic life is the day spent in the library or the archive; and there are the entrepreneurial professors of rodomontade, whose time is spent in writing grant applications. Some see themselves as educating an elite, whereas others are social engineers who wish to remedy the defects of secondary education and to use the university to combat social inequalities. Most of these types have their prototypes in the nineteenth century. As the university context was transformed, so academics at Oxford and Cambridge had the opportunity to reimagine what it meant to be a don. This was the era which saw the invention of the tutorial as the centrepiece

---

[24] Engel, *From Clergyman to Don*; Sheldon Rothblatt, *The Revolution of the Dons: Cambridge and Society in Victorian England* (London: Faber and Faber, 1968).

[25] Brock and Curthoys (eds.), *Nineteenth-Century Oxford*, Parts 1 and 2.

[26] Some of the varieties of donnishness are explored by Noel Annan, *The Dons: Mentors, Eccentrics and Geniuses* (London: HarperCollins, 1999).

of an Oxford education, and this was accompanied by the emergence, in the wake of Newman, of the pastoral conception of the don. Some college fellows saw their role as akin to that of schoolmasters, and indeed in the later Victorian period it was quite possible to move from a mastership at a public school to a fellowship at a college, from a fellowship of a college to the headship of a school, or from the headship of a school to the headship of a college.[27] Colleges generally thought it desirable to have one or two tutors at least who would maintain close relations with the undergraduates, and not just their own pupils, perhaps by means of a sustained interest in the rowing club or other college sports. Former schoolmasters were thought particularly good at performing this role. Others, such as Benjamin Jowett at Balliol, revelled in the opportunities they had to train their pupils for examination success and to form the governing elite. Jowett and his like were not hearty, schoolmasterly dons, for they assumed that the governing elite should also be an intellectual elite. But they took 'usefulness in life' as the measure of their success, and construed their role as shaping men who would go out into the world and be worldly successes.[28]

Pattison was not a great university reformer, as Jowett and Sidgwick among his contemporaries could justly claim to be. He was no administrator, and declined the opportunity to act as Oxford's vice-chancellor when it was his turn. He shaped no institution which serves as his memorial. He matters because he stood for a particular vision of what it meant to be a don, and this was grounded in a sense that the university had a noble purpose to serve. He was quite clear what distinguished his vision from Jowett's. 'The separation between Jowett & myself consists in a difference upon the fundamental question of University politics – viz. Science & learning v. School keeping. Two men who are opposed on this point, cannot, as things are now, be in sympathy on any other.'[29] He was harsh in reducing Jowett's conception of his role to school keeping, but what emerges strongly from this quotation is not just his animosity towards his great rival, but also his sense that the University was riven by conflicts

[27] On the experience of former headmasters as college heads, see M. C. Curthoys, 'The colleges in the new era', in Brock and Curthoys, *Nineteenth-Century Oxford*, Part 2, pp. 128–9. In 1886, however, Henry Sidgwick complained of 'the snub given to academic work' when the headmaster of Harrow was translated to the mastership of Trinity College, Cambridge: Sheldon Rothblatt, *Tradition and Change in English Liberal Education: An Essay in History and Culture* (London: Faber and Faber, 1976), p. 183.

[28] Annan, *The Dons*, p. 62.

[29] Pattison to Meta Bradley, 22 May 1881, Pattison papers, Bodleian Library, MS Pattison 121 ff. 129–30.

over the very nature of the academic vocation. Pattison had a much more vivid sense of that vocation than any of his contemporaries. The academic vocation was a calling to the lifelong task of mental cultivation for its own sake.

Where did this conception of the academic vocation come from? It strongly resembles the idea of the philosophical life expounded by the German idealists and neohumanists – by Kant and Fichte, Schleiermacher and Humboldt. Pattison made a number of visits to German universities from the 1850s onwards, was certainly influenced by Fichte's writings on the vocation of the scholar, and became known as a proponent of the German idea of the university. But this study also highlights an enduring influence about which Pattison was distinctly more ambivalent: that of the Oxford Movement (Tractarianism) in general and of Newman in particular. This might strike the reader as surprising. The Tractarians were resolute in their defence of the local traditions of Oxford against the invasion of German scholarship, which they regarded as rationalist in temper, and against the institution of a professorial mode of instruction. Their leader, Dr Pusey – himself a professor, although he eschewed the title – thought that there was something idolatrous about the attempt to magnify professorial teaching.[30] Today, the Humboldtian idea of the 'research university' continues to be contrasted with Newman's tutorial conception of the university: indeed, the current vice-chancellor of the University of Oxford has made this point more than once in his public pronouncements on the 'conceptual foundations' of today's 'research-led' universities.[31] But there were more similarities between Humboldt's and Newman's visions of the university than this account suggests, and Pattison was led to his own distinctive understanding of the academic life through his profoundly important encounter with the Oxford Movement in the 1830s and 40s.[32] At the end of his career he was, though an Anglican priest, a thoroughly secular don; but his donnishness was permanently shaped by the clericalism of the Tractarians. On the mantelpiece of his study he kept, to the end of his life, a framed photograph of Newman.[33]

---

[30] W. R. Ward, 'From the Tractarians to the Executive Commission, 1845–1854', in Brock and Curthoys, *Nineteenth-Century Oxford*, Part 1, p. 328.

[31] John Hood, Sir Robert Menzies Oration on Higher Education, University of Melbourne, 11 October 2001, quoted in *Oxford Today* 17.1 (Michaelmas 2004), 14.

[32] R. D. Anderson, *European Universities from the Enlightenment to 1914* (Oxford: Oxford University Press, 2004), p. 197.

[33] [T. F. Althaus], 'Recollections of Mark Pattison', *Temple Bar* 73 (1885), 32.

Pattison is important because no other British thinker has reflected so compellingly and with such seriousness on the nature of the academic vocation and the proper purpose of a university. In the last twenty years British universities have undergone an upheaval comparable in scale to that which the ancient English universities experienced in Pattison's lifetime. But whereas Victorian university reform was nourished by a remarkable quality of reflection on what universities were for, university policy today is apparently pragmatic and unenlightened by any philosophical consideration of the purpose of the 'higher education sector'. 'Research' is more important to universities than ever before, and claims a larger share of their budgets; but one can hardly imagine that Pattison, the apostle of the 'endowment of research', would have been gratified by the outcome. A 'vibrant research culture' dominated by monitoring of 'outputs' and by research projects with discrete 'aims and objectives' as required by funding bodies would have seemed to him just as alien to the philosophical life as were the endless board and committee meetings and the examination and prize-awarding culture of Victorian Oxford; 'all the objects of science and learning, for which a university exists, being put out of sight by the consideration of the material means of endowing them'.[34] The urge to be busy – whether in marking scripts and attending examination boards, or in giving an endless round of international conference papers and completing the latest research outputs – is always, Pattison would have thought, a betrayal of the academic's vocation to *think*. He was too much of an idealist, and too easily repulsed by pragmatic compromise, to be an effective reformer; and he offered no practical blueprint for change. His insistence on the spiritual and ascetic aspects of the academic's vocation seems remote from today's concerns. But in his ability to articulate an ideal of academic life he had a prophetic quality which remains as resonant today as it was to the Victorians. He warns us not to become so caught up in the machinery by which academic life is conducted that we forget the ends for which it exists.

There is a literature on Pattison, but it belongs essentially to the 1950s and 60s, and is dominated by the work of two memorable Oxford college heads, John Sparrow and Vivian Green.[35] There was no hagiographical 'life and letters' published in the shadow of his death: his widow, who quickly

---

[34] Mark Pattison, *Memoirs* (London: Macmillan, 1885), p. 90.

[35] John Sparrow, *Mark Pattison and the Idea of a University* (Cambridge: Cambridge University Press, 1967); V. H. H. Green, *Oxford Common Room: A Study of Lincoln College and Mark Pattison* (London: Arnold, 1957); V. H. H. Green, *Love in a Cool Climate: The Letters of Mark Pattison and Meta Bradley 1879–1884* (Oxford: Oxford University Press, 1985).

remarried, had too painful a memory of the marriage to want to dwell on her late husband's life, and she certainly felt that in bringing his *Memoirs* to publication she had fulfilled her duty to him. That volume painted such an unappealing portrait of its author that interest in him was stifled. Furthermore, there is something curious about the literature that does exist on Pattison. He was a man who was devoted to the life of the mind, who prized fundamental intellectual inquiry above all things; yet no study of him has engaged centrally with the nature of his intellectual endeavours or with the substance of his thought. Both Green and Sparrow were more interested in the man than in his ideas. Sparrow professed to explore Pattison's 'idea of the university', but in fact showed remarkably little interest in Pattison's work and his thought, and the section of his book which has attracted most attention was the chapter in which he offered some controversial conjectures on his representation in literature. Sparrow long contemplated a major biography of Pattison, and it has been specu-lated that this might have been 'a masterpiece of intellectual history, like Noel Annan's Leslie Stephen'.[36] But in fact he eschewed a direct engage-ment with Pattison's writings, excepting only the *Memoirs*, an edition of which he prepared but did not bring to publication. The cache of Pattisonia he left to Lincoln College includes his extensive notes on the Bodleian manuscripts, but neither there nor in his papers at All Souls is there even a single note, so far as I have discovered, on any of Pattison's writings. He prepared an elaborate genealogy of the Pattisons, and assembled a remarkable collection of photographs and autographs of family members; but nowhere, it appears, did he make a systematic record of Pattison's published writings. Yet, given that so much of his work was published anonymously, that has to be the starting point for anyone aiming to get to grips with Pattison's thought.

Pattison's life was lived too much in the mind for a straightforward biography to be possible. But thought was so intimately bound up with the man that a monographic study of his thought would be equally unsatis-factory. His importance was not just that he expounded a particular idea of the university but that in his person he stood for a distinctive conception of the academic's vocation. He was regarded by those who knew him as a striking and remarkable personality. 'It was almost universally felt', wrote a distinguished pupil, 'that the Rector was an uncommon and original man; that he was not a copyist or echo of any individual or coterie, and that when he delivered a judgment no one gained by neglecting to attend to

---

[36] Geoffrey Wheatcroft, 'A lazy life lived grandly', *New Statesman*, 25 September 1998.

it.'[37] Like Annan's famous study of Leslie Stephen, this book therefore aims to combine a strong biographical framework with a detailed analysis of ideas. The first part of the book combines a biographical account of his life with an exploration of a variety of representations of that life: his self-representation in his *Memoirs*, his public reputation both in his own day and posthumously, and some of the fictional representations of the man. The second part focuses on Pattison the thinker. It begins by tracing the evolution of his sense of the vocation of the scholar: this remained deeply ascetic, and I argue that it was enduringly shaped by the Tractarian phase which Pattison himself was inclined to represent as a diversion from his vocation. His life of Isaac Casaubon is analysed here as his maturest statement of his understanding of the nature of scholarship. Chapter 5 assesses Pattison's distinctive contribution to the debates on university reform, and shows that that contribution has been distorted by his assimilation to the 'endowment of research' party which he inspired. And finally I consider Pattison as one of the pioneers of the study of the history of ideas, and suggest that for him intellectual history was not merely a discipline or sub-discipline, but was integral to his whole conception of the life of the mind.

A study of Pattison's thought must proceed rather differently from the usual approach of the intellectual historian. He did not expound a doctrine, and indeed was resistant to the appeal of intellectual systems. So it is not possible to organize such a study around the elucidation of a logically ordered body of thought. Moreover, although he regarded it as incumbent upon the philosopher to be up to date with the latest movements of thought, he also had a horror of platitude and was inclined to react against intellectual fashions and preferred to derive his inspiration from the history of thought rather than from his contemporaries. It is therefore not easy to contextualize him by showing how he intervened in the polemics of the day. Instead I have set out to evoke an intellectual temper, a cast of mind which, in spite of its antipathy to cut-and-dried systems, spoke with a remarkable consistency in a range of contexts over a period of thirty years. That intellectual temper is best communicated not through paraphrase, but in Pattison's own words. He was an eminently quotable writer with a gift for a pithy epigram which could encapsulate the nub of an issue or the strengths and weaknesses of a thinker or a body of thought. I make no apology for frequent recourse to direct quotation in this book. The flavour of Pattison's writings could not otherwise be conveyed at all.

[37] James Cotter Morison, 'Mark Pattison. In Memoriam', *Macmillan's Magazine* 50 (Oct. 1884), 401.

PART I

*Lives*

CHAPTER I

## *'No history but a mental history'*

'The existence of an autobiography', Friedrich Hayek once speculated, 'may be the cause of our knowing less about its subject.'[1] Certainly the student of Pattison's career has to address the difficult question of how to construct a biographical account that makes proper use of his own testimony as an authority, while at the same time reading it critically and probing its limitations. The same problem has confronted biographers of other famous autobiographers, from St Augustine to Mill. Augustine's most recent biographer has observed that if we are to understand his life we need to avoid the snares he has laid for posterity, but also to respect his own version of the story. 'If we will wring a real confession or two from him against his will, we must first listen to the story he wants to tell us.'[2] This is wise counsel that can be applied to other subjects too. Both Mill and Pattison were intellectuals who wrote their autobiographies as histories of a mind, and it is for that reason that their autobiographies present peculiar problems for later historians. Reading autobiographies critically is an everyday task for the historian, who has to address not only the fallibility of memory but also the desire of their subjects to present their own lives in the most favourable possible light and so to weave webs of myth in which later generations have become entangled. Historians of nineteenth-century Oxford have of course had to read Pattison's *Memoirs* critically in order to use the volume as a source on Tractarianism or the quality of education in the University prior to the era of reform. But the intellectual biographer of Pattison has to be centrally concerned with his subjectivity, and for this purpose the *Memoirs* are an unrivalled source which cannot easily be tested by reference to sources of other kinds. But that cannot mean accepting the authority of the beguiling narrative that Pattison constructs. That narrative

---

[1] F. A. Hayek, *John Stuart Mill and Harriet Taylor: Their Friendship and Subsequent Marriage* (London: Routledge & Kegan Paul, 1951), p. 16.
[2] James J. O'Donnell, *Augustine, Sinner and Saint: A New Biography* (London: Profile, 2005), p. 37.

certainly constitutes a reflection upon his lifetime's quest to make sense of his identity as one who lived for the life of the mind. But it was also an integral part of that quest.

THE WILD BOY OF WENSLEYDALE

Mark Pattison was born in Hornby, a small village of two or three hundred inhabitants some three miles from Catterick in the North Riding of Yorkshire, on 10 October 1813. He was the first child of Mark James Pattison, curate of the parish of Hornby, and his wife Jane, the daughter and heiress of Francis Winn, a banker who had served as mayor of the nearby town of Richmond. His father was a Devonian, born in Plymouth, but the Pattison family claimed French ancestry, and had once spelt their name Patisson. The forename Mark was most unusual in the nineteenth century, but it had been a 'distinguishing praenomen' in the family for 'many generations': as the Rector of Lincoln would later proudly insist, it 'distinguishes us from innumerable Pattisons Scotch'.[3]

Mark James Pattison, a graduate of Brasenose College, Oxford, combined evangelical religion with social pretensions: his favourite reading, apart from the *Oxford University Calendar*, was *Debrett's*.[4] A large part of the attraction of the curacy to him must have been the proximity of the parish to Hornby Castle, seat of the duke of Leeds.[5] The vicar of the parish, one George Alderson, was non-resident, so the curate acted also as chaplain to the duke. The curate of Hornby was, his son recalled, 'a man of great general ability, of popular talents, & great conversational powers', and became a favourite at the castle and even a 'confidential adviser' to the duke.[6] In those days Anglican livings were of greatly varying values and nomination to them commonly rested with lay patrons (sometimes individuals, sometimes corporations such as colleges), and advancement in the church depended heavily on lay social connections.[7] The curate of Hornby

---

[3]  Pattison to Anne Stebbing, 19 October 1874, Lincoln College MS/PAT/1.

[4]  Pattison, *Memoirs*, p. 24.

[5]  The parish was in the peculiar jurisdiction of the Dean and Chapter of York. This is why Pattison told his father in 1840 that 'You know that I have set my heart upon being ordained in the diocese within the territorial limits of which, if not within the jurisdiction – I was born.' Pattison to M. J. Pattison, 16 March 1840, Lincoln College MS/PAT/III. By this he meant the diocese of Ripon, which had in fact been created in 1836. At the time of Pattison's birth Hornby (and Hauxwell too) belonged, curiously enough, to the diocese of Chester.

[6]  Bodleian MS Pattison 138, ff. 10–11.

[7]  The fullest study of the operation of ecclesiastical patronage is Peter Virgin, *The Church in an Age of Negligence: Ecclesiastical Structure and Problems of Church Reform 1700–1840* (Cambridge: James Clarke, 1989), especially pp. 171–90. He finds (p. 173) that 48 per cent of advowsons (or rights of

would certainly have hoped that his relations with the duke would bring him preferment to a lucrative parish.

The ducal family was in fact absent from the castle for much of Pattison's childhood: they lived in Naples from 1816 to 1823, perhaps because gambling debts had forced the duke to rein back his expenditure. During the family's absence the steward and bailiff of the castle would frequently consult the curate, who thus came to wield 'much of the power of the castle'. The Pattison children – eventually there would be two boys and ten girls – were able to use the castle grounds as their private playground, and it was in playing in the woods and ponds there that the young Mark 'insensibly imbibed the love of natural objects, & of animal life' which, he recalled towards the end of his life, 'has been one source of never failing pleasure to me'.[8]

That privilege was lost, at least for a part of the year, on the family's return from Naples in 1823, but their return brought the curate many invitations to dine, and no doubt renewed his hopes of preferment. The duchess ('a foolish woman', Pattison recalled) grew close to Mrs Pattison, and was godmother to her first daughter, Jane. Mark would play several times a week with the second son of the duke and duchess, Lord Conyers Osborne, who was just a year or two older. 'Shields & javelins to hurl at each other, such as we were reading of in Virgil, were our chief delight.'[9] Lord Conyers seems to have been Mark's closest boyhood friend, and was 'a lively, bright, well-mannered, and gracious young man', in contrast to his elder brother.[10]

In the event, preferment did not come from the duke. In 1825 the curate of Hornby was offered the nearby parish of Hauxwell, where he would remain for the rest of his life. The village and rectory of Hauxwell would have a profound and formative influence on the young Pattison's character, even though they were to be his permanent home for only seven years until he went up to Oxford in 1832. The village had only about two hundred inhabitants, and the Pattisons were physically remote even from the hub of village life: the manor of West Hauxwell, which had almost vanished, had only four houses in addition to the rectory and the hall. Pattison, who was not sent to school of any kind, but was educated at home by his father, can have had little contact with boys of his own age. He was already an

nomination to livings) were held by private individuals. 9 per cent belonged to the Crown and 7 per cent to schools, colleges and corporations. The remainder were held by bishops, parish clergy or cathedral chapters.
[8] Bodleian MS Pattison 138, ff. 13–14, 16–17.    [9] Bodleian MS Pattison 138, f. 19.
[10] Pattison, *Memoirs*, p. 20.

undergraduate when his only brother, Frank, was born. His closest friend, and intellectual sparring-partner, was a female cousin, Philippa Meadows, who lived a few miles away at Ainderby. Only once did he even leave Yorkshire before he went up to Oxford. His boyhood was evidently in many ways a strikingly solitary one, in spite of the crowded home. In the *Memoirs* Pattison records at some length his youthful enthusiasm for natural history and for country sports, especially fly fishing, which remained lifelong passions. It was, he surmised, his 'delight in rural objects' that fed the development of his Wordsworthian poetic sensibility. 'When I came in after years to read *The Prelude* I recognised, as if it were my own history which was being told, the steps by which the love of the country boy for his hills and moors grew into poetic susceptibility for all imaginative presentations of beauty in every direction.'[11]

In his *Memoirs*, Pattison would dwell on the enduring effects of his isolated upbringing and would emphasize, in particular, his naïvety as an Oxford undergraduate. But, for someone of his background, a home education was by no means as unusual in the early decades of the nineteenth century as it would become later in the century. To send his son to one of the major public schools would have been a serious financial commitment for the rector of Hauxwell, and in any case at this time they constituted a 'ramshackle and partly discredited form of education available for relatively small numbers of the aristocracy, gentry, clergy, and professional classes'.[12] They were prey to numerous abuses, and evangelicals such as Pattison's parents generally regarded them as brutal and barbaric institutions that undermined the moralizing influence of the home. Among Pattison's near contemporaries, Macaulay and Ruskin were both denied the benefits of a public school education by the scruples of their evangelical parents.[13] On the other hand there were alternatives: Richmond Grammar School, just a few miles away, was a distinguished endowed grammar school which had a strong tradition of sending pupils to Oxford or Cambridge. But a formal schooling was not yet regarded as an essential part of a middle-class upbringing, and country clergy in particular would quite commonly educate their children at home. Copleston and Keble – two of the formative influences on the college Pattison entered in

---

[11] Pattison, *Memoirs*, pp. 33–5.
[12] J. R. de S. Honey and M. C. Curthoys, 'Oxford and schooling', in Brock and Curthoys (eds.), *Nineteenth-Century Oxford*, Part 2, p. 545.
[13] John Tosh, *A Man's Place: Masculinity and the Middle-Class Home in Victorian England* (New Haven and London: Yale University Press, 1999), pp. 104, 117.

1832 – were themselves the products of a home education in a country rectory or vicarage.[14]

If the absence of formal schooling did not make Pattison's upbringing an exceptional one for an Oxford undergraduate, the lack of regular contact with young males would certainly have exacerbated his sense of shock on entering the all-male society of an Oxford college. It is now something of a historiographical commonplace that the middle-class sense of manliness and masculinity was formed by the contrast between the domestic environment, in which the female influence was strong, and the 'public' environment of the all-male institution such as the public school or the college.[15] In Pattison's case the home environment was exceptionally dominated by females and his entry into an all-male institution was unusually late: for it is worth remarking that whereas he was eighteen on arriving at Oxford, Keble had been just fourteen and Copleston fifteen. The crisis he experienced in his early months at Oxford, which he would remember vividly to the end of his life, was in part a crisis of manliness – of the passage from boyhood to adulthood. But it was at least as much about establishing a masculine identity.[16]

OXFORD: DISCOVERING THE SELF

In the *Memoirs* Pattison treats his boyhood only cursorily, although it had been his hope to return to this period at greater length.[17] Instead he announces that he will begin with his arrival in Oxford in 1832. The justification is in large measure that his father had groomed him from boyhood to go to Oxford and to win a fellowship.

There never was any question as to my destination. It was assumed from the cradle upwards that I was to go to Oxford, and to be a Fellow of a college. From about 1825 onwards a Fellowship of Oriel was held up to me as the ideal prize to which I was to aspire. I was never diverted or distracted from this goal of ambition by any alternative career being proposed to me.[18]

[14] Honey and Curthoys, 'Oxford and schooling', p. 548.
[15] See the contributions to Michael Roper and John Tosh (eds.), *Manful Assertions: Masculinities in Britain since 1800*, (London: Routledge, 1991) especially Peter M. Lewis, 'Mummy, matron and the maids: feminine presence and absence in male institutions, 1934–63', pp. 168–89.
[16] The distinction between masculinity and manliness is emphasized by Boyd Hilton, 'Manliness, masculinity and the mid-Victorian temperament', in Lawrence Goldman (ed.), *The Blind Victorian: Henry Fawcett and British Liberalism* (Cambridge: Cambridge University Press, 1989), pp. 60–70.
[17] Pattison, *Memoirs*, p. 1.     [18] Pattison, *Memoirs*, p. 8.

For Mark James Pattison, his undergraduate years had been the high point of his life. That was the time when he had mixed with the social elite; since then, his career had been a disappointment to him, and he no doubt felt that he had not made the most of the opportunities his Oxford education had presented to him. The University evidently loomed large in his conversation, and this helped fire his son's imagination. The young Pattison assiduously studied his father's copy of an Oxford guide book, so that when he and his father visited Oxford to put his name down for admission to Oriel, he impressed his father by knowing where each college was.[19]

It seems likely that the isolation of his upbringing meant that Oxford, and the idea of a university education, bewitched Pattison's youthful imagination far more than they would have done had he been at a public school which routinely sent pupils to one of the universities.

I thought that now at last I should be in the company of an ardent band of fellow-students, only desirous of rivalling each other in the initiation which the tutors were to lead into the mysteries of scholarship, of composition, of rhetoric, logic, and all the arts of literature.[20]

He had probably never met an undergraduate before the visit to Oxford in 1830. On that visit he spoke with Lord Conyers Osborne, his childhood friend, who was by now an undergraduate at Christ Church. Osborne told him that Oriel and Balliol, the colleges which far surpassed the rest in examination success and intellectual distinction, were known in his circle as 'the two prison-houses'. Pattison, however, was not to be put off: 'I was eager to doom myself to either of the prisons'.[21]

He duly matriculated at Oriel in April 1832, and entered into residence there the following month. His undergraduate years are treated at great length in the *Memoirs*, and are well documented both in his diaries and in his correspondence with his parents and sisters. There are two interlocking central themes in Pattison's narrative of this period: on the one hand, he emphasizes his social awkwardness when he went up to Oxford at the age of eighteen, and the acute self-consciousness that afflicted him when thrown into college life; and on the other hand he highlights the gap that separated his high expectations of what a university should be from the reality of Oxford in the 1830s. Historians disagree as to whether they should accept the account Pattison gives of Oriel in the 1830s. They increasingly appreciate that Oxford had reformed itself from within in the first decade of the

[19] Pattison, *Memoirs*, p. 14.    [20] Pattison, *Memoirs*, p. 53.    [21] Pattison, *Memoirs*, p. 23.

nineteenth century, and that the new examination statutes of 1800 and 1807 entailed 'a genuine tightening up in academic standards and discipline'.[22] Along with Balliol and Christ Church, Oriel had been at the forefront of the reforming movement and was certainly the most intellectually high powered of the colleges. Perhaps it was because he knew of Oriel's reputation that Pattison's expectations were so high, and hence were so sharply disappointed. The letters he wrote home as an undergraduate make it clear that the account he gives in his *Memoirs* was an authentic reflection of the impression Oriel made on him at the time, and was not a mere retrospective construction. 'This morning I went to my first lecture at 9', he wrote to his father towards the beginning of his first term, 'and so far from not being put on, had most to do of any body, the others not knowing a word of it.' The dean, Dornford, knew his mathematics only 'like a Parrot, as it is in the book'.[23] As his *Memoirs* emphasize, Pattison was unfortunate in the timing of his arrival at Oriel: three remarkable tutors, headed by Newman, had just been ousted from their tutorships in a dispute with Provost Hawkins over the character of the tutorial arrangements in the college.[24]

We have seen that Pattison had an extraordinarily isolated childhood, which gave him little experience of boys of his own age or of relations with social superiors. As a result of his unfamiliarity with social interaction, his character was underdeveloped. Having arrived in Oxford 'a mere child of nature, totally devoid of self-consciousness, to such a degree that I had never thought of myself as a subject of observation', he now developed 'a self-consciousness so sensitive and watchful, that it came before me and everything I said or did'. This 'became a canker in my character for years afterwards'.[25] This characterless and acutely self-conscious young man was moulded by his surroundings, because imitation was the only way in which he could respond to his fellow men, and he 'succumbed to or imitated any type or set, with which I was brought into contact'.[26] In short, 'I was trying to suppress that which was, all the time, my real self, and to put on the new man – the type by which I was surrounded'.[27] In the *Memoirs* he sets out to show how 'nervous self-consciousness' gave way to 'the substantial development of the real self'.[28]

---

[22] P. B. Nockles, 'An academic counter-revolution: Newman and Tractarian Oxford's idea of a university', *History of Universities* 10 (1991), 137.

[23] Pattison to M. J. Pattison, 7 May 1832 and 21 May 1832, quoted by F. Nolan, 'A study of Mark Pattison's religious experience 1813–1850', D. Phil thesis, University of Oxford, 1978, pp. 27–8.

[24] Pattison, *Memoirs*, pp. 85–8.   [25] Pattison, *Memoirs*, p. 49.   [26] Pattison, *Memoirs*, p. 48.

[27] Pattison, *Memoirs*, p. 54.   [28] Pattison, *Memoirs*, p. 56.

But what was that 'real self'? It was a self fundamentally committed to the life of the mind. Even the gauche and naïve boy from Hauxwell had glimpsed that ideal, which he already thought it was the role of a university to sustain. Why else had his father fondly repeated a sentence from the Eton Latin grammar, the proverb, Pattison wrote, that 'presided over my whole college life': 'Concessi Cantabrigiam ad capiendum ingenii cultum', 'I went to Cambridge to acquire cultivation of mind'?[29] He imagined a university to be 'an honourable company of rivalry in the pursuit of knowledge'.[30] Yet that ideal was utterly remote from the practice of most dons and undergraduates in Oxford in the 1830s, even at Oriel, the college which, with Balliol, represented the intellectual cream of the University. They had no notion of the kind of intellectual curiosity which Pattison had formed even in the desert of Hauxwell.

Such was my simplicity that I had believed that no one went to college but those who were qualified, and anxious, to study. Nor was the difference between the passman and the honour-man a sufficient clearing up of the paradox, for such it seemed to me, that men should flock to a university not to study.[31]

Although the seed of the ideal of intellectual self-improvement had long been planted in Pattison's mind, it did not begin to grow until the long vacation of 1833, after he had spent four terms at Oriel. It was then that he started to keep what he called a 'student's journal' in which he began by setting out a plan of study. It was to that moment that, in retrospect, he traced 'the first stirrings of anything like intellectual life within me'. For his plan of study – absurdly ambitious though it was – had the merit that it was 'a scheme of self-education, rather than of the hand-to-mouth requirements of an examination'. This was the moment when his 'boy's intelligence, receptive of anything I read or heard' gave way to 'the new idea of finding the reason of things'. Pattison had found his real self: 'the principle of rationalism was born in me, and once born it was sure to grow, and to become the master-idea of the whole process of self-education, on which I was from this time forward embarked'.[32]

As he recounts in the *Memoirs*, the grandiose project of self-education which he set out for himself in July 1833 was, from a practical point of view, counter-productive. Its merit was precisely that it soared above the demands of the examiners; but this was also its practical defect. 'I had strongly the desire of knowledge, but not at all the desire of that particular knowledge which the examination test prescribes.'[33] Even when he took a

---

[29] Pattison, *Memoirs*, p. 22.    [30] Pattison, *Memoirs*, p. 105.    [31] Pattison, *Memoirs*, p. 53.
[32] Pattison, *Memoirs*, pp. 120–1.    [33] Pattison, *Memoirs*, p. 133.

private tutor, or 'coach', he made the mistake of engaging C. P. Eden of Oriel, a 'science coach' who 'wanted to reconstruct my education fundamentally, from the bottom upwards', whereas what he really needed was 'one of those routine professionals, who just supply your memory with the received solutions of the patent difficulties of philosophy, as current in the schools at the time'. Later he switched to a 'scholarship coach', whose focus was on the practical demands of the examination, but more time had been wasted.[34] He deferred sitting his finals, but even so when he did he found himself under-prepared and graduated with a second-class degree. He recalls that he was lucky the outcome was not worse.

Pattison says he was despondent at the outcome: 'I saw I must give up my darling dream of getting a fellowship and living a life of study in a college'.[35] In fact things must have been more complicated. He must have known, and his father reminded him, that a first was by no means a prerequisite for a fellowship.[36] For one thing, celibacy restrictions meant that the turnover of fellowships was rapid, and the number of fellowship elections each year far exceeded the number of firsts awarded annually.[37] Each college set its own fellowship examination, and Oriel, in particular, had a reputation for taking no notice of the results of the public examinations when electing to fellowships, since it placed more reliance on its own distinctive and rigorous examination. Newman, famously, had been elected fellow of Oriel in spite of his mediocre degree, which was worse than Pattison's. Pattison was placed in the same class on the same list as J. M. Wilson, who would rise to be president of Corpus Christi. When Pattison was elected at Lincoln his two most junior colleagues had both taken thirds; four other fellows had not taken honours at all, and only two had taken firsts. So the account given in the *Memoirs* over-dramatizes the significance of his degree class. It was probably his intellectual pride that was hurt, and the injury would have been all the more acute given that examinations were, in those days, genuinely public events: not only were other members of the University allowed to attend, but they would actually do so, since no one could enter as a candidate in the Schools without having first attended two examinations.[38] He also knew that most colleges

---

[34] Pattison, *Memoirs*, pp. 139–42.    [35] Pattison, *Memoirs*, p. 155.

[36] M. C. Curthoys, 'The "unreformed" colleges', p. 170.

[37] The number of firsts in Greats each year was around thirteen at the time Pattison graduated, whereas on average forty fellowships would fall vacant in a typical year: Curthoys, 'The "unreformed" colleges', p. 164; information in firsts from the *Oxford University Calendar*; see also W. R. Ward, 'From the Tractarians to the Executive Commission, 1845–1854', in Brock and Curthoys (eds.), *Nineteenth-Century Oxford*, Part 1, p. 319.

[38] Curthoys, 'Examination system', p. 345.

habitually elected fellows from their own members, which restricted opportunities, and that his own college's fellowships were the most open and the most fiercely competitive. In any case Pattison persuaded his father to allow him to stay in Oxford to stand for fellowship elections. He stood unsuccessfully at Oriel, at Balliol, and twice at University College, before he was finally elected fellow of Lincoln in November 1839, more than three years after his graduation. 'No moment in all my life has ever been so sweet', he recorded, wholly authentically.[39]

The published text of the *Memoirs* suppresses any reference to an important dimension of Pattison's life at this time, and for long after: the family difficulties stemming from his father's mental illness. In the summer of 1834 he had been committed to a private lunatic asylum near York. This was a traumatic experience and an assault on his dignity: the asylum was, he wrote, 'the most nauseous den to which a clergyman of the Established Church, and that clergyman a gentleman, could have been consigned'. On his return to Hauxwell the rector exercised a tyrannical authority over the family. He attempted, for instance, to forbid any of his daughters to marry, and denounced them from the pulpit.[40]

Religious issues exacerbated this family strife. It was during this period that Pattison became associated with Tractarianism, that movement of High Church renewal in the Church of England that was peculiarly identified with Oriel. His *Memoirs* owed much of their celebrity to the account they offered of his encounter with the Oxford Movement, and to the end of his life Pattison was known as one who had very nearly 'gone over' to Rome with Newman. Most of his sisters followed his lead and adhered to the Tractarian cause, and this exacerbated the rector's erratic behaviour and his sense of being persecuted in his own household. 'Will you take your dinner with the Papists in the dining room', he would ask visitors, 'or with the poor persecuted Protestant here?'[41] He blamed his elder son for infecting the household with heretical doctrines, and for some years banned him from visiting.

## INTO THE TRACTARIAN WHIRLPOOL: NEWMAN AND HIS IMPACT

In the *Memoirs* Pattison has very little to say about his religious upbringing, except for the observation that his father was an evangelical, and that the

---

[39] Pattison, *Memoirs*, p. 183.    [40] Sparrow, *Pattison*, pp. 34–5.
[41] Sparrow, *Pattison*, p. 35.

religious books available to him at Hauxwell were all of that stamp.[42] But the nature of that upbringing has been much illuminated in an important doctoral thesis by Fergal Nolan, which remains unpublished. Nolan stresses the key role played by Jane Pattison, rather than her husband, in shaping the domestic religion of the Hauxwell rectory, and makes extensive use of her commonplace books – to be found among her elder son's papers – to define the nature of that religion. There was a note of spiritual earnestness to be found here, along with a sense of the pettiness of the rewards and achievements of this world in contrast to the blessings of the world to come. Here was something of the asceticism that would colour her son's intellectual life and would be deepened by his encounter with the Oxford Movement.[43]

All that Pattison says about his undergraduate religious beliefs is that he tended towards liberalism, so that he was an ostentatious admirer of Hampden's Bampton Lectures, which generated one of the *causes célèbres* of the time: 'the dissolving power of nominalist logic applied to the Christian dogmas was wholly to my mind'.[44] What he does not mention is the difficulty that this incipient liberalism caused him at home, but Nolan has shown that it almost cost him his academic career. The great majority of fellowships at Oxford at the time were clerical fellowships: that is, their tenure depended upon eventual ordination. A layman who had no intention of proceeding to ordination might hold a fellowship for a few years until such time as the statutes required him to take orders, but that was of little use to Pattison, who saw a fellowship as the means to allow him to fulfil his vocation of a lifetime devoted to study. He took it for granted that that vocation implied ordination.

That, of course, was his parents' understanding too. But for evangelicals such as the rector of Hauxwell and his wife, ordination was a step of the utmost spiritual significance, and must be preceded by signs of a lively faith. Already by May 1834 the rector seems to have been persuaded that his son had become a liberal. He refused to read the Greek Testament with him, because 'I should be contributing my aid to a measure of which I do not approve – your undertaking without direct call of The Spirit of GOD – office of a minister – a sin wh[ich] if you commit – I can tell you from bitter experience you will never cease to deplore thro' your whole life.' In November 1835, when Pattison was preparing to sit his final examinations, the rector insisted that his son must read for the bar on graduation, rather

---

[42] Pattison, *Memoirs*, pp. 15, 173.
[43] Nolan, 'Pattison's religious experience', especially pp. 12–14.  [44] Pattison, *Memoirs*, p. 170.

than remaining in Oxford to seek election to a fellowship. The reason was, again, that he was persuaded that Pattison had become lax in his religious observance and was therefore unfit for ordination.[45] 'That boy of ours', the rector told his wife, 'is perhaps not aware that a fellowship will not avail much unless he takes orders – otherwise he cannot hold it more than seven years'. 'Of this I said you were perfectly aware', reported Jane Pattison to her son, 'but I could not say what your intentions with regard to orders might be. I had never heard your opinion on that subject, nor could I tell what other line you thought of.'[46] Pattison's parents clearly understood that he sought a fellowship to support a life of study, and not simply to launch him in a non-academic profession. Equally clearly, he had been remarkably reticent about the prospect of ordination.

In the *Memoirs* Pattison records his dilemma after graduation as follows:

> At the end of the Long [Vacation, 1836] I went back to Oxford to take my B. A.; as the pursuit of fellowships was but a precarious one it was necessary to choose a profession. My father rather seemed to want me to go to the bar, for which I had myself a great aversion; I acquiesced, however, on the understanding that I was to remain for a year in Oxford and try to get on the foundation of some college.[47]

The impression given here is that Pattison's father wanted him to read for the bar if he were unable to win a fellowship. But correspondence between them at the time suggests that the story was more complicated. The rector of Hauxwell was still unwilling to accept that his son was fit for ordination, and acquiesced in his trying for a fellowship only on the understanding that the bar would be his goal: in other words, that he would hold a fellowship only for a limited period while he established himself in his profession. But Pattison continued to press his father to accept his goal of a 'studious life', should he be elected to a fellowship. He did so in words which are remarkable for the sense of self that they articulate. The idea of a life given over to study, which would constitute the organizing narrative of his *Memoirs* half a century later, was no retrospective construction, but was already embedded in Pattison's consciousness:

> I have lived such a life more uninterruptedly than 1 in a thousand for the whole of my past life, and it is not easy to me to change now so entirely – to fit myself for a life of active business of dealings with men.[48]

---

[45] Nolan, 'Pattison's religious experience', pp. 60, 57.
[46] Jane Pattison to Pattison, 10 March 1836, Bodleian MS Pattison 43, ff. 114–15.
[47] Pattison, *Memoirs*, p. 159.
[48] Nolan, 'Pattison's religious experience', p. 74, quoting Pattison to M. J. Pattison, 7 December 1836, now in Lincoln College MS/PAT/III/1.

This time, his father yielded, and Nolan has persuasively speculated that this was a response to definite signs of a religious awakening in his son from the summer of 1836 onwards. His diary, for example, records his feeling of 'spiritual enthusiasm' in October 1836.[49] By December 1837, when he told his parents of his intention to prepare for ordination, he was living in the house Newman had rented on St Aldate's to accommodate a group of graduates of Tractarian sympathies. There could no longer be any doubt of his earnestness, much as his parents might disapprove of his mentor's churchmanship.[50] Newman's Christianity was not that of Hauxwell, Jane Pattison warned in January of that year. Still, his father no longer objected to his ordination, though his mother continued to urge 'the necessity of an attentive, a searching investigation of the reasons and motives which induce you to think of taking orders'.[51]

The Oxford Movement, or 'Tractarianism', was born in the senior common room of Pattison's own college, Oriel, during his undergraduate years. Its key figures, Newman, Keble and Pusey, were all current or former fellows of the college, and Newman had just been ousted from his tutorship when Pattison arrived. Keble's Assize Sermon, from which the Oxford Movement is conventionally dated, was delivered in Oxford on 14 July 1833, at the end of Pattison's fourth term. It was Newman, as vicar of the University Church of St Mary the Virgin, who was the great charismatic influence: 'I do not believe there has been anything like his influence in Oxford, when it was at its height', wrote Gladstone, 'since Abelard lectured in Paris.'[52] But there is little evidence that the movement had much impact on Pattison during his undergraduate career; and neither did he come under Newman's personal influence in this period.

The movement began as a defence of the rights of the church against state interference. In particular, it sprang from a reaction to the Whig government's decision to suppress ten Irish bishoprics and to divert funds to secular educational purposes. But it went far beyond a mere conservative defence of the status quo against a reforming government, for the assertion of the rights of the church against the state led its proponents to a rediscovery of the spiritual essence at the heart of the institutional church. In broader European terms, it can be understood as the local and Anglican

---

[49] Nolan, 'Pattison's religious experience', pp. 71–7.
[50] Jane Pattison to Pattison, 11 December 1837, Bodleian MS Pattison 43, f. 189, referring to the contrast between Hauxwell and 'the society of the O[riel] common room & Dr Pusey's'.
[51] Nolan, 'Pattison's religious experience', pp. 79–80, 102.
[52] Quoted by C. S. Dessain, *John Henry Newman*, 3rd edn (Oxford: Oxford University Press, 1980), p. 43.

counterpart of the revival of Ultramontanism – or the assertion of papal supremacy – within the Roman Catholic Church in the wake of the French Revolution.[53] For prescriptive privilege alone was insufficient to defend the church against the assertion of parliamentary sovereignty. Instead, the church must rest its claims on its apostolic authority: and that meant a reassertion of its catholicity. Like the Ultramontanes, the Oxford Movement was at once reactionary and radical: its defence of historic claims led it to espouse far-reaching renewal.

What drew Pattison towards Newman and the Tractarians? It is difficult to think of Pattison as a naturally Christian soul, and from 1846 onwards he seems to have been interested in Christianity only from an historical point of view. Geoffrey Faber thought that 'his Tractarianism was only an interlude between the crude Evangelicalism of his youth and the learned polished Agnosticism of his old age'.[54] In fact, however, there is more of a puzzle than Faber acknowledges. Conversions from evangelicalism to Tractarianism were common enough: this was the path Newman himself had followed. Conversions from the kind of religious liberalism that Pattison seems to have espoused as an undergraduate were much less so. Newman defined his entire clerical career as one of resistance to religious liberalism, by which he meant the application of rational criticism to religious dogma. In embracing Tractarianism, was Pattison not deviating from the journey he had begun as an undergraduate? That was the story he told in the *Memoirs*: the whole episode – which lasted almost a decade – was a deplorable lapse of judgement in which the rationalist spirit that he was beginning to embrace as an undergraduate was subdued and almost extinguished. As he depicted it in the *Memoirs*, the Oxford Movement stood in opposition to everything he came to cherish most closely. Newman himself was depicted as a merely reactionary influence who, had he had his way, would have turned Oriel into a seminary.[55]

This same picture of the Oxford Movement as an anti-intellectual force recurs in the works of other apostates: J. A. Froude, for instance, asserted that 'famous as the Tractarian leaders were to become, their names are not connected with a single effort to improve the teaching at Oxford or to

---

[53] In writing this, I am not forgetting that as a cardinal Newman (unlike his fellow convert, Manning) would become a staunch opponent of the Ultramontane party in the Roman church.

[54] Geoffrey Faber, *Oxford Apostles: A Character Study of the Oxford Movement* (London: Faber and Faber, 1933), p. 433.

[55] Pattison, *Memoirs*, p. 87; A. Dwight Culler, *The Imperial Intellect: A Study of Newman's Educational Ideal* (New Haven: Yale University Press, 1955), p. 74.

mend its manners.'[56] But this is a crude and indefensible caricature. In fact, given Pattison's precocious sense that the University stood in need of renewal, one thing that may well have attracted him to the Tractarians was the fact that they were radicals who deplored the formalism and laxity of current academic practices and stood for their rejuvenation. Far from insisting on a narrow defence of the status quo, they were 'motivated by a vision and ideal of a university'.[57] This would have appealed to Pattison, who had a 'restless desire' for improvement, and who all his life identified with the cause of reform.[58] When he describes his early years as a fellow of Lincoln, Pattison explicitly associates the cause of religious seriousness with that of academic reform. 'The juniors, Green, Kay *junior*, Perry, and myself, formed an opposition contending for discipline, decency, order, and religion (outward).'[59] The division here was not one of churchmanship: whereas Pattison was a Tractarian, the younger Kay was a staunch evangelical. It was a generational rift in which academic conservatism was identified with religious laxity. In some respects the Tractarian campaign for the renewal of the University and a heightened sense of its purpose appealed across boundaries of churchmanship, to the 'juniors' – that is, chiefly, younger fellows of colleges – against their seniors.[60] Pattison was an idealist who could not easily tolerate the kind of messy practical compromise which any kind of institutional life demands. It was natural for him to side with those – whether they were radicals or counter-revolutionaries – who stood for spiritual seriousness. The Tractarians were not alone in representing that cause, but for Pattison's generation of young Oxford men they were quintessentially identified with it. In Cambridge, the Apostles, whose characteristic ideal was that of 'personal growth through contemplation', played a comparable role. Their chief intellectual mentor was F. D. Maurice, and their religious orientation was very different from that of the Oxford Movement, but like the Tractarians they had a deep sense of 'the moral bankruptcy of the educational status quo'. They stood for the revitalization of the role of the tutor, much as the Tractarians did in Oxford.[61] As one of Pattison's contemporaries, Dean Church, recalled, the Oxford Movement attracted 'all that was deepest and most vigorous, all

---

[56] Quoted by Culler, *Imperial Intellect*, p. 115.   [57] Nockles, 'Academic counter-revolution', 148.
[58] Pattison, *Memoirs*, p. 254.   [59] Pattison, *Memoirs*, p. 218.
[60] P. B. Nockles, ' "Lost causes and … impossible loyalties": the Oxford Movement and the University', in Brock and Curthoys (eds.), *Nineteenth-Century Oxford*, Part 1, p. 197.
[61] Bart Schultz, *Henry Sidgwick: Eye of the Universe* (Cambridge: Cambridge University Press, 2004), p. 51.

that was most refined, most serious, most high-toned, and most promising in Oxford'.[62]

Given his deep loneliness, Pattison undoubtedly gained some gratification from the sense of belonging to a tight-knit group bound together by ascetic habits of self-denial. The Tractarians fostered a spirituality rooted in self-discipline. Habits of external obedience, they believed, nurtured an inward disposition of submission to God, and Pattison's diaries from this period suggest that he threw himself into the pursuit of this spiritual life with enthusiasm. He fasted on Fridays, and was disgusted at John Hannah, a colleague at Lincoln, for ordering mutton chops on that day.[63] 'I see a great deal of degrading superstition, of fasting and attending endless religious services', he recalled in his *Memoirs*, on reading these diaries from forty years before.[64] Pattison was a regular visitor to the community Newman had established at Littlemore, a village just to the south of Oxford which formed an outlying part of his parish.

It must have strengthened the appeal of the Tractarians to Pattison that, at least in the person of Newman, the group was identified with the cause of learning. This aspect of the Oxford Movement has often been obscured too, not least by Pattison himself, who recalled that the influence of the Tracts had been to suspend 'all science, humane letters, and the first stirrings of intellectual freedom which had moved in the bosom of Oriel'.[65] But when he wrote in more considered vein, he acknowledged that the Tractarian movement had instigated 'a revival of the spirit of learned research', and pointed out that some of its early critics complained that it seemed to make learning the road to salvation, which would thus be blocked to the uneducated.[66] The religious spirit with which Newman and his allies sought to infuse Oxford was anti-rationalistic, but it was not anti-intellectual, and still less was it opposed to the cause of learning.[67] As he describes in his *Memoirs*, Pattison's first scholarly projects were undertaken at Newman's instigation, and these enabled him to acquire not just the taste for research, but also some of its techniques. He collaborated on the edition and translation of Aquinas's *Catena Aurea*, or 'golden chain', an anthology of commentaries on the Gospels by the church fathers. Pattison

[62] R. W. Church, *The Oxford Movement: Twelve Years 1833–1845* (London: Macmillan, 1904), p. 182.
[63] Green, *Oxford Common Room*, p. 102. Hannah was a Tractarian sympathizer, though not a committed Newmanite.
[64] Pattison, *Memoirs*, p. 189.    [65] Pattison, *Memoirs*, p. 101.
[66] Pattison, 'Learning in the Church of England', *National Review* 16 (1863), reprinted in *Essays by the late Mark Pattison sometime Rector of Lincoln College*, ed. Henry Nettleship (Oxford: Clarendon, 1889) II, pp. 269–70.
[67] Culler, *Imperial Intellect*, p. 117.

undertook the section on St Matthew, which stretched to three volumes, and this enabled him to display his bibliographical acumen for the first time. Because Aquinas did not give precise references, Pattison's research for this edition enabled him to acquire a familiarity with 'the whole range of patristic bibliography', and he 'established quite a Bodleian reputation for finding my way about among the writings of the Fathers, genuine and suppositious'.[68] He then contributed two substantial biographies – Stephen Langton and Edmund Rich – to Newman's series of *Lives of the English Saints*. These, he recalled, rested on 'an amount of research, of which no English historian at that time had set the example'. Indeed, the work on the life of Langton stretched over nearly two years in all, and made much use of original sources.[69] Pattison's commitment to the cause of intellectual culture would later induce him to diverge sharply from doctrinal orthodoxy, and in his mature scholarly work he would depict a basic conflict between learning and ecclesiastical authority. But for a time Tractarianism certainly nurtured his commitment to learning, and while he regarded the intellectual quality of some of his fellow Tractarians with disdain, he warmly respected the power of Newman's mind.[70] It would be misleading, then, to suppose that Pattison's Tractarian phase can be interpreted in terms of the temporary ascendancy of the religious impulse over the intellectual, although the *Memoirs* give that impression at times. The alternative narrative offered in the *Memoirs* – that of his intellectual history as a history of continuous growth – is more satisfactory. Under Newman's aegis his commitment to learning blossomed to the point where it could no longer be contained by orthodoxy.

The first phase of the Oxford Movement came to a close on 9 October 1845, when Newman was received into the Roman Catholic Church by Father Dominic Barberi, an Italian Passionist priest. Shortly beforehand he had resigned his fellowship at Oriel, and he now left Oxford for good. 'I have never seen Oxford since', he recalled in 1864, 'excepting its spires, as

---

[68] Pattison, *Memoirs*, p. 181.
[69] Pattison, *Memoirs*, p. 186. Pattison says he wrote two of the lives; R. C. Christie in the *Dictionary of National Biography* says he wrote Langton and Rich. But A. W. Hutton, in appendix II to his 1900 edition of the *Lives*, attributes Ninian and Langton to Pattison, and Edmund Rich jointly to Pattison and Dalgairns. To confuse matters still further, in *Notes and Queries* ser. 7 vol. I (15 May 1886), 395, one of Pattison's sisters, Eleanor Mann, responding to a query, firmly attributed the life of St Augustine of Canterbury to Pattison, and doubted whether he wrote any others. But the diary, Bodleian MS Pattison 128, ff. 30, 34, 43, 54, 63, 101, makes it clear that Langton can be positively attributed to Pattison. MS Pattison 128, ff. 101, 108, 111, makes it clear he also wrote Rich ('St Edmund'), whether on his own or jointly (f. 111: 'Came back and wrote the last of S. Edmund to my great relief', 13 Sept. 1845).
[70] Pattison, *Memoirs*, pp. 209–10.

they are seen from the railway.'[71] Although the conversion is sometimes represented as a watershed, it had been widely expected for two years, when he had resigned the living of St Mary the Virgin; and in some sense it had been inevitable since 1841, when Tract 90, the last and most controversial of the tracts, had been condemned by the bishops of the Church of England. 'It is impossible to describe the enormous effect', wrote Pattison, 'produced in the academical and clerical world, I may say throughout England, by one man's changing his religion. But it was not consternation; it was a lull – a sense that the past agitation of twelve years was extinguished by this simple act.'[72]

It was also, Pattison added, 'a lull of expectation to see how many he would draw with him'.[73] Many expected that Pattison would be one of them, and so some comment is needed here on the nature of his recoil from the Oxford Movement. It was widely believed among his friends that Pattison had been on the verge of converting to Rome in 1845–6. The legend circulated that he would have done so had he not missed a vital coach or train and thus had time to reconsider the decision.[74] Whether or not the legend is true, Fergal Nolan has shown why it was reasonable for his friends to have expected him to convert. Pattison was not just a committed Tractarian; he was clearly identified, from the early 1840s, with the most Romanizing group within the Tractarian party – men such as W. G. Ward, Frederic Oakeley, Charles Seager, J. B. Morris, J. D. Dalgairns and J. R. Bloxam.[75] Ward, Dalgairns and Seager had converted even before Newman. So had Pattison's gifted cousin Philippa Meadows, who had been his closest intellectual companion in his youth. Pattison was seen as a man who was inclined to push arguments to their logical limits, and who was therefore unlikely to remain content with the Anglican *via media*.

The corollary of this analysis is that once he had decided not to convert, Pattison could not but react violently against that same *via media*. There is little to suggest that he had ever possessed that warm and rooted love of the Church of England that was so important, notably, to Keble. As a Tractarian he had become outspokenly critical of Anglicanism. Once he had decided not to have recourse to the authority of Rome, he would

---

[71] John Henry Newman, *Apologia pro vita sua* (Harmondsworth: Penguin, 1994), p. 213. He would revisit Oxford in February 1878, on being made an honorary fellow of his undergraduate college, Trinity. Pattison was one of the guests at the dinner held to mark the occasion.
[72] Pattison, *Memoirs*, pp. 212–3.     [73] Pattison, *Memoirs*, p. 213.
[74] For this legend, see e.g. Goldwin Smith, *Reminiscences*, ed. Arnold Haultain (New York: Macmillan, 1910), pp. 84–5.
[75] Nolan, 'Pattison's religious experience', p. 136.

inevitably take reason as his ultimate principle in matters of religion. Already in 1846 two friends who urged him to convert, Jack Morris and the Brussels priest, the Abbé Donnet, both remarked on the emergence of what Morris called 'scepticism' in Pattison's thinking.[76] This accords with the account given in the *Memoirs*, where Pattison observes that he was led away from Puseyism not by any arguments, but by 'the slow process of innutrition of the religious brain and development of the rational faculties'.[77]

One of the most precious items among Pattison's papers in the Bodleian is a commonplace book that he began in October 1845. The final entries were made in the 1860s, but the early entries can be dated more or less precisely to the crucial period 1845–7. A particularly revealing one was written in January 1846, and has rightly been highlighted by Nolan. This is what Pattison wrote:

There is now a struggle going on within me between love of the world and conviction – but how much more dreadful would not the struggle be should my mind enter on a new phase, and any serious doubts arise of the claims of the church … The most subtle argument against Rome I have yet thought of, stole into my mind tonight (Jany. 14. 1846) and I do not think it right to suppress it – but may God keep me from harm while I write it – Suppose the theory of tradition and development true and granted, suppose the Ch[urch] of Rome to be the true genuine representative of the Ch[urch] of the 1st Cent and the claims of the Protestants as against her to be unfounded – all that is proved is that here is a consistent growth and body of opinion directly swinging from the apostles – but what then? Is the all-comprehensive Being, the Father of all, to be tied and limited by any system, however harmonious, consistent, ancient and apostolic? And if he has given to any individuals the powers of mind to embrace, and the moral nature to rest in, a mental system more comprehensive than this dogmatic one, may he not have intended that system for such persons, just as he has intended the Roman system for those who find in it all they want?[78]

Pattison was here wrestling with two kinds of conflict. On the one hand, there was the conflict between his conviction of the truth of the claims of the Roman Church, and on the other his worldly interests, for it was now apparent that there would be no wholesale 'conversion of England', or reunion with Rome, and that individual conversion on his part would entail the loss of his fellowship and livelihood and the abandonment of his dream of a life of study. But on the other hand he also highlighted the

---

[76] Nolan, 'Pattison's religious experience', p. 387. [77] Pattison, *Memoirs*, p. 208.
[78] Bodleian MS Pattison 7*, pp. 39–41. This volume is numbered by page and not by folio.

tension between any kind of doctrinal orthodoxy and the free life of the mind. Whatever the validity of its apostolic claims, he could be sure that Rome would fetter his intellectual freedom far more tightly than the Church of England would do. The question that faced him was this: was he more convinced of the truth of the claims of the Roman Catholic Church than he was convinced that his own selfhood rested on the free exercise of his mind? This was as much an existential choice as a matter of belief. It was when exercising one's reason, he had written, that one felt one's own personality most keenly.[79] For the time being he was intellectually persuaded by Catholic doctrine as taught by Rome. But what if he were subsequently to come to the conclusion that it was mistaken? To submit to Rome would mean not only resigning his fellowship and hence abandoning his livelihood; it would also mean shackling his intellect and so sacrificing a commitment which for more than a decade he had regarded as constitutive of his very identity.

One of the books that helped him confront these choices was the autobiography of the Spanish-born émigré theologian, Joseph Blanco White. White (1775–1841) had had one of the most curious spiritual journeys of the nineteenth century. The descendant of an Irish merchant who had emigrated to Spain early in the eighteenth century, he was educated in Seville and ordained a priest in the Roman Catholic Church, but lost his faith and migrated to England where he edited a Spanish-language newspaper, with Foreign Office backing, to urge self-government and liberal constitutional reform for the Spanish-American dominions. This won him a pension from the British government.[80] He also embraced Christianity again: ordained in the Church of England, he warned the British public against the dangers of Roman Catholic priestcraft. Elected a member of the Oriel common room, he was close to the group of liberal-minded Oxford Anglicans known as the Noetics. Later, however, he embraced Unitarianism. In his autobiography he vindicates his intellectual integrity in the face of the obvious accusations of inconsistency and apostasy. The book was published in 1845, and Pattison began reading it in August 1846. What struck him in particular was White's insistence on the inherent conflict between free inquiry in matters of religion and submission to credal orthodoxy. This was one of the passages Pattison noted down in his commonplace book:

---

[79] Bodleian MS Pattison 74, f. 104.
[80] G. Martin Murphy, 'White, Joseph Blanco (1775–1841)', *Oxford Dictionary of National Biography*, Oxford University Press, 2004 [http://www.oxforddnb.com/view/article/29260, accessed 12 May 2005].

I feel every day more convinced that as long as I submitted to the yoke, lightly though I bore it, of a Church Creed, I was not in a fair condition to take a correct view of the complicated and much obscured subject of religion. Let no one who calls himself member of an establishment think that he shall be able to judge correctly of such matters.[81]

The speed with which Pattison's theological stance was shifting under the impact of the 'crash' of 1845 was evident in the sympathy he was already expressing for White's Unitarianism:

There is much truth in B. W.'s observation that, 'if Christianity is to become a living power in the civilized parts of the world, it must be under the Unitarian form'. It is the form best adapted to man when his mind is formed by an education which aims only at cultivating the understanding, & does not claim to discipline & direct the affections towards a Deity of definite attributes. As discarding mystery, and all that is unintelligible it finds it's [sic] place readily in refinement founded on the mastery of the mind over all that surrounds it. He says again, 'In the infancy both of each man and of mankind, conviction by reasoning is very difficult, and, if produced, very feeble. The convinced child forgets his conviction in a moment; so it happens with all persons who have not thoroughly practised & applied their mental faculties; so again we see it, whenever disease or low spirits weaken those powers. The only way to convince persons & nations who are in the infant state of mind is awe & astonishment.'[82]

There could be no question of Blanco White's honesty and integrity: 'his life was a martyrdom in the cause of freedom of thought'.[83] It was perceptive of Dean Church to notice White's significance when he recalled how some of Newman's followers – and he surely had Pattison foremost in his mind – responded to their leader's conversion in 1845. 'In others,' he wrote, 'the break-up of the movement under such a chief led them on, more or less, and some very far, into a career of speculative Liberalism like that of Mr. Blanco White, the publication of whose biography coincided with Mr Newman's change.'[84]

Pattison was here engaging with practical questions of the kind that had been raised in abstract terms more than half a century before by Immanuel Kant in his famous essay, 'An answer to the question: what is enlightenment?' Kant took rationality to be fundamental to what makes us human, and he denounced the 'self-incurred immaturity' that made us accept beliefs on trust rather than having the courage to use our own reason. But he was concerned with the problem of the clergyman's obligations towards the church he served. Since the church was held together by common beliefs,

---

[81] Bodleian MS Pattison 7*, p. 79.    [82] Bodleian MS Pattison 7*, p. 84.
[83] Bodleian MS Pattison 7*, p. 87.    [84] Church, *Oxford Movement*, p. 402.

should not the clergyman be obliged to uphold those common beliefs? Kant distinguished – in a way many have found puzzling – between the private use of reason, which could indeed be circumscribed by restrictions of this kind – and its public use, which must be sacrosanct. The clergyman must teach what his church teaches, but he cannot be obliged to believe it, and any oath imposed by church or state authorities requiring him to commit himself to certain dogmas must be regarded as null and void, because it would close off forever 'all further enlightenment of the human race'.[85] Pattison was not faced with the prospect of an oath of this kind. But he was faced with the prospect of a course of action which, though it might coincide with what his reason told him *now*, would effectively – especially if he opted for ordination in the Roman church – cut him off from the possibility of a life devoted to the free cultivation of his mind.

The Victorian age was famous for its crises of faith, many of which were related in autobiographical or fictional form. The striking thing about Pattison's religious evolution, however, is that he passed from Tractarianism to something resembling unbelief without experiencing a crisis of faith or a conversion experience. The nearest thing to a conversion chronicled in his *Memoirs* was not a religious conversion at all, but the moment he defines as that when his mind awoke. After the crisis of 1846 his diaries never again reveal Pattison wrestling with questions of religious belief. He had made his existential choice, for intellectual freedom over credal conformity: henceforth the consequences of that choice simply had to work themselves out in his mind.

THE COLLEGE TUTOR

As a fellow of Lincoln Pattison enjoyed a small stipend in the region of two hundred pounds a year, but this was his for life on condition of proceeding to holy orders and remaining unmarried. It imposed no obligation to teach, or to engage in research, or to undertake any kind of work within the University. The syllabus was largely undifferentiated and each college could therefore manage with two or three tutors drawn from among the resident fellows: fewer than one in eight college fellows at the time were engaged in educational work in Oxford.[86] Lincoln had a small fellowship,

---

[85] Immanuel Kant, 'An answer to the question: what is enlightenment?' [1784], translated by James Schmidt, in James Schmidt (ed.), *What is Enlightenment? Eighteenth-Century Answers and Twentieth-Century Questions* (Berkeley and Los Angeles: University of California Press, 1996), pp. 58–64.

[86] Engel, *From Clergyman to Don*, appendix 8, p. 292.

however, and in 1842 Pattison was appointed college tutor.[87] He later represented this as decisive in preventing him from following Newman in 1845: his tutorial work gave him 'a serious object in life, beyond holding up one of the banners of the Puseyite party'.[88] The work of a college tutor, as Pattison depicts it, was certainly intensive: it consisted in the main of catechetical college lectures, for these were the days before the institutionalization of the individual tutorial based on a student's essay. He records that in one term he had four consecutive hours' lectures each day. In these lectures, which might be attended by about fifteen students, the tutor would ask the students in turn to translate and to construe extracts from the prescribed text, and he would intersperse these exercises with comments on the text and its subject matter. As tutor, Pattison instituted a number of important innovations. Holding the Newmanite conception, which he never lost, of university teaching as the personal influence of one mind on another, he began the practice of seeing his pupils individually after dinner to discuss the progress of their work. Along with contemporaries such as Jowett at Balliol, Richard Congreve at Wadham and H. L. Mansel at St John's, he thus pioneered the individual tutorial as a formal part of the Oxford system of education.[89] He took groups of pupils on vacation reading parties – lasting as long as a month – to the Lake District or the Scottish Highlands, where he would seek to expand their literary and intellectual interests. Above all, he adopted a time-consuming and mentally draining approach to lecturing. In teaching Aristotle's *Ethics*, for instance, he sought to move away from the merely textual and formulaic mode of lecturing that was the norm, and instead sought to get his students to engage with Aristotle's doctrines as 'real truths, which could be assimilated with such ideas on morals and psychology as the student could be said to possess'.[90] In other words, he aimed to instil in his students the ethic of self-improvement which he would also drill into them in his college sermons. Their learning should not consist merely of the acquisition of such formulaic knowledge as would impress their examiners, but should take the form of a continuous rethinking of their view of the world. He called this 'real knowledge'.

---

[87] J. Radford to Pattison, 15 October 1842, Bodleian MS Pattison 60, ff. 8–9. In the *Memoirs*, p. 136, Pattison mistakenly gives the date of the appointment as 1843.

[88] Pattison, *Memoirs*, p. 187.

[89] M. C. Curthoys, 'The "Unreformed Colleges" ', p. 152. These were a varied group of tutors: Mansel was a High Churchman and a Tory, whereas Congreve was a prominent Comtist. Neither was a Platonist nor homosexual, so confounding the argument of Linda Dowling, *Hellenism and Homosexuality in Victorian Oxford* (London: Cornell University Press, 1994), ch. 2.

[90] Pattison, *Memoirs*, pp. 261–2.

Pattison was always an idealist who set high standards both for himself and for others. He conceded that he was not the most successful tutor in terms of the production of firsts, although he nevertheless insisted that Lincoln became known for the efficiency of its tuition. He certainly possessed a charismatic authority that left a lasting imprint on many of his students, some of whom – Richard Christie and William Stebbing, for instance – became his lifelong friends. He writes that he became aware of possessing a 'magnetic influence' over his students which enabled him to acquire a 'moral ascendancy' in the college.[91] The source of this authority did not lie in the dramatic quality of his teaching, but instead in the students' sense of his unique qualities: this was a man, they sensed, who lived for the life of the mind in a way that few others did. Recollections of Pattison commonly observed that he made an unforgettable impression on those who encountered him, and this personal quality was put to best effect in his tutorial work. Some of his former pupils would write to him in extraordinarily reverential terms. This was written by the vicar of Fen Drayton, Cambridgeshire, a decade after his graduation:

You were the first who held out a hand to raise me fr: the slough-of-despond of an extreme (at least intellectual) self-depreciation. You were the man – the very Angel of God – who led me back, by leading strings I cd. neither see nor feel, to the ways of reason & freedom, just as I was blundering on to the brink of spiritual suicide – just as I, under notions of duty, was about to change the name of <u>man</u> for that of machine: of 'free born son of God', for that of 'an obedient child of the Church'.[92]

At the same time Pattison had begun to launch his literary career, writing for High Church periodicals such as the *British Critic* and the *Christian Remembrancer*, chiefly on historical subjects. The connection with the *Christian Remembrancer* was an important one. It was, he subsequently recalled, a party organ; but 'though it discussed questions of criticism from a party, and not from a scientific, point of view, yet [it] did so with candour and moderation'.[93] Its editors, the pioneering ritualist William Scott and Pattison's Oriel contemporary J. B. Mozley, were forceful in urging him to curb his lifelong tendency to brevity and to write more expansively. 'I will tell you what we all think of your articles', Scott wrote in April 1845, when Pattison had published only two pieces for him.

Every one is pleased with them – nothing can be more satisfactory – except their length. Each of them might well be doubled. As somebody said – a <u>fact</u> – the

---

[91] Pattison, *Memoirs*, p. 221.

[92] Frederick Shaw to Pattison, 17 Aug. 1859, Bodleian MS Pattison 52, f. 478.

[93] Pattison, 'Learning in the Church of England', p. 278.

impression is that all our type must be exhausted, you pull up so suddenly. You bring your readers into a delightful country – and then presto! The scene closes as soon as opened.

When Mozley wrote a year later to suggest a piece comparing the French and English 'schools of history', he again urged him to develop his ideas at greater length. 'You ought however not to write a short Article, but a good long one. It is only long articles that tell. This is rather odd, but I can assure you, it is true. Quantity is wanted to tell.'[94] Pattison had a gift for the terse and luminous essay, and this was one of a number of respects in which his own qualities were perhaps not best suited to the age in which he lived. The Victorians valued big books and big articles, because they bore patent testimony to the industry on which they rested.

Pattison wrote here as a Tractarian, and one of Romanizing tendencies. Reviewing Dr Charles Wordsworth's *Diary in France*, which consisted mainly of reflections on French education and religion, he supports the French Catholics' campaign for *liberté d'enseignement*, and suspects Wordsworth of a tendency to Gallicanism in looking to Louis-Philippe to restore the position of the church. 'It is quite humiliating to hear a Christian minister talking in the undisguised way in which Dr Wordsworth does, of making the Church subservient to political ends – and such an end, too, as that of maintaining Louis Philippe on his throne.'[95] At this stage Pattison's European interests were concentrated on France, rather than Germany, and this was in particular because the struggle for the freedom of church was at its most acute there. In his review of Thiers's *History of the Consulate and Empire* he dwelt at some length on the significance of the Napoleonic Concordat. This was a topic dealt with cursorily in most histories of the period, but this must change: 'the Church and the Church's affairs, from filling the last and most obscure corner in our books of history, have come to occupy the most prominent page in them'.[96]

Pattison's later public persona was so laced with anti-clericalism that it is striking to find in these early articles anticipations of many of his distinctive qualities as a critic, and of many of the characteristic opinions of his maturity. Just a few months after Newman's conversion, for example, we find him deploring the influence of 'the blighting spirit of party' over the

---

[94] William Scott to Pattison, 7 August 1845, Bodleian MS Pattison 47, ff. 5–6; J. B. Mozley to Pattison, 14 April 1846, Bodleian MS Pattison 47, ff. 24–6.

[95] [Pattison], 'Wordsworth's Diary in France', *Christian Remembrancer* 10 (1845), 376.

[96] [Pattison], 'Thiers' History of the Consulate and Empire', *Christian Remembrancer* 10 (1845), 123.

activities of the Clarendon Press. This stifled what might otherwise have been 'the most magnificent institution for the purposes of literary publication in Europe'. Instead of being devoted to the publication of works of erudition, the resources of the Press were 'frittered away on school and prize-books'.[97] His enduring interest in the impact of institutional forms on scholarly practices was apparent here. Another characteristic of his mature reviewing was anticipated in these early reviews: a confidence in contextualizing the work under discussion by means of, for example, perceptive comments on the social context of reading, or on what we might today call the history of the book.[98]

It was not his literary work, however, but his remarkable success as tutor, and the standing it gave him in the college, that made him a credible candidate for the headship. John Radford, rector of Lincoln since 1834, died on 21 October 1851. The death was not unexpected: the rector was around seventy, his health had been poor for at least a year, and the prospect of an election of a successor had been the subject of common room speculation for some time.[99] The election that followed was to scar Pattison's mind and spirit for the rest of his life.

In the Victorian period – much more than today – a college headship was a position to which it was natural for a fellow to aspire. Within the University the heads had real power, and nationally they had access to social elites. Their income greatly exceeded that of a fellow, even a fellow who held a college office such as tutor or bursar. And unlike fellows they were allowed to marry. Any fellow would jump at the opportunity to be elected head.

Pattison had evidently formed aspirations to the headship even before Radford's death. The field of potential candidates was small, being limited by statute to present and former fellows of the college. Pattison was the senior tutor and sub-rector and had been the effective power in the college for some years, and other sources confirm his opinion that under his direction Lincoln had become one of the best managed of Oxford colleges.[100] His successful service as an examiner in 1848 and the cogent and forceful evidence he gave to the 1850 Royal Commission had made him a significant figure in the University too. His only rival in terms of ability was Richard Michell, who, having vacated his fellowship on marriage, had

---

[97] [Pattison], 'The Oxford Bede', *Christian Remembrancer* 11 (1846,), 331.
[98] [Pattison], 'Thiers' History', 105.    [99] Bodleian MS Pattison 129, ff. 50–1, 24 September 1851.
[100] Balliol College: Jowett Papers II.1.8, Jowett to an unknown correspondent, 18 May [1855?].

become vice-principal of Magdalen Hall, the ancestor of Hertford College. He was ineligible for the rectorship because the statutes excluded those who held, or had held, the fellowship confined to natives of the Wells diocese.[101] On the other hand, Pattison was by now identified as a liberal and a reformer; the fellowship was divided between reformers and the old guard; and Pattison's acerbity, and perhaps also the touch of priggishness about him, had made him personally unpopular with the old guard. Michell, whose contacts with Lincoln remained strong, was certainly set against Pattison: he was a Tory and an evangelical, and an opponent of reform.

As things turned out he was defeated as a result of a sequence of events which his own *Memoirs* have made so famous that they helped inspire C. P. Snow's fictional account of the election to the headship of a Cambridge college in his novel *The Masters*. Pattison appeared at one point to be in possession of a sure majority, with five votes including his own out of nine fellows eligible and able to participate. But one of the five, a non-resident barrister, J. L. R. Kettle, announced at the last moment that he had switched sides, in spite of his long-standing commitment to the cause of university reform. He had evidently been persuaded by the machinations of Richard Michell behind the scenes, and had decided to vote for William Kay senior, who had emerged as the candidate of the conservatives. Pattison's party then decided that if they could not get their own candidate elected they might be able to avert the triumph of their opponents. They therefore floated the candidacy of James Thompson, whom they knew to have the backing of one member of the old guard; and Thompson was elected, by five to two, although he had the positive backing of only one fellow. This was an intriguing outcome which provides food for thought for theorists of voting behaviour. Perhaps that is why it so fascinated the eminent mathematician G. H. Hardy, who drew Pattison's account of it to Snow's attention. Certainly Pattison, who voted for him, had no illusions about Thompson, 'a mere ruffian' whose election represented 'the return to the reign of the satyrs and wild beasts'.[102]

In the event it did Pattison no good that his party had been instrumental in Thompson's election. His relations with the new rector deteriorated rapidly, and four years later Pattison resigned the office of tutor. In the *Memoirs* Pattison places the blame squarely with Thompson: 'he treated

---

[101] The rectorship, and eleven of the twelve fellowships, were restricted to natives of the dioceses of Lincoln and York.

[102] Pattison, *Memoirs*, pp. 288, 290.

me as Hawkins treated Newman. He wanted to get me out as an uncon-
formable element in the mechanical system of government which was now
substituted for the human and personal relations into which I had entered
with each undergraduate individually. He offered me such hard terms as to
the tutorship that I indignantly threw it up, and, to earn some income for
the moment, fell back on private tuition.'[103] This one-sided version is
unlikely to commend itself to the dispassionate reader of the correspondence between the rector and Pattison in 1855. Disagreement seems to have
arisen in the first place from Pattison's non-attendance at chapel, which he
presented as a protest against mere formalism in religion and as a mani-
festation of his unwillingness to associate himself too closely with the
establishment in college, given his disapproval of the way it was run. To
this offence the rector added Pattison's absence from scholarship examinations and elections, which was a clear violation of the duties of the senior
tutor.[104] As V. H. H. Green comments, even a more sympathetic head than
Thompson could hardly neglect to require the senior tutor to carry out his
duties.[105]

Deprived of the income from the office of tutor, Pattison was still able to
draw on his fellowship. This, he recalled, was enough to live on at a time
when the style of life in college was frugal.[106] He continued to take some
pupils from other colleges. Jowett, in particular, was helpful in sending him
undergraduates from Balliol. One, Charles Bowen, would become a judge
of the Court of Appeal, and another, Albert Venn Dicey, would become
Vinerian professor of English Law and the most eminent of English
constitutional lawyers. Like many of Pattison's pupils, Dicey remained a
friend. Pattison earned perhaps fifty pounds a year through teaching,
which he confined to two terms. He had little to do with the undergraduates at Lincoln, one of whom, John Morley, recalled the awe with
which they regarded 'the inscrutable sage in the rooms under the clock'.[107]
He was free to spend the spring and summer months indulging his lifelong
passion for the countryside on lengthy rambles in Germany and fishing
expeditions to Yorkshire and Scotland. It was also his practice to take a
summer curacy in a rural parish during the incumbent's absence: this
would supplement his income and give him a base away from Oxford.

---

[103] Pattison, *Memoirs*, p. 299.
[104] James Thompson to Pattison, 12 and 13 November 1855, Bodleian MS Pattison 51, ff. 143–6.
[105] Green, *Oxford Common Room*, p. 195.   [106] Pattison, *Memoirs*, p. 295.
[107] John Morley, 'On Pattison's *Memoirs*', *Macmillan's Magazine*, April 1885, reprinted in his *Critical Miscellanies* (London: Macmillan, 1909), vol. III, p. 156.

EUROPE'S SPECULATORS: THE ENCOUNTER WITH GERMANY

Pattison took advantage of the leisure afforded by his freedom from tutorial responsibilities by spending a good deal of time in Germany in the late 1850s. The Black Forest had for some time been established as one of his favourite locations for walking tours, but now he began to make serious contacts with German scholars for the first time. He would become known – though this was a half-truth, as we shall see – as one of the great Victorian advocates of German learning and the German model of the university.

It is hard to be certain when Pattison's interest in Germany took root. As an undergraduate he engaged a German tutor with whom he had twelve lessons, but he represents this as a symptom of his indiscriminate quest for self-improvement rather than, for instance, a step arising from his sense that Germany was the intellectual power-house of the world.[108] The year after graduating he ranked learning Italian along with German among his priorities. He certainly read German books in this period, but when he read Schiller's *Fiesko* in 1837 he felt that his reading in German was not yet fluent enough for him to form a confident judgement of something so difficult to appraise as a play.[109] He does not come across as a Germanophile at this time. The 'pains-taking German scholar' was something of a cliché, and a pejorative one, in his diary from around the time of his election to his fellowship. He was contemptuous of 'the muddled German plodder who has waded through every sheet of printing or manuscript to be found in all the libraries of all the universities of Europe, with a view to his new edition of Dictys Cretensis'.[110]

This kind of hackneyed representation of German scholarship was common in the Oxford of the 1830s. At this time there was only the most superficial understanding of the flowering of learning in the wake of the creation of the new University of Berlin. On the one hand the German professor was thought to be a narrow and dull specialist, the sort of man who 'directs the whole force of his mind to the investigation of the habits of the Scarabaeus major, to the utter neglect of all other beetles'. On the other hand (and perhaps incompatibly) he was thought to be dangerously addicted to speculation: 'an inveterate theorist, an intellectual cardhouse builder'.[111] This

---

[108] Pattison, *Memoirs*, p. 114.    [109] Bodleian MS Pattison 5, f. 6.
[110] Bodleian MS Pattison 6, ff. 39, 80.
[111] Quotations from Walter C. Perry, *German University Education*, 2nd edn. (London: Longmans, 1846), pp. 4–5. Perry is here summarizing the clichéd English view of the German professor, which he set out to correct.

latter representation of German thought dates from the conservative response to the French Revolution, when journals such as Canning's *Anti-Jacobin Review* concluded that German intellectual life had become infected with the vices of French 'philosophism'. 'A German writer', the journal pronounced, 'is, in general, a man that is discontented with every thing about him; his chief happiness, and glory consist in publishing a successful journal.' Not a single German professor was to be found who 'dares admit the existence of a God'.[112] When the Roman historian Niebuhr was translated into English, the *Quarterly Review* denounced him as a 'pert, dull scoffer' who evinced a disrespect for tradition and authority that would inevitably spill over from classical into biblical scholarship.[113] In Pattison's Tractarian days the rationalist German professor remained a familiar trope in High Church discourse. Thomas Acland, during a visit to Berlin University in 1834, told F. D. Maurice that the theology professors there 'all seem to think <u>Wissenschaft</u> more important than soundness of creed'.[114] The Puseyites in particular assumed that disinterested research must mean free inquiry loosed from its moorings in religious orthodoxy: once it was taken as the foundation of academic life, there was no telling what depths of doctrinal depravity might be plumbed. Pusey himself had, curiously enough, been one of the first Englishmen to study in German universities – in 1827, at the instigation of his Oxford mentor Dr Charles Lloyd, afterwards Bishop of Oxford. Lloyd had urged his young protégé to learn German and to study in Germany, the better to be able to combat the alarming developments in biblical scholarship there. He heard the biblical scholar Eichhorn lecture in Göttingen and met Schleiermacher in Berlin. The result was *An Historical Enquiry into the Probable Causes of the Rationalist Character Lately Predominant in the Theology of Germany*, published in 1828. But the book was not read carefully. Pusey was supposed to be sympathetic to German rationalist theology, and as a result he never allowed the book to be reprinted. Neither did he think it necessary to re-visit the German universities. It was not just in theology that he distrusted the spirit of rationalism. 'The scepticism as to Homer', he thought, 'ushered in the scepticism as to the Old Testament.'[115]

[112] James Schmidt, 'Inventing the Enlightenment: Anti-Jacobins, British Hegelians, and the *Oxford English Dictionary*', *Journal of the History of Ideas* 64 (2003), 432–3. The quotations date from 1800.
[113] Quoted by Norman Vance, 'Niebuhr in England: history, faith, and order', in Benedikt Stuchtey and Peter Wende (eds.), *British and German Historiography 1750–1950: Traditions, Perceptions, and Transfers* (Oxford: Oxford University Press, 2000), p. 88.
[114] Quoted by Asa Briggs, 'Oxford and its critics, 1800–1835', in Brock and Curthoys (eds.), *Nineteenth-Century Oxford*, Part 1, p. 139.
[115] Quoted by Vance, 'Niebuhr in England', 89.

In the 1840s a fuller appreciation of the German academic world became possible as a result of works such as *German University Education* (1845) by the Unitarian minister W. C. Perry, who had studied for a doctorate at Göttingen in the 1830s and had subsequently settled in Berlin. Thomas Arnold had long been interested in Niebuhr's work, and his lectures during his brief tenure of the Regius chair of modern history (1841–2) helped introduce an Oxford audience, including Pattison himself, to German historical scholarship.[116] In this respect Oxford lagged behind Cambridge, where an influential circle of liberal-minded Anglicans around Julius Hare at Trinity had been among the first in England to discover the new understanding of history being developed in Germany.[117] But on the whole the early Germanizers were theologically heterodox: the Unitarians, for instance, were particularly strongly drawn to the German tradition of free inquiry in religious matters, and a number of their leaders, such as John Kenrick, John James Taylor and James Martineau, made prolonged study visits to Germany.[118] Pattison's background was very different, and there is no clear evidence of his being drawn especially to the German intellectual world until the 1850s. The immediate impetus came from the publication in 1855 of a biography of Joseph Justus Scaliger by Jacob Bernays, a German-Jewish scholar more than ten years Pattison's junior.[119] Pattison was himself planning a biography of Scaliger, to form the centre-piece of his 'Lives of the Scholars' of the French Renaissance, and he read Bernays's book promptly.[120] He must have made contact with Bernays soon afterwards: we have a sequence of letters from Bernays to Pattison in 1856, the first one dated 10 February, although Pattison's side of the correspondence does not survive from this period.[121] In September of the same year he met Bernays for the first time, during an extended visit to Heidelberg, and was most impressed: 'a wonderful man – his power makes

[116] Pattison reports his attendance at Arnold's lectures in an undated letter to his sister Eleanor, presumably from 1842: Lincoln College MS/PAT/II/A.
[117] The classic study is Duncan Forbes, *The Liberal Anglican Idea of History* (Cambridge: Cambridge University Press, 1952).
[118] Howard M. Wach, 'A "still, small voice" from the pulpit: religion and the creation of social morality in Manchester, 1820–1850', *Journal of Modern History* 63 (1991), 430, 449.
[119] The relations between Pattison and Bernays are discussed in Arnaldo Momigliano, 'Jacob Bernays', *Koninklijke Nederlandse Akademie van Wetenschappen*, n.s. 32, no. 5 (1969), 151–78, reprinted in A. D. Momigliano, *Studies on Modern Scholarship*, G. W. Bowersock and T. J. Cornell (eds.) (London: University of California Press, 1994), 121–46.
[120] In his diary he records reading it on 1 September 1855: Bodleian MS Pattison 129, f. 181.
[121] Bodleian MS Pattison 51, ff. 194–5, 252–3, 322. At his death, Bernays directed that his collection of letters received should be returned to their senders, and Pattison's letters, covering the period 1860–81, ended up in the Bywater papers in the Bodleian.

itself felt in ½ a hours [sic] conversation'.[122] Thanks to a letter of intro-duction from his Oxford friend W. C. Lake, he also made the acquaintance of the Chevalier Bunsen, the diplomat and liberal theologian. Bunsen, who was married to an English woman, had previously served as Prussian ambassador in London and had close contacts with English liberal Anglican theologians. The three men evidently discussed what form Pattison's work on Scaliger should now take. Bernays wanted Pattison to translate his book into English, whereas other German scholars – such as Johannis Brandis – encouraged Pattison instead to use Bernays's book but to 'write it over again'. This was what Pattison preferred: he wanted to present Scaliger in a way that would make sense to the English public. He tried to persuade Bernays that owing to 'the weakness of English science & scholarship' his book was simply not adapted to the English public. But Bernays insisted, and contrary to the account given in Pattison's *Memoirs*, Bunsen seems to have supported him. Pattison acquiesced, but as soon as he started on a translation found that the book 'does not run at all well into English'.[123] Whether or not that was the reason, the translation never appeared.

Although Pattison initially found Bernays a rather difficult man to deal with, their friendship blossomed. 'I learn more from him in an hour, than in a weeks [sic] reading', he noted later during that first visit to Heidelberg.[124] They began a correspondence that continued intermittently until Bernays's early death in 1881: in 1863 Bernays dedicated his study of Aristotle's lost dialogues to Pattison, who in 1872 took his wife to meet Bernays in Bonn.[125] Bernays admired Pattison's study of Casaubon, which appeared in 1875: 'You have built', he wrote, 'a fine monument to solid knowledge, strict relevance, and a noble mind, and have opened up for specialists a rich pantry in the whole of the intellectual and cultural history of the sixteenth century.'[126] Pattison's friendship with Bernays created opportunities for a series of Oxford classicists and ancient philosophers to make contacts with the world of philological scholarship in Germany: Henry Nettleship, Ingram Bywater, Charles Appleton and D. B. Morris were all introduced to Bernays by Pattison.[127]

[122] Bodleian MS Pattison 137, p. 5.
[123] Bodleian MS Pattison 137, pp. 5–9, 17 (this volume is numbered by pages rather than by folio).
[124] Bodleian MS Pattison 137, p. 66.   [125] Bodleian MS Pattison 137, pp. 163–4.
[126] Jacob Bernays to Pattison, 5 February 1875, MS Bywater 61, ff. 41–2 (my translation from the German).
[127] Pattison to Bernays, 28 March 1865, 5 July 1868, 10 July 1869, 18 June 1870, MS Bywater 61, ff. 6, 10, 12, 14.

On that first visit Pattison took the opportunity of attending the theologian Richard Rothe's course on dogmatics at Heidelberg. He was impressed: there were no rhetorical flourishes, but Rothe proceeded methodically and undemonstratively, and 'one feels in the hands of a master, who knows where he is, & what he is coming to'.[128] He met a number of other German scholars, including the historian of philosophy Kuno Fischer, who had just published a study of Francis Bacon, and Bernays's mentor, the Latinist Friedrich Ritschl, who would later teach Nietzsche at Bonn and Leipzig. The philosopher Eduard Zeller became, like Bernays, a lifelong friend. Pattison was sufficiently impressed by his first-hand encounter with the German academic world to observe, in an essay published in 1857, that 'it so happens that, at present, European speculation is transacted by Germans, as our financial affairs are by Jews'.[129]

Pattison would spend a further extended period in Germany in 1858–9, at first serving as the Berlin correspondent of *The Times*, and then as Assistant Commissioner for the Newcastle Commission on Popular Education, producing a report on German schools in parallel with Matthew Arnold's report on France. Both appointments testify to the reputation he was beginning to acquire as an authority on German affairs, and not simply on German scholarship. It is unclear how the arrangement with *The Times* arose, but it occurred at a crucial period in Prussian politics: the advent of Prince William's regency and the liberal surge in the elections of November 1858 marked the beginning of a 'new era' not just in Prussia, but more generally in Germany. *The Times* would have been particularly pleased to have its own correspondent in Berlin at such a time, and the arrangement was evidently a success: 'it is the unanimous wish of all here', wrote George Dasent, the assistant editor, at the conclusion of the connection, 'that you should resume your correspondence when you return to Berlin'. Pattison declined that invitation, but the staff of *The Times* tried hard to keep him: he had acquired a mastery of 'all the intricacies of Prussian politics', wrote the newspaper's manager, Mowbray Morris, who urged Pattison at some point to 'resume a correspondence which has reflected credit both upon you & The Times'.[130] This was not mere flattery. An article on the subject of foreign correspondents in

[128] Bodleian MS Pattison 137, pp. 128–30; Pattison, *Memoirs*, p. 301.

[129] [Pattison], 'The present state of theology in Germany', *Westminster Review* 67 O.S. (1857), reprinted in *Essays* II, p. 216.

[130] G. W. Dasent to Pattison, 11 Jan 1859; Mowbray Morris to Pattison, 27 Jan 1859 and 14 March 1859, Bodleian MS Pattison 52, ff. 290–1, 302–3, 340–1.

the *Saturday Review* in January 1859 drew attention to 'the present Prussian Correspondent of the Times' as an 'excellent instance of the best kind of correspondent'. This was because his reports typically dug beneath the surface of events to contextualize them and to make their significance clear to the English public. So, in reporting the elections of November 1858 'he sent home a series of most instructive essays, in which enough, and not too much, was given to explain the position of the different parties, and the constitutional process by which their battle was decided'. He was regarded as 'master of the wider features of the system, and the remoter bearings of the affairs on which he is called to comment'.[131]

For a period of nearly three months Pattison dispatched regular reports, on average every second day, and often at some length: his more substantial pieces could stretch to four thousand words or more. The *Saturday Review* was right to see an unusual depth of analysis and breadth of perspective in these reports. One of the obstacles that always faces the reader who wishes to follow foreign news in the press is the difficulty of getting a sense of the recent historical background: journalists typically record the news and rarely have space to dwell on the context, while historians have not yet turned their attention to such a recent period. Pattison made sense of current developments in Prussia with the aid of a powerful analytical grasp of nineteenth-century German history. For example, he analysed the nature of the reaction that had dominated Prussian politics since 1850: this sought to sweep away the work of the 1848 revolution, in its constitutional as well as its democratic aspects. It was therefore inclined to overturn even the achievements of the Stein-Hardenberg period at the beginning of the century.[132] Pattison was especially acute in his observations on the Prussian civil service, or *Beamtenthum*. Unlike the French bureaucracy this had not, historically, been a weapon in the armoury of arbitrary power. Rather, Pattison maintained, the civil service had been the most important bulwark against the tendency to the arbitrary exercise of power. The spirit of independence and sense of rectitude displayed by the officials discharged some of the functions performed in a free country by public opinion and the press. But this had changed in the wake of the Manteuffel era: governments had sought to reduce 'the independent *Beamtenthum* into a moral police, to be employed against the people'.[133]

Pattison was recruited to assist the Newcastle Commission by one of its members, W. C. Lake, a fellow of Balliol and Somerset vicar who would

---

[131] 'Foreign correspondents', *Saturday Review* 7 (15 Jan. 1859), 65.
[132] *The Times*, 17 December 1858, p. 7.    [133] *The Times*, 7 December 1858, p. 8.

shortly be appointed prebendary of Wells and later dean of Durham. He was asked to provide 'a very succinct general account of popular education in the various countries which you visit': this need not involve 'minute details of the management of schools', but 'only such as are essential to an accurate estimate of the educational system'. This was to be accomplished in four months, and for this he would be paid fifty pounds a month, together with travel expenses and a *per diem* allowance of fifteen shillings to cover hotel bills.[134] There had been the possibility of an appointment to report on English schools, but Lake told Pattison that the foreign appointment would maximize his contribution to the Commission's work: had he been appointed to report on English education he might have encountered theological difficulties, whereas in Germany 'you will do for the country in this matter as much, I feel more, as any man could.' At the same time he offered some advice which casts light on the way in which Pattison was regarded by his contemporaries. He should be careful not to include too much 'theory' in the report. 'Your critics on all sides admitting fully your ability charge you with a certain amount of "crotchettyness", and even in this matter I have been warned "only to prevent Pattison from letting crotchets get hold of him".' In a report of this kind, Lake added, 'practical men & hostile critics, will be glad to expose anything which they wd call *mere theory*'.[135]

Pattison's report did not have the magisterial quality of Matthew Arnold's more famous report, which was to germinate some of the key ideas he would later expound in *Culture and Anarchy*.[136] Although Arnold dealt with Holland and the French-speaking cantons of Switzerland as well as with France, his focus was on France and to that extent he had an easier task than Pattison, who evidently found the heterogeneity of Germany a challenge and left Catholic education to one side. Likewise he found himself unable to include the German cantons of Switzerland, which the commissioners had asked him to consider. Lake, having warned Pattison to avoid 'theory', in retrospect wished that he had felt able to be more discursive, as Arnold was. Nevertheless, the commissioners were grateful to him for providing 'an authoritative account of German Education' which was characterized by 'evident accuracy' and 'precise information'.[137]

[134] W. C. Lake to Pattison, 9 Feb. 1859, Bodleian MS Pattison 52, ff. 311–13.
[135] W. C. Lake to Pattison, 7 Oct. 1858, Bodleian MS Pattison 52, ff. 179–82.
[136] Stefan Collini, *Arnold* (Oxford: Oxford University Press, 1988), pp. 69–71; F. G. Walcott, *The Origins of 'Culture and Anarchy': Matthew Arnold and Popular Education* (Toronto: University of Toronto Press, 1970).
[137] W. C. Lake to Pattison, Bodleian MS Pattison 52, ff. 564–6.

By the end of the 1850s, then, Pattison had established himself as an authority on Germany: her theology, her scholarship, her politics and her educational system. This was a very important dimension to his public profile as it would develop during the rest of his career. His contemporaries, John Stuart Mill and Matthew Arnold, were both able to enhance their authority as cultural critics by deploying their knowledge of French thought and institutions and contrasting England unfavourably with her rival across the Channel.[138] Pattison was able to do the same with his knowledge of Germany. As we shall see, he would often present himself as a critic of English middle-class public opinion, which he would represent as too narrowly commercial in its view of the world. The English middle class, he thought, had no interest in education for its own sake. Likewise the English reading public had little interest in true scholarship. Germany served as a counterpoint to England: German culture, whatever its faults, could not be convicted of superficiality. Moreover, since the era of reform that followed the remodelling of the University of Berlin at the instigation of Wilhelm von Humboldt in line with neohumanist ideals, German universities had taken as their animating principle the idea of *Wissenschaft*: the disinterested pursuit of systematic knowledge for its own sake. Pattison would come to see this as the ideal to which he had been striving since his intellectual awakening as an undergraduate.[139]

He recognized, however, that to invoke the 'German professor' was as good as to discredit any proposal for university reform in nineteenth-century England.[140] Pattison was by no means an uncritical Germanophile. How could he be, when so many of his German contacts gave him a negative view of German universities? Bonn and Göttingen were the only two which were flourishing, Kuno Fischer told him in 1856.[141] He was critical of the aristocratic bias and reactionary political influence on academic appointments in Germany.[142] In his *Times* reports he made some of the characteristic observations of a Victorian liberal on administrative centralization in Prussia and on the role of the police. He found Prussian political culture illiberal, notably in its treatment of the Polish question: 'Every party here, even the Liberal, has yet to learn the lesson of toleration

---

[138] Stefan Collini, *Public Moralists*, pp. 133–4; Georgios Varouxakis, *Victorian Political Thought on France and the French* (Basingstoke: Palgrave, 2002), especially p. 47.

[139] The fullest account of the Humboldtian model and its place in the history of European universities in the nineteenth century is Marc Schalenberg, *Humboldt auf Reisen? Die Rezeption des 'deutschen Universitätsmodells' in den französischen und britischen Reformdiskursen* (1810–1870) (Basel: Schwabe, 2002).

[140] Schalenberg, *Humboldt auf Reisen?*, p. 273 n. 257.    [141] Bodleian MS Pattison 137, p. 44.

[142] Bodleian MS Pattison 137, pp. 106–7, 165.

of its opponents.'[143] He even felt ambivalently about German scholars: he admired their depth but deplored their lack of clarity.

> How vastly greater would be the circulation among us of the really solid and valuable books published in Germany, if they were only so written that we could understand them . . . the periodic sentence, as the Germans now construct it, is an insuperable obstacle in the way of our reading their books. No knowledge of the language can supply the superhuman attention necessary to carry the mind through such a labyrinth of clauses.[144]

All his life Pattison sought a synthesis of the German idea of the dignity of *Wissenschaft* with the English model of the man of letters. Friedrich Ritschl, the Latinist, was 'abounding in knowledge, but cannot write an intelligible page'.[145] Volkmann's *Rhetorik*, which he read in November 1882, was 'a truly German muddle of facts & quotations'.[146] The Germans' merits and defects were the reverse of those of the French, on whom he was consistently harsher. Pattison typically portrayed France as the home of a 'superficial idea of education', where 'genuine erudition', a rarity, was unappreciated even when it did exist. It was a country where superficial mental polish and 'diversified information' were widely diffused, notably by 'the facile process of lecture-hearing'; and where 'no real questions' were debated.[147] Perhaps only the Dutch got the balance right, he reflected: they united 'the scientific temper of the German philology, with the practical sense of the English'.[148]

### COINING THE ORE INTO SIXPENCES: THE WRITER AND HIS PUBLIC

It was in the 1850s, following the 'catastrophe' of the rectorship election, that Pattison laid the foundations of his literary career. At the time of the 1851 election Pattison's reputation, though high in Oxford, did not really extend any further. He had published quite extensively, but only in High Church periodicals such as the *British Critic* and the *Christian Remembrancer*. And he had not yet made any one subject his own. In the *Christian Remembrancer* his reviews – they were all reviews, but lengthy ones – ranged from Robert Hussey's edition of Bede to John Stuart Mill's

---

[143] *The Times*, 14 Dec. 1858, p. 7.

[144] [Pattison], 'Theology and philosophy', *Westminster Review* 67 o.s. (Jan. 1857), 258.

[145] Bodleian MS Pattison 130, f. 75.    [146] Bodleian MS Pattison 134 f. 2, 5 Nov. 1882.

[147] PP 1852 no. 1482, vol. xxii, p. 45; [Pattison], 'Theology and philosophy'.

[148] Bodleian MS Pattison 130, f. 74, 15 Feb. 1874.

*Principles of Political Economy*. It was the events of 1851 that impelled him to take his literary work much more seriously, and to become one of the most prominent literary dons of the time.[149] The article that launched this phase of his career was his piece on Isaac Casaubon's diary in the *Quarterly Review* of 1853. This was not only his first contribution to one of the great literary reviews, but it was also the first time he had touched on what was to become his life's focus, the modern history of classical learning, or even, more broadly, on the intellectual history of modern Europe. It was here that, for the first time, Pattison truly found his voice as a scholar. It would be to the *Quarterly* that he would turn to publish his most substantial essays on the history of classical learning: on Huet in 1855, Montaigne in 1856, Scaliger in 1860 and the Estiennes in 1865.

The choice of the *Quarterly* deserves some comment: it was a Tory journal, and one might have expected Pattison to regard it with distrust if not disdain. It was not his first choice, for he offered the Casaubon piece in the first instance to the Whiggish *Edinburgh Review*. But the *Edinburgh* was unable to take it, and owing to a chapter of accidents, including the appointment of its editor to government office, Pattison never did publish there. He seems to have found the *Quarterly* congenial because its editor, the Norfolk rector Whitwell Elwin, was a man of scholarly tastes, as Pattison gratefully recalled.[150] Elwin was quick to identify the article as possessing 'the elements of unusual ability', indicating that its author had the potential to become an 'eminent writer'.[151] Even so, their correspondence from the 1850s indicates that the relationship of author and editor was by no means an easy one. Pattison clearly resented editorial changes made without his express consent. 'Had letter today fr[om] Elwin', he noted in his diary on 14 October 1853,

complimenting me very highly, and making a sort of apology for the stabbing & maiming he has inflicted. My line will be to return a courteous, but very cold answer, abstaining fr[om] a word of complaint, and equally fr[om] a word of approbation. And my present resolve is never to write in the Q[uarterly] again without a guarantee ag[ain]st similar treatment.[152]

---

[149] In a classic study, Altick found that academics constituted only a minute fraction of the large sample of nineteenth-century British authors whose backgrounds he was able to trace: Richard D. Altick, 'The sociology of authorship: the social origins, education and occupations of 1,100 British writers, 1800–1935', *Bulletin of the New York Public Library* 66 (1962), 389–404.

[150] Pattison, *Memoirs*, 319.

[151] Whitwell Elwin to Pattison, 13 October 1853: Bodleian MS Pattison 50, f. 255.

[152] Bodleian MS Pattison 129, f. 121.

Pattison contributed to a remarkably wide range of periodicals: over twenty in all, including newspapers (*The Times, The Guardian*), an academic journal of a new kind (*Mind*), and a foreign periodical (the *North American Review*). This range should not blind us to certain patterns in his literary activity. The first period, as we have noted, consisted of his association with High Church publications, and chiefly the *Christian Remembrancer*. This connection was at its closest in the crucial years 1845–6, but spanned the period 1844–8, with some isolated contributions in the early 1850s. It relaxed as he broke free of the Oxford Movement in the late 1840s. The failure of his candidature for the rectorship in 1851 impelled him to turn his back on clerical Oxford and to look instead to the metropolitan press as an outlet for his literary activity. In 1855 he began an association with the radical *Westminster Review*, then under the editorship of the charismatic John Chapman, which lasted until 1863. For the first four years this connection was particularly intense: not only did Chapman publish major pieces by Pattison, such as his articles on German theology (April 1857) and Buckle's *History of Civilisation in England* (October 1857), but Pattison undertook surveys of recent literature in theology and philosophy (1855–7) and then in history and biography (1857–8). At the same time he began his relationship with the *Saturday Review*, to which we shall return in a moment. This relationship quickly faltered but was re-established once Pattison had broken with the *Westminster*: in the period 1864–8 the *Saturday* was the main outlet for his critical writing. From 1869 his closest connection was with the *Academy*, the foundation of which he helped to inspire. Finally, in the period 1877–81 John Morley induced him to contribute several substantial pieces to the *Fortnightly Review*, by then the foremost organ of advanced liberal opinion. In Morley's words, the *Fortnightly* aimed at 'the diffusion and encouragement of rationalistic standards in things spiritual and temporal alike'. Its spirit was 'the spirit of Liberalism in its most many-sided sense'.[153]

The volume as well as the range of Pattison's writing deserves emphasis, given that he has the reputation of having produced little. To the research assessors of the twenty-first century an output founded chiefly on reviews looks feeble, but Pattison's major essays, such as those on Casaubon, Huet and Scaliger, each of which exceeded twenty thousand words, dwarfed modern academic papers in their scale. Other essays, such as his contributions to *Oxford Essays* (1855) and *Essays and Reviews* (1860) were conceived on a still more ambitious scale, and were widely noticed: each of these two

---

[153] John Morley, *Recollections* (London: Macmillan, 1917), I, p. 86.

pieces exceeded 25,000 words. These writings fill two fat volumes in the posthumous collection of his *Essays* brought to publication by his friend Henry Nettleship. Eight hundred citations in the first edition of the *Oxford English Dictionary* testify to an extensive body of published work.

Pattison's time in the academic wilderness coincided with a remarkable period of expansion of the British press stimulated by the removal of the tax on advertisements in 1853, the abolition of the stamp duty in 1855, and finally the lifting of the paper tax in 1861. These changes not only unleashed a dramatic growth of the daily press, but also facilitated the establishment of new weekly periodicals, including some important ones which competed with the *Spectator* and the *Athenaeum* for the allegiance of the educated public.[154] The most important in its day was the *Saturday Review*, founded in 1855, the year Pattison resigned his tutorship. Its editor, John Douglas Cook, was scarcely an intellectual: John Morley, who admired him as 'a wonderfully successful editor-manager', nevertheless thought him 'almost illiterate'.[155] But Cook had an eye for literary talent and was one of the first editors to set out to recruit such talent from the universities: James Fitzjames Stephen and Henry Maine were two notable contributors. Cook approached Pattison at an early stage, encouraging him to suggest political subjects on which he would like to write. Although Pattison expressed interest, he did not take Cook up on this invitation to extend his range, and he would have been out of sympathy with the editor's conservative politics. He did, however, review regularly for the *Saturday*, on philosophical, classical and historical subjects, over the next two decades. The *Saturday* was famous for its pugnacious house-style – it was nicknamed the 'Saturday Reviler' – and Pattison soon learned to sharpen his pen. One of his earliest pieces was a contemptuous review of a new edition of Aristotle's *Ethics* by an Oxford contemporary, the pre-Tractarian high churchman W. E. Jelf of Christ Church. Pattison thought it was an egregious instance of Oxford as it had been before the era of reform: the Oxford he had encountered as an undergraduate. 'Mr Jelf must surely have turned out of some neglected drawer in his study his old undergraduate "notes," and sent them off to the printer as they stood. In no other way can we account for the prodigious folly of printing such a book as this.' He concluded with a fine demonstration of the art of a Saturday Reviewer:

---

[154] Malcolm Woodfield, 'Victorian weekly reviews and reviewing after 1860: R. H. Hutton and the *Spectator*', *Yearbook of English Studies* 16 (1986), 74–6.
[155] F. W. Hirst, *Early Life and Letters of John Morley* (London: Macmillan, 1927), p. 38.

We are glad to find one thing about the book which we can commend, and that is the plan of securing a margin for pencil notes by printing the duodecimo text in an octavo page. And as the notes are printed by themselves at the end, any one can convert this into a lecture-room edition by cutting out the English notes and throwing them into the fire. They cannot be of use to any human being.[156]

Not surprisingly, Jelf took umbrage at this, and wrote to challenge Pattison to deny his authorship of the review.[157] We do not know whether Pattison replied to this, but the following month he formed the suspicion that Jelf, an examiner, had exacted his revenge by blocking the award of a First to one of Pattison's pupils, the future church historian Charles Abbey. One of Jelf's co-examiners had to assure Pattison that this was not the case.[158]

Even Pattison's shorter reviews, such as those he wrote for the *Saturday Review*, would run to several thousand words and would typically include masterly mini-histories of the subject under discussion, not abstracted from the book under review but feeding on Pattison's own learning to contextualize the book in question. A good example was his review in 1866 of a new edition of Aristotle's *Ethics* – evidently a great improvement on Jelf's – by Sir Alexander Grant, another Oxford contemporary who had become vice-chancellor of the University of Bombay. This review stretches to about 3,500 words. It begins with a typically tart Pattisonian sketch of commonplace attitudes to the relevance of the study of Aristotle:

The blame and the praise are probably both equally misplaced. To the modern man, the creature of his day, impatient, because ignorant, of the past, it is enough that Aristotle was an 'ancient', and wrote in Greek, and was very ignorant of 'modern science'. The conservative clergyman, on the other hand, imagines that somehow 'Catholic truth' is involved by implication in Aristotelian philosophy, and has been imbibed therefrom by successive generations of University students.

Pattison then goes on to provide a compact but authoritative synopsis of the place of Aristotle in the Oxford curriculum from the middle ages to the revised Examination Statute of 1850, which left the *Ethics* as the sole remnant of what had once been a comprehensively Aristotelian curriculum. He follows this with some observations on the value of the *Ethics* as a prescribed text. The book is, he observes, 'one of the most precious monuments of classical antiquity which has been preserved to us'; but it is also, in itself, a philological problem, and the textual challenges it presents mean that it does not easily provide a springboard into wider philosophical

---

[156] [Pattison], Review of W. E. Jelf (ed.), *Aristotle's Ethics*, *Saturday Review* I (8 March 1856), 378–9.
[157] W. E. Jelf to Pattison, 12 Apr. 1856, Bodleian MS Pattison 51, f. 222.
[158] A. S. Farrar to Pattison, 6 May 1856, Bodleian MS Pattison, 51, f. 225.

teaching or study. It is, however, pre-eminently an examinable book, and that, says Pattison, is the chief reason for its durability. Finally, Pattison the historian of the book speaks, and gives the reader a learned and critical history of the various Oxford editions of the *Ethics* since Wilkinson's edition of 1716, which Pattison thinks has been unduly disdained: in fact Wilkinson's was 'by no means a contemptible performance, and for the time in which it appeared it is a highly respectable one'. A number of later editions receive characteristic Pattisonian dismissal: Cardwell's, for instance, scarcely rose above 'the level of a school-book', while another nineteenth-century editor, Brewer, was 'a scholar . . . who might have done better things', but who 'sat down to produce a lecture-book, and he did it'. All in all, this review is a *tour de force*, and a classic of its kind, combining terse judgements, wide perspective, and deep learning.[159]

Pattison attached a high and noble significance to his role as a critic. Like Matthew Arnold, he saw the critic as an educator of the public mind and the public taste: a 'public instructor', as he put it in a review of the essays of one such critic, John Morley.[160] Pattison was one of those critics who sought to break with what they regarded as the amateurish (though often brilliant) reviewing that had prevailed in the age of Macaulay and before. Pattison thought this style of reviewing was sustained by the educational methods deployed in the public schools and universities, which 'would seem to have as its end and aim the production of article-writers'.[161] These trained 'article-writers' could turn out an piece on any subject, according to the editor's needs; and, he observed to one editor, 'Don't you notice how they all write in the same style, with the same clever varnish!'[162] In place of this clever generalism he asserted the principle that the critic must be as much an expert as the author of the book under review: 'There is no such art as the universal art of judging', he wrote in riposte to Ruskin. 'A man can only estimate values with which he has long been conversant.'[163] He was one of the architects of Charles Appleton's journal, *The Academy*, which pioneered specialist reviewing of this kind in a period just preceding the establishment of the first of the academic periodicals.[164] As Pattison understood it, the role

---

[159] [Pattison], Review of Sir Alexander Grant, *The Ethics of Aristotle. Illustrated with Essays and Notes*, *Saturday Review* 21 (1866), 563–4.

[160] Pattison, Review of John Morley, *Critical Miscellanies*, 2nd series, *The Academy* 12 (13 Oct. 1877), 353.

[161] Pattison, Review of Morley, *Critical Miscellanies*, 353.

[162] Quoted by Mrs Oliphant, *A Memoir of the Life of John Tulloch, DD, LLD.* (Edinburgh & London: Blackwood, 1888), p. 359.

[163] Pattison, Review of John Ruskin, *Arrows of the Chace*, *The Academy* 19 (12 Feb. 1881), 110.

[164] Pattison, Review of Matthew Arnold, *Mixed Essays. The Academy* 15 (17 May 1879), 425.

of critic was a demanding one which required a rigorous regime of training: 'his education is not complete till he has in his mind a conception of the successive phases of thought and feeling from the beginning of letters'.[165] He respected Morley as a critic because having begun, like other reviewers, 'with no other idea than that of wreaking his cleverness upon the language', he had risen above it by means of 'honest labour', indeed twenty years of 'self-education and self-discipline'.[166] Likewise, Leslie Stephen stood out from 'the crowd of clever writers who make the pages of our magazines and reviews brilliant with wit and wisdom', because he wrote with 'more matured intellectual shape and solid foundation in character than the generality of those to whom we look for periodical instruction'.[167]

Pattison's reviewing was fundamental to his propagation of the ideal of learning as he understood it. He represented this as a counter-cultural ideal, in the sense that he saw it working against the grain of public opinion. He saw learning as a mode of life that was under threat from the sway of democracy, in Tocqueville's sense; and in particular, in England, from the philistine values of a commercially minded middle-class opinion. He was fond of telling Jacob Bernays that there was no reading public in England for the kind of book Bernays wrote: 'you know our English circumstances. We must write that which will pay. 'Tis yours to draw the ore from the mine, we can but coin it into sixpences & distribute to the crowd.'[168] In a critical review of R. C. Jebb's edition and translation of Theophrastus's *Characters*, he conceded that it was not Jebb's fault that 'the conditions of publication in a "practical" country have forced him to do inferior work': in other words, to produce what Pattison called a 'schoolbook' rather than a critical edition.[169] In his review of Morley he observed that 'for political philosophy – i.e. for wisdom and learning applied to public affairs – the English public have a distinct disrelish'. This constrained what Morley could achieve. 'He has now raised himself to the highest point of comprehensive view to which a public writer can rise in this country without forfeiting his popularity. One step further in the direction of political philosophy and he must lose his audience.'[170]

---

[165] Pattison, 'Books and Critics', *Fortnightly Review* 28 O. S. (1877), 669.
[166] Pattison, Review of Morley, *Critical Miscellanies*, 353.
[167] Pattison, Review of Leslie Stephen, *History of English Thought in the Eighteenth Century*, *The Academy* 10 (2 Dec. 1876), 533.
[168] Bodleian MS Pattison 137, p. 17, 11 Sept. 1856; MS Bywater 61, ff 4–5, Pattison to Bernays, 23 Oct. 1860.
[169] Pattison, Review of *The Characters of Theophrastus*, trans. and ed. by R. C. Jebb, *Academy* II (1870), 52–4.
[170] Pattison, Review of Morley, *Critical Miscellanies*, 353.

Because Pattison was acutely sensitive to the social context of his literary work, he was also intensely conscious that the demands of readers and editors – and not just their demands, but also his own literary vanity – threatened his primary commitments to truth and the development of his own mind. Morley criticized Macaulay for his deficiency in the disinterested love of truth that marked the genuine scholar. He lacked 'that spirit of inwardness which has never been wholly wanting in any of those kings and princes of literature with whom it is good for men to sit in counsel'. Pattison certainly shared Morley's conception of the true scholar and probably identified himself as the antithesis of Macaulay in this respect. But he nevertheless sprang to the historian's defence:

Doubtless this is true of Macaulay. But of which of us all who undertake to instruct the public, monthly, weekly, daily, is it not true? Which of us possesses 'the spirit of inwardness', so that we can devote our life to our own mental architecture? The literary life as lived in this 'epoch rich in tremendous and far-sounding phrases' is not a life of recueillement, not the 'chercher en gémissant' of Pascal. What we are all striving after, we who write, is, not to know the thing that is true, but to get listened to.[171]

There was one other literary venture, in some respects the most important of Pattison's career, in this phase of Pattison's career prior to his election as rector. This was involvement in *Essays and Reviews*, a collection of liberal theological studies published in 1860. This volume generated perhaps the stormiest theological controversy of the Victorian period: it sold twenty thousand copies in two years, went into thirteen editions in five years, and more than four hundred books, pamphlets and articles were written in response. Two of the seven contributors were tried for heresy, and although they were finally acquitted, the book was condemned by both houses of Convocation, and half the clergy of the Church of England signed a declaration against it. Pattison's own essay, on eighteenth-century religious thought, aspired to be purely historical and provoked less controversy than some of the others, but the income it brought him greatly exceeded the yield of any of his other pieces of literary work.[172] Moreover, its presence in *Essays and Reviews* firmly identified him with the cause of theological liberalism: he was one of the 'seven against Christ'. Agitation in the religious press, led by the Tractarian newspaper, the *English Churchman*, prevented his proceeding to a doctorate of divinity following

---

[171] Pattison, Review of Morley, *Critical Miscellanies*, 354.
[172] The intellectual significance of Pattison's essay, and its place in his conception of the history of ideas, are discussed in Chapter 6.

his election as rector, as an ordained head of house would usually do.[173] And Pattison did indeed play a crucial role in the genesis of the volume.

In the mid-1850s he became editor of the theological section of the *Westminster Review*, the radical periodical once owned by John Stuart Mill. His editorial role chiefly involved writing an extended survey of new publications in the field of theology, but Pattison, at least for a time, entertained wider ambitions.[174] He hoped to use this position to turn that periodical into an organ of radical theology; a review that would 'lead thinking men in Theology and Religion'.[175] The editor, John Chapman, was unwilling to go along with this proposal: from a commercial point of view he thought it imprudent to include more than one theological or religious article per issue. In any case, as a freethinker he was happy to publish provocative work on religious subjects, but not to make the *Westminster* into a theological journal. At the same time as Pattison was dissatisfied with Chapman, so was H. B. Wilson, who had been antagonized by Chapman's decision to publish an article on the 'Religious weakness of Protestantism' by Francis Newman, the increasingly rationalist brother of John Henry. Wilson judged this article to be anti-Christian. It was Wilson and Pattison who were central to the genesis of *Essays and Reviews*, Wilson as editor and Pattison as the man who was most committed to the project of creating what was intended to be a periodical, or regular series of publications, promoting 'scientific' theology.

Pattison was not much given to intellectual collaboration, since what mattered most to him was not outward intellectual productions but the inward culture of the mind. So what was he seeking to do in working with Wilson to bring this project about? Because Pattison told Chapman that he wanted the *Westminster* to 'lead' theological opinion, and because Chapman responded by stressing that 'thinking men' would always diverge, it has been argued that Pattison wanted to make the *Westminster Review*, in Chapman's words, the instrument for the dissemination of a new 'constructive creed'.[176] But we possess only Chapman's side of the correspondence, and not Pattison's, and we have to be cautious in what we can deduce about what Pattison said from the arguments used by

---

[173] James Heywood to Pattison, 5 February 1861, Bodleian MS Pattison 54, ff. 243–4.
[174] The account that follows relies chiefly on Mark Francis, 'The origins of *Essays and Reviews*: an interpretation of Mark Pattison in the 1850s', *Historical Journal* (1974), 797–811, modified by Martha S. Vogeler, 'More light on *Essays & Reviews*: the rôle of Frederic Harrison', *Victorian Periodicals Review* 12 (1979), 106, and Josef L. Altholz, 'Periodical origins & implications of *Essays and Reviews*', *Victorian Periodicals Newsletter* 10 (1977), 153 n. 31.
[175] Chapman to Pattison, 9 Oct. 1857, Bodleian MS Pattison 51, ff. 386–90.
[176] Francis, 'Origins of *Essays and Reviews*', 805–6.

Chapman to refute him. It is true that Pattison, like many mid-Victorians, characterized the age as one of 'much dissolution of opinion, no fruitful fermentation of thought'. Whereas some of the sharpness of sectarian conflict had been blunted, he noted, the historical peculiarities of the sects stood in the way of the emergence of religion based on 'ideas purely spiritual'.[177] But did he really want to forge a new orthodoxy? To 'lead' opinion is an ambiguous expression. It might mean to *construct* doctrine, or it might simply mean to go *in advance of* opinion. It seems much more likely that Pattison meant the latter. After all, that was what *Essays and Reviews* would attempt to do, whereas the contributors had no intention of propounding a connected doctrine. The book was prefaced by an explicit assertion that each contributor was responsible for his own, and only his own, contribution; and there was a striking lack of coordination. At the end of September 1859 Wilson wrote to Pattison to chide him for the lateness of his paper, which, along with Jowett's, was delaying the appearance of the volume, which had originally been advertised with a publication date of February 1859. Remarkably enough, just six months before actual publication, Wilson enquired of Pattison what the subject of the essay would be.[178] These were the two men who were chiefly responsible for the whole project. This letter hardly suggests that the propagation of a reconstructive theological system was their aim.

Rather, what Pattison had in mind was a forum for the articulation of 'scientific' theology – what we might, today, call academic theology, unconstrained by churchmanship or party. To understand what he had in mind, we should turn to the essay on German theology that he published in the *Westminster Review* in 1857. Noting Germany's ascendancy in other branches of science and scholarship, Pattison identified the anomaly that 'German Theology has been long under a ban' in Britain.[179] This ban was now ridiculous, because German theology was no longer animated by a 'revolutionary spirit', but had reached a state of maturity characterized by 'a habit of careful research, governed by a conscientious spirit, and armed with all the resources of knowledge, direct and collateral'. Far from being 'wild and capricious', as Dr Pusey thought, now '[i]ts own intense consciousness of the laws of logical method checks it at every turn'.[180]

[177] [Pattison], 'Theology and philosophy', *Westminster Review* 63 o.s. (Jan. 1855), 206.
[178] H. B. Wilson to Pattison, 27 Sept. 1859: Bodleian MS Pattison 52, ff. 508–9.
[179] Pattison, 'Present state of theology in Germany', p. 211.
[180] Pattison, 'Present state of theology in Germany', pp. 214–15.

Pattison depicted the kind of critical-historical theology that had come to the fore in Germany as a logical completion of the Reformation: a historical necessity, therefore, in contrast to Pusey's focus on its arbitrary and capricious character. This was because Pattison interpreted the significance of the Reformation, in world-historical terms, as 'the insurrection of the human reason against the yoke of authority'. Reliance on the authority of scripture was an unstable stopping point: it was inevitable that rational criticism should, in time, be applied to scriptural texts to determine their credibility.[181]

Pattison wanted the *Westminster Review* to be an organ for free critical inquiry in matters of religion and theology, on the German model. This was not a matter of partisanship: the whole point about the Tübingen School that he so much admired was that it subordinated theological speculation to the critical method, whereas previously 'philological criticism had been an instrument of speculative theology'.[182] When Chapman declined to increase the theological content of his periodical, Pattison turned instead to other options to achieve the same goal: specifically, to *Essays and Reviews*. Although we know it as a one-off publication, Pattison and Wilson planned it, in the first instance, as a quarterly general periodical, and when that seemed to entail too great a financial risk, they thought in terms of a series of annual volumes comparable to the series of *Oxford Essays* and *Cambridge Essays* which had been appearing since 1855. Wilson did most of the organizational work, but Pattison was instrumental in securing Jowett's involvement. He also tried, unsuccessfully, to engage others in the project, notably J. B. Mozley, his old Oriel contemporary who had been a fellow inhabitant of Newman's house on St Aldate's. He had distanced himself from narrow Tractarianism, but by no means as far as Pattison, and even though his own thought had been evolving 'so completely in a liberal direction', he declined to participate on the ground that what he would write would be 'a little too dogmatic' for the other contributors.[183]

If the contributions had a common spirit, that spirit can best be defined in terms of a shared belief that disinterested scholarship had the capacity to unite people who were divided by churchmanship. Pattison's own study of the eighteenth-century deistical controversy began by deploring the partisanship that shaped the writing of religious history in England: 'We have

[181] Pattison, 'Present state of theology in Germany', pp. 221–2.
[182] Pattison, 'Present state of theology in Germany', p. 226.
[183] J. B. Mozley to Pattison, 27 July 1858, Bodleian MS Pattison 52, ff. 114–5.

not yet learnt, in this country, to write our ecclesiastical history on any better footing than that of praising up the party, in or out of the Church, to which we happen to belong.'[184] But it was Jowett's essay 'On the interpretation of scripture' that articulated this approach most potently. Jowett was certainly not central to the genesis of the volume, and he was the last to submit his essay; but his contribution provides an insight into the essayists' intentions. It was and is much misunderstood, chiefly because of the author's repeated insistence that the bible should be read 'like any other book'.[185] Those who know no more of Jowett's essay than that assume – as many of his contemporaries did – that it encapsulates his whole meaning. The essay must have been written to liberate biblical criticism from the straitjacket of literalist orthodoxy. 'In the literature of human freedom', one authority has written, 'Jowett's essay deserves a place besides Milton's *Areopagitica*.'[186]

This is not wrong, but it does mislead. Jowett did not find the biblical scholarship of his time to be in thrall to a crabbed literalism; neither did he consider it to be characterized by a narrow orthodoxy. He did not seek to throw wide the gates to a thousand different readings of each text; rather, he hoped to set out a method that would generate a greater degree of agreement in the reading of scripture. Above all, he had no intention of undermining the sacred status of scripture. Instead, he wanted to enhance its 'moral power' by establishing its 'true meaning' more clearly.[187] This was a liberal project; but the reason why it was liberal needs to be unfolded. Jowett was certainly not saying: let a thousand opinions clash. Rather, he deplored the fact that the interpretation of the bible was a battleground. It was not biblical criticism, but ecclesiastical partisanship that had made it a site of conflict. The point of a properly scientific method of biblical interpretation was, paradoxically, 'to get rid of interpretation, and leave us alone in company with the author.'[188] The modern interpreter of scripture should not hide the discrepancies in the text, for 'the acknowledgment of them is the first step towards agreement among interpreters'. Rather, 'he would restore the original meaning, because "seven other"

[184] Pattison, 'Tendencies of religious thought in England, 1688–1750', *Essays and Reviews* (London: Parker, 1860), p. 255.
[185] Benjamin Jowett, 'On the interpretation of scripture', *Essays and Reviews* (London: Parker, 1860), p. 377.
[186] Josef L. Altholz, *Anatomy of a Controversy: the Debate over 'Essays and Reviews', 1860–1864* (Aldershot: Scolar, 1994), p. 31.
[187] Jowett, 'On the interpretation of scripture', p. 425.
[188] Jowett, 'On the interpretation of scripture', p. 384.

meanings take the place of it; the book is made the sport of opinion and the instrument of perversion of life.'[189]

Jowett's essential point was that an accumulation of traditional interpretations, encrusted with partisan attempts to twist scriptural passages to prove controversial doctrines, got in the way of the original meaning of the text. Until the scholarly interpretation of scripture established its ascendancy, disagreement would remain.

> The Protestant and Catholic, the Unitarian and Trinitarian will continue to fight their battle on the ground of the New Testament … Apparent coincidences will always be discovered by those who want to find them. Where there is no critical interpretation of Scripture, there will be a mystical or rhetorical one. If words have more than one meaning, they may have any meaning. Instead of being a rule of life or faith, Scripture becomes the expression of the ever-changing aspect of religious opinions. The unchangeable word of God, in the name of which we repose, is changed by each age and each generation in accordance with its passing fancy. The book in which we believe all religious truth to be contained, is the most uncertain of all books, because interpreted by arbitrary and uncertain methods.[190]

Jowett and Pattison would later come to stand for rival conceptions of the university, and their relations were soured by their intellectual differences. But in the 1850s and early 60s university politics and religion tended to unite rather than divide them. Pattison shared Jowett's frustration at the way in which ecclesiastical partisanship frustrated the search for truth. He was despondent at the controversy generated by *Essays and Reviews* because it was dominated by precisely the kind of partisanship it was designed to overcome. Reviewers were critical of his own essay either because they detected in it a sympathy for rationalist theology of the kind he was seeking to examine historically, or because they saw his historian's neutrality as a cowardly evasion of the responsibility of the writer to state his own position. 'So wholly extinct is scientific theology in the Church of England', he concluded, 'that the English public could not recognise such a thing as a neutral and philosophic inquiry into the causes of the form of thought existing at any period. Our clergy knew only of pamphlets which must be either for or against one of the parties in the Church.'[191]

[189] Jowett, 'On the interpretation of scripture', p. 376.
[190] Jowett, 'On the interpretation of scripture', pp. 371–2.   [191] Pattison, *Memoirs*, p. 314.

# CHAPTER 2

# 'Into the abysses, or no one knows where'

At the point that the *Essays and Reviews* controversy broke, Thomas Hughes's novel, *Tom Brown at Oxford*, sequel to the more famous *Tom Brown's Schooldays*, was in the midst of being serialized by the recently founded monthly, *Macmillan's Magazine*. Hughes had been an undergraduate at Oriel a decade after Pattison, and he set the novel in the 1840s. He recounts a conversation between his hero and a puzzled young woman who asks which is worse: a Tractarian or a Germanizer. Tom Brown has no doubt of the answer:

The Germanizer, of course ... because one knows the worst of where the Tractarians are going. They may go to Rome, and there's an end of it. But the Germanizers are going into the abysses, or no one knows where.[1]

Pattison had been a Tractarian, but had narrowly avoided going to Rome. For many of his critics, the course of the remainder of his life vindicated Tom Brown's view that the fate of the Germanizing rationalist was far worse. Towards the end of his life Pattison was sometimes inclined to that view himself, but that was hardly how things would have seemed to him in the early 1860s. In the midst of the controversy over *Essays and Reviews*, he would win the prize that had been denied him a decade previously.

### THE PRIZE: ELECTION TO THE RECTORSHIP

It is curious that whereas Pattison's *Memoirs* dwell to an inordinate extent on the events of October and November 1851, they tell us nothing at all of his election to the rectorship in January 1861. Yet the outcome of that election was in its way just as extraordinary as that of ten years before.

---

[1] Quoted by Briggs, 'Oxford and its critics', p. 138. This chapter was first published in the September 1860 issue of *Macmillan's Magazine*, at a time when general periodicals such as *Fraser's Magazine* had begun to review *Essays and Reviews*.

How Pattison contrived to win is something of a mystery. As in 1851, there were nine voting fellows. Whereas in 1851 Pattison had a distinct body of fellows (four, including himself, out of nine) who formed his 'party', in 1861 it is difficult to identify any of the fellows, apart from himself, as his supporters. Whereas the party that opposed him in 1851 remained largely intact, the three fellows who had supported him then had all since resigned. His correspondence in January 1861 shows him to have been deeply pessimistic about the outcome. When one of his sisters reassured him that he would have some supporters, the one she named was John Iles, a former pupil of Pattison's, now rector of Wolverhampton. But a week later Iles wrote to Pattison to say not only that he was surprised that Pattison was offering himself as a candidate, but also that he would certainly not be supporting him:

I think it only right to state, why I cannot on any consideration support you. I have considered your intellectual, religious, and social qualifications:
1. Intellectual. – very few men could have higher.
2. Religious. – I cannot even guess what your religion is, and no one, whom I have asked, is able to enlighten me – years ago, when Undergraduate and Bachelor, in Lincoln men speculated on the same subject, with no better success: – in those days we laughed over this matter, admired your intellect, and would have had you as our Rector – but as grown men, we take a more serious view, and I at least could never recommend to my Relatives and Friends, the College, where you, still the same mysterious Pattison, were the Head.
3. Social. – I first became acquainted with you in Michaelmas Term 1847: my impression is, that you have never during all the time since then, been entirely on friendly terms with the governing body of the College: it is difficult then to believe, that another step in position would at once alter your social character.
With such opinions in my head, I feel that if I vote for you, I vote against Lincoln College.[2]

The letters of congratulation Pattison received following his election likewise indicate that his friends had been pessimistic about the outcome: their tone is one of surprised elation. Elizabeth Gaskell, for instance, had been led to believe that 'you were not likely to obtain that honour, which (may I say it?) all your friends knew you so well deserved'. The former fellow George Perry observed apologetically that he had put himself forward as a candidate only because he supposed Pattison to be out of the contest. And Edward Poste was all the more pleased because 'I had heard in Oxford a clear demonstration of the impossibility of such an event'.[3]

[2] J. Hodgson Iles to Pattison, 8 January 1861, Bodleian MS Pattison 54, ff. 17–18.
[3] Elizabeth Gaskell to Pattison, 26 January 1861; George Perry to Pattison, same date; Edward Poste to Pattison, 25 January 1861, Bodleian MS Pattison 54, ff. 93–4, 118–9, 67–8.

There were in fact two leading candidates in January 1861: Richard Michell and Thomas Fowler. Michell was now eligible under the new statutes and was the front-runner, with an identifiable bloc of four voters. This must have been no surprise to Pattison: at least three of these had been fellows in 1851 and had declined to vote for Pattison then; he could hardly have expected to win their support now. His pessimism was based, apparently, on the fact that the liberals had come out for Fowler, a 28-year-old Merton graduate elected to his fellowship not six years before.[4] Pattison's former pupils such as Richard Christie thought Fowler's claims presumptuous, given his youth; but Pattison evidently had good reason to suppose that Fowler and not he had emerged as the liberals' candidate.[5] That was why he sought to enlist the help of university liberals such as Jowett and Goldwin Smith, chiefly to bring pressure to bear on W. W. Merry, a Balliol man elected fellow of Lincoln in 1859, who would eventually succeed Pattison as rector in 1884. Both Jowett and Smith felt that the intervention of outsiders would be counter-productive, although Jowett offered more useful advice than Smith, who urged Pattison to leave Oxford and pursue a literary career in London.[6]

So what happened to bring about Pattison's election? We have an apocryphal version of the story in the form of an oral account given by Henry Sidgwick to his Cambridge colleague, Henry Jackson, the Regius professor of Greek. Jackson made a note of this account in his copy of the *Memoirs*. The Cambridge University Librarian, A. F. Scholfield, who acquired that copy, passed the note on to John Sparrow.[7] Jackson's account – which is uncertain as to the total number of electors, and does not identify Pattison's rivals – suggests that Fowler had four first-choice supporters; Michell three; and Pattison two. According to Jackson, Pattison secured election by threatening Fowler that he and his supporter would vote for Michell, who would thus be elected. At that point Fowler withdrew, and he and his supporters helped elect Pattison. In some details, this account is certainly inaccurate: Jackson does not name the second-placed candidate, but simply calls him a 'non-resident'. But Pattison and Fowler were, it seems, the only current fellows who presented themselves in 1861; Michell was not a non-resident, but a former fellow.

[4] Green, *Oxford Common Room*, pp. 200–2, curiously fails to mention Fowler's candidacy.
[5] R. C. Christie to Pattison, 16 January 1861, Bodleian MS Pattison 54, ff. 32–3.
[6] Jowett to Pattison, two undated letters [January 1861], Bodleian MS Pattison 54, ff. 3–4, 15–16; Goldwin Smith to Pattison, 6 January 1861, MS Pattison 54, ff. 11–14.
[7] See A. F. Scholfield to John Sparrow, 2 December 1956, Lincoln College MS/PAT/III/10.

Apocryphal though it is, this account is worth taking seriously, however, since it offers a credible explanation, and perhaps the only credible explanation, of how Pattison's election arose from an apparently hopeless balance of forces. In one respect Jackson's account is surely wrong: Michell was almost certainly ahead of Fowler in terms of first-choice backers. Pattison told his former pupil, Octavius Fox, that Michell had four supporters, and Fox replied that he thought he could guess who they were.[8] Pattison's correspondence also makes it clear that the liberals in college were lining up behind Fowler: in fact the same letter from Fox, which expresses astonishment that Michell was unable to 'detach any one of Fowler's supporters', implies that Fowler had at least three if not four supporters, including himself. This picture of the balance of forces is broadly supported by Jowett's first (undated) letter of January 1861. There he says 'I believe what you say about Merry that he has a goodwill to you & would support you against Michell quite as zealously as Fowler.'[9] There is a grammatical ambiguity about this sentence: is Fowler a subject ('as Fowler would') or an object ('as he would support Fowler')? The latter is much the more likely, but either version would offer support to Jackson's account. The question Pattison and Jowett were evidently pondering is whether Fowler's supporters would stick to their guns if it were clear that their candidate could not stop Michell, whereas another candidate might.

There is one further piece of evidence: the animosity that existed between Pattison and Fowler throughout Pattison's rectorship. This was apparently purely personal: the two men had very similar intellectual outlooks, and Fowler was evidently much influenced by Pattison's idea of the university. Pattison was certainly suspicious of Fowler long before January 1861, but just two months earlier they had collaborated in support of Max Müller's unsuccessful candidature for the professorship of Sanskrit.[10] After the rectorship election their relations were consistently bad, and yet Fowler was, in the words of one colleague, 'the kindest and best natured man I have almost ever known'; which may help explain why the college liberals were inclined to think of him as a serious candidate in spite of his youth.[11] In 1865 Fowler spoke up at a college meeting against a proposal to reimburse Pattison for part of the cost of the repair and

---

[8]  Octavius Fox to Pattison, 11 February 1861, Bodleian MS Pattison 53, ff. 66–7.
[9]  Jowett to Pattison, n.d. January 1861, Bodleian MS Pattison 54, ff. 3–4.
[10]  Bodleian MS Pattison 130, f. 32.
[11]  William Warde Fowler, *Reminiscences* (Privately published, 1921), p. 27. W. W. Fowler, who was no relation to Thomas, was a scholar and then a fellow of Lincoln when Pattison was rector and Thomas Fowler sub-rector. He succeeded to the sub-rectorship when his namesake was elected president of Corpus Christi. Of all the fellows of Lincoln he was closest to Pattison.

refurbishment of the drawing room in the rector's lodgings. 'The debate', wrote Pattison in his diary,

> was the occasion of Fowler's betraying the real state of his feeling towards me, which it is of importance to me to bear in mind. He has never forgotten the disappointment of the rectorship. I have for 4 years done all in my power to soften it for him, and by resigning the whole management of the men to him to give him importance, and not to let him feel that he had lost anything by the change of Rectors.

Pattison had thought that their relations were becoming more amicable, but he now realized that 'his rancour is as intense as ever beneath. He hates not so much me personally, as the rectorate, and by reflexion from it all authorities and powers in the University'.[12] Even after Pattison's death Fowler could not be induced to say a good word about him.[13] This degree of animosity is difficult to explain by a straightforward defeat in a three-cornered election: after all, Fowler was only twenty-eight at the time, and must have known that his time would come, as it did. What enraged Fowler was a sense that Pattison had deployed underhand tactics, and above all that through Pattison's unscrupulous willingness to engage in what the French call 'la politique du pire' he, Fowler, had been forced to put Pattison in the rectorship by his own vote.

This was not as scandalous an election as that of 1851 had been: all three contenders in 1861 were worthy of the headship, and indeed the two defeated candidates subsequently succeeded to headships at other colleges. But it is extraordinary that Pattison was able to secure election in spite of having the positive support of, at most, only one fellow other than himself. Pattison was not a man of business, but this incident shows him to be practised in the lower arts of politics. He had evidently learned from the experience of 1851, when he and his followers had deployed 'la politique du pire' for purely negative ends. Now he used the threat of it to get his own way. There is something heroically unscrupulous about this. But it is also worth reflecting on how it worked. Why did Fowler's party not call Pattison's bluff? Did they really believe he would be prepared to vote for Michell, whom he certainly regarded as his enemy, whereas he had no reason at this stage to be antagonistic towards Fowler? The answer may be that the events of 1851 showed that Pattison might very well do just that. In that sense, the folk memory of tactics employed to elect Thompson in 1851 may have been what made Pattison's tactics work a decade later.

---

[12] Bodleian MS Pattison 130, f. 61, 22 December 1865.
[13] Thomas Fowler to T. F. Althaus, 25 April 1885, Lincoln College MS/PAT/I.

The other question is why Fowler's party were prepared to switch *en bloc* to Pattison in the face of his own unscrupulous behaviour towards them. Sheer partisanship seems to hold the key: Michell was a Tory and an opponent of university reform; Pattison, isolated as he had been from college affairs for five years, was strongly identified with university liberalism, and with religious liberalism too. 'The defensive strength of liberalism at Oxford is at least doubled by your election', wrote one staunch liberal to Pattison in the aftermath of the vote.[14] He was also a man of national distinction – much more so than he had been a decade earlier. They preferred Fowler not because of any political differences between him and Pattison, but simply because Fowler was the current head of the reforming party in college, as Pattison had been in 1851. If they knew that they could not have Fowler, it made sense to go for Pattison.

Even if we accept this story, there are still some puzzles. Who exactly were the four who voted for Michell against Pattison? On the face of things there were no fewer than five who should have preferred Michell to Pattison. Calcott, West and Metcalfe were all conservatives in national and university politics and had opposed Pattison in 1851. Kettle was a liberal in politics but no friend to Pattison, whose cause he had deserted ten years before: in any case, he wrote to Pattison to tell him that he regarded Michell as the best candidate, although he implied that he would prefer Pattison to Fowler and assured him that 'if you are elected I for one shall feel proud that we have so able & distinguished a man for our Head'.[15] Finally, as we have seen, John Iles had firmly told Pattison that he could never vote for him. Iles was evidently a liberal in politics: at least, we know that he voted for Gladstone against Chandos in the election for the university seat in 1859.[16] It is possible that he followed the rest of Fowler's party and voted for Pattison against his better judgement. But it is also possible, as V. H. H. Green supposes, that West, having opposed Pattison in 1851, supported him from the outset in 1861.[17] Certainly he and Pattison enjoyed a cordial relationship in spite of their political differences, for Pattison admired West's astute business sense as college bursar. If Pattison's one positive backer was not a liberal, it helps explain why

---

[14] Frederick W. Walker to Pattison, n.d. [January–February 1861], Bodleian MS Pattison 54, ff. 221–2. Walker was a classical philologist and High Master of Manchester Grammar School.

[15] J. L. R. Kettle to Pattison, 23 January 1861, Bodleian MS Pattison 54, ff. 51–4.

[16] Green, *Oxford Common Room*, p. 199 n. 3.

[17] V. H. H. Green, *The Commonwealth of Lincoln College 1427–1977* (Oxford: Oxford University Press, 1979), p. 467.

Fowler's party came to regard their position as hopeless and hence capitulated in the face of Pattison's tactics.

One final question to pose is this: why did Pattison want the rectorship so badly that he was prepared to act in so ruthless a manner? As I have suggested, at the time it was an office to which it was natural for an eligible candidate to aspire, and at least three former fellows, in addition to Michell, seem to have offered themselves as candidates without attracting support.[18] But in the course of a decade Pattison had had plenty of time to reflect on the prospect of the rectorship, and it is striking that several of his friends were prepared to suggest to him, in the days and weeks leading up to the election, that it was perhaps not the job for him. Goldwin Smith thought he would be well advised to cut his losses and concentrate on his writing: 'If you write a book that will live, as well you may, nobody will ask whether you were Rector of Lincoln; & if they do, it will only be to condemn the College.'[19] Frederick Shaw, a former pupil who almost idolized his old tutor, was highly critical of the list of names being discussed and urged Pattison not to care about the outcome: but he did so in words that implied that he thought that Pattison's gifts were not those of a head of house. 'Can you think of any Collegiate or Corporate Body for which the absolutely best <u>man</u>, would be the best head?'[20] Another former pupil, Edward Lowe, was even blunter: he wished Pattison well, but 'I do not feel absolutely sure, whether yr election wd be altogether for the interests of the College'.[21] Yet in spite of all these hints, Pattison clearly did want to be elected.

Pattison was a man who never forgot an injustice, and it could be that he wanted the post in 1861 simply because he felt, reasonably enough, that he had deserved to be elected in 1851. Had he been elected then we can speculate that he would have been a vigorous head, at least to begin with. As things turned out he was a notoriously inactive rector. He preferred to leave most college business to his sub-rector, Thomas Fowler, and justified this course to himself by saying that he did not want Fowler to feel that he had lost any of his status or power as a result of Pattison's election, as he himself had felt that Thompson's election had deprived him of the influence he had had under Radford. But when Fowler left, Pattison treated his successor, William Warde Fowler, in a similar way.[22] He never ceased to

---

[18]  These were Hannah, Espin and Green. Espin, along with Pattison, Michell and Fowler, was spoken of as a candidate in *The Times*, 7 January 1861, p. 6.
[19]  Goldwin Smith to Pattison, 6 January 1861, Bodleian MS Pattison 54, ff. 11–14.
[20]  Frederick Shaw to Pattison, 8 January 1861, Bodleian MS Pattison 54, ff. 19–20.
[21]  Edward C. Lowe to Pattison, 15 January 1861, Bodleian MS Pattison 54, ff. 28–31.
[22]  William Warde Fowler, *Reminiscences*, pp. 58–9.

regard college business as a tiresome distraction. 'Audit, whole day consumed in vanity & nothingness', he wrote in a typical diary entry.[23]
Pattison had in fact persuaded himself that college headships should
properly be regarded as sinecures – pensions, in the eighteenth-century
sense – for men of high literary or scientific distinction, to enable them to
pursue their work free from distraction. It was an interpretation of the
office that he would articulate expressly in his most important intervention
in debates on university reform, his *Suggestions on Academic Organisation*
of 1868.

### THE DREAM OF HAPPINESS

There was one obvious opportunity that his elevation opened up to him.

In Pattison's day, most college fellowships at Oxford were held on
condition of celibacy: most fellows were in holy orders, and a fellow who
wished to marry would usually wait for an attractive college living to fall
vacant, or perhaps take a schoolmastership.[24] Prior to the late-Victorian
growth of a non-academic middle class in the city, Oxford society was
therefore overwhelmingly male. The only dons who could marry were
college heads and professors: heads were then practically a separate caste,
and professors were few in number before the reforms of the 1850s, and
were under no obligation to reside. 'When I was scholar and fellow',
recalled E. A. Freeman, who was just a few years younger than Pattison,
'we very seldom saw the inside of a house as distinguished from a college.'[25]

Pattison was brought up in the company of ten sisters and he was very
close to several of them, especially Eleanor and Rachel. He also had a
curiously intense cerebral relationship with his remarkable cousin, Philippa
Meadows, which he relates in the *Memoirs*. But apart from his relatives
female friendship seems to have been wholly absent from his life until 1861.
Moreover, apart from a fleeting interest in the possibility of a chair at one
of the newly established Queen's Colleges in Ireland in the late 1840s, he
seems never to have sought escape from his fellowship.[26] He must have

---

[23] Bodleian MS Pattison 132, f. 39, 22 Dec. 1879.
[24] A Lincoln fellow might marry, however, if he took one of the two parochial chaplaincies in Oxford –
All Saints or St Michael's – which were attached to the college. Pattison could have taken
St Michael's in 1849 or All Saints in 1852. But neither living was valuable and in each case it was
taken by a relatively junior fellow. See Green, *Commonwealth of Lincoln College*, p. 707.
[25] E. A. Freeman, 'Oxford after forty years – 1', *Contemporary Review* 51 (1887), 611.
[26] In 1851, shortly before the first rectorship election, he fleetingly considered taking the valuable
college living of Waddington in Lincolnshire. But his colleagues evidently took it for granted that he
would turn it down: Green, *Commonwealth of Lincoln College*, pp. 448–9.

been almost unique among Victorian clerical dons in his indifference to ecclesiastical preferment – which may be another way of saying that he increasingly came to regard his clerical status simply as the necessary and irksome condition of his academic career.

Yet within eight months of his election to the rectorship in January 1861, Pattison would marry. 'I see in the papers that Mark Pattison is married!', wrote Newman to the Duchess of Norfolk. 'Sic transit Gloria. He will never come to us.'[27] It would be one of the most remarkable marriages, and one of the most tragic, of the Victorian era. Pattison was a melancholic, a hypochondriac and hugely self-centred, while his wife – much more of an altruist – was strong-willed, principled and highly ambitious.

Emily Francis Strong was just 21 when she married the Rector of Lincoln, who was then approaching his 48th birthday. The age difference was, famously, the same as that which separated the Casaubons in *Middlemarch*. But commentators have tended to make too much of it. Victorian professional men commonly married late, and large age differences were by no means unusual. To take just two instances from Pattison's Oxford contemporaries, Frederic Harrison and James Bryce both married women twenty years their junior. Of the five of Pattison's collaborators on *Essays and Reviews* who married, all except Wilson were over forty on marriage: Temple married a woman twenty-four years younger, and Powell twenty-eight. It was not the age difference, but the personalities involved, that made the Pattison marriage so striking.

Francis, as she was known up to the end of her first marriage (when she adopted the name 'Emilia', as a more sophisticated and cosmopolitan version of her first name), was by any standards an exceptional woman.[28] She achieved distinction and international renown as an art historian who specialized in French art of the Renaissance and after. At the same time she was an active social reformer who was particularly associated with the cause of women's trade unionism.

Francis was the third of five daughters (and the fourth of six children) of an Indian army officer, Captain Henry Strong, who on his retirement from the service lived for a time in Ilfracome, where Francis was born in 1840, and then entered into the employment of the London and County Bank (an ancestor of NatWest). He was appointed to manage the bank's Oxford branch, newly opened in the High Street, in 1841. For many years the

[27] Quoted in Frank M. Turner, *John Henry Newman: The Challenge to Evangelical Religion* (New Haven and London: Yale University Press, 2002), p. 428.
[28] She will be referred to as Francis here.

family lived in an apartment above the bank, just around the corner from Lincoln; but they later settled in Iffley, a couple of miles from Oxford, in a large house called The Elms which is now the home of the Hawkwell House Hotel. Since Pattison had an account with the London and County Bank, we may surmise that it was as his bank manager that Captain Strong encountered him. Strong wrote in January 1861 to congratulate Pattison on his election to the rectorship, and since the congratulations were offered in the name of the whole family it can be inferred that there had already been some social interaction. The Strongs were guests at a dinner party in the rector's lodgings in May 1861.[29] The family certainly moved in Oxford academic circles, and counted among their friends William Ince, fellow of Exeter, Goldwin Smith of University College, and especially Henry Acland, Regius professor of medicine, and his wife Sarah. Francis's elder sister, Rosa, had already married a fellow of New College, William Tuckwell, who officiated at the Pattisons' marriage at Iffley church on 10 September. Perhaps the younger sister wished to outdo Rosa by marrying a head of house. Francis herself was formidably well connected for such a young woman, having already turned down an offer of marriage from William Holman Hunt. But scarcely anything specific is known of how Pattison and Francis Strong became intimate.

Captain Strong was a keen amateur painter and Francis inherited his talent to such an extent that her youthful drawings impressed John Ruskin, a close friend of the Aclands, when they were shown to him, and he persuaded her to study at the National Art Training School at South Kensington, the forerunner of the Royal College of Art. She studied there from 1858 to 1861, in the course of which time she made the acquaintance of another art student, Charles Dilke. Later, as Sir Charles Dilke, and a controversial politician on the advanced wing of the Liberal party, he would become her second husband. They were fellow members of a South Kensington club which played the Kent pub game of 'trap and bat' in the orchard of Gore House under the eyes of a spectator of the eminence of W. M. Thackeray, whose daughters were also members.

There is disagreement, as we shall see shortly, as to whether Pattison and Francis Strong may be taken as the originals of Edward Casaubon and Dorothea Brooke in George Eliot's *Middlemarch*. Francis certainly resembled Dorothea in her extreme devotion. Her mother brought her up on solid 'Church principles' which Francis, as was her wont, pushed to

[29] Henry Strong to Pattison, n.d. [but evidently January 1861], Bodleian MS Pattison 54, f. 72; MS Pattison 14 (engagement diary).

the extreme of out-and-out Puseyism of a relentlessly ascetic kind. As a student at South Kensington she would shock her fashionable friends with her insistence on undertaking works of supererogatory penitence such as lying for hours on a bare floor for the most trivial misdeed.[30]

The Pattisons' marriage is curiously lacking in first-hand documentation. None of Pattison's letters to Francis survive, and he kept only the letters she wrote in 1875–6. Pattison's diary is strikingly sparse for the 1860s – much sparser, in fact, than for any other part of his adult life. The main surviving source of information on the marriage is the collection of letters Francis wrote in the last nine years of the marriage to Eleanor Smith, who contrived to remain on good terms with both parties.[31] For that reason, a number of misapprehensions have grown up which are difficult, but not impossible, to dispel. Foremost among these misapprehensions is the belief that the marriage went wrong almost from the outset. Even Sparrow took this view, which makes it hardly surprising that scholars with a more passing interest have endorsed it.[32] Both of Francis's biographers agree, and suppose, quite wrongly, that Pattison (or perhaps Francis) destroyed his diary for 1861 in order to avoid exposing the secrets of the early marriage.[33] It was certainly true that, according to her own account, Francis found the sexual relationship unfulfilling from the outset, but though the modern assumption is that this must have been decisive, there is in fact no evidence that the marriage lacked personal intimacy in the early years. 'The marriage was not ill-assorted', wrote Lady Dilke's obituarist, who clearly knew the couple, 'nor, though it had its trials for both parties, was it other than one of personal affection and intellectual

---

[30] Sir Charles W. Dilke, 'Memoir [of the author]', in Lady Dilke, *The Book of the Spiritual Life* (London: Murray, 1905), p. 9.

[31] Eleanor Smith was the sister of Pattison's friend, the mathematician Henry Smith. She was a notable Oxford figure in her own right, and a pioneer of women's higher education.

[32] Sparrow, *Pattison*, p. 11. A typical example of assumptions about the marriage is the brief discussion in an otherwise very good article by Philippa Levine, ' "So few prizes and so many blanks": marriage and feminism in later nineteenth-century Britain', *Journal of British Studies* 28 (1989), 159. In a mostly inaccurate paragraph, Levine accepts the conventional view that for Francis the marriage was 'a miserable experience', which is a very short abridgement of a rather complex story.

[33] Kali Israel, *Names and Stories: Emilia Dilke and Victorian Culture* (Oxford: Oxford University Press, 1999), p. 76, says that Pattison's diary for 1861 was 'probably destroyed by him', but gives no evidence for this perverse judgement. It seems to be derived from Betty Askwith, *Lady Dilke: A Biography* (London: Chatto & Windus, 1969), p. 10, who, having noted Francis's penchant for applying the eraser or the scissors to manuscripts, says that Pattison's diary for 1861 and the whole of 1862 is 'missing'. What she might have said is that the diary resumes in September 1862 on the reverse of the page used for December 1860: no pages have been removed from that book. See Bodleian MS Pattison 130 f. 33. Incidentally, it is by no means the case that Francis (if indeed it was she) sought to remove only derogatory references to her: she tried to erase all mention of her, even quite innocent references to reading books 'aloud to F': e.g. MS Pattison 130, ff. 91, 94, 98, 108, 114, 180.

sympathy at the outset.'[34] The belief that their personal relationship went awry from the outset seems to derive not from any evidence relating to the Pattisons, but instead, perversely enough, from George Eliot's portrayal of the Casaubons' marriage. There is no doubt that Francis came to regret the marriage and constructed it retrospectively as a disastrous mistake. 'For nineteen years', she wrote in 1881, 'I have been struggling to keep down the longing for deliverance'.[35] What is less clear is exactly when she came to be conscious of the desire for deliverance. If this happened before 1875 there is nothing to prove it. Outwardly the marriage was successful up to that point.

'Mark Pattison did not write a story of his marriage', says Kali Israel, the most recent biographer of his wife.[36] But in fact he did, at least in fragments, in his letters to Meta Bradley, the young woman who became his intimate friend in his last years. Pattison's crucial letter, in which he announced to Meta that 10 September (the date of his marriage in 1861) was 'an anniversary which depresses me to the lowest depths of misery', has largely been excised, presumably either by Meta herself or by Pattison's protégé, T. F. Althaus, to whom she left the letters at her death.[37] In the missing part Pattison evidently told Meta the story – his story – of the marriage. But his narrative can largely be reconstructed from Meta's side of the correspondence. V. H. H. Green, in his study of the Pattison – Bradley correspondence, skips over this rapidly on the ground that 'Mark's account of his married life, so uncritically accepted by Meta, was one-sided and partisan'.[38] Of course it was one-sided, but its significance is precisely that it was *his* narrative of the marriage, and the only version of his narrative that we possess. The story that emerges there is quite clear on this point: Pattison distinguished explicitly and sharply between 'the long years of such loving-companionship as I imagine few people are capable of' and 'their successors [which were] the darker by contrast'. Meta enquired: 'Perhaps some day you'll tell me what built up such a wall of ice between you – tho somehow I fancy that you don't even know yourself. I'd have thought any misunderstanding impossible after so many years of most intimate communion.'[39] Pattison replied to say that 'I feel that you have not only taken in the situation, so far as I have disclosed it, but have exactly

---

[34] 'Lady Dilke', *The Times*, 25 October 1904, p. 4.
[35] E. F. S. Pattison to Eleanor Smith, 30 March 1881, Bodleian MS Pattison 118, f. 63.
[36] Israel, *Names and Stories*, p. 76.
[37] Bodleian MS Pattison 119, ff. 144–7, Pattison to Meta Bradley, 12 September 1880.
[38] Green, *Love in a Cool Climate*, p. 45.
[39] Bodleian MS Pattison 119, ff. 148–9, Meta Bradley to Pattison, 14 September 1880.

estimated the feeling which urged me to make the avowal to you'; but he declined to explain the formation of the 'wall of ice', 'partly on account of the difficulty of putting such a history on paper; partly because to have said as much as I have done has been such a wrench to my reserve, that I have not the force to make a second effort. That must be adjourned.'[40] The following month he repeated the stark contrast between the last few years and the earlier years of the marriage: 'My birthday was 10 October last Sunday, we have usually had a plum pudding, and latterly, that has been the only celebration – though in the days of my happiness it was made a regular fête, and gift day.'[41]

Pattison never did explain, or date, the formation of the 'wall of ice', but it seems clear from this exchange that for him the years of 'intimate communion' had been many and the 'dark years' relatively few. That helps us make an informed guess that, in Pattison's eyes, the wall had formed around the period 1875–6. Indeed, the fact that he kept a collection of Francis's letters from this period, and included them – in the file of letters he deemed of special interest – among the papers he deposited in the Bodleian, is highly significant. He evidently regarded them as illuminating the turning point in the marriage, and he perhaps thought they cast his wife as the wrongdoer. It was also in the mid-1870s that his diary-keeping resumed an intensity it had not had since the 1850s: the period from the beginning of 1861 to the beginning of 1876 is sparsely covered in about a hundred pages, whereas we have over three hundred pages on the last seven years of his life: three times as much on a period of half the length. In Pattison as in other diary-keepers, such as his Oxford contemporary Arthur Hugh Clough, intense diary-keeping was a sure indication of inner unhappiness and loneliness.[42] So what happened?

Early in 1875 Francis Pattison revived her friendship with Dilke; and from the summer of that year, ostensibly on medical advice, she took to living chiefly on the Continent, first in Wildbad in Germany, then in Nice, and finally in Draguignan.[43] Pattison reacted badly to her absence, just as, she thought, his father had when one of his daughters was away from Hauxwell. Already in August 1875 she found his letters exasperating.

---

[40]  Bodleian MS Pattison 119, ff. 155–60, Pattison to Meta Bradley, 19 September 1880.

[41]  Bodleian MS Pattison 119, ff. 201–2, Pattison to Meta Bradley, 15 October 1880.

[42]  Anthony Kenny, *Arthur Hugh Clough, A Poet's Life* (London: Continuum, 2005), p. 54; also Anthony Kenny (ed.), *The Oxford Diaries of Arthur Hugh Clough* (Oxford: Clarendon, 1990).

[43]  Sparrow, *Pattison*, p. 44, gives the date when Francis started living abroad as 1867. Sparrow presumably intended to write 1876, but I have a copy of the book in which Sparrow made typographical corrections by hand, and he did not correct this.

Sometimes he appeared to blame her for getting ill on purpose in order to make her absence necessary; at other times he self-pityingly lamented that 'my home is broken up & all my dream of happiness in the closing years of my life vanished'. Francis had, he supposed, 'arranged' that her life would henceforth be lived without him.[44] Early in 1876 she wrote the devastating letter from which the marriage would never recover, when she told Pattison that she had come to find sexual relations with him 'insufferable'.[45]

We can only guess at the sequence of events and emotions here, but it seems likely that the renewal of her friendship with Dilke – though there is no evidence that it was ever adulterous – strengthened Francis's distaste for the sexual side of her marriage and induced her to flee to her continental retreat. Pattison clearly took this very badly, and evidently accused her of desertion, and even of feigning illness as a pretext for her desertion. Francis's reference to her physical aversion to sexual intercourse was first made in January 1876, explicitly in the context of an attempt to reassure Pattison of her continued love:

My dear dear Mark. Oh how I wish I were with you to prove to you that I am in no wise really changed to you – that my first and constant thoughts are devoted to you, that I value to the full all the goodness, & care you shew for me. You say I am 'free as to my movements'. The <u>only</u> wish & intention I have is to return <u>to you</u> to <u>Oxford</u> as soon as the weather, & my health permits – to settle down there quietly & work by your side for the summer as in past years – I do not think I can promise to face the winter. I am so delicate the slightest cold & change affects me instantly, & seriously. If it rains in the morning both my hands are stiff – but I have not the least desire to absent myself more than is absolutely necessary, & I do believe that when you see that you have all my thought, & anxiety to be your companion, & comfort the disappointment you feel at the state in wh I have now confined [sic] will be softened.

I will not attempt to defend myself agst the accusations either stated or implied wh you bring agst me. But you cannot forget that from the first I expressed the strongest aversion to that side of the common life, during 73–4 this became almost insufferable – but I tried to conceal it hoping that it might settle itself. You had told me constantly all along that it w^ld soon [change?] & when I thought it had by Acland's directions I rejoiced because I felt saved from any chance of wounding or distressing you. For believe me I wld suffer a great deal rather than give you a slight pain – much less a pain w^h is I feel <u>not</u> a slight one.

I almost wish now that I had not told you since I see how I have grieved you – anyway anything of the sort in my state of health must be impossible for a long

---

[44] E. F. S. Pattison to Eleanor Smith, n.d. and 9 Aug. 1875, the latter quoting a letter from Pattison: Bodleian MS Pattison 118, ff. 22–3 and 24–5.

[45] Bodleian MS Pattison 60, ff. 128–9, E. F. S. Pattison to Pattison, date unclear [probably January 1876].

time to come. All I meant when I said 'a fear preoccupied me' was that when you were with me I have often refrained from shewing you the affection I feel on that account. I cannot but think I am differently constituted to most, & that the excessive nervous irritability w^h is always engendered by the malady under w^h I suffer is the reason for the distress I laboured under throughout '74. You know you were greatly annoyed with me at le Locle, at Geneva, & in Paris, & I was trying hard for self control.[46]

It is evident that the difficulties of the Pattisons' marriage quickly became notorious, at least in Oxford: indeed, Francis's prolonged absence made this unavoidable. Jowett, always inclined to gossip, thought he had detected in one of Francis's reviews in the *Academy* a disguised attack on her husband, although it is difficult to be sure he was right. He certainly thought the increasingly acerbic tone of Pattison's interventions in academic politics – usually directed against Jowett and his allies – was to be explained by his bitterness at his marital problems, which left him 'in a state of irritated sensibility against all things'.[47] Perhaps Pattison had his own marriage in mind – certainly Jowett thought so – when he wrote of the failure of Milton's marriage. 'His poet's imagination ... had pictured for him the state of matrimony as an earthly paradise, in which he was to be secure of a response of affection showing itself in a communion of intelligent interests. In proportion to the brilliancy of his ideal anticipation was the fury of despair which came upon him when he found out his mistake.'[48]

Pattison can hardly have been thinking of Francis, however, when he wrote that Mary Milton was 'a dull and common girl'.[49] Neither did he share Milton's belief in sexual inequality. But a striking and curious feature of the early phase of the Pattisons' marriage is that the relationship of husband and wife blurs into that of tutor and pupil. Sir Charles Dilke, whose memoir is properly reticent about the trials of his widow's first marriage, writes of her 'schooling' by Pattison, and says that on her marriage she 'began to work for and with her husband'.[50] To the modern ear this is likely to sound rather repulsive, and at the time there were mutterings to the effect that Pattison was using his wife as an unpaid research assistant; but it should be said that if that was indeed how she

[46] Bodleian MS Pattison 60, ff. 128–9, E. F. S. Pattison to Pattison, date unclear [probably January 1876].
[47] Balliol College Jowett Papers III M 67, Jowett to Morier, 22 October 1876. The review in question was her review of Gustave Desnoiresterres, *Voltaire et la Société Française au XVIII Siècle*, *Academy* 9 (8 January 1876), 25–6. 'Tout savant est un peu cadavre', she quotes on p. 26.
[48] Pattison, *Milton* (London: Macmillan, 1879), pp. 56–7. Balliol College: Jowett papers H38 ff. 73–5, notes on Pattison's *Milton*.
[49] Pattison, *Milton*, p. 56.     [50] Dilke, 'Memoir', 18.

was used we might have expected some manuscript remains to demonstrate it. Even if she assisted him in his work he certainly encouraged her to develop scholarly interests of her own. 'It was put before me that if I wished to command respect I must make myself the authority on some one subject which interested me', was how she recalled the advice. 'I was told, and it was good counsel, not to take hack-work, and to reject even well-paid things that would lead me off the track.'[51] This was authentic Pattisonian advice: he told a pupil who had recently taken a First and who hoped to win a fellowship that he must 'choose some one special subject' to teach, rather than offering to 'read with' pupils on whatever they required. That was the route to 'true superiority', for '[m]en distinguish excellencies – much more than they used – & only the vulgar talk of "a very clever man".'[52] Francis was certainly able to pursue her own work on their long summer journeys to the continent: on one occasion in Vienna she found herself, fortuitously, being escorted around the Albertina Museum by Archduke Albrecht.[53] She launched her literary career, no doubt building on Pattison's contacts, by writing for the periodicals to which he contributed: the *Saturday Review*, the *Quarterly Review* and the *Academy*.

While Francis was incontestably independent in mind and spirit, she and Pattison had a great deal in common intellectually, and he participated in a number of her enthusiasms. These included her activity as a social reformer campaigning with and on behalf of working women through organizations such as the Women's Protective and Provident League, which she served as a Council member for many years. Mrs Nettleship pointed out that 'In this matter she had, far more than has been generally supposed, the sympathy, and, indeed, the most active assistance of the Rector of Lincoln.'[54] Late in his life we find him presiding at a meeting of the League. Sir Charles Dilke indeed speculated that 'it was originally the influence of Mark Pattison's diatribes on the uselessless of mere monasticism which turned his wife from speculative theology to more human forms of devotion'.[55] Like his wife, Pattison was an early supporter of the campaign for the enfranchisement of women. Conversely, she shared his views, rather than Dilke's, on such issues as the endowment of research in universities. When she counselled her niece, Gertrude Tuckwell, about her intellectual endeavours she spoke in recognizably Pattisonian tones.

[51] Quoted in Dilke, 'Memoir', pp. 26–7. Dilke here quotes from an undated letter Francis wrote to Gertrude Tuckwell, Bodleian MS Pattison 140, f. 87.
[52] Pattison to William Stebbing, 3 August 1854: Times Collection, Harry Ransom Center, University of Texas at Austin.
[53] Dilke, 'Memoir', 26.     [54] Quoted by Dilke, 'Memoir', 43.     [55] Dilke, 'Memoir', 43.

'Religion in the hierarchy of human knowledge', she wrote, 'seems to me to put these truths in an emotional form, & to enable those who have not or cannot develop the <u>speculative</u> powers of their intellect to apprehend in a different medium the "truths" of metaphysics.' This doctrine – that religious orthodoxy could be understood as an instrument to enable those who cannot grasp metaphysical ideas in their full abstraction to encounter them in a more digestible form – had been formulated by Pattison as early as the mid-1840s, when he faced a choice between submission to Rome and the freedom to follow the light of his own intellect. Francis was aware that she was simply echoing advice her husband could give with greater expertise: 'On all this however I speak entirely as a <u>lay</u> critic – the Rector has most deeply studied the subject & could help you with an authority I cannot pretend to.'[56]

In many ways the Pattisons' marriage, for its first decade or more, was a fine example of the companionate marriage celebrated by John Stuart Mill:

The man no longer gives his spare hours to violent exercises and boisterous conviviality with male associates; the two sexes now pass their lives together; the women of a man's family are his habitual society; the wife is his chief associate, his most confidential friend, and often his most trusted adviser.[57]

Husband and wife shared many interests and respected each other intellectually. It is difficult to accept that the breakdown of their sexual relations was the central cause of the marital difficulties. By this time Pattison was in his sixties, and many men of that age might have accepted a life of *de facto* celibacy with little difficulty.

In her study of five Victorian literary marriages, Phyllis Rose makes an important suggestion. She sees each of the marriages she studies as consisting of two 'narrative constructs'.

In unhappy marriages, for example, I see two versions of reality rather than two people in conflict. I see a struggle for imaginative dominance going on. Happy marriages seem to me those in which the two partners agree on the scenario they are enacting, even if, as was the case with Mr and Mrs Mill, their own idea of the relationship is totally at variance with the facts.[58]

To see how this thesis might be applied to the Pattisons, we need to turn to the thorny topic of George Eliot's supposed representation of their

[56] E. F. S. Pattison to Gertrude Tuckwell, 27 February 1882, Bodleian MS Pattison 140, ff. 45–6.
[57] Mill in the House of Commons, 20 May 1867, quoted by Tosh, *A Man's Place*, p. 53.
[58] Phyllis Rose, *Parallel Lives: Five Victorian Marriages* (Harmondsworth: Penguin, 1983), p. 15.

marriage as that of Edward Casaubon and Dorothea Brooke in *Middlemarch*.

Was Casaubon Pattison? The question has been discussed so often, and often so profitlessly, that one hesitates to scratch old wounds once more. But the identification has played such an important role in the survival of Pattison's reputation that the question of its credibility has to be revisited. We have to begin by unpicking the question, which can be separated out into the following questions. First, did Eliot's Casaubon resemble Pattison? If so, were the resemblances central or peripheral to the character as portrayed in the novel? If there were similarities, could they have been accidental, or did Eliot paint Casaubon from life? And if she did, did she do so in the knowledge that some of her readers would draw the conclusion that Casaubon was indeed Pattison?

As for the first question, John Sparrow said practically all that needs to be said. Like Pattison, Casaubon married a woman twenty-seven years his junior, and one who was drawn to her husband because she saw him as the personification of learning. Like Casaubon, Pattison looked older than he was, and the 'bitterness in the mouth and . . . venom in the glance' found in Casaubon could be detected in the Rector of Lincoln too. Both Casaubon and Pattison found difficulty in expressing affection and in evoking affection in return. Both men were known to be engaged in a great scholarly undertaking, and, like Casaubon, Pattison died leaving his great projected work unfinished – although George Eliot could not have known that would happen when she wrote.

Nevertheless, Sparrow found himself entrapped in a prolonged academic controversy, first in *Notes and Queries* following a review of his book by Eliot's American biographer, Gordon Haight; and then in the letters columns of the *Times Literary Supplement*, following a speculative piece on 'Dorothea's husbands' by Richard Ellmann. At the heart of the controversy was this: did George Eliot intend her readers – or some of them – to identify Casaubon with the Rector of Lincoln? Sparrow thought she did: 'George Eliot had Pattison in mind when she created Casaubon, and . . . she wished her readers to identify the two'.[59] His evidence for imputing to Eliot the intention that her readers would identify her character with Pattison rested essentially on the choice of name: although Pattison had not yet published his biography of Isaac Casaubon, he was known to be working on him, and had published his first major article on him as long ago as 1853. As Sparrow's colleague A. L. Rowse put it in a private letter,

---

[59] John Sparrow, letter in *TLS*, 16 March 1973, p. 296.

'the <u>name</u> Casaubon is so revealing to anyone who knows the processes' by which real writers write.[60] Furthermore, the resemblances cannot have been wholly accidental, for Sir Charles Dilke, in his memoir of his widow, wrote:

To deal once and for all with a subject always distasteful to my wife, Dorothea's defence of her marriage with Casaubon, and Casaubon's account of his first marriage to Dorothea in the first book of *Middlemarch*, are as a fact given by the novelist almost in Mark Pattison's words. Here the matter ends.[61]

This is rather confusingly expressed: how can Dorothea's defence of her marriage be given in Pattison's words? But in the manuscript version of the memoir he was clearer and more explicit. How did he know this 'as a fact'? Not because of his wife's testimony, but because of that of the novelist:

Casaubon's letter to Dorothea at the beginning of *Middlemarch* from what George Eliot herself told me in 1875, must have been very near the letter that Pattison actually wrote, and the reply very much the same.[62]

Is this case convincing? Ellmann thought not: Sparrow's evidence was 'singularly unpersuasive'.[63] Haight (though not Ellmann) actually contested the proposition that the name Casaubon was drawn from Pattison's interests: it was in fact, he argued, drawn 'from her own studies of the seventeenth century before she met Pattison'.[64] He also contested the reliability of Dilke's testimony: Eliot 'always refused to discuss her novels with her most intimate friends'; Dilke was never one of that circle; and he first met Eliot in 1878, three years after the alleged conversation.[65] In any case, Eliot had already conceived and drafted a pedant's proposal of marriage as early as 1846, and it is therefore unclear what Pattison's letter, if indeed she had seen it or had its contents paraphrased to her, could have added to what her imagination had already supplied. Finally, the verbosity and circumlocutions of Casaubon's letter bear no resemblance at all to Pattison's prose style, which was, as Betty Askwith put it, 'lucid' and 'sinewy'.[66]

[60] A. L. Rowse to Sparrow, 23 April 1969, Lincoln College MS/PAT/III/10.
[61] Dilke, 'Memoir', p. 17.
[62] British Library Add MSS 43932, quoted by Gordon S. Haight, *TLS* 1 June 1973, p. 616.
[63] Richard Ellmann, *TLS* 30 March 1973, p. 352.
[64] One reviewer of *Isaac Casaubon*, the Renaissance historian J. A. Symonds, actually thought that Eliot had set out to depict Isaac Casaubon, and not his biographer, in the person of Edward Casaubon: *The Academy* 7 (1875), 207–8.
[65] Haight, *TLS* 1 June 1973, p. 616.
[66] Askwith, *Lady Dilke*, p. 16. Sparrow, interestingly, was unusual in not admiring Pattison's prose style.

The various antagonists agreed on a good deal here. All agreed that there were some similarities between Casaubon and Pattison, although Haight thought they went little further than the fact that each married a woman twenty-seven years his junior. All agreed that the similarities were not fundamental: whereas Casaubon was a charlatan who wrote little and was out of his depth in the world of learning, Pattison was internationally acknowledged to be a man of true learning. He also wrote much more widely than has been appreciated. Whereas, in the novel, Casaubon's literary infertility is implicitly connected with sexual impotence, we can surely infer from Francis's letters that Pattison, whatever his inadequacies as a lover, was certainly not impotent.

What was at issue was essentially whether George Eliot intended the identification to be made. We can be certain that the identification was made, for many contemporaries commented on it, although they always stressed how absurd it was.[67] We can also be certain that Francis Pattison recognized herself in *Middlemarch*, which is surely why she avoided discussion of the novel by denying (falsely) that she had read it. But no one has ever really offered a credible explanation of why Eliot should have set out to injure two friends of hers in this way; nor, indeed, of why she apparently remained on good terms with the Pattisons afterwards.

For my part, I take the view that George Eliot had no intention of offending the Pattisons, although in choosing the name Casaubon she was probably having some kind of joke with them. There is no good reason for Dilke's view that she secretly disliked Pattison. So why did Francis Pattison take so badly to the novel – much worse than her husband, who (if the identification is accepted) had much more reason to complain? Was it because George Eliot had broken a confidence? Perhaps; but then the evidence that she did so is tenuous. Sparrow, the arch-conservative opponent of the admission of women to All Souls, appears to offer what looks like a proto-feminist account of the whole affair. Francis 'may have sanctioned or even encouraged' the breach of confidence, and 'may even have felt grateful for the sympathetic literary presentation of her case'; while George Eliot, 'the confidant [sic] of the suffering wife', must have meant Pattison to suffer in his turn. She was an Amazon springing to the defence of the ill-treated and suffering wife. 'The story, in fact, is of strong action by one high-minded woman on behalf of another.'[68]

---

[67] For example: *Manchester Guardian* 31 July 1884, p. 5; *Daily Telegraph*, 1 Aug. 1884; *Academy* 26 (9 Aug. 1884), 94; Morley, 'On Pattison's Memoirs', 165.
[68] Sparrow, *Pattison*, pp. 16–17.

But this account rests on the belief, which Sparrow apparently shared, that the Pattisons' marriage was a failure from the start, to such an extent that by the early 1870s Francis resented her husband sufficiently to connive in his public humiliation. As we have seen, the evidence for this is practically non-existent. Furthermore, Sparrow's account is self-contradictory. He has Pattison forced to 'suffer in silence' and to 'endure seeing his own stilted proposal of marriage reproduced almost word for word and held up to ridicule, in the knowledge that his wife had repeated it *verbatim* to her friend the novelist'. But then he also observes that Pattison's diary 'shows that Middlemarch was one of the books from which he gave private "readings" in his study to his female disciples'.[69] How can these two propositions be squared? If a novelist holds an acquaintance up to ridicule and so forces him to 'suffer in silence', is that acquaintance likely to respond by holding private readings from the offending novel?

It seems to me possible that whereas George Eliot intended to have no more than a joke at the Pattisons' expense, it backfired in the sense that Francis saw much more of herself, and her marriage, in the novel than Eliot had intended.[70] It is far from unknown for people to interpret their experience, even their experience of marriage, through a prism provided by fictional models.[71] So *Middlemarch* began, almost against Francis's will, to shape the way in which she understood her marriage. In other words, Sparrow gets the story the wrong way round. Whereas he posits the possibility that the novel was, from one point of view, a battle in an ongoing conflict between two warring spouses, I would suggest instead that it helped precipitate the drift to war.[72] From that point onwards Francis began to see herself as Dorothea and to seek an escape from the confines of the marriage. Needless to say, Pattison saw little of himself in Casaubon and therefore saw no reason either to break off his relations with Eliot and G. H. Lewes, or to refuse to mention the novel.

---

[69] Sparrow, *Pattison*, pp. 17, 15.

[70] It seems to have been clear to her contemporaries that Francis saw herself as Dorothea: e.g. Mrs Oliphant to Frank Wilson, 20 February 1879, in Mrs Harry Coghill (ed.), *The Autobiography and Letters of Mrs M. O. W. Oliphant* (Edinburgh: Blackwood, 1899), p. 277.

[71] Rose, *Parallel Lives*, pp. 14–15.

[72] Nuttall hints at this possibility: A. D. Nuttall, *Dead from the Waist Down: Scholars and Scholarship in Literature and the Popular Imagination* (New Haven & London: Yale University Press, 2003), pp. 78–9.

## UNRIVALLED LEISURE: THE RECTOR OF LINCOLN

Pattison imagined the rectorship as a pension conferred on him as a man of learning, and used it to support a life devoted to study. The office afforded him 'unrivalled academic leisure', he wrote.[73] He deplored the tendency of colleges, in electing to headships, to prefer 'the man of business and social habits' to 'the man of culture and learning', and he intended to use his office for what he regarded as its proper purpose.[74] 'He has been a very good Rector – never interfered in any one's business', said one of the fellows of Lincoln, during Pattison's last illness.[75] On two separate occasions in the 1870s he was alarmed at the prospect of having to take on the vice-chancellorship of the University, and when the Chancellor offered it to him in 1878 he refused it.[76] He came to resent not only college business but also the duty to entertain. Such were the demands it made on his nervous powers, he reflected, that the business of entertaining might usefully be given over exclusively to those with nothing better to do: people, he meant, 'who have no inner life'.[77] All his life he found that intellectual pursuits demanded solitude and freedom from commitments. Even when an old and valued friend called to stay, his pleasure was qualified by 'the bitter resentment against the thief of my precious leisure'.[78] His diary echoed that of Isaac Casaubon, whose life he would write: 'When the claims of business or society have taken up any considerable part of a day, his outcries are those of a man who is being robbed'; but when he has read from dawn to dusk, 'to-day I have lived'.[79] 'Chapter Day. The whole day perished!' was how Pattison expressed the same sentiment in his own diary.[80]

In the *Memoirs* Pattison wrote that, unlike most autobiographers, 'I have seen no one, known none of the celebrities of my own time intimately, or at all'.[81] But that was something of a literary affectation. It would be wrong to think that Pattison lived a life of retirement from the world, however much he might represent that as the life he coveted. In Oxford he was active in the affairs of the Bodleian Library, of which he was a curator, and of the Clarendon Press, which he served for many years as a delegate. He also acquired a taste for London life and was regularly in Town. He examined for

[73] Pattison, *Memoirs*, pp. 323–4.
[74] Pattison, 'Learning in the Church of England', p. 300.    [75] [Althaus], 'Recollections', 43.
[76] Bodleian MS Pattison 130, ff. 91–2 and 197; MS Pattison 131, f. 34: diary entries for 20 November 1874, 19 Oct. 1877, 15 June 1878.
[77] Bodleian MS Pattison 130, f. 72, 24 November 1873.
[78] Bodleian MS Pattison 130, f. 104, 3 March 1875. This was R. C. Christie.
[79] Pattison, *Isaac Casaubon 1559–1614* (London: Longmans, 1875), p. 102.
[80] Bodleian MS Pattison 130, f. 90, 6 November 1874.    [81] Pattison, *Memoirs*, p. 1.

the Indian Civil Service and for the University of London and served on the councils of Bedford College and of University College, Aberystwyth: in 1868–9 he even chaired Bedford's committee of management, which ran the college in the interregnum prior to the new constitution of 1869; thereafter he chaired the council for a decade, and for a time held the office of visitor.[82] He was active in the affairs of the London Library, where he served on the committee with, among others, Herbert Spencer. He knew most of the literary and intellectual elite, whom he would have encountered, for instance, at the *Saturday Review*'s summer dinner. Towards the end of his life we find him serving as one of the original committee members of William Morris's Society for the Protection of Ancient Buildings, along with Carlyle, Ruskin, Burne-Jones and Holman Hunt.[83]

Pattison particularly valued his membership of the Athenaeum, the club of the higher intellectual elite, famous for having the best club library in London as well as the worst food.[84] He was elected in 1865 under its 'Rule II', which empowered the committee to elect each year to immediate membership not more than nine men considered to be 'of distinguished eminence in Science, Literature, or the Arts, or for Public Service'. He involved himself closely in the club's affairs, both on its library committee and on its general committee, where he used his position to secure the election of, among others, Henry Sidgwick and Henry Smith.[85] The club was one of his favourite places. Its library, which held more than thirty thousand volumes, was 'the most delightful place in the world – especially on a Sunday morning'.[86] At the beginning of 1884, when he knew he was dying, he wrote sadly to a friend, 'I feel I shall never ascend the staircase of the Athenaeum again'; 'though I suppose', he added, characteristically and in self-parody, 'that by living over the 1st of Jan. I have incurred the liability for the subscription for the year in wh. we have entered.'[87]

---

[82]  Margaret J. Tuke, *A History of Bedford College for Women 1849–1937* (London: Oxford University Press, 1939), pp. 59, 114, 120.

[83]  John Delafons, *Politics and Preservation: A Policy History of the Built Heritage 1882–1996* (London: Spon, 1997), p. 20.

[84]  He also belonged, for a time, to the Savile Club, which was founded in 1868 and tended to attract a similar pattern of membership to the Athenaeum. W. D. Rawlins to Pattison, 23 October 1872, Bodleian MS Pattison 57, ff. 18–19; Neil Duxbury, *Frederick Pollock and the English Juristic Tradition* (Oxford: Oxford University Press, 2004), p. 19, n. 27.

[85]  Bodleian MS Pattison 132, ff. 6, 9. On the significance of the Athenaeum in late-Victorian intellectual life, see Collini, *Public Moralists*, pp. 15–21.

[86]  L. A. Tollemache, 'Recollections of Pattison', in Tollemache, *Stones of Stumbling*, 2nd edn (London: William Rice, 1885), p. 188.

[87]  Pattison to J. R. Thursfield, 2 January 1884, Bodleian MS Pattison 139, ff. 16–17. At that time the subscription was eight guineas.

Stefan Collini has identified the Athenaeum as one of the sites where 'the higher intellectual stratum of London society' gathered. Pattison's election, together with his participation in groups such as the Metaphysical Society, confirmed his national status as a member of the intellectual elite, which, as Collini has again shown, was particularly compact and homogeneous at this time.[88] In the days before academic conferences it was at the Athenaeum that Pattison would renew his acquaintance with Scottish university figures such as Alexander Bain, John Tulloch and Thomas Spencer Baynes, who, as he did, used the club as their London base.[89] It also enabled him to rub shoulders with literary and scientific men from outside the universities – to breakfast with Matthew Arnold, for instance, in December 1878. Rather less to his taste was the prospect of encounters with bishops. The Archbishop of York (William Thomson, formerly provost of Queen's) was 'offensively patronising' at breakfast in February 1877.[90] Another bishop would come and sit next to him at lunch and ask 'simple questions, just like a little boy, about evolution and other modern speculations'.[91]

In the last decade of Pattison's life we can trace the first signs of the fragmentation of that compact intellectual elite of mid-Victorian society. Academic specialization and professionalization were to be the main agencies of that process. Pattison himself occupies an intriguingly liminal place in these developments. He made his reputation writing about what would today strike us as esoteric themes of little interest beyond the academy, notably the history of classical learning; but he wrote about them for a general rather than a specialized readership. He wrote for the great generalist periodicals, and he published his loss-making biography of Casaubon with Longmans, and not with the Clarendon Press which, at his instigation, had established a fund for the subsidy of learned works which would not be likely to prove commercially viable. But he also had a role in some of the early forays into academic professionalization that began in the 1870s. He was actively involved in *The Academy*, a periodical founded in 1869 which occupied an intermediate position, since its subject coverage was broad but it insisted on employing specialist reviewers. He applauded the critic who fulfilled the role of public educator, but he was sceptical of the claims of those, such as his friend John Ruskin, who sought to exercise their authority as critics over the whole range of topics of public concern, from

---

[88] Collini, *Public Moralists*, p. 19.
[89] Pattison to Alexander Campbell Fraser, 9 March 1881, National Library of Scotland Dep 208 Box 9.
[90] Bodleian MS Pattison 130, f. 167.   [91] Tollemache, 'Recollections', p. 188.

field sports to Shakespeare. 'It is not that upon any of these things Mr Ruskin may not have something good to say, but that he cannot expect to transfer to any of these subjects the *prestige* which his special knowledge has justly conferred on his opinions on art. On art topics Mr Ruskin is a prophet or an oracle; on economical subjects he is but one of us.'[92] When, a few years after the creation of *The Academy*, Alexander Bain and Croom Robertson established Britain's first specialist philosophical periodical, *Mind*, Pattison was one of the big names whose advice and collaboration they solicited. Significantly, Bain and Robertson attached particular importance to the international standing of their periodical. They sought 'the co-operation of the foremost workers in Germany and elsewhere', and emphasized the need for the journal to report in detail on the international periodical literature. Unlike today's academic journals, however, they paid for contributions, and paid quite generously: up to a pound a page. Pattison would therefore have been paid of the order of fifteen pounds for the much-remarked piece he contributed to the first issue of *Mind* in January 1876.[93] The fact that they paid well was an indication that the founders saw themselves as competing for contributors with the general periodicals.

It is, however, revealing that Pattison was involved in initiatives in academic professionalization not only in philosophy, but also in classics. He was active in the Oxford Philological Society, and, more importantly, was a member of the council of the Society for the Promotion of Hellenic Studies from its foundation in 1880 until his death. There, however, he would have sat alongside not just academic Hellenists such as Richard Jebb, Henry Jackson and Ingram Bywater, but also a more diverse group of enthusiasts who included Oscar Wilde, the publisher Frederick Macmillan and several bishops. That Pattison was involved in professional initiatives both in philosophy and in classics testifies to his own catholicity of interests, but also to the porosity of disciplinary boundaries at this time.

Pattison never felt the lure of the political life that was felt by so many of the 'lights of liberalism' studied by Christopher Harvie – dons of a slightly later generation which had not experienced the Tractarian crisis at first hand.[94] He had a lifelong aversion to 'party spirit', which he first denounced in an undergraduate essay and continued to lament in his

[92] Pattison, Review of Ruskin's *Arrows of the Chase*, 110.
[93] G. Croom Robertson to Pattison, 2 February & 6 March 1875, Bodleian MS Pattison 57, ff. 32–33 & ff. 46–7.
[94] Christopher Harvie, *The Lights of Liberalism. University Liberals and the Challenge of Democracy 1860–86* (London: Allen Lane, 1976).

*Memoirs* half a century later.[95] But there is no question that his own sympathies were firmly Liberal. He was a member of the Oxford Political Economy Club and was an active member of the Social Science Association, that distinctive mouthpiece for mid-Victorian Liberal opinion. He was a member of Gladstone's election committee in 1865, when the future Prime Minister unsuccessfully defended his seat as member of parliament for the University of Oxford.[96] In fact he seems to have been ambivalent in his attitude to Gladstone. 'I am very sorry Gladstone fights for such an object as the University seat', he told Stebbing in 1853, before Gladstone was clearly identified with Liberalism. 'It ought to be quite the other way – we ought to be proud to retain him – he is only too great for his constituency to appreciate.'[97] But he was dismissive of Gladstone's Homeric scholarship, and we later find him using 'Gladstonian moonshine' as a term of criticism.[98] Because he regarded democracy with a somewhat elitist disdain he has been characterized as a Whig. But unlike most Whigs he was an enthusiastic and improbable supporter of Gladstone's campaign against the Bulgarian atrocities, a campaign which typically attracted Evangelicals and Anglo-Catholics rather than Liberal Anglicans or sceptics. This was an issue that found him alongside the High Churchmen Liddon and Pusey and against his former Broad Church allies Stanley and Jowett.[99] He also backed James Bryce's campaign on behalf of the Armenians in the Ottoman Empire, and in 1879–80 backed a call for an inquiry into the conduct of the Afghan War which cited 'certain acts committed by the British authorities ... contrary to the practices of civilized warfare'. His lack of sympathy for patriotism and nationalism rendered him immune to the appeal of Disraelian jingoism and imperialism.[100] On the outbreak of the First Boer War in 1880 he wrote: 'The Transvaal business is shameful. Shall we never again know what it is for England to be on the side of right and justice?'[101]

[95] Nolan, 'Pattison's religious experience', pp. 58–9; Pattison, *Memoirs*, p. 332.

[96] Bodleian MS Pattison 130, f. 59: diary 30 May 1865.

[97] Pattison to William Stebbing, 7 January 1853. Times Collection, Harry Ransom Center, University of Texas at Austin.

[98] Bodleian MS Pattison 132, f. 10, diary for 11 April 1879.

[99] Richard Shannon, *Gladstone and the Bulgarian Agitation* (London: Nelson, 1963), pp. 182–4, 212–15, 220.

[100] *The Times*, 21 March 1878, p. 10; Tollemache, 'Recollections of Pattison', 157–8; L. T. Hobhouse and J. L. Hammond, *Lord Hobhouse: A Memoir* (London: Arnold, 1905), pp. 125–7.

[101] Pattison to William Stebbing, 28 December 1880, Times Collection, Harry Ransom Center, University of Texas at Austin.

One cause to which Pattison showed a consistent commitment in the last two decades of his life was that of the emancipation of women. He was, for instance, active in the campaign for women's suffrage.[102] But he had a particular commitment to the cause of women's education, on which he gave evidence to the Taunton Commission in 1866. He was called, in the chairman's words, because he had 'specially directed [his] attention to the subject of the education of girls of the middle classes', but the chairman was surprised to discover that Pattison had never visited a girls' boarding school, nor, apparently, any kind of girls' school. Rather, Pattison avowed,

I have had no other means of knowing the classes of whom I speak than any other English clergyman has had who is 50 years old, and is married, and has had many sisters, and has been resident in a great variety of English counties, and has seen the farming class and the clerical class, and something also of the daughters of shopkeepers.[103]

He was able to refer, however, to his involvement in teaching a German class as part of a scheme of lectures for young women established in Oxford by Eleanor Smith in 1866.[104] A decade or so later, he gave a donation of one hundred pounds which was crucial to the establishment of the Association for Promoting the Higher Education of Women in Oxford. At a time when the women's halls – Somerville and Lady Margaret Hall – functioned simply as hostels, the Association was responsible for making educational provision for the students by drawing on and extending the existing lecture scheme. Pattison's diary in his later years frequently records his attendance at meetings of the Association, whether general meetings or council meetings.[105] We have already noted his close involvement in the affairs of Bedford College, also at the instigation of Eleanor Smith. After his death, Francis gave his collection of books on botany and mathematics to Bedford, and Somerville received a gift of four hundred volumes, selected by Ingram Bywater from among Pattison's literary and historical collection.[106]

[102] Bodleian MS Pattison 131, ff. 20, 26, March–April 1878.
[103] Schools Inquiry Commission, House of Commons Parliamentary Papers 1867–8 vol. xxviii Pt. 4, pp. 944. Pattison would later rectify his lack of direct acquaintance with girls' schools, at least to the extent of visiting Cheltenham Ladies' College with its head, Dorothea Beale, during the Social Science Congress at Cheltenham in 1878: Bodleian MS Pattison 131, f. 48.
[104] Schools Inquiry Commission, 947. See also Janet Howarth, ' "In Oxford but . . . not of Oxford": the women's colleges', in Brock and Curthoys (eds.), *Nineteenth-Century Oxford*, Part 2, p. 238.
[105] Examples include: 20 November 1879, 26 November 1879, 14 & 15 March 1881, 3 November 1882, 27 Sept. 1883: Bodleian MS Pattison 132, ff. 33–4, MS Pattison 133, f. 37, MS Pattison 134, ff. 2, 45.
[106] Tuke, *History of Bedford College*, pp. 266–7; the information on the donation to Somerville was supplied by Miss Pauline Adams, fellow and librarian of the college.

As early as 1857 we find Pattison commending Michelet for defying convention in recognizing that women too have a history.[107] There is no reason to suppose that his interest in women's education owed anything to Francis's influence, for she seems to have taken little specific interest in the cause, and Pattison's involvement in the Association coincided with the couple's semi-estrangement. It was a cause for which many prominent academic liberals worked enthusiastically, T. H. Green in Oxford and Henry Sidgwick in Cambridge being distinguished examples. Given Pattison's progressive sympathies and educational interests, his sympathy for the cause is not surprising; but given his aversion both to campaigning and to practical organization, the extent of his involvement in the movement calls for explanation. From the 1860s onwards he was deeply alienated by the effects of university reform on Oxford. While the University had become hugely more efficient, it had, to his mind, lost sight of its proper vocation. Liberal education had been marginalized by the obsession for examinations. It could well be that Pattison got interested in girls' education precisely because he thought that a truly liberal education might be possible for girls and young women whereas it no longer was for boys and young men. Because middle-class girls were not focused on careers there was no reason for their education to be hamstrung by the need to prepare for examinations. Young women who came to Oxford would do so, he assumed, out of a disinterested quest for knowledge. This, he told the Taunton Commission, had been his experience in teaching on the ladies' lecture scheme: whereas boys have to some degree to be driven to learn, 'the girls come to you and want to learn'.[108] Just as Henry Sidgwick urged that Newnham should not try, like Girton, to ape the men's colleges but should instead beat an innovatory path of its own, so Pattison valued women's higher education not simply or even mainly for egalitarian reasons, but because he saw in it the possibility of doing something which had proved impossible in the men's colleges. That was why he urged the Schools Inquiry Commission to ensure that girls' education should not be over-shadowed by an examination system: 'I should be sorry to engage female education, which is now at its beginning, in a system which will bring with it what we see it has brought with it in the case of boys.'[109] On the council

---

[107] [Pattison], 'History, biography, voyages and travels', *Westminster Review* 68 o.s. (Oct. 1857), 578.
[108] Schools Inquiry Commission, p. 952.
[109] Schools Inquiry Commission, p. 952. On Sidgwick's position, which contrasted sharply with that of Emily Davies, the founder and first mistress of Girton, see the editor's introduction to Emily Davies, *The Higher Education of Women*, ed. Janet Howarth (London and Ronceverte: Hambledon, 1988), p. xliii–xliv.

of Bedford College he argued against the college's decision to enter its students for the London University examinations.[110]

Until his marriage just short of the age of forty-eight, Pattison had lived almost exclusively in male company with the exception of his female relatives. By contrast, from 1861 he moved increasingly in mixed circles. This was partly a consequence of being married, and partly a consequence of being, as rector, head of a household capable of entertaining mixed company. It was also connected with the diversification of Oxford society, and with a shift towards mixed patterns of sociability in late-Victorian upper-middle-class society. A particularly striking feature of his leisure pursuits during his rectorship is that he was an active practitioner of the two games that were most associated with this new pattern of sociability: croquet and lawn tennis.[111] Croquet was introduced into England in the 1850s, and the Pattisons seem to have taken it up early in their marriage, and certainly by 1864. The Rector, who was already a keen player of racquets and fives, threw himself into this new pursuit with apparently inexhaustible enthusiasm: in May 1867 he was instrumental in the creation of the Oxford University Croquet Club, and one day the following month he played for six hours, from 3 to 9 p.m.[112] In his sixties he would compete at the All-England Croquet Club at Wimbledon. Something in the game appealed to his mind, and he was said to be able to diagnose the mental biases of his fellow players from the tactics they used. Such was his proficiency at the game that he came close to becoming national champion.[113] Towards the end of his life croquet was losing something of its appeal and was being supplanted by lawn tennis as the game played at upper-middle-class garden parties. Pattison took up the game with some zest, playing it, for example, with Professor Bartholomew ('Bat') Price and his wife and daughters at their home on St Giles, or with the family of Arthur Johnson, a fellow of All Souls, in Norham Gardens. One malicious obituarist wrote that he 'made the mistake of trying to pose as a modern Brummell and superannuated butterfly', and that it was pathetic to see such a distinguished man of letters 'dressed in flannels and trying to be

[110]  Bodleian MS Pattison 131, f. 16, January 1878.

[111]  Richard Holt, *Sport and the British: A Modern History* (Oxford: Oxford University Press, 1989), pp. 124–8.

[112]  Pattison to William Stebbing, 2 June 1867, Times Collection, Harry Ransom Center, University of Texas at Austin. For racquets and fives, see the letters of 26 May 1856 and 31 July 1857 in the same collection.

[113]  William Tuckwell, *Reminiscences of Oxford* (London & New York: Cassell, 1900). p. 221. L. A. Tollemache, 'Recollections of Pattison', pp. 173–4.

agreeable to girls scarcely out of their teens'.[114] But that is probably to underestimate the seriousness with which Pattison took the game, which he certainly did not confine to summer garden parties. In December 1880 he played lawn tennis for eighteen hours on seventeen different days.[115] The game was not necessarily strenuous, but this is quite impressive for a man of sixty seven. When A. D. Nuttall dismisses the idea of Pattison the sportsman, insisting (wrongly) that 'the horse-riding and the angling belong to Pattison's youth', he misses an important dimension of Pattison's personality.[116] He certainly looked older than he was, and was always a hypochondriac, but he was physically active even towards the end of his life.

This transformation of his, and Oxford's, patterns of sociability certainly had a profound impact on Pattison's life. As rector he developed a reputation for enjoying the company of women, especially but not exclusively of intelligent young women. He was inclined to regard an all-male dinner party as 'dreary in the extreme'.[117] He became close to a whole series of such women. One of the first, and certainly the most distinguished, was Mary Arnold, the daughter of Matthew Arnold's brother Thomas: following her marriage to a Brasenose don she would later achieve fame as the novelist Mrs Humphry Ward. She recalled that in the period 1868–72, when she was just entering adulthood, the Pattisons 'mattered more to me perhaps than anybody else', and she would often dine with them on Sunday evenings.[118] Pattison encouraged her scholarly interests in Spanish literature – 'Choose a subject, and know everything about it!', he urged – and secured her access to the Bodleian.[119] He later suggested that she should translate a book that made a profound impact on his last years, the *Journal Intime* of the Swiss critic and philosopher Henri-Frédéric Amiel. She would paint the best, and most affectionate, fictional portrait of Pattison in her international best-seller, *Robert Elsmere*. Other female novelists were prominent in Pattison's circle: Rhoda Broughton, who took revenge for a disagreement between them by penning a savage depiction of him as Professor Forth in *Belinda*; and the Irish writer May (Mary) Laffan, whose entertainingly gossipy letters he classed with those possessing 'special interest'. He was also, briefly, close to an American widow, Mary

[114] *The World*, 6 August 1884.
[115] Bodleian MS Pattison 133. Two days were too wet for tennis, and another was audit day, consumed by college business.
[116] Nuttall, *Dead from the Waist Down*, p. 76. Pattison says that he took up riding in his mid-thirties: *Memoirs*, pp. 234–5.
[117] Bodleian MS Pattison 131, f. 56, Dec. 1878.
[118] Mrs Humphry Ward, *A Writer's Recollections (1856–1900)* (London: Collins, 1918), p. 103.
[119] Ward, *A Writer's Recollections*, p. 105.

Carroll, whom he met while travelling in Italy, and at whose death he recorded that she was 'the only woman, except F., to whom I could say anything I wished to say, with the certainty that it would not be misapprehended'.[120] Some of her letters too were classed as possessing special interest.

Broughton and Laffan were in their thirties or forties when they knew Pattison, and Mary Carroll was much older. Obviously it was not they to whom Walter Pater was referring when he maliciously described Pattison as 'romping with great girls among the gooseberry bushes'.[121] But Pattison also evidently enjoyed close, but semi-pedagogical relations with a number of younger women: to some extent his own two nieces, but especially with Francis's niece, the tall and attractive Gertrude Tuckwell. His letters to her, written when she was aged 18–20, are intellectual gems which shed a powerful light on Pattison's thought at the end of his life. In these letters he speaks with the voice of a teacher, and he certainly regarded Gertrude, or 'Gee', as worthy of his attentions: 'she is wonderfully intelligent, but deficient in interests – has the air of a girl who is blasé by having had a wide surface presented to her view, & not habituated to penetrate to the inside of anything.'[122] He treated her, she later recalled, as 'a person of equal intellectual standing [who] merited the most careful and searching response'.[123] She was evidently a woman of great ability: a Christian Socialist like her father, she ended her life a Companion of Honour, a recognition of the philanthropic work with and on behalf of working women which she began as secretary to her aunt.

Pattison's oddest relationship was with a very different kind of woman, Meta Bradley, niece of the Master of University College. She was neither clever nor attractive, comes across as prematurely middle-aged, and with the exception of Pattison no one, least of all her family, seems to have had a good word to say for her. Yet she and Pattison conducted a five-year relationship which, while almost certainly chaste, was intimate to the point of scandal. Pattison's letters to her constitute by far the largest surviving cache of his correspondence. Vivian Green has published a rich narrative of the relationship based intensively on the two sides of this correspondence.[124]

[120] Bodleian MS Pattison 131, f. 8. The exception made for 'F[rancis]' here is important, since this was December 1877, more than a year into their estrangement.
[121] Green, *Love in a Cool Climate*, p. 26.
[122] Pattison to Meta Bradley, 1 Aug. 1880, Bodleian MS Pattison 119, ff. 106–7.
[123] Lincoln College MS/PAT/III/5b.　　[124] Green, *Love in a Cool Climate*, passim.

This was a strange and intriguing relationship which loomed so large in Pattison's later years that some comment on it is needed here. Pattison was, throughout his life, a profoundly lonely man who found warm human relationships difficult and who tended to alienate those who loved him, notably most of his sisters. His marriage promised to give him the kind of companionship he yearned for, and, as I have argued, for more than a decade it largely did so, even if the relationship looked very different from Francis's perspective. The rupture with his wife left him desolate, and it was after the events of 1876 that he formed close relations with other women. The relationship with Meta worked for him because she was so uncomplicatedly unselfish as to devote herself to his welfare, and because she had no real interests to distract her from him. Although she was of mediocre intelligence, she possessed intellectual interests, or at least sought to cultivate such interests to allow her to communicate more effectively with him.

Pattison's literary productivity in the course of his rectorship disappointed the many admirers of his literary qualities. 'What he left in literature', wrote Matthew Arnold, 'hardly satisfies, perhaps, the estimate which his friends had and retain of him.'[125] He published three books in this period: his *Suggestions on Academical Organisation* in 1868, his great life of Isaac Casaubon in 1875, and a slim life of Milton in 1879. In addition he published two editions of Pope (the *Essay on Man* in 1869 and the *Satires and Epistles* in 1872), both with the Clarendon Press, which reissued them frequently, and an edition of Milton's sonnets at the invitation of his friend, the publisher Kegan Paul. It is curious to find that Pattison, who attached such importance to depth of learning, published little at his own initiative and was more likely to commit himself to print as a result of commissions or in the form of *pièces d'occasion*. The biography of Casaubon was the obvious exception: it had a long gestation and was, in a sense, the fruit of nearly a quarter of a century's work and thought. But the *Suggestions on Academical Organisation* – the focus of Chapter 5 – began as a report which Pattison was commissioned to produce on behalf of a group of academic reformers, while the study of Milton was commissioned by John Morley, the series editor, for the English Men of Letters series published by Macmillan. He wrote eight entries, all biographical articles on scholars, for the ninth edition of the *Encyclopaedia Britannica*. These were all incisive and elegant, but absorbed more time and effort than they were worth. That on Erasmus, for instance, took him more than four

---

[125] Matthew Arnold to T. F. Althaus, 5 January 1885, Lincoln College MS/PAT/I/C.

weeks to write at the end of 1877, and he thought it too good for the Encyclopaedia – 'though I could, with time, make it very much better'.[126]

The book on Milton was one of the first volumes to appear in a series which would have an enduring place in English literary culture. The series did much to define – both by its range of subjects and by its range of contributors – what the late Victorians understood by the category of 'men of letters'. Significantly, both Morley and Macmillan were keen to recruit writers they perceived as not only famous but also 'respectable', and no doubt Pattison's reputation as a heavyweight scholar as well as his position as a head of house helped confer gravitas on the series, as did the presence of his old Oxford contemporary, the dean of St Paul's, R. W. Church. 'The highest respectability – and the highest capacity – an impossible union, O my Macmillan', wrote Morley on 5 October 1877. 'But I accept your command all the same.'[127] Morley failed to recruit Matthew Arnold or George Eliot, but his contributors included T. H. Huxley, Trollope and Henry James, as well as critics such as R. H. Hutton, Leslie Stephen and Froude.

Payment for this series was relatively slight: a hundred pounds per volume, although George Eliot was offered several times that sum. This was less than Pattison earned for his contribution to *Essays and Reviews*. But the incentive to write was the honour of belonging to a distinguished company.[128] It also offered Pattison access to a wider reading public: the volumes were priced very affordably at 2s 6d and, as Alexander Macmillan wrote to Dean Church, 'we would hope for a sale on Railway Stalls and the like'.[129] As Morley recalled, the aim of the series was to bring 'knowledge, criticism and reflection … within reach of an extensive, busy, and pre-occupied world'.[130] The series rapidly became something of a national institution, and for two generations, writes John Gross, it 'remained an unfailing standard for harassed teachers and conscientious students'.[131]

It might be asked why Pattison was invited to write on Milton, rather than on (say) Bentley, Pope, or Gibbon, any one of whom he might reasonably have claimed. Although he had written on Milton, he did not have the expertise of David Masson, professor of Rhetoric and English

---

[126] Bodleian MS Pattison 131, f. 6.
[127] Quoted by John L. Kijinski, 'Professionalism, authority, and the late-Victorian man of letters: a view from the Macmillan archive', *Victorian Literature and Culture* 24 (1996), 232.
[128] Kijinski, 'Professionalism', 233–4.
[129] Quoted by Kijinski, 'Professionalism', 236.    [130] Morley, *Recollections*, vol. I, p. 92.
[131] John Gross, *The Rise and Fall of the Man of Letters: Aspects of English Literary Life since 1800* (London: Weidenfeld, 1969), p. 107.

Literature at Edinburgh, who was in the middle of a huge multi-volume biography of Milton. One part of the answer to that question is that the ethos of the series was, as it were, 'men of letters on men of letters'; particular scholarly expertise was less important than the sense that here was a contemporary man of letters writing about a past writer whom he identified as a kindred spirit.[132]

Pattison was not, in fact, straightforwardly a 'man of letters', if we use Kijinski's definition of that category: 'Neither a "Victorian sage", nor a specialist speaking to other specialists, nor even primarily a journalist, the man of letters was a professional writer who attempted to earn a living by selling "serious" writing to what he still considered a general, middle-class readership.'[133] Pattison was not a professional writer, for his writing did not constitute his major source of income, but merely supplemented his income from his fellowship and later the rectorship. He also objected to those cultural critics, such as Ruskin, who claimed a general intellectual authority on the basis of what was, in fact, a specialized cultural expertise. But Pattison certainly expected to make money from his pen, and sought to write seriously for a general readership. In Heyck's terms, he 'shared a market relationship with a general reading public'.[134] To that extent the label 'man of letters' is not inappropriate.

The prominence of poets and poetry in his later works deserves some comment, not least because his book on Milton had a far greater longevity than anything else he wrote. Appraisals of this book have varied. Pattison was hurt by two critical reviews, including one by the historian S. R. Gardiner, who he thought was exacting revenge for an academic dispute.[135] Among more recent commentators, Sparrow thought the book 'excellent', just as he considered the editions of Milton and Pope 'first-rate'; but Nuttall is less sure, considering it the work of (in this respect) a 'gifted amateur, getting some things right, some wrong'.[136] Oliver Edwards, discussing the Men of Letters series in *The Times* in 1955, contrasted the few disappointments in the series, such as Trollope's *Thackeray*, Froude's *Bunyan* and Stephen's *George Eliot*, with, at the other extreme, those contributions which 'have become so famous that they exist almost outside it'. Pattison's *Milton* was the first he listed in this second category.[137] He never intended it to rival the monumental six-volume life of Milton by

---

[132] Kijinski, 'Professionalism', 237.     [133] Kijinski, 'Professionalism', 229.
[134] Heyck, *Transformation of Intellectual Life*, p. 25.     [135] Bodleian MS Pattison 132, f. 36.
[136] Sparrow, *Pattison*, p. 1; Nuttall, *Dead from the Waist Down*, p. 107.
[137] Oliver Edwards, 'The slim red line', *The Times* 15 September 1955, p. 13.

David Masson, whose publication, begun in 1859, was approaching completion. Pattison, who always scorned prolixity, was explicit about his aim, which matched the purpose of Morley's series: 'The present outline is written for a different class of readers, those, namely, who cannot afford to know more of Milton than can be told in some two hundred and fifty pages.'[138] It was tangential to the area of his real expertise, but the project's attractions to Pattison are apparent. He was drawn to the study of any man who framed his life in accordance with a deeply felt intellectual vocation. Milton, he writes, in his 'delicious retirement of Horton', in Buckinghamshire, 'laid in a stock ... of wide and accurate knowledge'; not knowledge for its own sake, but useful knowledge, by which Milton understood 'that which conduced to form him for his vocation of poet'. This was not Pattison's vocation, but he certainly felt an affinity.[139]

Poetry had in fact been a lifelong passion of his, and he took great pleasure from evenings spent reading aloud, usually in the company of women friends. He valued the best poetry as a means of spiritual education which helped cultivate the ability to see the world as it really is. Like the project of intellectual improvement to which he devoted his life, it exposed one to new perspectives on life and so combatted narrowness and prejudice. He spoke of this in his last public address, 'On reading poetry', given at Bedford College in October 1883 to commemorate the start of the new session. It was reported in *The Times*, and the Dean of St Paul's wrote that 'Nothing so true and so real has been said for a long time.'[140] 'All aesthetic emotion', said Pattison, 'has this high moral quality, that it is unexclusive; it helps to keep the soul alive and open, and to prevent it from shutting itself up, like an oyster, in a little world of its own fixed opinions and prepossessions.' He took poetic feeling to be an innate capacity which all possess in varying degrees, but which can be nourished or stifled by education and the social environment. He proceeded to discuss the hindrances to its development. Criticism, even good criticism, was one, because it interposed itself between the poem and the reader, and so got in the way of a direct appreciation. The mass of good criticism which the Victorian period had produced 'creates a kind of haze through which we habitually come to look on the poet's writings and which prevents our seeing them as they are'. Moreover, the cultivation of poetic feeling, like the cultivation of the mind, demanded freedom from the constant pressures of a busy life.

---

[138] Pattison, *Milton*, p. 2.    [139] Pattison, *Milton*, p. 15.
[140] Quoted by Tollemache, 'Recollections of Pattison', p. 177.

Life in great towns makes leisure and solitude more and more rare and difficult to obtain; and yet without these it is difficult to cultivate the poetic emotion. The habit of living at high pressure even makes leisure and solitude insupportable when we can get them; as with alcoholic stimulants, when the high pressure is removed the nerve-force collapses.[141]

It is striking that theology, which had been at the heart of Pattison's preoccupations in the 1850s, features only peripherally in the bibliography of his writings after 1860. In the *Memoirs* he explains this by saying that the reception accorded to *Essays and Reviews* had demonstrated to him that the English reading public could simply not comprehend the idea of a scientific theology, as distinct from partisan religious polemic. Defining the precise nature of his religious beliefs following his drift away from liberal Anglicanism is difficult because of his public and even private reticence about his heterodoxy. We know that he continued to attend college chapel regularly, and to preside at the eucharist, and indeed that when in Yorkshire he would assist his brother-in-law, the rector of Richmond. He was, in other words, punctilious about maintaining the outward forms of religious profession. He could hardly do otherwise, given that the tenure of his office required him to be in Anglican orders. But in private he was acerbic about the clergy. 'Priests are generally professional quacks trading in beliefs they don't share', he told Gertrude Tuckwell.[142] As for bishops, he despaired: 'After a man has been consecrated ten years, he loses all sympathy with the modern spirit.'[143] That was a characteristic and revealing remark. What mattered to Pattison was the continuing onward quest for truth, and from 1845 onwards he ceased to believe that that could be reconciled with a previous commitment to the maintenance of a doctrinal orthodoxy. He thought that the demands of intellectual integrity entailed a commitment to the postulate of the uniform operation of natural laws, which excluded a belief in miracles; but that did not exclude the possibility of an intelligent and spiritual first cause. Indeed he seems to have looked upon this possibility favourably. 'The real puzzle is how *anything* comes to exist.'[144] Perhaps his position was a modernized version of eighteenth-century deism – the movement he studied in his contribution to *Essays and Reviews*.

The ethics of outward conformity was a subject of sustained interest to many of Pattison's contemporaries in the serious intellectual world of the

[141] *The Times*, 11 October 1883, p. 6.
[142] Pattison to Gertrude Tuckwell, 25 June 1881, Bodleian MS Pattison 141, f. 19.
[143] Tollemache, 'Recollections of Pattison', p. 188.
[144] Tollemache, 'Recollections of Pattison', p. 193.

high Victorian period. Their interest was not just speculative, but practical, since religious tests loomed large in the academic landscape until the 1870s. There were some notable sacrifices of career ambition to intellectual integrity among Pattison's friends and acquaintances. The poet Arthur Hugh Clough resigned his tutorship and then his fellowship at Oriel in 1848 for reasons of religious doubt. The following year J. A. Froude, a fellow of Exeter College, resigned his fellowship when the head of his college denounced his novel, *Nemesis of Faith*, which was itself an exploration of the ethics of conformity and a protest against the requirement to take orders. Two decades later Henry Sidgwick resigned his Cambridge fellowship because he felt he could no longer in conscience subscribe to the Thirty-Nine Articles. His college, Trinity, kept him on as a lecturer, but Sidgwick characteristically continued to dwell on the ethical issues involved.[145] So too did John Morley, who left Oxford with a pass degree when he lost his faith and his father cut off his allowance. In his *On Compromise*, first published in 1874, he pursued a Millite investigation into 'the limits that are set by sound reason to the practice of the various arts of accommodation, economy, management, conformity, or compromise'. He urged 'the abandonment of those habits of hypocritical conformity and compliance which have filled the air of the England of to-day with gross and obscuring mists'.[146] These were questions with which Pattison declined to wrestle, at least in public. In his case the stakes were high, for by the time he ceased to regard himself as an Anglican he was well established as head of his college and alternative career directions were not obvious. But, in addition, he regarded himself as an academic by vocation in a way that the others, with the exception of Sidgwick, did not.

Pattison died at Harrogate on 30 July 1884, after a painful struggle with stomach cancer, which his eminent doctor had diagnosed as depression.[147] Others diagnosed pernicious anaemia, the condition that had killed his father. He had accomplished some kind of reconciliation with Francis, who had returned to care for him in his last months, once she had overcome the cynicism produced by her long experience of his hypochondria. They had left Oxford some six or seven weeks before, when his doctors advised him that the iron water of Harrogate might do him some good. Francis rented a house there which he thought 'truly commodious' and

---

[145] For example, Henry Sidgwick, *The Ethics of Conformity and Subscription* (London: Williams and Norgate, 1870).

[146] John Morley, *On Compromise* (London: Macmillan, 1888), pp. 1, 200.

[147] J. A. Stirke to D. S. MacColl, 30 Dec. 1883, Glasgow University Library MS MacColl S441, transcript at Lincoln College MS/PAT/III/9.

'in the finest situation', although he could not help commenting, as if in self-parody, that it was 'very expensive £10.10.0 per week'.[148] To the end he kept a close eye on his finances. 'It is clear that the Argentine republic, & not Brazil, is the country into wh. one ought to put one's money', he noted in May,

and apropos of their assertion of the decay of Brazil, comes to me the Report of the English Bank of Rio announcing an 8 per % div instead of the customary 10 per %. These contretemps and the disaster of the U. S. Rolling stock will knock off £300 from my income this year, besides endangering nearly £3,000 of capital.[149]

Equally, however, and still more fundamentally in character, even in his last months he continued his lifelong quest for knowledge: 'I am impelled by an invisible force to be always refilling the vessel of Danaides.'[150] On his deathbed he made a final statement of his religious outlook. Francis took down his words, which were uttered, she noted, 'with a passionate energy', in spite of the state of his health. They are in fragments, rather than in an ordered sequence, but they nevertheless cast light into Pattison's inner life. 'The true philosopher', he pronounced, 'is so oppressed by his consciousness of the vast space around him that he is always modest, but he possesses in the life of the soul the worthiest thing of all worthies. That is the idea to which we give the name of God.'[151] Francis felt that these rather pantheistic utterances would preserve 'the highest aspect of his', and would counteract the impression of cynical unbelief which Pattison conveyed in his last years, and especially in the *Memoirs*. She therefore planned to publish the 'Confession of Faith' as an appendix to the *Memoirs*. Her co-executor, Frank Pattison, objected, thinking its open heterodoxy might offend the religious sensibilities of the rest of the family.[152] Instead she copied Pattison's words to various friends – Eleanor Smith, William Stebbing, her brother-in-law William Tuckwell. They were evidently authorized to circulate the Confession privately.[153] Francis's own copy appears among the Pattison papers. 'To the philosopher', Pattison continued, 'God means the highest conceivable value, it is the thing per se, it is intellect. Whether it belongs to an individual or is a diffused essence like . . . we don't know.'

---

[148] Bodleian MS Pattison 134, f. 65.     [149] Bodleian MS Pattison 134, f. 63.
[150] Bodleian MS Pattison 134, f. 62.     [151] Bodleian MS Pattison 112, ff. 102–3.
[152] E. F. S. Pattison to Eleanor Smith, 11 Dec. 1884, Bodleian MS Pattison 118, ff. 115–116.
[153] The reviewer of the *Memoirs* in the *British Quarterly Review* 81 (1885), 442–3, had evidently seen it, and took it to be 'a document of true philosophical value, as well as an evidence of deep personal religion'.

For Pattison there was no separation between the spiritual life and the life of the intellect. He separated his position from that of the Baconian and the positivist. They were interested only in the fruits of knowledge: how had the operation of the intellect added to the sum of human happiness. But this 'conquest of nature by the intelligence' was merely 'the substratum or basis of the grand development of thought w$^h$ provides not only for my seventy years of life, but for the past & present, w$^h$ pervades all things'. He held that the highest life was the philosophical life, and the philosophical life consisted in the cultivation of the intellect not for any practical benefits, but for the inherent good of truth. 'The true slavery', he maintained, 'is that of the "doers" to the free idle philosopher who lives not to do, or enjoy, but to know.'[154]

In his later years Pattison was a figure of nationwide renown. His public speeches were commonly recorded in the newspapers and he was much in demand, especially for educational causes. Lord Aberdare, the former Home Secretary, wrote that 'all must feel that one of the lights of Oxford & of England is extinguished'.[155] That was in a private letter of condolence to Francis, but Pattison's death was widely noticed in the daily and periodical press too. The obituaries bordered on the fulsome. *The Times*, which in those days carried about as many obituaries in a month as today's newspaper carries in a day, devoted three full columns (about five thousand words) to its obituary notice: this was as much space as it would give Arnold in 1888 and Jowett in 1893, and was certainly not a simple recognition of Pattison's position as a head of house, since others of that rank (such as his rivals, Michell and Fowler) got just a few paragraphs. The obituarist declared that with his passing 'the University of Oxford has lost one of its most eminent scholars and the English world of letters a master mind'. 'In range of study and amplitude of learning', the writer continued, 'he had very few rivals among his contemporaries, and fewer still perhaps in that maturity of judgment, that comprehensive breadth of view, which are the notes not merely of profound knowledge but of the truly philosophic mind.'[156] Pattison had long-standing connections with *The Times*, and Dean Church thought its obituary a 'panegyric', but other newspapers, such as the *Manchester Guardian*, broadly echoed this verdict.[157]

---

[154] Bodleian MS Pattison 112, ff. 103–6.
[155] H. A. Bruce, 1st Baron Aberdare, to E. F. S. Pattison, 2 August 1884, MS Bywater 61, ff. 117–8.
[156] *The Times*, 31 July 1884, p. 6.
[157] R. W. Church, 'Mark Pattison', *The Guardian*, 6 August 1884, reprinted in R. W. Church, *Occasional Papers Selected from the Guardian, the Times, and the Saturday Review 1846–1890* (London: Macmillan, 1897), vol. II, p. 354.

J. C. Morison, a former pupil, pointed to the contrast between Pattison's 'secluded habits' and 'the extent and quality of his fame during the last ten or fifteen years'.[158]

Pattison's death was even noticed in the United States, although he had never crossed the Atlantic and held a low opinion of American intellectual life.[159] The *New York Times* carried an obituary, and Morison's appreciation of him in *Macmillan's Magazine* was reprinted in *Littell's Living Age*, a weekly journal which brought notable articles from the British periodical press to the attention of American readers. In the early months of 1885 Littell's would also reprint Althaus's 'Recollections of Mark Pattison' from *Temple Bar*, and John Morley's major review of Pattison's *Memoirs* from *Macmillan's Magazine*. So, in the words of one American commentator, 'many Americans heard for the first time the name of this Oxford scholar when they read in the English weeklies of his death, and found the papers for weeks afterward occupied with reminiscences and characterizations'.[160]

The next chapter will explore the nature of Pattison's posthumous reputation, and the role of his own *Memoirs* in shaping the way in which he was remembered. There is a striking contrast between the amount of press interest that attended Pattison's death and the subsequent neglect that befell his memory. It is a story that casts intriguing light on the ways in which reputations are made and sustained.

---

[158] Morison, 'Pattison', 401.
[159] Pusey House, Oxford, Mrs Humphry Ward papers: Pattison to Mary Augusta Ward, 17 October 1883. '[The Americans] always seem to me to be the slaves of fashion, & to pretend to admire what they are told is admirable.'
[160] 'Two English men of letters', *Atlantic Monthly* 56 (1885), 121.

CHAPTER 3

# Memoirs and memories

The survival of names and reputations depends not only on objective achievement but also on a variety of contingencies. Among these are bequests. Pattison was a wealthy man, who by means of lifelong frugality accumulated a fortune of over £46,000. This is roughly the equivalent of two million pounds today, and, excepting those who inherited a substantial fortune, it is not easy to find a wealthier Victorian intellectual.[1] It was certainly in his power to use this wealth to perpetuate his name and to associate it with a cause he cherished. In April 1881 Meta Bradley urged Pattison not to alter his will in her favour, as he proposed, but instead to leave a substantial legacy for the advancement of research. This would have the advantage of attaching his name to some lasting memorial. 'I s[houl]d like my grand-nieces' generation to be familiar with y[ou]r name in connection with something at Oxford', she wrote.[2] Since the work of the university commissioners he was disinclined to leave money to the college, as he had previously intended, not least because the Bishop of Lincoln, as the college's visitor, had successfully defended his right to nominate to one fellowship, which thus continued to be confined to clerics. Pattison was also now unsympathetic to the direction taken by the campaign for the endowment of research, which had been launched in the first place at his inspiration. 'As to endowing research', he wrote, 'I would not do it even if I could, as I am at present minded.'[3] As a result, no institution, monument, or building commemorates Pattison, in Oxford or elsewhere.[4] In this

---

[1] The *Oxford Dictionary of National Biography* gives wealth at death as a standard piece of information in all entries. In round figures, Ruskin left £10,000, Sidgwick £12,000, Arnold £1,000, Jowett £20,000, Mill £14,000, Carlyle under £40,000, Spencer £19,000, Leslie Stephen £16,000. Pattison had inherited a small sum from his mother in 1860, but only a small devise of land from his father: Sparrow, *Pattison*, pp. 36, 54.

[2] Bodleian MS Pattison 121, ff. 49–50, Meta Bradley to Pattison, 17 Apr. 1881.

[3] Bodleian MS Pattison 121, ff. 61–5, Pattison to Meta Bradley, 23 April 1881.

[4] Althaus founded a Mark Pattison Exhibition at Lincoln in 1933, but this seems to have been awarded only sporadically.

respect he differs from many of his Oxford friends and contemporaries. His greatest rival is commemorated by a street name, for Jowett's Walk passes the Balliol sports ground, once known as 'the Master's Field' in his honour. Pattison's sister, Dorothy – who, having joined an Anglican sisterhood, achieved celebrity for her work as a nurse in the Black Country – was commemorated by the Sister Dora Hospital in Walsall, and a statue in the town centre. Pattison's pupil and close friend Richard Christie left his books to form the basis of the University of Manchester Library: the Christie Library now houses a bistro ('Christie's'), and at the entrance diners pass a stained-glass window which depicts Christie in academic dress at his books.

If Pattison did not perpetuate his name through his will, he did leave a volume of *Memoirs* which generated an extraordinary amount of interest in the short term. Its longer-term influence on his reputation was, however, much more complex.

## THE SUBJECTIVE LIFE OF THE SCHOLAR

Pattison engaged in a lifelong 'conversation' with intellectuals and scholars of the past, through their diaries, their autobiographies and other ways in which they recorded their interior lives. The *Memoirs* were the product of this conversation. This fact has important implications for the way in which we understand the intertextual dimensions of the book, and, indeed, for our reading of the rest of his work. It is commonly, and plausibly, suggested that many of Pattison's writings have a strongly autobiographical element. This is true, most importantly, of his largest work, the biography of Isaac Casaubon. But it could equally plausibly be argued that his voracious appetite, from undergraduate days onwards, for volumes of autobiography and diaries by scholars and intellectuals is to be explained by his search for ways of making sense of his own identity. So if it is indeed true that Pattison's Casaubon was remarkably like Pattison, as he depicted himself in the *Memoirs*, this was in large measure because Pattison shaped his own self and interpreted his own self in the light of his understanding of Casaubon.

The poet Robert Southey was the first to use the term 'autobiography', just four years before Pattison's birth, and the genre blossomed under the influence of the romantics and their interest in subjectivity.[5] Pattison was

[5] Nicholas Capaldi, *John Stuart Mill: A Biography* (Cambridge: Cambridge University Press, 2004), p. 237.

by no means straightforwardly a romantic, but he shared this fascination with the interior life and the self. In particular, he had a lifelong interest in intellectual self-representation: in the ways in which scholars, thinkers and writers record their mental development in diaries and memoirs. These literary genres formed a significant part of his reading throughout his adult life, and we should therefore recognize him as a notably self-conscious diarist and autobiographer whose own *Memoirs* were shaped by the auto-biographies of others, and whose diaries were influenced by the various models of scholars' diaries with which he was familiar. The authors of these diaries and autobiographies constituted that 'freemasonry' which helped him discover his own self. Perhaps only Goethe, of nineteenth-century autobiographers, came to the task of writing his own life with a deeper knowledge of the history of the genre.[6]

Pattison's attitude towards autobiography was, however, ambivalent. He was irresistibly drawn to it; but there was also something about the genre that he found repellent. Was it not egotistical to parade one's self before the world? In his biography of Milton – one of his last works, written not long before Meta Bradley began to prod him into writing his own memoirs – he asks 'why it is that a few men, Gibbon or Milton, are indulged without challenge to talk about themselves, which would be childish vanity or odious egotism in others'. His answer was not simply that these are men of 'confessed superiority', but that in these rare cases 'the gratification of self-love, which attends all autobiography, is felt to be subordinated to a nobler intention'. What was important in Milton's autobiographical sketches was not his own self, but his dedication to the 'high and sacred calling' of the poet.[7] It is difficult to avoid calling Pattison's *Memoirs* to mind when we read those words. Their justification lay not in their author's importance, but in his devotion to the philosophical life, or the life of the mind. But he had to be persuaded that the story of his intellectual life was worth telling. In December 1883, when he was in the midst of the composition of the *Memoirs*, he exchanged letters with his former pupil William Stebbing on the subject. Stebbing evidently urged Pattison to concentrate on the development of his own intellect. Pattison demurred, although he was in fact already set on that track. 'Your hint as to the direction, wh[ich] the Reminiscences should take, is of such importance that I have pondered it much. I must say that the thing had not occurred to

---

[6]　Eugene L. Stelzig, *The Romantic Subject in Autobiography: Rousseau and Goethe* (Charlottesville and London: University Press of Virginia, 2000), pp. 132–3.
[7]　Pattison, *Milton*, p. 79.

me in that light, & even now I am not quite able to come into your view. The egotism of so writing appalls me. Do you think it possible that there are many people who would care to read a long drawn history of the growth of an individual mind?'[8]

Pattison's interest in autobiography can be traced as far back as his undergraduate years, when he read not only Gibbon's autobiography but also other famous examples of the genre, such as Thomas De Quincey's *Confessions of an English Opium-Eater*, which he found charming.[9] Towards the end of his life, the period when he was first contemplating and then composing his *Memoirs* was a period of particularly intense reading and re-reading of autobiographies. A significant number of these are mentioned in the *Memoirs*. While two – by Mozley and Cox – are cited as sources for the events Pattison narrates, the rest are cited for what they have to say about the nature of autobiography itself, or the nature of the intellectual life. Besides Gibbon, they include Harriet Martineau, Rousseau, George Sand, Quinet, Wordsworth and Blanco White, not to mention Goethe, whose autobiography, *Dichtung und Wahrheit*, is quoted right at the end. Other works he read during the short period when he was composing his own included the autobiographies of Adamantios Koraes, the leading philosopher of the Greek Enlightenment, and of Peter Daniel Huet, the seventeenth-century French philologist about whom Pattison had written in the *Quarterly Review* nearly three decades earlier.[10] He also read Abraham Hayward's life of Goethe, the *Souvenirs de Jeunesse* of Charles Nodier, the French romantic novelist and bibliophile, and lives of a number of scholars of the eighteenth century, including Daniel Wyttenbach, David Ruhnkenius and Richard Bentley. But Pattison's interest focused above all on intellectual autobiographies which narrated, first, lives devoted to study and to the cultivation of the mind, and, second, lives characterized by intellectual evolution, especially in religion, which others might characterize as inconsistency or apostasy, but which in another sense could be read as *development*. 'Autobiography', it has been said, 'wills the unity of its subject',[11] and it was important to Pattison to be able to depict his own religious life in this way:

---

[8] Pattison to William Stebbing, 23 December 1883, Times Collection, Harry Ransom Center, University of Texas at Austin. Pattison added: 'P. S. Do you happen to know any other autobiography except Gibbons [sic], wh is framed on the plan you recommend?'

[9] Bodleian MS Pattison 2, f. 3, diary 12 Jan. 1835.

[10] Bodleian MS Pattison 134, ff. 58, 60–1, 25 November and 7 December 1883.

[11] John Sturrock, *The Language of Autobiography. Studies in the First Person Singular* (Cambridge: Cambridge University Press, 1993), p. 5.

Slowly, and not without laborious effort, I began to emerge, to conquer, as it were, in the realm of ideas. It was all growth, development, and I have never ceased to grow, to develop, to discover, up to the very last ... I seemed to my friends to have changed, to have gone over from High Anglicanism to Latitudinarianism, or Rationalism, or Unbelief, or whatever the term may be. This is not so; what took place with me was simple expansion of knowledge and ideas. To my home Puritan religion, almost narrowed to two points – fear of God's wrath and faith in the doctrine of the atonement – the idea of the Church was a widening of the horizon which stirred up the spirit and filled it with enthusiasm. The notion of the Church soon expanded itself beyond the limits of the Anglican communion and became the wider idea of the Catholic Church. Then Anglicanism fell off from me, like an old garment, as Puritanism had done before ... There was no conversion or change of view; I could no more have helped what took place within me than I could have helped becoming ten years older.[12]

Or, as he put it in a draft: 'To the world I seem to have changed from high-church, & even romanising to rationalist, – to myself I feel only to have grown.'[13]

Gibbon and Blanco White met the two criteria most fully. Both were devoted to the life of the mind, and both had experienced more than one religious conversion. Gibbon, famously, converted to Roman Catholicism as an undergraduate at Oxford; was brought back within the Protestant pale thanks to the efforts of a Calvinist minister in Lausanne into whose care his father entrusted him; and subsequently came to adopt an enlightened scepticism towards all religious orthodoxies. In his autobiography he portrays his first conversion as the product of his inquisitive mind when combined with the negligent tutorial arrangements he experienced at Magdalen, and he refused to be ashamed of 'an honest sacrifice of interest to conscience'.[14] Blanco White had a still more curious religious odyssey which took him from Roman Catholicism in Spain through a period of unbelief to Liberal Anglicanism, association with the Oriel Noetics, and thence to Unitarianism. In his autobiography – the volume which was instrumental in stiffening Pattison's resolve not to convert to Rome in 1845–6 – White vindicated himself against the obvious accusation of inconsistency, and argued that his religious evolution was a simple development guided by his consistent pursuit of a life of intellectual integrity.[15] 'The internal sources, the seeds which have been unfolded into my present

[12] Pattison, *Memoirs*, pp. 325–7.
[13] Bodleian MS Pattison 138, f. 3, Notes for Autobiography.
[14] Edward Gibbon, *Memoirs of my Life and Writings*, A. O. J. Cockshut and Stephen Constantine (eds.) (n.p., Ryburn, 1994), p. 90.
[15] Pattison read it in August 1846: Bodleian MS Pattison 128, ff. 127–30.

convictions', he wrote, 'may all be found, I may say, in every one of my writings.'[16]

Like Gibbon, White kept a journal, and quoted from it liberally in his autobiography. Naturally this caught Pattison's attention.

B. White's Journals are indeed the history of a <u>mind</u>, not of a <u>man</u>. We have in them not the workings of the same mind on the external world, – such is the auto[bg] of Gibbon e.g. – but the progress & development of a mind, the same yet unceasingly growing . . . As the work advances we have a sort of pleasure in seeing the unflinching consistency with which he carries out the work of rejection; we feel that his views are enlarging, that we have to do with one in whom the free play of the intellect is unclouded by those secular influences that so hamper the majority of even thinking men.[17]

One further icon of the life of the mind exercised a particularly imme-diate influence on the composition of Pattison's *Memoirs*. The *Journal Intime* of the Swiss critic and philosopher, Henri-Frédéric Amiel, was published posthumously in 1882–3 under the editorship of Amiel's friend, the critic Edmond Scherer. Pattison read it almost immediately – in June–July 1883 – and recorded that he found it 'a very striking mental revelation'.[18] He drew it to the attention of one of his protégées, Mary Ward, who published an English translation in 1885. She told her publisher that Pattison had recommended it 'by saying that in *importance* it seemed to him that nothing of its kind had equalled it since Rousseau's *Confessions*'.[19] He amplified this remark in a letter he wrote to Scherer, whom he had met some years before. After Pattison's death Scherer published the letter in *The Times*. As Mary Ward observed, 'the words have a strong and melancholy interest for all who knew Mark Pattison'. This is what Pattison wrote:

I wish to convey to you, sir, the thanks of one at least of the public for giving the light to this precious record of a unique experience. I say unique, but I can vouch that there is in existence at least one other soul which has lived through the same struggles, mental and moral, as Amiel. In your pathetic description of the *volonté qui voudrait vouloir, mais impuissante à se fournir à elle-même des motifs*, – of the repugnance for all action – the soul petrified by the sentiment of the infinite, in all this I recognise myself. *Celui qui a déchiffré le secret de la vie finie, qui en a lu le mot,*

---

[16] John Hamilton Thom (ed.), *The Life of the Rev Joseph Blanco White written by himself with Portions of his Correspondence* (London: John Chapman, 1845), pp. 3, 399–400.
[17] Bodleian MS Pattison 7*, pp. 87–9.   [18] Bodleian MS Pattison 134, f. 38, 13 July 1883.
[19] Quoted by John Sutherland, *Mrs Humphry Ward: Eminent Victorian, Pre-eminent Edwardian* (Oxford: Oxford University Press, 1990), p. 98.

*est sorti du monde des vivants, il est mort de fait.* I can feel forcibly the truth of this, as it applies to myself!

It is not, however, with the view of thrusting my egotism upon you that I have ventured upon addressing you. As I cannot suppose that so peculiar a psychological revelation will enjoy a wide popularity, I think it a duty to the editor to assure him that there are persons in the world whose souls respond, in the depths of their inmost nature, to the cry of anguish which makes itself heard in the pages of these remarkable confessions.[20]

Pattison urged Lionel Tollemache, and many other friends, to read the *Journal Intime.* Tollemache – who became close to Pattison in the last two years of his life – offered a plausible conjecture about what he found so important in Amiel:

May not his relish for Amiel's moral self-dissection have been due to his sympathy for one who suffered from great mental depression – depression aggravated by considering how much had been expected from him, and how little he had performed?[21]

The reader of Amiel's journal who is familiar with Pattison can hardly fail to hear Pattison speaking on almost every page, which may be why some writers have (mistakenly) seen Pattison in Mary Ward's Edward Langham, the protagonist's tutor in *Robert Elsmere.*[22] In fact Mrs Ward acknowledged that Langham was a sort of English Amiel, a man paralysed by a sense of 'the uselessness of utterance, the futility of enthusiasm, the inaccessibility of the ideal, the practical absurdity of trying to realise any of the mind's inward dreams'.[23] Pattison recognized himself in Amiel's depiction of the enfeeblement of the will and incapacity for action generated by pursuit of universal knowledge and universal sympathy: 'I feel a terror of action', wrote Amiel, 'and am only at ease in the impersonal, disinterested, and objective life of thought.'[24] But the intellectual content of Amiel's thinking is also very Pattisonian. In particular, we find the antithesis between inner freedom and compliance with external forces which, as we shall see, stood at the heart of Pattison's moral outlook.

[20] Mrs Humphry Ward (ed.), *Amiel's Journal. The Journal Intime of Henri-Frédéric Amiel* (London: Macmillan, 1885), pp. x–xi.
[21] L. A. Tollemache, 'Recollections of Pattison', p. 131.
[22] Maurice Cowling, *Religion and Public Doctrine in Modern England.* Volume III: *Accommodations* (Cambridge: Cambridge University Press, 2001), p. 144; William M. Calder III and Daniel J. Kramer, *An Introductory Bibliography to the History of Classical Scholarship chiefly in the XIXth and XXth Centuries* (Hildesheim, Zurich and New York: Georg Olms, 1992), p. 310; and, more tentatively, A. N. Wilson, *God's Funeral* (London: Murray, 1999), p. 124.
[23] Mrs Humphry Ward, *Robert Elsmere* (Edinburgh: Nelson, 1952), p. 55.
[24] Ward (ed.), *Amiel's Journal*, p. 49.

Without religion, Amiel wrote, there can be no inner life; and without inner life, no 'resistance to circumstance'. The man who 'has no refuge in himself' lives 'in the outer whirlwind of things and opinions', and is really 'an anonymity, but not a man':

He who floats with the current, who does not guide himself according to higher principles, who has no ideal, no convictions, – such a man is a mere article of the world's furniture – a thing moved, instead of a living and moving being – an echo, not a voice. The man who has no inner life is the slave of his surroundings, as the barometer is the obedient servant of the air at rest, and the weathercock the humble servant of the air in motion.[25]

In a fascinating passage written in 1852, Amiel lamented the tendency of the age 'to substitute the laws of dead matter (number, mass) for the laws of the moral nature (persuasion, adhesion, faith)', and he defined negative and positive liberty in a way which would surely have rung a bell for Pattison. Negative liberty 'has no law in itself, and recognises no limit except in force', while positive liberty is 'action guided by an inner law and curbed by a moral authority'. These themes – moral freedom juxtaposed with dependence upon material circumstances – are ones we shall encounter as central themes of Pattison's sermons. In the antitheses between materialism and spiritualism, and between socialism and individualism, Amiel saw 'the eternal antagonism between letter and spirit, between form and matter, between the outward and the inward, appearance and reality'. He added, in a declaration that might easily have come from Pattison, that 'the test of every religious, political, or educational system, is the man which it forms. If a system injures the intelligence it is bad. If it injures the character it is vicious. If it injures the conscience it is criminal.'[26]

The relevance of Amiel's journal to the history of the composition of Pattison's *Memoirs* does not depend upon conjecture alone. We can track it in detail through Pattison's diary and other manuscript material. In January 1881 Meta Bradley urged him to 'give an account of y[ou]r real inner self', so that she might understand 'how you have become yr present self', and Pattison wrote from Paris to tell her that 'Renan has been doing in the Rev[ue] d[es] d[eux] mondes what you advise me to do – giving his souvenirs de jeunesse – explaining how, he being destined to the sacerdoce came to be the man he is'.[27] He evidently responded to her that he had long thought of writing an autobiography, though he originally envisaged it for

---

[25] Ward (ed.), *Amiel's Journal*, p. 114.  [26] Ward (ed.), *Amiel's Journal*, p. 27.
[27] Meta Bradley to Pattison, 15 Jan. 1881; Pattison to Bradley, 20 Jan. 1881: Bodleian MS Pattison 120, ff. 37–40, 44–45.

private distribution only.[28] The diary, together with some of his correspondence, gives us a precise chronology of the composition. Yielding to Meta's pressure he began thinking about it in the summer of 1881, when staying at Richmond, but got no further than reading Wordsworth's *Prelude*, which was the nearest example he could find there of 'the history of a mind – the only history I have to tell'.[29] He made a false start in November 1882, but abandoned the effort. He resumed the task eleven months later (21 October 1883), when he knew he was dying, and it became his chief literary preoccupation: in late November and early December he was writing or dictating more or less every day. We know from his correspondence that by 6 December he was 'still at Oriel', but in December and January he dictated the rest, covering the period to 1860, that is, the eve of his election as rector, and including 'a few general paragraphs in conclusion, summarily touching upon the later life'. Indeed, on 30 December he informed Meta that he had finished the *Memoirs* and that Macmillan had agreed to publish them; and on 6 January 1884 he told a confidante that he had finished his autobiography a fortnight previously.[30] So we can be certain that the text as we know it was composed in the last ten weeks of 1883.

It is crucially important, then, to know that Pattison re-read Amiel at exactly the time he was writing the *Memoirs*; and, to be more precise, the part dealing with his life up to and including his undergraduate days at Oriel. His diary records that he was reading Amiel on 16 November, 17 November, 23 and 24 November, and on three of these occasions the reference to reading Amiel is followed immediately by an entry recording work on the *Memoirs*.[31] An entire sheet of the diary, covering the period 20–23 November, has been excised, and there may, obviously, have been further references to reading Amiel on the missing days. On finishing Amiel's journal for the second time on 24 November, he described it as 'quite a unique book of confessions in its frankness & subtle probing of a man's soul by himself – some of the critiques – such as those on V. Hugo, and Chateaubriand, are masterpieces of objective criticism'.[32] In addition, two quotations from Amiel's journal are to be found among some autobiographical fragments, composed at some point in 1883, which survive in manuscript.[33]

[28] Meta Bradley to Pattison, 11 Aug. 1881, Bodleian MS Pattison 121, ff. 219–23; Pattison to Bradley, 20 Aug. 1881, MS Pattison 122, ff. 1–4.
[29] Pattison to Meta Bradley, 29 July 1881, Bodleian MS Pattison 121, ff. 211–18.
[30] Pattison to Mrs W. D. Hertz, 6 Jan. 1884, Bodleian MS Pattison 144, f. 66.
[31] Bodleian MS Pattison 134, ff. 56–8.    [32] Bodleian MS Pattison 134, f. 58.
[33] Bodleian MS Pattison 138, ff. 29, 31.

### THE *MEMOIRS*

Pattison's autobiography is a curious volume. Because it was written in a hurry, and for the most part dictated, at a time when he was suffering from the cancer that ultimately killed him, it is not written with the spare elegance that characterized most of his writing. His epigrammatic brilliance is on show, but the book lacks the rigorous organization and economy with words that usually marked his work. It is therefore difficult to endorse the verdict of the reviewer – a friend and protégé of Pattison's – who remarked on the book's 'artistic unity' and 'the beauty of the style'.[34] Like all his writings, it is studded with pithy judgements, but it contains a number of infelicities which would no doubt have been weeded had he been able to see it through to publication.[35] The volume is also incomplete: it really covers only the period from his matriculation at Oxford in 1832 to the eve of his election as Rector of Lincoln in 1861: less than thirty years out of a life that spanned more than seventy. Indeed, almost nine-tenths of the book is devoted to the period up to 1851, and almost half to his undergraduate years. It was rumoured after its publication that a second volume would shortly appear, much to the alarm of some of his Oxford colleagues: Thomas Fowler, by then President of Corpus Christi, feared that he was to be attacked from beyond the grave and said he had prepared some recollections of his own to exact revenge.[36] In fact, it would seem that Pattison never had any intention of dealing with the period of his rectorship: he said this was because he would have to deal with people who were still alive, but his more specific reason was surely that he would have to discuss his marriage, and that was too painful and, in any case, unlikely to be tolerated by his widow. It was his 'boyish years' he planned to deal with in a later volume, if he were to be spared time to do this.[37] In spite of these defects it made a powerful impact when it was first published and, as we shall see, did much to shape the way in which Pattison was remembered.

Roy Pascal has written that 'in the autobiography proper, attention is focused on the self, in the memoir or reminiscences on others'.[38] On these

---

[34] H. Nettleship in *Academy*, xxvii (28 March 1885), 215.

[35] This point was noted by the review in *British Quarterly Review* 81 (1885), 442–3, but has been overlooked by those scholars, including even Sparrow, who have pounced on an egregious mixed metaphor as if it were typical of Pattison's writing: Sparrow, *Pattison*, pp. 23–4.

[36] Michael Sadleir, *Michael Ernest Sadler (Sir Michael Sadler K.C.S.I.) 1861–1943. A Memoir by his Son*, (London: Constable, 1949), pp. 75–6.

[37] Pattison, *Memoirs*, p. 1.

[38] Quoted by A. O. J. Cockshut, *The Art of Autobiography in 19th and 20th Century England* (New Haven & London: Yale University Press, 1984), p. 2.

definitions, Pattison's book would be better classed as an autobiography than as a set of memoirs, for he professed (misleadingly) to 'have seen no one, known none of the celebrities of my own time intimately, and have only an inaccurate memory for what I hear'; but like one born to be an autobiographer he engaged in a lifelong exploration of his own self.[39] One qualification, however, should be made to this statement: although he was constantly drawn to autobiography, he also found self-revelation exhausting. Late in life he told his friend Lionel Tollemache that he disapproved of auricular confession because it made people examine themselves too closely.[40] But he spoke as one who was by nature inclined to intense self-examination. Few writers in the history of the genre of autobiography can have been as intensely preoccupied with their own identity, with their own subjective self. One particularly perceptive obituarist wrote that Pattison 'was perpetually questioning and cross-questioning books and persons in order to learn the mystery of himself, his own mind and being'.[41] His *Memoirs* were a quintessential instance of the autobiography as narrative of a quest; and like other 'questers' he had an unshakable sense of his own uniqueness.[42] He could have echoed Rousseau's declaration: 'I am made unlike any one I have ever met; I will even venture to say that I am like no one in the whole world.'[43] But that is not to say that he was possessed of a bold and proud independence of spirit: far from it. As an undergraduate, his initial response to his sense of his difference from others was an attempt to imitate them. The *Memoirs* narrate, and his journals document, a lifetime's struggle to construct an identity for himself. He set out to construct that identity by devouring the autobiographies and journals of anyone he identified as, potentially, like him. The key to this quest may be found, perhaps, in a letter he wrote to Meta Bradley in 1880:

In saying I must be 'lonely mentally', you have struck upon a truth vital to me. It is so. On the other hand there is a kind of freemasonry among people who have passed through it all, of which I get the benefit wherever I go, all over Europe. We know each other, & feel easy in each other's society, even without exchanging ideas, or touching on the burning questions. I am getting more & more every year to know people of this kind. They are not very numerous, but no part of the world – not even Oxford – is wholly without them.[44]

[39] Pattison, *Memoirs*, p. 1.     [40] Tollemache, 'Recollections of Pattison', p. 145.
[41] *Athenaeum*, 2 August 1884, pp. 147–8.     [42] Cockshut, *Art of Autobiography*, ch. 8.
[43] Jean-Jacques Rousseau, *Confessions*, trans. J. M. Cohen (London: Penguin, 1953), p. 17.
[44] Bodleian MS Pattison 119, ff. 209–13: Pattison to Meta Bradley, 18 October 1880.

That mental loneliness is unmistakable in the *Memoirs*; but those *Memoirs* were themselves the culmination of a lifelong effort to gain access to the 'freemasonry' he refers to here. He sought to do so by literary communion with those figures in the past whom he identified as sharing that single-minded devotion to the cultivation of the intellect which set him apart from other men, and who left records of that devotion in the form of diaries or autobiographies.

Reviewers of the *Memoirs* took the text to be an unconscious recognition of the importance of character in human affairs: Pattison's failure to realize his full potential was to be ascribed to weakness of character and enervation of will. But for the author too character was a central analytical category in the story of his life: in a crucial passage in the first chapter, the word 'character', and derivatives such as 'characterless', appear six times in three paragraphs, in each case with reference to Pattison himself.[45] In framing his life story around the formation of his own character he was by no means unique among Victorian autobiographers: John Stuart Mill, for instance, famously recounted the mental crisis he experienced when he came to feel that he was a 'manufactured man', not self-made but the product of the unique education his father had given him.[46] Like Mill, Pattison did not attend school, but was educated by his father. But whereas Mill, on reaching adulthood, was haunted by the sense that his character had been made for him, Pattison tells the story of a youth who simply had no character. 'Surely no boy ever reached eighteen so unformed and characterless as I was!'[47] Such was the solitude of his upbringing that he had, prior to his arrival in Oxford, little sense of his own difference from other boys: he had therefore little sense of his own identity.

This is why, unusually, Pattison begins his narrative with his arrival at Oriel. He depicts his undergraduate self as lacking in character. It was marked by 'mutability and chameleon-like readiness to take any shade of colour', with the result that he failed to assert 'my own right to be what I was'.[48] The *Memoirs* recount the way in which he came to exercise that right. That required him to free himself from 'the bondage of unreason' and from 'the traditional prejudices which, when I began first to think, constituted the whole of my intellectual fabric'.[49] Pattison depicts his formation in a way that is curiously reminiscent of the conjectural anthropology of the *Discourse on Inequality*, in which Rousseau speculates on how

---

[45] Pattison, *Memoirs*, pp. 47–9.
[46] A. O. J. Cockshut (ed.), *The Autobiography of John Stuart Mill* (Halifax: Ryburn, 1992), p. 85.
[47] Pattison, *Memoirs*, p. 49.    [48] Pattison, *Memoirs*, pp. 47–9.    [49] Pattison, *Memoirs*, p. 2.

man progressed from a state of natural freedom to the social state, which brought with it self-consciousness and hence dependence, inequality and subjection; and on how he might reconquer a new kind of rational and civil freedom.[50] In his childhood in a remote country parish in North Yorkshire Pattison lived, as it were, in the state of nature, 'much like Caspar Hausser [sic] in the Bavarian wilds'.[51] He was 'a mere child of nature, totally devoid of self-consciousness, to such a degree that I had never thought of myself as a subject of observation'.[52] His arrival in Oxford at the age of eighteen brought him his 'first contact with my species', and he was overcome with a morbid self-consciousness born of an acute sense of his 'unlikeness to others'. 'I found, what I had not been prepared for, that the differences between myself on the one side, and all the rest on the other, were greater than the resemblances; the points of antipathy more numerous than the points of sympathy.'[53] He reacted on the one hand with disgust for his peers, but on the other hand with an exaggerated desire for their approval, which he tried to win by a 'constant personation'.[54] His self-consciousness was exacerbated, and his quest to assimilate hampered, by an ignorance of the usages of polite society. 'I had been turned out upon the world without the most elementary knowledge of the rules of etiquette', he writes. 'I didn't know I ought to leave a card after hospitality; I doubt if I had any visiting cards to begin with.'[55] He recounts his disastrous attempt to give a wine-party in the autumn of 1832, after which he was convinced that his 'clownishness' had left him 'ostracised, black-balled, expelled from society'.[56]

This sense of exclusion made Pattison still more vulnerable to the tyranny of society. He was, as he depicts himself, peculiarly vulnerable to 'all the social distractions to which a youth lodged in college rooms is liable', as well as, in the vacation, a 'lazy acquiescence in the home circle'.[57] The *Memoirs* narrate the transition from the state of nature to the state of

---

[50] It is not clear whether Pattison ever read the *Discourse on Inequality*; but he certainly encountered and noticed similar ideas in idealist accounts of the philosophy of history such as Fichte's *Characteristics of the Present Age*: Bodleian MS Pattison 7*, pp. 115–6.

[51] Pattison, *Memoirs*, p. 104. See also p. 36: 'But I was not spoiled, as a boy is who has been brutalised by a school; I was only rude, unfledged, in a state of nature.'

[52] Pattison, *Memoirs*, p. 49.    [53] Pattison, *Memoirs*, p. 46.

[54] Pattison, *Memoirs*, pp. 104, 48, 56. More than a quarter of matriculants were under eighteen, so Pattison, who was half way through his nineteenth year when he matriculated, was by no means young: see Lawrence Stone, 'The size and composition of the Oxford student body 1580–1910', in Lawrence Stone (ed.), *The University in Society* (Princeton and London: Princeton University Press, 1974), I, p. 98.

[55] Pattison, *Memoirs*, p. 59.    [56] Pattison, *Memoirs*, p. 144.

[57] Pattison, *Memoirs*, pp. 132, 116.

bondage to society, but also, more importantly, the process of emancipation from those bonds by a discovery of his rational self or his 'real self'.[58] He traces the beginning of this process to a specific moment, 'the dawn of intellect in me', which occurred in the Long Vacation of 1833, four terms into his undergraduate career. This was the moment at which the autobiographer finds 'the first stirrings of anything like intellectual life within me'. Crucially, this was the moment when he began to keep a journal of his reading and thinking: 'a student's diary', he writes, 'on the same plan as I have kept up, with intervals, to the present date'.[59] And he spells out the essential nature of that intellectual life, distinguishing it from education as simple acculturation. 'Hitherto I had had no mind, properly so called, merely a boy's intelligence, receptive of anything I read or heard. I now awoke to the new idea of finding the reason of things.'[60] He 'enforced' on himself a 'new principle . . . that of never allowing myself to be the passive recipient of any one's thoughts or opinions, but to think out for myself every statement, and to stop upon it until I had found if it ranged with what I had already accepted'.[61]

Pattison's account of this moment when he began to discover the true meaning of the intellectual life is akin to an account of a conversion experience. For one thing, it was a moment when he started to sense that old beliefs had to be shed: 'I began to suspect I might have much to unlearn as well as to learn, and that I must clear my mind of much current opinion which had lodged there.'[62] Furthermore, it was effectively the start of the rest of his life, the moment when he discovered the principle which would thenceforth govern his existence: 'the principle of rationalism was born in me, and once born it was sure to grow, and to become the master-idea of the whole process of self-education, on which I was from this time forward embarked'.[63]

What Pattison is telling here is the story of his acquisition of a true or rational freedom. In the 'state of nature' of Wensleydale he possessed a natural freedom, the freedom of the 'wild boys' who exercised such fascination over eighteenth- and nineteenth-century thinkers: he compares himself not only with Caspar Hauser, the wild boy of Bavaria, but also with Peter, the wild boy of Hanover.[64] But his encounter with society on his

---

[58] For 'real self', see Pattison, *Memoirs*, pp. 54, 56.
[59] Pattison, *Memoirs*, pp. 119–20. This journal begins (in July 1833) at Bodleian MS Pattison 115.
[60] Pattison, *Memoirs*, pp. 128, 121–2. See also p. 38: 'I was already [c. 1831] marked out for the life of a student, yet little that was in the books I read seemed to find its way into my mind. There was no mind there!'
[61] Pattison, *Memoirs*, p. 124.  [62] Pattison, *Memoirs*, p. 121.
[63] Pattison, *Memoirs*, p. 121.  [64] Pattison, *Memoirs*, p. 56.

arrival in Oxford brought with it self-consciousness and hence (as in Rousseau) dependence on others. His 'growing anxiety as to what others were thinking of what I said and did' fastened 'the yoke of moral tyranny' around his neck.[65] The discovery of the life of the intellect was the means he found to emancipate himself from this tyranny. For Pattison the philosophical life was the truest form of freedom. That was what he meant when he told Francis on his deathbed that the men of action are the real slaves, whereas true freedom belongs to the 'idle philosopher' who lives not to do but to know.[66] The nature of true freedom was a theme he would explore most fully in one of his finest essays, on Calvin at Geneva, published in the *Westminster Review* in 1858. There too he offered a Rousseauian account of freedom, distinguishing 'the natural instinct of the free man' from 'the liberty of a truly free will': the latter, unlike the former, depended on consciousness. 'The roving savage and the citizens of a Republic are both free, but in a different sort'; the latter was a fuller liberty, for 'true liberty is only realized through self-control, when "the weight of chance desires" has been felt, and been shaken off by an effort of the will'. This was a vindication of the civic freedom of Calvin's Geneva, but for Pattison this was itself a stunted freedom, for Calvin, who 'had a passionate desire to live as a free man under the law of God', nevertheless 'felt no corresponding necessity for intellectual emancipation'.[67]

The central narrative of the *Memoirs*, then, consisted of an account of Pattison's acquisition of rational freedom through his consecration of himself to the philosophical life. The adoption of the principle of rationalism gave meaning to his life. Needless to say, Pattison – who in his maturity was committed to an empiricist epistemology – did not understand rationalism in the Cartesian sense. He employed the term in its everyday sense of a commitment to reason and observation, as opposed to faith or tradition, as the road to truth. His main challenge as an autobiographer would be to explain the appeal of Tractarianism to one in whom the 'principle of rationalism' had already been born.

Pattison devoted an important and much-studied section of the *Memoirs* to the Oxford Movement. He depicts this phase of his life as a relapse into superstition: Tractarianism was a 'whirlpool' into which he was drawn, as it were, against his will. Escape came only when 'my brain had consolidated itself, and the forces of reason were slowly beginning to reassert themselves against the masses of imported superstition or native tendency to pietism,

[65] Pattison, *Memoirs*, p. 60.    [66] Bodleian MS Pattison 112, f. 105.
[67] [Pattison], 'Calvin at Geneva', *Westminster Review* 70 o.s. (1858), reprinted in *Essays* II, pp. 39–40.

which had hitherto had it all their own way'.[68] One thing that weakened the movement's hold over him was his intellectual disdain for most of his fellow Tractarians. Likewise the appeal of Rome faded once he had visited Paris and encountered French Catholicism at first hand. In the English Catholic convert and scholar Kenelm Digby, whose *Mores Catholici* he admired, he found 'there was no mind underneath; it was all accumulation in support of Catholic dogma'. In other words, learning was an instrument in the service of apologetics, and not an end in itself. Among Parisian Catholics he found 'a spirit of credulity so vulgar that it could not have existed had it ever been brought into the light of day'.[69] As we shall see in Chapter Four, Tractarianism had a more enduring influence on Pattison's conception of the intellectual life than he was willing to admit. But for the moment the key point is this: for Pattison the autobiographer, the struggle to discover his own self was fundamentally a struggle to release his intellect from its fetters.

Pattison's narrative of his own life is put into relief by his account of his cousin, Philippa Meadows, for her story was more or less the inverse of Pattison's, as he tells it. Philippa (referred to in the *Memoirs* simply as 'a female cousin') was the daughter of Mary Meadows, the widowed sister of Mark James Pattison. She was some three years older than Pattison. During Pattison's boyhood they lived at Ainderby, a neighbouring parish to Hauxwell, and she and Pattison developed a close but (he insists) platonic friendship founded on a shared passion for books. But whereas Pattison constructs his life's story around the painfully slow growth of the intellectual life and the gradual shedding of the shackles of superstition, Philippa's trajectory – as he recounts it – was the reverse. She outshone her younger cousin, at least in his recollection. She 'early developed a masculine understanding'. As a young woman she possessed a clearly defined character of mind: 'a speculative activity which urged her, would she or would she not, through all the abysses of philosophic thought', combined with a 'perseverance in learning' which equalled her speculative powers. 'I have known some of the wittiest, the ablest, and the best read men of my time', wrote Pattison, 'but I do not exaggerate when I say that this woman at about thirty-five was a match in power and extent of knowledge for any of them'.[70]

His choice of thirty five was not an arbitrary one, for that was the age at which Philippa (together with her mother) was received into the Roman

[68] Pattison, *Memoirs*, pp. 182, 208.   [69] Pattison, *Memoirs*, pp. 209–11.
[70] Pattison, *Memoirs*, pp. 223–4.

Catholic Church. They eventually settled in Paris, where Pattison would visit them. 'But all intellectual intercourse between myself and cousin was at an end', he recalled. 'Her conversation had come to be a passionate invective in monologue against Protestantism, Anglicanism, and everything except what was Roman.' In her the principle of rationalism had developed early but had been swept away in a tide of religious enthusiasm. 'Can such a wreck of a noble intellect by religious fanaticism be paralleled?' her cousin asked.[71]

### THE VICTORIAN RECEPTION OF THE *MEMOIRS*

The *Memoirs* were published on 4 March 1885 and became a minor literary sensation. They were widely reviewed in the daily press (*The Times*, the *Daily News*, the *Manchester Guardian*, the *Standard*, the *Pall Mall Gazette*), in the weeklies (the *Athenaeum*, the *Spectator*, the *Academy)* and in the monthly and quarterly periodicals (*Macmillan's Magazine*, *Temple Bar*, the *British Quarterly Review*, the *London Quarterly Review*, the *Journal of Education*).[72] Practically all the reviews were substantial. Even the dailies spared the space for generous quotations from the text: the review in the *Times* was spread over two weeks, and that in the *Manchester Guardian* ran to about five thousand words. The first two print runs were quickly exhausted and by April the volume was into its third run. Sales were therefore of the order of three thousand or more within weeks, which was far more than Macmillan had expected.[73] It was also in demand with patrons of Mudie's circulating library, and Pattison well knew this to be an indication of a popular readership, for 'Smith and Mudie . . . look only to what is most asked for'.[74] This level of circulation did not make the *Memoirs* a best-seller, but – to put it in perspective – it far exceeded that of *Essays and Reviews* in its early weeks.[75] This reception deserves comment, since the *Memoirs* do not have the immediate appearance of a literary classic, being 'brief, fragmentary, and uneven', as one reviewer observed.[76]

[71] Pattison, *Memoirs*, p. 228.
[72] *The Times* also carried a rebuttal by Travers Twiss of Pattison's account of the University College election of 1839: 3 April 1885, p. 4.
[73] R. F. Steff (Macmillan Company Secretary) to John Sparrow, 7 June 1971, Lincoln College MS/PAT/III/15.
[74] *Journal of Education* n.s. 7 (1885), 427–8; Pattison, 'Books and critics', 673.
[75] It took *Essays and Reviews* three months to exhaust its first print run of one thousand copies: Altholz, *Anatomy of a Controversy*, p. 36.
[76] *Pall Mall Gazette*, 6 March 1885. The generous print layout of the Victorian period may mislead today's readers, but the book was not much more than fifty thousand words long.

Yet almost all reviewers, whether or not they thought Pattison, as revealed in his autobiography, a sympathetic personality, pronounced the *Memoirs* or their author 'remarkable', a word that recurs with striking frequency in Victorian appreciations of the man and his work. The *Daily News* thought Pattison 'a very remarkable character', while the *Standard* judged the *Memoirs* 'one of the most remarkable books of the season' and the *Athenaeum* called it 'a book of remarkable power'.[77] The *Journal of Education* observed that if he had been to public school Pattison 'would probably have been a happier and a less remarkable man'.[78] Public interest reached to the highest levels. When Gladstone dined with the Archbishop of Canterbury and others in March 1885, Pattison's *Memoirs* were a central topic of the table talk: the Prime Minister, recorded Archbishop Benson, was 'absolutely lost in Mark Pattison's Life', several sentences of which he was able to quote verbatim.[79]

Gladstone was no ordinary prime minister, least of all in the intensity and catholicity of his literary, scholarly and theological interests; but the extent of his fascination is worth dwelling upon. He first read the *Memoirs* on 12 March 1885. Six days later the conversation with Benson took place, which prompted the Archbishop to read the *Memoirs* over Easter; and on 23 March he transcribed a number of passages from the book, which still survive among Gladstone's papers in the British Library. On 29 March Pattison featured, alongside George Eliot, in a conversation he had with Sir John Seeley, Regius Professor of History at Cambridge, and on Easter Day (5 April) Pattison still dominated the Prime Minister's mind. Nor was this all. He probably read Althaus's recollections of Pattison, and certainly read Tollemache's twice, and we know that he re-read the *Memoirs* in 1890. He also discussed the book with Mary Ward when he met her in 1888 to discuss her *Robert Elsmere*, a novel which exerted a still greater hold over his mind and which had an important Pattisonian connection.[80] He told Mrs Ward that he reckoned the *Memoirs* 'among the most tragic and the most memorable books of the nineteenth century'.[81]

---

[77] *Daily News*, 6 March 1885; *Standard*, 10 March 1885; *Athenaeum* no. 2994 (14 March 1885), 335–6; all cuttings at Lincoln College MS/PAT/1/B. See also Goldwin Smith, *Reminiscences*, ed. Arnold Haultain (New York: Macmillan, 1910), p. 84, who considers Pattison 'the most remarkable figure' among the academic liberals of the 1850s.

[78] *Journal of Education* n.s. 7 (1885), 149.

[79] Arthur Christopher Benson, *The Life of Edward White Benson, sometime Archbishop of Canterbury* (London: Macmillan, 1900) vol. II, p. 50.

[80] William S Peterson, 'Gladstone's review of *Robert Elsmere*: some unpublished correspondence', *Review of English Studies* xxi (1970), 450.

[81] Ward, *A Writer's Recollections*, p. 106.

The combination of Gladstone's marginal annotations to his copy of the *Memoirs*, and his separate notes on the book, provide us with some evidence on the basis of which we can speculate on the reasons for his fascination, and we can hazard a few guesses about the passages he was able to quote to the Archbishop of Canterbury.[82] Gladstone scholars will not be surprised to learn that the passages on the Tractarians in general, and Newman in particular, were heavily marked. He evidently queried Pattison's assertion that Newman's conception of the tutorial relation, had it been realized at Oriel in the 1830s, would have turned the college into 'a mere priestly seminary and not an agent of the university'.[83] The comments on Bishop Butler, one of Gladstone's intellectual heroes and a lifelong scholarly passion of his, were also noted for future reference, and the Prime Minister clearly had a lively interest in Dorothy Pattison, Sister Dora of Walsall. The rectorship election of 1851 was, of course, impossible to avoid: '271–90. The disgraceful history of the election to the headship (Told without a twinge!).'[84]

Gladstone was, not surprisingly, centrally concerned with Pattison's religious evolution. He expressed his disapproval of passages voicing scepticism or rationalism, notably the assertion that religion is a good servant but a bad master, and others which excluded the operation of divine providence.[85] What particularly concerned him was the conflict that the *Memoirs* highlight between religious orthodoxy and learning. To admit such a conflict would have been to remove a pillar of Gladstone's life's work. So his pencil marks highlighted passages in which Pattison asserted or assumed this conflict. These included the proposition that talent was much scarcer in Oxford before the secularization of the University, and the accusation that Gladstone's own college, among others, was 'corroded ... by the canker of ecclesiasticism ... which excludes all intelligent interests'.[86] Gladstone saw civilization as 'a thing distinct from religion, but destined to coalesce with it', and he found in ancient Greece, and especially in Homer, the first articulation of the values of a civilized society. His classical learning was thus a supplement to his religious studies, and not a distraction from them.[87] He therefore deplored the suggestion that Christian values overturned, rather than transcended, the values of

[82] The system of marginal annotations used by Gladstone is elucidated by Ruth Clayton, 'W. E. Gladstone: an annotation key', *Notes and Queries* 246 (N. S. 48) (June 2001), 140–3.
[83] Pattison, *Memoirs*, p. 87. Gladstone placed a question mark in the margin here.
[84] British Library Add MS 44792 f. 54.
[85] Pattison, *Memoirs*, pp. 97, 328.    [86] Pattison, *Memoirs*, pp. 69, 89.
[87] H. C. G. Matthew, *Gladstone 1809–1874* (Oxford: Oxford University Press, 1988), pp. 153–4.

classical antiquity. He baulked at the reference to 'the degenerate and semi-barbarous Christian writers of the fourth century', and highlighted the passages where Pattison identified in the patristic era 'the saddest moment in history – the ruin of the painfully constructed fabric of civilisation to the profit of the church', and where he portrayed Tractarianism as a new Counter-Reformation which 'suspended, for an indefinite period, all science, humane letters, and the first strivings of intellectual freedom which had moved in the bosom of Oriel'.[88] As we shall see, he would return to these themes in his Romanes Lecture at Oxford in 1892.

Gladstone evidently had a special concern with Pattison's assertion that whereas others might see inconsistency and tergiversation in his intellectual journey, he himself saw only growth. In Gladstone's pencilled index to the key passages in the *Memoirs*, we find the entry '328, 9 Development'. This refers to the passage in which Pattison describes his intellectual evolution as an organic growth:

An ovum was deposited in the nidus of my mind, blind, formless, with no quality but life. Incubation warmed it; it differentiated itself into logical members, then threw out tentacles, which grasped with avidity all matter which they could assimilate from their environment, till the whole conception presented itself organically complete and articulate.

In his notes Gladstone transcribed this passage, along with the lengthy passage that occurs three pages before, in which he specifically describes his religious development in these evolutionary terms: 'slow as the steps were, they have been all forward'.[89] He doubted this story. Quoting the passage, immediately before the first of these two extracts, in which Pattison illustrated this developmental account of his intellectual life with reference to the growth of his idea of the university, from 'the most rudimentary notion, the personal relation between teacher and taught', Gladstone objected:

In developing the idea [i.e. the idea of the university], he seems wholly to have lost the personal side of its [the university's] teaching office – & this he censures without seeing how he was censuring himself.[90]

This may be an unjust critique of Pattison's later conception of the university; but it illustrates Gladstone's unwillingness to accept that there was nothing but organic growth in Pattison's mental history.

---

[88] Pattison, *Memoirs*, pp. 97, 96, 100–1.    [89] Pattison, *Memoirs*, p. 326.
[90] British Library Add MS 44792 f. 58.

Gladstone had a wider interest in Pattison's work. He did not encounter the *Suggestions on Academical Organisation* until more than five years after publication, but when he did he immediately wrote to his Chancellor of the Exchequer,

Do you know Pattison's book on Academical organisation? I have only now become acquainted with it, & think it the most powerful & searching (though not free from exaggeration) that I have seen. On his practical proposals there is a great deal to be said; but it may be called a gallant scheme.[91]

His own copy of the book is heavily annotated. He bought Pattison's biography of Casaubon immediately on its appearance in 1875 and thought it 'remarkable' (that adjective again). He made extensive notes on it, and it absorbed his attention for an unusual length of time: according to the diaries he first looked at it on 1 March, and, having met Pattison at Mrs Grote's on 8 May, read it again on 10, 11, 13, 14, 15, 17 and 19 May.[92] He wrote to an American correspondent of the book's 'great merits'.[93] His fascination with Pattison endured beyond the rector's death and the immediate impact of the *Memoirs*. In his *Studies Subsidiary to the Works of Bishop Butler* he engaged closely with Pattison's comments on Butler, chiefly in the *Memoirs*.[94] When Gladstone gave the first Romanes lecture at Oxford in 1892, under the title 'An academic sketch', his aim was, he later recalled, 'to combat Pattison's statement that the extinction of the Pagan civilisation by the Church was a great calamity'.[95] His lecture was a grand survey of the history of European universities, and indeed of the relations between religion and learning from the fall of Rome to his own day. The University and the Church certainly stood in tension, but Gladstone insisted that they were not adversaries or antagonists, 'in any other sense than as two rowers, one on the right, and the other on the left,

[91] Gladstone to Robert Lowe, 17 April 1883: H. C. G. Matthew (ed.), *The Gladstone Diaries* vol. VIII (Oxford: Oxford University Press, 1982), p. 317. Gladstone read the book on 10 and 17 April: *Gladstone Diaries* vol. XIV (Index), p. 511.

[92] H. C. G. Matthew (ed.), *The Gladstone Diaries* vol. IX (Oxford: Oxford University Press, 1986), pp. 17, 35–7; the notes are at British Library Add MSS 44792, f. 53, 44794, f. 186. In this case Gladstone did not annotate his own copy.

[93] Quoted in Hall Harrison, *Was the Revised Constitution of the Diocese Legally Approved? Or is it Null and Void? A Letter to the Right Reverend William Woodruff Niles, D. D., Bishop of New Hampshire* (Boston: Williams, 1879), pp. 39–40.

[94] W. E. Gladstone, *Studies Subsidiary to the Works of Bishop Butler* (Oxford: Oxford University Press, 1896), pp. 76–7.

[95] Asa Briggs (ed.), *Gladstone's Boswell. Late Victorian Conversations by Lionel A Tollemache and Other Documents* (Brighton: Harvester, 1984), p. 107.

portions of whose force neutralise one another, unite nevertheless to propel the boat'.[96]

Why did Pattison's *Memoirs* fascinate not just Gladstone, but also the wider educated public? Some reasons are straightforward and relate to the subject matter dealt with. Pattison offered an original and first-hand perspective on the Oxford Movement, and more generally on the battle of ideas in Victorian Oxford, and these were subjects which had an obvious appeal to the educated public of the late Victorian period. The *Pall Mall* reviewer observed that

No chapter in the history of opinion is more attractive than the record of the struggle between Liberalism and Clericalism at Oxford in all the various phases which it has passed through during the last half-century, and on all of them these memoirs have something luminous and incisive to say.

He commented that the account of Newman was particularly interesting, no doubt because it was more sympathetic than the account Pattison offered of the other major figures in the Oxford Movement.[97] The *Manchester Guardian* endorsed this view, and considered Pattison's remarks on the Tractarian movement to be 'of the highest value'.[98] The impact of the Oxford Movement, especially on Oxford, was 'a profoundly important phase of thought', according to *The Standard*;[99] and reviewers recognized that a history of the ideas that formed the present age is the hardest kind of intellectual history to write, and that Pattison was uniquely well equipped to write such a history, both because of his personal involvement and, more especially, because of his distinctive interest in and aptitude for '[t]he filiation of ideas, the movement of thought'.[100]

At the same time, reviewers thought that the volume had a powerful human interest, which sprang in part from Pattison's candid self-revelation, and in part from his fiercely introspective personality. The reader would not need to find the author a sympathetic character to feel the book's power, which depended at once on its 'charm' and its 'strangeness'.[101] The reviewer in the *Daily News* perceptively commented that the book might have been entitled 'Annals of a Subjective Life': he stressed, as others did, that Pattison made a memorable personal impression, whether

---

[96] W. E. Gladstone, *The Romanes Lecture, 1892, An Academic Sketch delivered in the Sheldonian Theatre, Oct. 24, 1892* (Oxford: Oxford University Press, 1892), p. 11.
[97] *Pall Mall Gazette*, 6 March 1885: this and the following newspaper cuttings are at Lincoln College MS/PAT/I/B.
[98] *Manchester Guardian* 16 March 1885, p. 6. [99] *The Standard*, 10 March 1885.
[100] *Athenaeum*, 14 March 1885, pp. 335–6. [101] *Pall Mall Gazette*, 6 March 1885.

positive or negative, on those who met him, and that while he 'did much good work', his fame and his importance owed much more 'to his character than to his performance'.[102] For that reason, another reviewer observed, the *Memoirs* were 'painfully interesting – the Confessions of an English Rousseau'.[103] They were important, wrote the *Pall Mall Gazette*, above all because they told the story of 'an intellect and temperament as extraordinary, and a life as unique in single-minded devotion to wisdom, as any that has been lived in our day'.[104] Pattison was unique; he sensed his uniqueness; and the *Memoirs* communicated something of that uniqueness.

But there are two more fundamental reasons which explain why Pattison's *Memoirs* were so absorbing to the late Victorian educated public. One reason was religious, and one was moral; and the two were intertwined.

From a religious perspective, Pattison's *Memoirs* were important in offering an account of the passage from belief to unbelief: to that degree, their impact can be compared to that of a best-selling novel such as *Robert Elsmere*, which also dealt with the crisis of faith. But the parallel should not be pressed too far: the message of *Elsmere*, where belief is transmuted into an ethic of service to others, could be held to be optimistic, whereas it was difficult for anyone, believer or unbeliever, to derive an optimistic conclusion from Pattison's account of his own mental development. It was Pattison's 'violent antichristianism' that struck, and appalled, Gladstone, as is clear not just from Benson's recollections but also from Gladstone's own manuscript notes on the *Memoirs* and, indeed, from his annotations to his own copy of the book. Nowhere in the *Memoirs* did Pattison in fact articulate an anti-Christian point of view, but he was pointedly anticlerical and implied that he had left Anglicanism behind him, as he had previously left Tractarianism behind him. The contempt for religious orthodoxy that struck Gladstone would have been all the more appalling given that the author was a priest of the Church of England.

The moral significance of the *Memoirs* also struck contemporaries, who drew lessons about the ethical consequences of the loss of faith. Pattison's manifest bitterness, his sense of failure, and his profound depression were seen as the results of the erosion of his religious belief and his loss of a spiritual sense. 'His cankered rationalism', concluded the Methodist *London Quarterly Review*, 'had blighted his whole soul and

[102] *Daily News*, 6 March 1885.   [103] *Journal of Education* n.s. 7 (1885), 149.
[104] *Pall Mall Gazette*, 6 March 1885.

life'.[105] For Archbishop Benson, the *Memoirs* were a compelling refutation of the humanist's assertion that secular philosophy could do as much as Christianity, if not more, to impart a softer moral character:

By many it is said that the belief in Christianity has nothing to do with forming the gentle noble temper, & grandeur towards adversaries and humility – that philosophy is the real mother of discipline within. The books which are beginning to appear, revealing the innerness of philosophies, do not bear this out. Carlyle, (*even* George Eliot) Pattison. It would have been a contradiction in the nature of things, had such a writer as Pattison even believed himself to be a Christian. But he assures us in every page towards the end that he was not so much a philosopher as philosophy.[106]

Benson's brother-in-law, the agnostic Cambridge philosopher Henry Sidgwick, could quite see the Archbishop's point. He had known Pattison as a fellow member of the Metaphysical Society and of the campaign for the 'endowment of research', and Pattison was instrumental in his election as a member of the Athenaeum. Though an agnostic, Sidgwick was inclined to worry about the moral consequences of unbelief. He read the *Memoirs* almost as soon as they were published. He recorded his reaction in his journal on 12 March:

Have just finished Pattison's Memoir; curious as an unconscious confession of sordid egotism, mingling with a genuine ardour for an academic ideal of life. Very odd that a man of so much intellectual calibre appears never to have turned on his own character the cold and bitter criticism that he applies to others. In spite of my sympathy with his views, I cannot but admit that his life is a moral fiasco, which the orthodox have a right to point to as a warning against infidelity. The fiasco is far worse than Carlyle's, though the fall is from a lower pedestal.

Some readers felt, as Sidgwick did not, that Pattison had in fact been unsparing of his own character and his journals suggest too strong rather than too weak a capacity for self-criticism.[107] But Sidgwick's comments were typical in dwelling on the moral significance of Pattison's tragic history. Of all the published reviews, it was the one in the *Spectator* that

---

[105] 'Mark Pattison', *London Quarterly Review* 64 (April–July 1885), 319. The word 'canker' was another one for which reviewers commonly reached: See *Journal of Education* n.s. 7 (1885), 149.

[106] Benson, *Life of Edward White Benson*, vol. II, p. 50. For a variant of this interpretation, see William Holden Hutton, *Letters of William Stubbs, Bishop of Oxford, 1825–1901* (London: Constable, 1904), p. 270. Stubbs thought the book would have been a '*reductio ad horribile*' of the life of intellectual selfishness', had it been a true picture of Pattison. But he did not believe it was.

[107] John Morley wrote: 'Of overweening egotism Pattison himself at any rate had none': Morley, 'On Pattison's Memoirs', p. 169. See also *Pall Mall Gazette*, 6 March 1885.

took this line most vociferously. The latter half of the book is painful reading, writes the reviewer,

for the impression it leaves upon us is that Mr Pattison, in throwing-off [sic] the fascination of a Romanising theology, threw-off also the moral restraints of all pure theology over the inner life, and gave himself up to the indolent melancholy and the vivid moroseness which the disappointment of legitimate hope had engendered in him, without making even the slightest moral struggle to turn his own wounded feelings into the sources of a nobler life than any he had lived before.[108]

It was a lesson, then, in the dangerous moral consequences of unbelief. In that sense, the *Memoirs* were important because they seemed to contribute, rather in defiance of their author's wishes, to an ongoing debate of the middle and late Victorian period on the ethics of belief and the moral consequences of unbelief. Just a few years before, in 1877, the newly founded quarterly, *The Nineteenth Century*, opened with what it called 'A Modern Symposium', in which Lord Selborne, James Martineau, Frederic Harrison, Dean Church and W. K. Clifford debated precisely these questions.[109] Could a non-believer live a morally good life? 'To most people', Owen Chadwick has written, 'the old truth that unbelief causes immorality appeared as obvious as ever.'[110] Certainly Pattison's account of his own passage from religious orthodoxy seemed to do the agnostics' cause no good whatsoever. Whereas Pattison asserted that religion is a good servant but a bad master, the *Spectator*'s reviewer thought otherwise:

We should say of this passage that the falsehood of the view it expresses is powerfully illustrated by the whole biographical fragment in which the passage is contained. If that story shows anything, it shows that the humanist view is not equal to the government even of a sedentary and studious life; that what Mr Pattison lost when he 'outgrew', as he represents that he outgrew, his Christianity, was infinitely more than what Mr Pattison gained, when he gained his conviction that man is merely one of the phenomena of nature, with an 'organism subject to the uniform laws' governing all other being. What he lost was moral strength and guidance. What he gained was an enervating creed which actually resulted in his own enervation.[111]

The same review also points to the relevance of another strand in the moral discourse of the later Victorian period: the central importance of the

[108] *Spectator*, 14 March 1885, pp. 356–7.
[109] The key contributions are reprinted in Michael Goodwin (ed.), *Nineteenth-Century Opinion* (Harmondsworth: Penguin, 1951), pp. 131–9.
[110] Owen Chadwick, *The Victorian Church*, 2 vols. (London: Black, 1966–70) vol. I, p. 121.
[111] *Spectator*, 14 March 1885, pp. 356–7.

concept of character, which was itself intimately related to the equally pivotal concept of manliness.[112] An American commentator wrote that Pattison's was 'a character ... divided in weakness and strength'.[113] As Pattison narrates his life, it was the defeat of his legitimate hopes of election to the rectorship in 1851 that ruined his life. The *Spectator* reviewer accepts that, in a just world, Pattison would have been elected, for his rivals were nonentities alongside him. But 'it was not an event which would have wrecked a strong man's life, and it might well have been one, if rightly used, to raise the whole level of a good man's character'.[114] The *Manchester Guardian* made much the same point: Pattison's moral collapse following the rectorship election laid bare a lack of a manly character. 'Instead of taking his disappointment like a man, he was plunged by it into the depth of misery.'[115] It was a commonplace in Victorian moral discourse that character was tested and strengthened by adversity. Yet Pattison responded with despair and abject moral collapse. 'He did not learn', wrote a bilious evangelical who knew him slightly, 'to bear a reverse with dignity or to trace his failures to his own deficiencies; they only threw him into a state of misanthropy and sulkiness.'[116] His narrative of his own life was therefore a kind of antithesis of the stories of heroic triumphs of character told in Samuel Smiles's *Self-Help*, *Character*, and numerous other works in the same vein. The *Temple Bar* reviewer, who thought that the 'canker of self-consciousness ate into his character', asserted, 'if his character had been as beautiful as his intellect was great he would have been one of the world's captains instead of only a vigorous kind of lieutenant'.[117]

The same theme is central to the lengthiest and most important review of the *Memoirs*, and one written from an agnostic point of view, that by John Morley in *Macmillan's Magazine*. Morley, later a Liberal cabinet minister and best known as the author of the classic biography of Gladstone, had been an undergraduate at Lincoln in the late 1850s, in the period between Pattison's resignation of his tutorship and his election to the rectorship. He was never intimate with Pattison as were some of his pupils, such as Richard Christie; but he knew him well both through

---

[112] On these concepts, see Stefan Collini, 'The idea of "character" in Victorian political thought', *Transactions of the Royal Historical Society* 5th series 35 (1985), 29–50, which is reprinted in Collini, *Public Moralists*, pp. 91–118; and John Tosh, 'Gentlemanly politeness and manly simplicity in Victorian England', *Transactions of the Royal Historical Society* 6th series 12 (2002), 455–72.

[113] 'Two English men of letters', *Atlantic Monthly* 56 (1885), 123.

[114] *Spectator*, 14 March 1885, pp. 356–7.     [115] *Manchester Guardian*, 16 March 1885, p. 6.

[116] Frederick Meyrick, *Memories of Life at Oxford, and Experiences in Italy, Greece, Turkey, Germany, Spain, and Elsewhere* (London: Murray, 1905), p. 105.

[117] [Eliza Lynn Linton], 'Mark Pattison', *Temple Bar* 74 (1885), 222, 236.

college lore and through subsequent literary connections: Pattison published for the *Fortnightly Review* during Morley's editorship, and his life of Milton appeared in Morley's series on 'English Men of Letters'. The two men shared a specialist interest in eighteenth-century thought. Morley was also a central figure in the Victorian debate on the ethics of belief: in an important work, *On Compromise*, published in the same year as the *Nineteenth Century*'s 'Modern Symposium', he argued that moral integrity required one to be true to one's own rational judgement, and alleged that articles of religion necessarily produced hypocrites. His review of Pattison has peculiar interest. It is a perceptive piece, which rightly recognizes Pattison's unique gifts as a critic, and vividly evokes the distinctive qualities of his mind; but it is relentlessly negative in its evaluation of his achievements judged in the light of his potential. 'Measured by any standard commensurate to his remarkable faculties, Pattison's life would be generally regarded as pale, negative, and ineffectual.'[118] The paucity of his achievements could be traced to moral causes: 'He was affected from first to last by a profound weakness of will and character', and while he had ability, he had 'no fight and no mastery in him'.[119] Morley thus follows the *Spectator*'s reviewer in reading Pattison's life, as recounted in the *Memoirs*, as a tale of spectacular moral failure. Again, the 1851 election, and Pattison's reaction to it, form the centrepiece: 'it must be pronounced', he writes in headmasterly fashion, 'a painfully unmanly and unedifying exhibition' of 'abject abasement'. Such 'weakness' and 'self-abandonment' might be excused in the event of close personal bereavement or profound spiritual crisis. 'But that anybody with character of common healthiness should founder and make shipwreck of his life because two or three unclean creatures had played him a trick after their kind, is as incredible as that a three-decker should go down in a street puddle.'[120]

Pattison's fame, then, was probably at its zenith in the aftermath of the *Memoirs*; but his reputation was damaged by the book. Jowett privately described it as 'a strange ill-natured book attacking now that he is dead many others who are dead.'[121] Most reviewers felt that the man emerged badly from the account he gave of his life. It was unfortunate that he had taken the opportunity 'to pour forth the hoarded bitterness of his own heart'.[122] The volume was a tragic account, they felt, of a great intellect

---

[118] Morley, 'On Pattison's Memoirs', p. 133.   [119] Morley, 'On Pattison's Memoirs', pp. 140, 143.
[120] Morley, 'On Pattison's Memoirs', pp. 153–4.
[121] Balliol College: Jowett Papers III. C116, Jowett to Lewis Campbell, n.d. [1885].
[122] 'Mark Pattison', *London Quarterly Review* 64 (Apr–July 1885), 309.

marred by a deeply flawed character; a story of enormous potential thwarted by enervation of the will. A man who could have been one of the pre-eminent literary figures of his age failed to bring his most cherished projects to completion. Morley thought he simply lacked fire in his belly.[123] 'He might have made a great name among contemporary writers had he so willed it', wrote another commentator a few years later. 'He did not so will it; and since the publication of his autobiography, if we may so call the volume that startled so many of us soon after his death, perhaps we are not astonished that he never realized the hopes that were formed of him by some who knew him best.'[124] The story Pattison told, and the way in which he told it, showed him to be unmanly; and there were few things the Victorians found it harder to forgive.

There are two further strands to the story of Pattison's immediate posthumous reputation. While she was editing the *Memoirs*, Francis had become secretly engaged to Sir Charles Dilke, whom she married in October 1885. After the engagement, but before its public announcement, Dilke had risen to prominence in the gossip columns when he was cited as co-respondent in the divorce case of Donald and Virginia Campbell. This case would bring an end to his ministerial, though not his parliamentary career. Francis's ostentatious support for Dilke brought her into the public eye, and some of the attention she attracted fell on her relations with her late husband. The comment implied that the estrangement of the Rector of Lincoln and his wife had been notorious, though it had been little commented upon at his death. One forum for political gossip, the *St Stephen's Review*, having initially praised Francis for her 'brave and noble act' in going through with the public announcement of the engagement, later came round to the view that she was worthy of neither of her husbands: 'If Mark Pattison was considered to have made a *mésalliance*, how can Sir Charles Dilke be held to have done otherwise?' The same journal oddly supposed that some of the excised passages in the *Memoirs* must have contained revelations concerning Francis, even though this was chronologically impossible, since the *Memoirs* cover the period before the marriage.[125]

The publication of a volume of his university and college sermons later in 1885, and Henry Nettleship's two-volume collection of his essays four years later, did much to restore Pattison's reputation and to sustain interest

---

[123] Morley, 'On Pattison's Memoirs', p. 173.    [124] *Notes and Queries* series 7 vol. VIII (26 Oct. 1889), 339.
[125] *St Stephen's Review*, 22 Aug. and 10 Oct. 1885; Lady Dilke to J. R. Thursfield, 1 Nov. 1886, Bodleian MS Pattison 140, ff. 88–9.

in him. The sermons did something to recapture the morally serious and idealistic side of Pattison which was lost beneath the acerbity and cynicism of the *Memoirs*. 'Readers who have been repelled', wrote the *Athenaeum*, 'by the traces of the petty jealousy and morbid self-consciousness which he determined to put on record [in the *Memoirs*], and have been tempted to take him at his own valuation, will be surprised by the earnestness of thought and real depth of feeling which characterize these pages'.[126] As for the collection of essays – most of which had been published unsigned, according to the custom – they revealed something of the quantity as well as the quality of Pattison's output. They were 'a complete vindication of their distinguished author', wrote the classicist and poet G. A. Simcox in the *Academy*. Contrary to the impression he gave in the *Memoirs*, Pattison did not selfishly store up his learning and keep it to himself.[127] According to the reviewer in *Notes and Queries*, the two fat volumes proved 'that those who had formed the highest opinion of Pattison's literary ability (we had almost said genius) were right after all'. That critic's particular favourite was the very first essay in the collection, on Gregory of Tours. That piece – which dated from Pattison's Tractarian period – revealed him already as 'a great master of style' as well as 'an extremely learned man'.[128]

LITERARY REPRESENTATIONS

We have seen that *Middlemarch* had an important place in the history of the Pattisons' marriage – not because it was intended as a representation of that marriage, but because Francis saw herself as Dorothea and henceforth could never look at her marriage in quite the same way as she had done previously. But the novel has also shaped the way in which Pattison has been remembered. To an unusual degree, Pattison has become 'known' to later generations through this, and other fictional representations, or suspected representations. In 1940, in an article marking the centenary of Rhoda Broughton's birth, *The Times* observed that, according to tradition, she had used 'the great Mark Pattison' as the model for her Professor Forth in *Belinda*; and went on to add that this was 'a book that might never have been written, perhaps, but for the example of "Middlemarch".'[129] That there was a connection between Pattison and *Middlemarch* could evidently be taken for granted.

---

[126] *Athenaeum* no. 3034 (19 Dec. 1885), 802–3.    [127] *Athenaeum* no. 3206 (6 Apr. 1889), 433.
[128] *Notes and Queries* series 7 vol. VIII (26 Oct. 1889), 339.    [129] *The Times*, 29 November 1940, p. 5.

In the aftermath of the publication of his study of Pattison in 1967, John Sparrow was drawn into protracted controversy with some eminent literary scholars about his supposed view that Pattison was the original of Edward Casaubon in *Middlemarch*. One cannot help thinking that the efforts of Sparrow's antagonists only served to reinforce in the reading public's mind the notion that there was a connection between Pattison and Mr Casaubon. The arguments were forgotten, but the connection remained in the mind – just as Stanley Baldwin famously connected Sir Henry Maine with some teachings about the relationship between societies based on status to societies based on contract, but could not remember whether Maine taught that status yields to contract or vice versa.

Sparrow and his critics agreed that if Pattison was the model for Casaubon, he was traduced in being represented in this way. The posthumous portrait presented by Mrs Humphry Ward in *Robert Elsmere* (1888) is another matter. Some critics have seen something of Pattison in Edward Langham, Elsmere's tutor; but, as we have seen, the evidence for this is dispelled once we realize that Mary Ward took that character largely from the pages of Amiel's *Journal Intime*, a book in which Pattison saw reflections of himself. The real portrait of Pattison in this novel is not one of the Oxford figures, but the rationalist squire, Roger Wendover. Mary Ward herself, in her autobiography, discussed the supposed likeness but was inclined to play it down: it was confined, she said, to 'a few personal traits, and the two main facts of great learning and a general impatience of fools'. She also highlighted a difference: 'If one could imagine Mark Pattison a landowner, he would certainly never have neglected his estates, or tolerated an inefficient agent.'[130] By contrast, she willingly acknowledged that T. H. Green was the model for Mr Grey, in whom she sought to reproduce the 'traits of a great thinker and teacher, who was also one of the simplest, sincerest, and most practical of men'.[131] There is, in fact, a separate allusion to Pattison – this time not in fictional guise – in connection with Grey. The narrator quotes what 'a well-known rationalist' had said of Grey: 'The Tories were always carrying off his honey to their hive.'[132] This is practically a direct quotation from a familiar passage in Pattison's *Memoirs*, where he emphasizes the conservative tendency of the revival of philosophical idealism in Oxford. This was a paradox, for it was a staunch Liberal, T. H. Green, who led the idealist revival. The anomaly was to be explained, Pattison wrote, by 'a certain

---

[130] Ward, *A Writer's Recollections*, p. 111.   [131] Ward, *A Writer's Recollections*, p. 132.
[132] Ward, *Robert Elsmere*, p. 64.

puzzle-headedness on the part of the Professor, who was removed from the scene before he had time to see how eagerly the Tories began to carry off his honey to their hive'.[133] When we then find Wendover, later in the novel, echoing these words, we might well wish to question the author's attempt to play down the resemblance. For Wendover tells Elsmere that he and Grey, though calling themselves Liberals and reformers, were in fact 'playing into the hands of the Blacks'; that is, of the clericals. 'All this theistic philosophy of yours only means so much grist to their mill in the end.' And he goes on to add that 'most men are puzzle-heads'.[134]

No one could take Wendover for an exact representation of Pattison. Wendover was a 'hermit', which Pattison certainly was not; he had also written 'books which had carried a revolutionary shock into the heart of English society', something which could hardly be said of Pattison. His particular expertise, in what is now called late antiquity, had not been of central concern to Pattison since his Tractarian days. But the affinities are much stronger than Mary Ward suggested. Wendover's biography mirrored Pattison's in crucial respects: he had been a Tractarian, and close to Newman in 1845; he had later studied in Germany – for ten years, in Wendover's case – and this accelerated his passage to scepticism and rationalism. But both men felt an ambivalence towards German scholarship: Wendover calls the Germans 'a nation of learned fools, none of whom ever sees an inch beyond his own professorial nose'.[135] Like Pattison, Wendover knew Renan; but unlike him, he admired current French scholarship. While Wendover's books had made more of a public impact than Pattison's, their themes were similar. The first, *The Idols of the Market-place*, was a critique of English religious orthodoxy. This perhaps mirrors Pattison's contribution to *Essays and Reviews*; and we might speculate that Mrs Ward derived the title from a passage in one of Pattison's published university sermons, where, in speaking of the contempt felt by the man of the world for the theorist, he refers to '[t]he maxims of the market-place and the court'.[136] For Pattison as for Wendover the 'market-place' was the site of the man of action and of antagonism towards the world of ideas. Wendover's second book, *Essays on English Culture*, attacked English ideals of education, and so mirrored *Suggestions on Academical Organisation*. Mary Ward evidently saw the counter-cultural quality of Pattison's mind and persona. Like Pattison, Wendover died leaving his great work incomplete: in Wendover's case, a history of

[133] Pattison, *Memoirs*, p. 167.    [134] Ward, *Robert Elsmere*, pp. 487–8.
[135] Ward, *Robert Elsmere*, p. 488.    [136] Mark Pattison, *Sermons* (London: Macmillan, 1885), p. 34.

evidence, or of 'testimony', conceived 'from the standpoint of evolution, of development'; and though Wendover's focus was on late antiquity, the theme of the changing character of testimony was a Pattisonian one.[137] Like Pattison, Wendover is essentially a student of the history of ideas, and that expression is used frequently in the novel. Wendover even wrote like Pattison, in a subtle, caustic and epigrammatic style. Above all, perhaps, each man was the possessor of a huge library – Wendover's grander than Pattison's, reflecting his greater wealth – and in each case the library was the mirror of the man, tracing, in particular, his intellectual evolution.

Wendover's personality traits mirror Pattison's in many respects. His manners are brusque, there is something un-English about him, and he is resentful of intrusions on his leisure. His conversation is acerbic and laced with anticlericalism; but he could be taciturn or evasive if asked deep questions about himself or his fundamental beliefs. Something of Pattison's cynicism is found in Wendover too. The arguments Wendover uses, for example, to try to persuade Elsmere to retain his living in spite of his religious doubts have much in common with those Pattison used, in private, to defend his retention of his rectorship, and hence his orders, in spite of his slide towards agnosticism. 'Why should you break up your life in this wanton way?'[138]

For all that, Wendover, memorable as he is in his way, is a rather flat character who has none of the complexity and vivid humanity that those who knew him well, such as Mary Ward, found in Pattison. What the author seems to have done is to condense one side of Pattison's character into Wendover, who serves a functional purpose in the novel rather than appearing as a rounded human being. Wendover is the sceptic who pours the icy water of learned cynicism over the energetic quest for practical improvement. He serves as the antithesis of that 'enthusiasm of humanity' that Elsmere has absorbed from his Oxford tutor, Grey. It struck many who knew him, especially late in life, that Pattison, too, was impervious to that ethical enthusiasm that was such a marked characteristic of the generation of T. H. Green and Mary Ward. But Pattison also tells us that, from boyhood, he was a natural reformer, always trying to think of better ways of doing things. That side of him is not captured in the personality of Wendover. Neither is Pattison's undoubted personal magnetism. Wendover comes across as cool and – until his final madness – in control

---

[137] See, e.g., Pattison to W. Tuckwell, 10 Jan. 1874, in my possession. Tuckwell had evidently asked Pattison for suggestions of what to read on this question.

[138] Ward, *Robert Elsmere*, p. 370.

of his passions. Pattison was known to have had a fiery temper and was certainly a man of deep passions. His poetry readings were said to be deeply felt and moving.[139] Whereas Wendover did not like women to talk about books, Pattison, as we have seen, set out to be a counsellor to women of intellectual interests, and many of them evidently found him warm and direct.

### AFTER THE VICTORIANS: SOME TWENTIETH-CENTURY SURVIVALS

John Betjeman was a pupil at the Dragon School in north Oxford at the end of the First World War. In his verse autobiography, he recalled bicycle rides around the roads of the academic suburbs.

> Here by the low brick semi-private walls
> Bicycling past a trotting butcher's cart,
> I glimpsed, behind lace curtains, silver hair
> Of sundry old Professors. Here were friends
> Of Ruskin, Newman, Pattison and Froude
> Among their books and plants and photographs
> In comfortable twilight.[140]

What exactly did Pattison's name come to represent in the twentieth century?

His name is not associated with any particular doctrine, nor even with the establishment of a particular discipline, and so once that generation who had had a personal attachment to him had gone – the 'sundry old Professors', such as Bywater, Sayce and Henry Nettleship, to whom he acted as a sort of academic patron – there could be no disciples to propagate his ideas and so ensure the survival of his reputation. But he was by no means forgotten, and it is worth pausing to reflect on the ways in which a reputation can survive.

There is some evidence that Pattison appealed to the theological modernists in the Church of England in the twentieth century. Their leader was Hastings Rashdall, dean of Carlisle, who made his academic reputation with a study of *The Universities of Europe in the Middle Ages*. Pattison was more or less the first Englishman to make a serious study of university history, and he may well have examined Rashdall's essay on the subject

---

[139]  Mrs Bertram Hunt (formerly Miss Willett) to T. F. Althaus, 21 Jan. 1885: Lincoln College MS/PAT/ I/C.

[140]  John Betjeman, *Summoned by Bells: A Verse Autobiography* (London: Murray, 2001), p. 46.

which won the Chancellor's English Essay Prize in 1883. It is not possible to establish in detail the nature of Rashdall's debt to Pattison, if indeed there was one. But in 1923 he wrote an interesting letter to an Anglican clergyman named Bartleet, who had evidently written to express an interest in Pattison, and to ask Rashdall about Pattison's later theological outlook. Rashdall declined, wisely, to rise to that challenge: 'He would be a bold man who attempted to say what M. Pattison's theological opinions were in his later years.' But he went on to comment on a paper on the afterlife which Pattison read to the Metaphysical Society in 1872, and concluded: 'M. Pattison attracts me too, in spite of his utter want of sympathy even with the best state of traditional Christianity, and his personal unfairness and ferocity towards people whom he disliked.'[141] Among Rashdall's contemporaries, the Bishop of Durham, Hensley Henson, shared his admiration for Pattison. Henson, a rather angular figure who constructed himself as an outsider, certainly shared Pattison's rationalist sympathies in matters of religion.[142] Oddly enough for a bishop, he even shared something of Pattison's anticlericalism. But, intellectually able though he was, he was not a man of learning in the way that Rashdall was.

Pattison's reputation has proved most resilient among classicists, and more specifically among those interested in the history of classical scholarship. He was, wrote an Oxford Regius professor of Greek, 'almost the only Englishman to have done distinguished work' in this field.[143] That distinguished work comprised the biographical essays on the French philologists of the Renaissance, collected posthumously in two 'great volumes', in the words of two American classicists; and, chiefly, the study of Casaubon: a 'great life', to quote those same American scholars.[144] The eminent German historian of classical philology, Rudolf Pfeiffer, applauded Pattison's studies on the French Renaissance scholars: these were 'exemplary' he thought, in spite of Pattison's religious bias, 'because his studies in detail are always informed by an awareness of the history of scholarship as a whole.'[145] It is the historians of classical scholarship who have, apparently, found Pattison's devotion to the life of learning most appealing and have

---

[141] Hastings Rashdall to the Rev. H. H. M. Bartleet, 6 April 1923, published in P. E. Matheson, *The Life of Hastings Rashdall D. D.* (London: Oxford University Press, 1928), p. 226. But Rashdall's recollection of the content of Pattison's paper was inaccurate.

[142] Cowling, *Religion and Public Doctrine*, vol. III, pp. 193–5.

[143] Hugh Lloyd-Jones, *Classical Survivals. The Classics in the Modern World* (London: Duckworth, 1982), p. 19.

[144] Calder and Kramer, *Introductory Bibliography to the History of Classical Scholarship*, pp. 260, 133.

[145] Rudolf Pfeiffer, *History of Classical Scholarship: from the beginnings to the end of the Hellenistic Age* (Oxford: Clarendon, 1968), p. ix.

been most absorbed by the account of it he offered in his *Memoirs*. For Hugh Lloyd-Jones, Pattison was an advocate of 'real learning', and his *Memoirs* 'give an astonishingly vivid picture of a mind which came to be deeply influenced by a desire for learning; and those who sympathise with that desire may find that the book exercises a powerful stimulus upon them'.[146] For the German-born Charles Brink, Kennedy professor of Latin at Cambridge, this was 'one of the great books of the nineteenth century . . . a poignant document of integrity in a life of doubt and, in spite of his self-torture, a refreshment of the spirit after the bland self-assurance of Jowett'.[147] Brink's remarks highlight one reason for the survival of Pattison's reputation: his rivalry with and antagonism towards Jowett and what Jowett stood for: for in this lineage Jowett was dismissed as an unscholarly man of letters. Jowett, noted Hugh Lloyd-Jones pointedly, 'defined a scholar as a man who read Thucydides with his feet on the mantelpiece'.[148] A much earlier Cambridge professor, Henry Jackson, Regius professor of Greek, had a distinctly lower opinion of Pattison, whom he had met: there was not much to be said for him except for his opposition to Jowett, who hated learning. 'This is a terrible book', he scribbled inside his copy of the *Memoirs*.[149]

Brink admired Pattison's idea of the university, which he continued to regard as 'basically the right one'.[150] But he was by no means blind to Pattison's defects: notably, he thought that Pattison was haunted by 'the ideal of universal knowledge', and so lacked 'the ability to delimit a vast subject sufficiently for appropriate conclusions'.[151] An earlier Cambridge classicist, A. E. Housman, had some striking affinities with Pattison – notably, a feeling of loneliness stemming from the sense that he saw the world as others did not – but he was still forthright about Pattison's defects. Pattison, he wrote, was 'a spectator of all time and all existence, and the contemplation of that repulsive scene is fatal to accurate learning'.[152]

Finally, Pattison occupied a important place in the background to twentieth-century British discussions of the purpose of the university. In

---

[146] Hugh Lloyd-Jones, 'Humboldt 2' and 'Greek studies in modern Oxford', in his *Blood for the Ghosts: Classical Influences in the Nineteenth and Twentieth Centuries* (London: Duckworth, 1982), pp. 69, 17.

[147] C. O. Brink, *English Classical Scholarship: Historical Reflections on Bentley, Porson, and Housman* (Cambridge: Clarke, 1985), p. 129.

[148] Hugh Lloyd-Jones, 'Max Müller', in his *Blood for the Ghosts*, p. 158.

[149] Jackson's notes, Lincoln College MS/PAT/III/9.

[150] H. D. Jocelyn, 'C. O. Brink and Liverpool,' *Liverpool Classical Monthly* 19 (1994), 46.

[151] Brink, *English Classical Scholarship*, pp. 131–3.

[152] Quoted by Brink, *English Classical Scholarship*, p. 132.

these discussions he was rivalled only by Newman among Victorians. Here Pattison stood for the view that the university existed for something more fundamental than the teaching of undergraduates: that 'something' being summed up by the word 'research', a term Pattison had used with reservations. When some reforming Edwardian dons published a series of articles in *The Times* on 'Oxford and the Nation', Pattison's *Suggestions on Academical Organisation* were a repeated point of reference – and Pattison was the only authority cited. Of the many contributions to Victorian debates on Oxford reform, his was the one that endured.[153] A few further examples should suffice to illustrate the survival of his reputation in this context.

Sir Walter Moberly was a philosopher and an important Anglican social thinker who served as vice-chancellor of the University of Manchester (1926–35) and chairman of the University Grants Committee (1935–49). There was no more important figure in university policymaking in mid-century. Unlike his counterparts today he thought seriously about what universities were for, and his thinking was historically as well as philosophically informed. He was the author of two books on universities in the aftermath of the Second World War: *The Crisis in the University* (1949) and *Universities Ancient and Modern* (1950). Pattison is cited in both books, in ways that indicate his iconic status. Moberly's awareness of Pattison is not surprising: he had been a fellow of Lincoln (1906–21) and was an important agent in the dissemination of the college's oral tradition about Pattison.[154] Much of this certainly came from Pattison's successor, W. W. Merry, who remained rector until his death in 1918 and who, as a young man almost sixty years before, had played a vital role in Pattison's elevation to the headship.

When Moberly was vice-chancellor at Manchester, his counterpart at another of the great civic universities, Birmingham, was Sir Charles Grant Robertson. Robertson was an Oxford historian and fellow of All Souls from 1893 to his death in 1948. While at Birmingham he wrote an interesting survey of *The British Universities* (1930). This is a slim volume of eighty pages which has correspondingly few references, but Pattison features as an icon of the research ideal. Both his *Suggestions on Academical Organisation* and the *Essays on the Endowment of Research* (attributed to Pattison alone)

---

[153] *The Times* 3, 5, 8, 13, 16, 20 and 29 April and 11 May 1907.
[154] Sir Walter Moberly to John Sparrow, 1 Feb. 1957, Lincoln College MS/PAT/III/10. Sparrow elsewhere recounts an anecdote about Pattison which he says he was told by 'an honorary fellow of Lincoln', who heard it from one of the undergraduates involved in the story. The honorary fellow was almost certainly Moberly.

were cited in the short bibliography. Robertson, incidentally, had known Rhoda Broughton in the early 1890s, when he was an Oxford undergraduate, and much later he would offer the opinion – not widely shared – that her Professor Forth was 'a much truer portrait' of Pattison than that drawn by Mrs Humphry Ward in *Robert Elsmere*.[155]

One of the fullest and fairest-minded of twentieth-century appraisals of Pattison and his *Memoirs* came from the pen of A. C. Benson, fellow and later Master of Magdalene College, Cambridge. It took fictional form, in one of the *Upton Letters* written by 'T. B.', a schoolmaster, to his friend Herbert. These were published in 1905, shortly after Benson had returned to Cambridge following two decades teaching at Eton. Benson was the eldest son and biographer of Archbishop Benson, who had formed such a low opinion of the *Memoirs*. It is not surprising, then, that – speaking through the voice of 'T. B.', he should have observed that the book had not been well received, and that

it is very difficult not to be influenced by current opinion in one's view of a book; one comes to it prepared to find certain characteristics, and it is difficult to detach one's mind sufficiently to approach a much-reviewed volume with perfect frankness.

He nevertheless found that his admiration for the book increased each time he read it. Benson, or T. B., was quite aware of Pattison's failings as disclosed in the book: his selfishness, his morbidity, and a lack of generosity towards others which led him to stress their weaknesses rather than their better qualities.[156] But he emphasized two notable qualities in the book.

The first was its 'absolute sincerity'. Whereas his uncle, Henry Sidgwick, thought that Pattison had failed to direct his critical judgement on his own character, Benson – rightly – saw that, on the contrary, Pattison was hugely self-critical. As an autobiographer he eschewed the temptation to adopt a pose and to paint his life 'in beautiful subdued colours'. Instead, 'he is quite as severe on himself' as on others, and 'shows clearly that the disasters of his life were quite as much due to his own temperamental mistakes as to the machinations of others'. He had 'no illusions' about himself, and was 'merciless' in chronicling his nervous collapse following the rectorship election of 1851.[157]

The second quality Benson identified was the 'extraordinary intellectual ideal' set forth in the book. 'I know of no other book', he wrote, 'which

[155] *The Times*, 9 December 1940, p. 5.
[156] T. B. [i.e. A. C. Benson], *The Upton Letters* (London: Smith, Elder, 1905), p. 217.
[157] [Benson], *Upton Letters*, pp. 217–18, 221.

displays in a more single-minded and sincere way the passionate desire of the savant for wide, deep and perfect knowledge, which is to be untainted by any admixture of personal ambition'. The book's effect, therefore, was to impress on him 'a high intellectual stimulus; it makes me realise the nobility and the beauty of knowledge, the greatness of the intellectual life'. Pattison's defects of character were obvious. He was notably lacking in 'practical power'. Nevertheless, 'the life presents a fine protest against materialism, against the desire of recognition, against illiberal and retrograde views of thought. Here was a great and lonely figure haunted by a dream which few of those about him could understand, and with which hardly any could sympathise'. The lesson of the book was 'to make me realise the high virtue of thoroughness'. That goal might indeed be unattainable amid the busy life of a schoolmaster, who must necessarily 'do a good deal of one's work sloppily and sketchily'. But the important thing was to have glimpsed the ideal. 'The true gain is to have been confronted with a real man, to have looked into the depth of his spirit, to realise differences of temperament, to be initiated into a high and noble ambition.'[158]

Much the most important influence on the representation of Pattison in the second half of the twentieth century was John Sparrow. Sparrow had a fascination with Pattison that lasted all his adult life. His correspondence with his mother makes it clear that his interest in Pattison had crystallized before he was thirty; and it may well have stretched back to his boyhood, for he was at Winchester with a nephew by marriage of the last surviving descendant of Pattison's parents, his niece Annie Elizabeth Mann. Sparrow wrote just one slim volume on Pattison, based on the Clark lectures he delivered at Cambridge in 1965. But for many years he projected a major biography – he suggested at one time that it might stretch to two volumes, although there is no evidence that he wrote any of it. He made more progress with a new edition of the *Memoirs*, something he worked on fitfully for thirty years, and which reached page proofs with Duckworth. The volume was never published, however, for it fell victim to a petty squabble between Sparrow and his editor at Duckworth, Colin Haycraft.

If Sparrow published little on Pattison, he certainly accumulated a great deal of material on him. More to the point, since Sparrow was best known as a conversationalist and wit, he also spoke a lot about Pattison, and in a way that clearly made an impact on his interlocutors. That Pattison crops

---

[158] [Benson], *Upton Letters*, pp. 219–20, 222–4.

up in Betjeman's poetry was certainly testimony to the power of Sparrow's advocacy. What is less clear is what precisely drew Sparrow to Pattison.

The two men certainly had affinities of a superficial kind. Both men held the headship of their college for a quarter of a century or thereabouts, having previously failed in a first attempt; although Sparrow, unlike Pattison, had no reason to be bitter about his initial rejection, and did not have to wait long for the fulfilment of his ambition. Both men owed much of their celebrity to their office, and were firmly associated in the public mind with that office, so that the educated public in the 1960s could be expected to know who was meant by 'the Warden of All Souls', as their predecessors in the 1870s could be expected to identify 'the Rector of Lincoln'. But neither was an active head: Sparrow from conservatism, Pattison from a depressive's reluctance to drive business through to its conclusion. Both were fundamentally selfish. Significantly, both refused the Oxford vice-chancellorship when the office was theirs by seniority, and while refusal, in each case, was unusual to the point of being a breach of convention, both men's friends thought they made the right decision. Finally, each man failed to bring his magnum opus to completion: Sparrow's projected biography of Pattison remained unwritten, just as Pattison's life of Scaliger existed only in fragments at his death.

That said, the contrasts between the two men are surely more important than these curious similarities. Pattison was, before all else, an academic, whose very identity was bound up with his Oxford life. He seldom contemplated an alternative, and when he did he turned his back on the possibility. But Sparrow was by profession a chancery barrister: only the peculiar status of All Souls gave him a foot in the academic world, and only in the loosest sense could he be labelled a 'don'. There is no evidence that he ever gave so much as a tutorial in Oxford, and as warden he caused offence by failing to maintain even the pretence of being interested in the research activities of the fellows of his college.[159] Pattison lived for the intellectual life and – in spite of his failure to write a history of eighteenth-century thought or a life of Scaliger – his literary output was substantial and his contribution to the Victorian intellectual world immense. Sparrow, by contrast, was a somewhat old-fashioned man of letters, a bibliophile but not in any sense an intellectual. He evaded any sustained engagement with Pattison's thought. Sparrow certainly prolonged Pattison's afterlife in British cultural life; but whether he was the right man to act as his advocate may be questioned.

---

[159] John Lowe, *The Warden: A Portrait of John Sparrow* (London: HarperCollins, 1998), 194.

# PART II

## *Ideas*

# CHAPTER 4

# *Manliness and good learning*

In his *Memoirs*, Pattison told the story of a life devoted from boyhood to the pursuit of self-improvement through study. His was to be a life consecrated to the cultivation of the mind, supported by a college fellowship. This goal was instilled in him by his father's loyalty to Oxford, and it was strengthened by his self-discovery as an undergraduate; and Pattison scarcely deviated from it for the rest of his life. This was no ordinary career ambition. When Pattison conceived his purpose the academic profession was unknown in England. College fellows who remained in residence for life would usually be considered failures. Rare were those, such as Newman, who envisaged 'perpetual residence even unto death in my University'.[1] So in taking the academic vocation as his life's purpose, Pattison was not choosing to play a role pre-determined for him by convention. On the contrary, the vocation of the academic or don was invented in Pattison's lifetime, and Pattison was one of those at the forefront of the effort to reimagine that vocation in an era of secularization. For Newman, the don's vocation was a subordinate aspect of the priestly vocation. But even at the height of his commitment to the Oxford Movement, that was never Pattison's understanding. On the other hand, the idea of a life of study certainly possessed a spiritual significance for Pattison, and he continued to invest it with a profound spiritual seriousness long after he had become detached from a working Christian faith.

Indeed the central preoccupation of Pattison's life was to probe what it meant to devote one's life to study and intellectual cultivation in a university. This preoccupation explains his lifelong fascination with the scholar's autobiography and the scholar's journal as literary forms: the subjective lives of scholars, writers and intellectuals enthralled him because they were bound up with his effort to invest his own vocation with meaning. It also explains why he would take the nature of the life of learning as the central

---

[1] Newman, *Apologia*, p. 213.

theme of his own intellectual inquiries, which focused on the lives of the classical philologists of the French Renaissance; and he would take this same theme as the central narrative of his own memoirs. But how did he understand the nature of the studious life, and why did he come to regard it in spiritual terms? Centrally, Pattison took the life of learning to be a voyage of self-exploration and self-development, and from this point of view he was obviously and deeply indebted to German neo-humanism and romanticism, the movements that inspired the resurgence of the German universities in the early nineteenth century. At the same time, there was something profoundly ascetic about his conception of learning, and here his continuing debt to the Oxford Movement was apparent.

We have seen in a previous chapter that in his deathbed 'Confession of Faith' Pattison articulated his conviction that the philosophical life, the life devoted to the intellect, was the highest life and possessed a spiritual value of its own. He also distinguished the disinterested life of the mind from those doctrines, such as positivism, which valued knowledge for the practical benefits it could confer in the conquest of nature, rather than for the intrinsic worth of truth. In the course of the Confession Pattison recalled:

Newman & the Lives of the Saints first put before me the idea of the life of the soul – but that view may be called the *Idea corruptrix* of the true, for it contains as a balance to its renunciations & its asceticism the set off of future reward – payment by results.[2]

This declaration contains two essential clues that allow us to understand the logic of the conception of intellectual culture that underpinned Pattison's mature thought. First, it draws attention to Newman's influence. In spite of the anticlericalism and religious heterodoxy of his old age, Pattison is known to have retained a profound respect for the Cardinal, and it is no surprise to find him drawing attention to Newman's enduring influence on his thought. But what is important here is that he refers specifically to Newman's *Lives of the English Saints*, the project in which Pattison had participated as a young fellow of Lincoln in the 1840s. In his *Memoirs* Pattison records his plan of writing the 'Lives of the Scholars', an aspiration he never brought to completion but which sums up his principal intellectual endeavours in the last three decades of his life. The 'Lives of the Scholars' could be understood as a secularized version of the *Lives of the English Saints*, and the deathbed confession bears out this speculation. The

---

[2] Bodleian MS Pattison 112, f. 103.

confession suggests, further, that the specific legacy of Tractarianism in Pattison's thought lay in its conception of holiness: something of the ascetic quality which the Tractarians looked for in the saint endured in Pattison's conception of the quintessential scholar.[3]

The confession also draws attention to the defect of the Tractarian conception of the soul: and it is significant that Pattison did not criticize the very concept so much as indicate that the Tractarians had an imperfect understanding of it. Specifically, they continued to attach the idea of the soul to an expectation of future reward, and this was a corrupted version of the true idea. Pattison put the matter tersely and colourfully: if this theodicy were correct, God would be operating a system of 'payment by results' comparable to that which Robert Lowe, as vice-president of the Board of Education, had instituted in English elementary schools in his Revised Code of 1862. For Pattison, as we shall see, the truly holy soul must be motivated by love of God apart from any hope of reward; and – more to the point – the true scholar must be moved by the love of learning for its own sake, and not by the hope of prizes, honours or fellowships. Pattison's ethical outlook was profoundly deontological: the good life must be its own reward.

The idea of holiness was by no means unique to the Oxford Movement, and the evangelicalism of Pattison's childhood would certainly have taught him to think of this world's rewards as negligible by the side of the far richer rewards awaiting him in the next.[4] But the quest for holiness through self-denial was certainly at the heart of Tractarian thinking.[5] Newman himself imbibed it in the course of his youthful conversion to evangelicalism, mainly through the writings of Thomas Scott.[6] He took to heart

---

[3] The ascetic quality of Pattison's conception of the scholar is noted by A. H. Halsey, 'Pattison: a prophet in need of rediscovery', *Times Higher Education Supplement* 18 Jan. 1974, 2. Most of this article is incorporated into A. H. Halsey, *Decline of Donnish Dominion: The British Academic Professions in the Twentieth Century* (Oxford: Oxford University Press, 1992), pp. 26–9, but the reference to the 'ascetic ideal' is omitted, perhaps because Halsey here sees Pattison and Newman as articulating antithetical ideas of the university. See also Goldwin Smith, *Reminiscences*, p. 85: Smith finds in one of Pattison's university sermons 'something like a regurgitation of the asceticism of his Newmanite days'.

[4] Nolan, 'Pattison's religious experience', p. 15.

[5] The Tractarian conception of holiness is discussed by Y. Brilioth, *The Anglican Revival. Studies in the Oxford Movement* (London, New York & Toronto: Longmans, Green, 1933); for a broader account encompassing other traditions, see David Bebbington, *Holiness in Nineteenth-Century England* (Carlisle: Paternoster, 2000).

[6] Pattison too was influenced by Scott, whose *Force of Truth* was in his father's library at Hauxwell. This was one of the 'religious books', mostly 'of an evangelical colour' on which he wasted many hours when he ought to have been preparing for the fellowship examination at Oriel: Pattison, *Memoirs*, p. 173. See also Bodleian MS Pattison 5, f. 6, 26 June 1837.

Scott's dictum, 'holiness rather than peace', and made it into something of a personal motto. Another important source may well have been the non-juror William Law, whose *Serious Call to a Devout and Holy Life* (1728) urged the Christian to adopt a life of temperance and self-denial, and to make public worship the expression of inward commitment as opposed to mere public duty. Even as an Anglican Newman had defended clerical celibacy as 'a higher state than matrimony', because marriage entailed 'interest in this world'.[7] He articulated this idea of holiness as a separation from worldly motivation in the first of his *Parochial and Plain Sermons*, entitled 'Holiness necessary for future blessedness', where he defined holiness as 'inward separation from the world'. For Newman, 'outward acts' were important not in themselves but by virtue of their tendency to foster 'inward habits', and holiness was to be understood as 'not merely the doing a certain number of good actions', but 'an inward character which follows, under God's grace, from doing them'.[8] This definition points to a further element in the Tractarian understanding of holiness: it was developed through the cultivation of right habits. 'Every act of obedience', declared Newman, 'has a tendency to strengthen our conviction about heaven. Every sacrifice makes us more zealous; every self-denial makes us more devoted.'[9] Specifically, the Tractarians sought to renew an ascetic spirituality in Anglicanism by means of a restatement of the monastic ideal of retirement from the world.[10]

Pattison was for a time strongly drawn towards the practice of this Tractarian spirituality. In a characteristic diary entry in October 1843 he warned himself against the dangers of worldly motivation – 'acting to be seen of others' – and merely formal and legal performance of religious duties.[11] He deplored relapses into his 'old commonplace worldly habits' and his tendency to seek 'happiness in the world'.[12] But even after he had broken with the Tractarians and indeed abandoned any recognizable form of Christian orthodoxy, his conception of scholarship and intellectual culture was infused with something of the spirit of the Oxford Movement. In particular, it was structured by a set of antitheses derived in large measure from the Tractarian idea of holiness. Peter Nockles has

[7] Quoted in Turner, *Newman*, p. 429.
[8] Geoffrey Rowell, Kenneth Stevenson & Rowan Williams (eds.), *Love's Redeeming Work. The Anglican Quest for Holiness* (Oxford: Oxford University Press, 2001), pp. 408–9.
[9] Quoted by Bebbington, *Holiness*, p. 23.
[10] Peter Benedict Nockles, *The Oxford Movement in Context. Anglican High Churchmanship, 1760–1857* (Cambridge: Cambridge University Press, 1994), p. 188.
[11] Bodleian MS Pattison 128, f. 15, 7 Oct. 1843.
[12] Bodleian MS Pattison 128, f. 27, 5 November 1843, and f. 34, 27 November 1843.

pointed out the counter-cultural qualities of Tractarian earnestness, which 'stressed self-denial, repose, introspection, quiet study' in a dynamic and bustling age which prized the active virtues.[13] Much the same can be said of Pattison's conception of learning. The pursuit of knowledge was to be understood, like the quest for holiness, as a vocation which set one apart from the world; and it depended chiefly on the inward character of the scholar, rather than on his outward achievements. Moreover, the devotion to the life of the mind was best inculcated through rigorous habits, for temptation constantly threatened to ensnare the aspiring student and to divert him from the pure pursuit of mental self-improvement.

Pattison is often caricatured as an exponent of the notion that learning and education are rival goals for universities, and as an advocate of the view that learning should be given priority. But this is a distortion of his position. It is important to emphasize here that the conception of intellectual culture which has just been sketched permeated his understanding of education as well as of the higher learning. We can now proceed to examine how it operated in those two contexts. We shall begin with education.

PREACHING THE LIFE OF LEARNING

The most important sources for Pattison's conception of education are his university and college sermons. These sermons deserve to be better known, because they present him in a more positive light than he presented himself in the *Memoirs*. Dean Church wrote that 'both his educated and his simple hearers thought [his sermons] unlike those of ordinary men in their force, reality, and earnestness'.[14] A volume of his nine university sermons, preached over the period 1850–71, and four college sermons from the period 1847–63, was published posthumously in 1885, a few months after the *Memoirs*. Reviewers commented on the contrast between the two volumes: the reader who came away from the *Memoirs* with a feeling of revulsion at Pattison's caustic gibes at his colleagues and contemporaries would be surprised, wrote the *Athenaeum*, by 'the earnestness of thought and real depth of feeling which characterize these pages'.[15] 'The Rector's sermons are splendid', wrote Claude Montefiore, later a leading light in liberal Judaism, in a letter to the philosopher Samuel Alexander.[16] These

---

[13] Nockles, 'Academic counter-revolution', 175–6.
[14] Church, 'Mark Pattison', p. 353.   [15] *Athenaeum* no. 3034 (19 December 1885), 802.
[16] Claude Montefiore to Samuel Alexander, 8 November 1885: John Rylands University Library, Manchester: ALEX/A/1/1/196/8. Alexander was then a fellow of Lincoln.

published sermons may be supplemented by an almost equally large collection of unpublished sermons which remain in manuscript form among Pattison's papers. These were preached either in college chapel, or in parishes where he held summer curacies. As Montefiore and other readers noted, the sermons were centrally concerned with the nature of a university education. Their theological content diminished as the years passed, but that is part of their fascination: they allow us to see the Tractarian ideal of holiness being transmuted into an ethic of the single-minded pursuit of knowledge.

One reviewer of the *Sermons* commented that they were less like sermons than 'essays delivered from the pulpit'.[17] Another observed that they were 'marked by the one quality which renders a modern sermon worth reading, for they convey the impression that the preacher had something to say about which he was in earnest, and which he tried to say as well as he could'. That reviewer drew attention to one sermon on the theme of self-improvement, which 'helps the reader to understand the principle on which Pattison deliberately framed his own course'.[18] And a major philosophical periodical took the view that the sermons constituted 'a real contribution to philosophy', at least in the sense that 'they disclose a more serious philosophical vein in their author's mind than any of his other writings'.[19]

The central proposition that Pattison develops in these sermons is that education, properly understood, must be ascetic; meaning, as a reviewer put it, 'not monastic or claustral, but disciplinary and formative'.[20] In defining a university education as ascetic, Pattison meant, in the first place, that it was a training of the whole person: a training of the character as well as of the intellect. In itself, that was not a radical position. It was the orthodoxy both in the English universities and in the reformed public schools that they offered an education of the character. Was this not the rationale of the cult of athleticism that Pattison so much despised?

Pattison knew that he was being provocative when he spoke of the formation of the character as an ascetic education. This adjective, after all, was more commonly associated with 'the ritual mortifications and debasing superstitions of the convent'; and aversion to 'monkery' was deeply rooted in English culture.[21] English Protestantism considered ascetic piety contrary to the gospel, and even the word 'virtue' savoured

---

[17] 'Last words of Mark Pattison', *Journal of Education* n.s. 7 (1885), 427.
[18] *Athenaeum* no. 3034 (19 December 1885), 802–3.
[19] *Mind* 11 (1886), 123.    [20] 'Last words', 426.    [21] Pattison, *Sermons*, 79.

of heathenism. Charles Kingsley and the 'muscular Christians' thought that Tractarian sacerdotalism encouraged an unhealthy tendency to introspection.[22] Pattison challenged this wholesale rejection of asceticism. 'In rejecting the monastic institute which is the caricature of religion, we need to be careful lest we let slip the reality with it. Ascetic piety is one thing, mortification of the flesh is another.'[23] Pattison's appropriation of the adjective 'ascetic' to describe his idea of a university education had the effect – and perhaps the intention – of highlighting its counter-cultural qualities. The higher education, and still more the higher learning, must in an important sense stand apart from the world. But in what sense exactly?

Pattison thought, to begin with, that the university was degraded if it allowed itself to be shaped by 'the world'; that is, by public opinion. He had been one of those Oxford tutors who wrote to the Prime Minister, Lord John Russell, in 1850 to urge him to establish a Royal Commission with the aim of reforming the University. He well understood that Parliament must intervene from time to time to align the use of historic endowments with the needs of the nation. He understood, and indeed insisted, that a university must be 'in vital connexion with the national intellect'.[24] But he believed it a symptom of the demoralization of the universities – of their lack of a sense of their noble purpose – if, once freed from the shackles of founders' intentions, they still needed to be reformed from without. 'If we were what we claim to be, surely it would belong to us to point out the way; to find the right road and to proclaim it, to lead others along it, ourselves in the van.'[25] Only if they stood apart from the spirit of the age could the universities reclaim their rightful supremacy in 'the intellectual guidance of England'.[26] Otherwise they would be moulded by 'a mere popular conception' of the utility of academic studies, and the higher purpose of universities would be lost:

Are we, here in our precious years of retirement, to know no more of the spiritual life than we can hope to do afterwards amid the pressure of public service, the strain of professional labours, or the still more distracting web of personal engagement which weaves itself round each one of us as life advances?[27]

Later, as he became more outspokenly anti-Catholic, Pattison was inclined to emphasize the anti-monastic character of the university, even

---

[22] David Newsome, *Godliness & Good Learning: Four Studies on a Victorian Ideal* (London: John Murray, 1961), p. 199.

[23] Pattison, *Sermons*, pp. 80–1.

[24] Pattison, 'Oxford Studies', *Oxford Essays* (London: Parker, 1855), reprinted in *Essays* vol. I, p. 429.

[25] Pattison, *Sermons*, p. 90.    [26] Pattison, *Sermons*, p. 91.    [27] Pattison, *Sermons*, p. 91.

in its medieval origins. But he continued to insist on the spiritual quality of a university education: 'the office of academical teacher', he declared in 1882, 'is eminently a spiritual ministration'. And the reason was to be found in the personal influence that was central to university education. As education progresses, he argued, the technique of teaching becomes less important and is replaced by 'the direct action of intellect on intellect, of character on character – the intellect and character of the teacher upon the intelligence and character of the pupil.'[28]

This was a quintessentially Newmanite conception of a university education. As a tutor at Oriel in the 1820s, Newman had persuaded his colleagues to reorganize college teaching so as to reassert the pastoral nature of the office of tutor. This, he thought, was in tune with the seventeenth-century Laudian statutes of the University, which declared the tutor to be 'not a mere academical Policeman, or Constable, but a moral and religious guardian of the youth committed to him'.[29] Newman himself had little interest in 'mere lecturing' in itself: the role of tutor interested him because it offered the opportunity of exercising a personal influence upon a group of pupils – those specially assigned to him, rather than shared with the other tutors. He wanted to be able to see his more serious pupils individually, and so to eliminate the harmful practice of hiring private tutors, whose influence would interfere with that of the official college tutor. It was this conception of the role of the tutor that led Newman and his colleagues into conflict with Provost Hawkins, with lasting consequences for Pattison's own education. But it remained at the heart of Newman's understanding of university education. A university is, as he inimitably put it, 'an Alma Mater, knowing her children one by one, not a foundry, or a mint, or a treadmill'.[30] No more than Newman did Pattison ever lose his conviction that a university education, properly understood, must be personal rather than simply mechanical.

Pattison, then, was insistent that if it was to be true to itself, the university must have the independence and self-confidence of purpose to stand at a critical distance from the world. This stance helps explain many of his most characteristic attitudes, and in particular his well-known loathing of the grip exercised on university education by the examination system.

---

[28] Pattison, 'What is a college?', *Journal of Education* n.s. 4 (1882), 71.
[29] Newman's words, quoted by Ian Ker, *John Henry Newman: A Biography* (Oxford: Oxford University Press, 1988), p. 39.
[30] John Henry Newman, *The Idea of a University Defined and Illustrated*, ed. I. T. Ker (Oxford: Clarendon, 1976), p. 129.

Academic standards in Oxford had been rising since the introduction of the examination statute of 1800, which introduced a formal system of university examination to replace the purely symbolic examination by two randomly chosen MAs that had prevailed in the eighteenth century. At first examinations were conducted orally, but pressure of numbers soon forced the introduction of written examinations with printed question papers. Pattison's arrival at Oxford thus coincided with the beginnings of the ascendancy of the examination system, of which he would become one of the most vocal critics. The new system had been subjected to criticisms on religious grounds from the outset: the evangelical William Wilberforce, for example, warned his sons of the dangers of 'emulation' which the class list created, and in 1829 a Hebdomadal Board committee acknowledged that there were 'strong objections on moral grounds' to the idea of a competitive order of merit of the kind used in the Mathematical tripos at Cambridge.[31] To some degree Pattison echoed these criticisms. He fully realized, of course, that the introduction of formal examinations had been instrumental in raising academic standards in the university; but he feared that the ascendancy of the examination was creating a new formalism in which outward attainments in the schools would be valued at the expense of the real intellectual qualities which the examinations were supposed to test.

For Pattison, the purpose of a university was to shape the inner man, and to light in him the inextinguishable flame of the desire for self-improvement, 'a high ideal of intellectual expansion and cultivation'.[32] That noble purpose was degraded if it depended for its operation on the offer of external rewards. The love of learning, of self-improvement, should be its own reward: it should not need to be rewarded in the examination schools, and if it is rewarded there then it could not be said to be its own reward:

To enforce study by examination is much on a par with compelling morality by public discipline, or restraining private extravagance by sumptuary laws. The outward actions are coerced by such enactments; the disinclination within remains what it was. What we wish to create is the disposition to self-improvement – *this* legislation cannot reach. The best contrived examination can only reach knowledge and acquirement; it cannot gauge character. We seek knowledge not for itself, but as a means for enlarging and building up the character. Something is wanted

---

[31] Curthoys, 'Examination system', p. 366. In the Mathematical tripos the candidates were not only placed in classes, but those in the first class (the 'wranglers') were themselves ranked, the top-performing candidate being known as the 'senior wrangler'.
[32] Pattison, 'Oxford Studies', p. 493.

for this purpose more than the compulsion of examinations to be passed, or the inducement of honours and rewards which may be won.[33]

The antagonism between true learning and the competitive drive was a recurrent theme in Pattison's sermons. Soon after his election to the rectorship, he exhorted his congregation in the college chapel: 'Let steady self-improvement be your end. Propose to yourselves as your guiding aim not a class, not a scholarship, not surpassing others, but the cultivation of your own mind through the instrumentality of the studies of the place.'[34] When he gave evidence to the Selborne Commission in 1877, he no doubt took some of the commissioners aback with his proposition that a clever boy starts to earn his living at fourteen, by virtue of being a good examinee, and that he will come to Oxford for the sake of its honours and prizes. As a result, the teacher was degraded into 'a mere coach'. Properly understood, he held, 'the office of an academical teacher is spiritual ministration': the more advanced education becomes, the more instruction as such is supplanted by 'the direct action of . . . the mind and character of the teacher upon the mind and character of the pupil'.[35]

Pattison was well aware that the ethic of lifelong self-improvement which he proposed as the proper function of a university to nourish was utterly remote from the great majority of dons and undergraduates, and that the gap between ideal and reality was enormous. Here he is in the first university sermon he preached as rector, in November 1861:

We step out of our studies with hearts dilated with the magnificent outlines of the Temple of Knowledge in which we dream we minister, and we find ourselves not in an academical auditory, but among the lower forms of a grammar school. Instead of a liberal curiosity, intellectual tastes, studious habits, and the frugal self-control of the scholar; instead of our ardour to teach being met by an equal ardour to learn, we find that we have to do with ignorance, stupidity, sensual tastes, laziness, indifference, an effeminate passion for amusement, self-indulgent habits, listless, aimless temperaments, inert rather than vicious, unenergetic, unheroic, unimpassioned. When to the generation of the stupid, the insensible, and the frivolous is added those whose understanding is frost-bound by the prejudices of a narrow sphere, or an artificial theological system, and those to whom the university course is a pecuniary speculation, the remnant is small indeed of those with whom we can hope to establish that intellectual sympathy between young and old which is the instrument of intellectual culture.[36]

---

[33] Pattison, *Sermons*, p. 95.    [34] Pattison, *Sermons*, pp. 271–2.
[35] University of Oxford Royal Commission, Minutes of Evidence: Parliamentary Papers 1881, Cmd 2868, lvi, 255–9.
[36] Pattison, *Sermons*, pp. 61–2.

This is a distinctive passage. In one who was accused, and accused himself, of weakness of character, we find some of the typical vocabulary of the Victorian discourse of character, along with the closely allied discourse of 'manliness'.[37] Character is heroic, energetic, passionate, whereas its antithesis is effeminate, lazy, and listless. The man of character possesses 'frugal self-control', whereas his antithesis displays 'sensual tastes' and 'self-indulgent habits'. Like many Victorians, Pattison feared that the virtues of the manly character were eroded by material progress: in a later sermon he spoke of 'the soft self-indulgent spirit which attends the diffusion of wealth and civilisation'.[38] The denunciation of the straitjacket of theological orthodoxy is quintessentially Pattisonian; but so too is the reference to the 'remnant', a term packed with meaning here, not least because of its biblical connotations. Pattison saw the university as necessarily elitist, but it was not concerned with a social elite or even with an academic elite in the conventional sense, since he was contemptuous of the prize-winners who entered the university as a 'pecuniary speculation', without any conception of intellectual culture. Rather, the university existed for a spiritual elite – a 'remnant' – who could commit themselves to an ethic of mental self-improvement without regard to the external rewards of the examination schools.

But at this point we need to pause to observe Pattison's ambivalent stance in relation to the 'manly virtues' so prized in the public discourse of the Victorian middle classes. Here we see him invoking them in support of the ethic of mental self-improvement: the intellectual life was nine parts 'strenuous and prolonged effort' to one part natural endowment.[39] But at the same time he challenged the hegemony of manliness in the Victorian moral universe, and urged the rival claims of the contemplative virtues. In a college sermon preached in 1863 he noted that 'keenness, vigour, boldness, skill, enterprise, readiness, hardiness, determination, solidity – the manly virtues of a trading and speculating people, are held in first honour among us'. He did not deny that they were honourable values: 'It is by their possession and exercise that our country holds among the kingdoms of Europe the position of which we are all so justly proud.' But he pleaded for a greater degree of pluralism, suggesting that these 'manly virtues' were 'too exclusively honoured', and that they tended 'to thrust out of sight the softer evangelical virtues of humility, patience, self-abnegation, prayer, devotion, charity'.[40] The Oxford Movement, itself often accused of being deficient in

---

[37] The classic account of this subject is Collini, 'The idea of "character"', 29–50.
[38] Pattison, *Sermons*, p. 93.    [39] Pattison, *Sermons*, p. 267.    [40] Pattison, *Sermons*, pp. 291–2.

manliness, had set out to nurture these softer and other-worldly virtues, and Pattison's respect for them was an enduring legacy of his Tractarian phase. We find the critique of the dominance of manly virtues recurring in his denunciation of the 'athletic furor' that gripped Oxford in the period of his rectorship.[41]

Equally rooted in his Tractarian phase was his antagonism towards formalism in education, and especially in university education. In March 1848, before he had broken decisively with the Oxford Movement, he regretted the need for the University, in a commercial age, to establish honours and prizes and so 'enlist the dangerous auxiliary ambition in the support of learning', and in June of the same year he warned members of his college against valuing 'the awards & honours of knowledge above the knowledge itself', and he specifically cited 'a love of obtaining prizes' as one form of the 'subtraction of our mental faculties from their appointed business'.[42] This was clearly a particular preoccupation of his at this time. Reviewing Mill's *Principles of Political Economy* for a High Church periodical in 1848 he observed that the development of the class and tripos systems at Oxford and Cambridge had the effect of 'giving commercial value to classical knowledge'; from which he inferred that there was insufficient public confidence in the remote benefits of mental cultivation, and that learning thrived only because the examination system had attached to it 'a ticket of merit, convertible at sight into specie in the money market'. For Pattison this was a degradation of the true ideal of a liberal education.[43] There is, significantly, an important diary entry from October 1843 which makes it clear that Pattison had already formulated his critique of this shallow competitiveness in a conversation with Newman, who in spite of his own experience was more sanguine about the effect of the system of degree classes in raising the standard of academic life in the university.[44] Even the quest for a fellowship, which dominated Pattison's life in the period 1836–9, was a betrayal of learning for its own sake. So, on the failure of his candidature at Balliol in 1838, he wrote that he must give up his hopes of a fellowship. As a result, he thought, 'my reading may now be turned into a completely new channel – no longer a means – but reading for reading's sake, for knowledge'.[45]

---

[41] Pattison, *Suggestions on Academical Organisation with especial reference to Oxford* (Edinburgh: Edmonston and Douglas, 1868), p. 316.

[42] Bodleian MS Pattison 71, ff. 28, 46–48.

[43] [Mark Pattison], 'Mill's Political Economy', *Christian Remembrancer* 16 (December 1848), 341.

[44] Bodleian MS Pattison 128; also recorded in *Memoirs*, 201–2.

[45] Bodleian MS Pattison 6, f. 61.

The critique of formalism in education fed on a critique of formalism in religion. 'The higher education', he wrote, 'can no more be committed to memory, and learnt by rote or by books, than religion can be transmitted by tradition or by a document.'[46] In his sermons Pattison was insistent that the Christian life did not hinge on conformity to an external discipline, but on obedience to an *inner* law: 'Christianity is a principle of action, not a set of rules.'[47] The Christian life was not about outward observance but about inward self-discipline: mere conformity with the external discipline of the church was not of the essence; instead it must be supplemented by enthusiasm and an ardour of the heart. The Christian life, he argued, should be understood as a quest for perfection after the pattern of Christ. In Pattison's sermons of this period there is a curious anticipation of Mill's *On Liberty*, over a decade before that famous essay was published and some years before it was first drafted; for Pattison insisted that nothing great can be achieved in the world without *thymos* – he deployed that Socratic concept meaning something like 'spiritedness' – and that the deadliest enemy of the Christian is conformity to habit or custom.[48] Before Mill, Pattison had conceived autonomy – genuine self-direction – as his basic ideal. And autonomy and self-direction were at the heart of his under-standing of character, just as they were for Mill. 'The great business of this place [the college]', he maintained, was 'the art of life, the self-formation, the building up a high-principled character by the light of distinct con-sciousness'. He told his congregation of undergraduates: 'the fabric of your own character is now placed in your own hands.'[49] Perhaps the central theme of Pattison's college and university sermons was the contrast between two conceptions of education: on the one hand, education as a form of social control or acculturation, by which younger members were absorbed into 'the extant habits and ideas of the community or the class'; and education as 'the culture and expansion of the man', the drawing out of the inner potential.[50] In the former, 'conformity to an external rule is the highest virtue', and this submission to 'the exterior conditions of our existence' was necessary if man were not to be 'in a state of habitual rebellion

---

[46] Pattison, 'Oxford Studies', p. 424.     [47] Bodleian MS Pattison 71, f. 29.

[48] Bodleian MS Pattison 71, f. 32, 5 March 1848: 'What great enterprize was ever conceived or executed without some share of that θυμος which is the animal basis of the moral habit Courage?'

[49] Bodleian MS Pattison 71, ff. 24–6. See the account of Cambridge reformers offered by Rothblatt, *Revolution of the Dons*, pp. 246–7. Rothblatt sees reformers from a range of different intellectual standpoints agreeing that a central objective of the university had to be the 'regeneration of the self' to overcome the enfeeblement of the English character. He notes that Pattison shared this point of view.

[50] Pattison, *Sermons*, pp. 46–7.

against law and usage'.[51] Pattison saw these as the essential functions of schooling, and especially of elementary schooling. The latter form of education, by contrast, acknowledged that 'Man has an active or creative power', and that mind is 'a reagent against society . . . exercising a dissolving force upon received opinion'. Here, in a university education, 'we are for the first time called upon to exert a force in an opposite direction – a reaction of the human soul against the barrier outside'.[52] Pattison recognized that these were ideal types, for any system of education must inevitably embrace both; but his main aim was to elucidate the logic and rationale of the latter conception, and to propound it as the foundation of all that is distinctive about university education.

This antithesis between forming oneself and being formed by external forces was crucial in shaping the way Pattison thought. This can be illustrated by examples from his other writings. In a fine essay on 'Calvin at Geneva', published in the *Westminster Review* in 1858, he articulates the distinction between external authority and inward self-discipline. Mere external authority, in the form of the modern state, 'a mere engine of police and property', cannot provide individual freedom. That requires virtue and ascetic self-discipline. Pattison later developed a strong aversion to philosophical idealism, but here he comes across as an exponent of the pure concept of positive liberty: 'true liberty', which 'is only realized through self-control, when "the weight of chance desires" has been felt, and shaken off by an effort of the will'.[53]

The profound sense of the ascetic quality of the vocation of the scholar continued to infuse Pattison's thinking long after he had detached himself from the Oxford Movement and even from any kind of orthodoxy in matters of religion. Indeed, much of his animosity towards Jowett's Oxford was on account of what he took to be its worldliness. It was too concerned with preparing students for a career in public service, for which the acquisition of a wide but shallow familiarity with the elements of knowledge would be enough, and insufficiently committed to helping students learn how to dig deeper and progress towards real knowledge or what he sometimes called 'progressive knowledge'.[54] So in 1863 he insisted that the main duty of teachers at a university was to introduce students to 'the one great art of life – the art of self-culture, self-discipline'. What – as shorthand, but *only* as

[51] Pattison, *Sermons*, pp. 105–6.
[52] Pattison, *Sermons*, pp. 109–112. See also Pattison, 'Oxford Studies', pp. 420–1.
[53] Pattison, 'Calvin at Geneva', p. 39. On idealism, see Pattison, *Memoirs*, p. 167.
[54] Pattison, 'Philosophy in Oxford', *Mind* I (1876), 88.

shorthand – we may characterize as Pattison's 'research ethic' consisted primarily in his sense that the academic had an absolute duty to be personally and actively engaged in a process of self-culture, and that, indeed, he would be deficient as a university teacher if he were not engaged in such a process. He had to set an appropriate pattern before his students, and 'unless our teaching be seconded by the interior discipline of our own life, it will be but sounding words'.[55] Elsewhere Pattison argued that we cannot 'teach from our recollections', and that 'the philosophical temper, – the last acquisition and the highest reward of the intellectual course, – can only be communicated by the mind which possesses it'.[56] He was scornful of the kind of education dispensed by reformed Oxford in the 1870s and 80s. This was provided by tutors whose sole qualification lay in the fact that they themselves were 'honour-men' and 'prize-men', and hence were equipped to train others in the winning of prizes and honours.[57] They produced a typical graduate who had acquired 'ready-made opinions' – not 'real knowledge' – from 'showy lectures' and manuals; and this graduate was not only intellectually but morally feeble. 'Having no root in itself, such a type of character is liable to become an easy prey to any popular charlatanism or current fanaticism', and the university was vulnerable to the vicissitudes of intellectual fashion.[58]

Pattison's understanding of university education was 'liberal' in that it was an education of the whole person, of the character as well as of the mind. The difficulty it presented was a moral much more than an intellectual difficulty: crucially, it demanded a discipline of the will.[59] In 1865 he reiterated that university education had not only an intellectual but also a moral aspect. This latter, he proposed, should be ascetic: in other words, it should be 'a discipline of character', which 'grasps at nothing less than the whole man.[60] But this did not imply a discipline from without, for what distinguished a university education from a school education was that the latter existed to allow society to reproduce itself by requiring conformity to an external rule as the highest virtue, whereas higher education begins when the mind begins to stir. The business of the university teacher is therefore 'not to inculcate truths but to force growth'.[61] Here Pattison sided with the cause of liberal education against both Catholic and positivist conceptions. They both understood university education to rest essentially upon the inculcation of truths. Pattison stood instead for education as the formation

---

[55] Pattison, *Sermons*, p. 70.   [56] Pattison, 'Oxford Studies', p. 422.
[57] Pattison, 'Philosophy in Oxford', 88.   [58] Pattison, *Memoirs*, pp. 240–1.
[59] Pattison, *Sermons*, p. 271.   [60] Pattison, *Sermons*, p. 103–4.   [61] Pattison, *Sermons*, p. 116.

of both mind and character; and, in higher education, their self-formation. A university education, he maintained, rests upon the idea 'that the character can be purified, strengthened, and raised to a heroic height by discipline, self-control, by a force exerted from within'.[62]

Like almost all of Pattison's most powerful writings, the sermons are deeply autobiographical. The antithesis between self-formation and being formed by external forces was a recurrent theme in the sermons. He urged his congregation to shun 'that worst of slavery, the resting your happiness on the good opinion of others'.[63] It was also central to the narrative of the *Memoirs*, as we saw in Chapter 3. The naïve and innocent boy who arrived at Oriel in 1832 was overcome by self-consciousness and a sense of his 'unlikeness to others', and he responded by allowing himself to be shaped by his environment. In his college sermons he repeatedly warned his undergraduate congregation against the thraldom of custom. This was what the church called 'the Spirit of the World', or the temptation to do 'as a matter of course what others do, what our own set do, whatever that set may be'.[64] In a college sermon preached on All Saints' Day, 1863, he identified 'the influence of example' as a chief cause of the 'spiritual barrenness' of the age.[65]

The *Memoirs* trace Pattison's emancipation from the bondage to society and custom, and, as we have seen, they date this to a precise moment in July 1833, the moment of 'the dawn of intellect in me'. He described this as if it were a kind of rebirth. The *Memoirs*, curiously enough, do not relate an experience of religious conversion or of loss of faith: they narrate an ongoing process of growth and development in his intellectual and spiritual life. But this moment of intellectual awakening was akin to a conversion experience. In his sermons he objectified this subjective experience of conversion to the life of the mind. In a university sermon preached in 1863, for example, he described the life of the student who had 'engaged in the struggle for self-formation'. This was evidently remarkably like the experience of spiritual rebirth. The struggle 'endows life with a purpose and a meaning which no other pursuit can give it'. Having found this 'rock' beneath his feet, the student now looks upon his fellow students in much the way, we imagine, an eighteenth-century evangelical or a Newmanite of the 1830s would have done:

He is astonished at the frivolous interests of those around him, their want of earnestness, their superficial hold on life, their apathy to the nobler objects of

---

[62] Pattison, *Sermons*, pp. 123–5.    [63] Pattison, *Sermons*, p. 263.
[64] College sermon 5 March 1848, Bodleian MS Pattison 71, ff. 33–4.
[65] Pattison, *Sermons*, p. 289.

human pursuit; the levity, monotony, and nonchalance of their conversation, betraying itself even in the tones of their voice. Though he does not seek diversions as they do, he finds that he enjoys life more than they, and can taste its pleasures with a relish which only a pure mind, a clear intention, and a vigilantly watched conscience can bestow. God, and the human destiny to which God has called him, is his presiding thought. The rule of his day is to be always making the best of himself.[66]

This is reminiscent of the account the *Memoirs* offer of the young Pattison's disdain for and disappointment in his fellow undergraduates at Oriel. 'I had not yet met with a single man who realised the idea I had formed of a university student.'[67]

Pattison's sense of the chasm that separated his vision of what a university education was properly about and the reality of undergraduate life for most students remained just as pronounced at the end of his Oxford life as at its beginning. 'How dismally ignorant these schoolboys are', he recorded in his diary after having an undergraduate to breakfast in April 1880. He was still more forthright following another such event in November or December of the same year. 'We have had an undergraduate to b.fast every morning. Today Thompson, a commoner, an utter dolt – to think that a University, with an apparatus of Professors & Libraries should exist for such African savages as that!'[68]

## IN DEFENCE OF THE PHILOSOPHICAL LIFE

Pattison scarcely preached after 1871, and no sermon preached after his Assize Sermon of that year survives. But the themes of the sermons – self-improvement as the lifelong commitment to be nurtured by a university; the university as a place of retirement, and so on – continued to preoccupy him and to infuse his writings and the various public addresses he gave on educational subjects. He would articulate them, for instance, in the article he published on 'Philosophy in Oxford' in the first issue of *Mind* in January 1876. This was a notable piece of work: G. H. Lewes and George Eliot thought it 'remarkable', and read it with gratification and delight.[69] But it had little to say about philosophy in the technical sense. Pattison always understood philosophy in something of a Platonic sense: 'a just and perfect judgment on the bearings and relationships of knowledge'.[70]

---

[66] Pattison, *Sermons*, pp. 96–7.  [67] Pattison, *Memoirs*, p. 147.
[68] Bodleian MS Pattison 133, f. 1.
[69] G. H. Lewes to Pattison, 27 December 1875, Bodleian MS Pattison 57, ff. 175–6.
[70] Pattison, 'Oxford Studies', p. 425.

The article set out to explain the stagnation of philosophical thought in contemporary Oxford. In retrospect this line of inquiry might strike the reader as perverse: T. H. Green, F. H. Bradley and Bernard Bosanquet were all resident fellows at the time, and in some ways the point at which Pattison wrote marked the beginning of the flowering of philosophy at Oxford which would culminate in the decades after the Second World War, when Oxford philosophy led the world. But Green had not yet been appointed to the chair of moral philosophy, which he assumed in 1878, four years before his untimely death; Bradley, always a recluse, published his *Ethical Studies* at the age of thirty, shortly before Pattison wrote; and Bosanquet did his most important philosophical work after his departure from Oxford in 1881. So perhaps Pattison, who was less than sympathetic to the idealists, can be forgiven for this judgement. The article developed a characteristically Pattisonian analysis. He eschewed abstract analysis of schools of philosophical thought, and instead explored the nature of philosophical inquiry and philosophical education and their social prerequisites. He did not attribute philosophical stagnation to the dominance of particular modes of thought, but instead imputed blame to the practical orientation of the academic environment. It should come as no surprise to read Pattison's definition of the nature of philosophical activity, which he regarded as the antithesis of the life of business and busy-ness:

The philosophic energy is of the nature of contemplation. It is always found to be in an inverse ratio to outward activity. It requires as its conditions retirement from strife, detachment from interests, above all mental freedom.[71]

Reformed Oxford of the 1870s, by contrast, was dominated by ecclesiastical partisanship; and its partisan battles were no longer fought out through the press, but carried out by means of the organization of academic parties with a view to victory in academic appointments and policymaking.

The dichotomy drawn here between philosophical inquiry and the active life underpinned Pattison's whole conception of the life of learning as a noble form of existence. He never undertook any work that could be defined as philosophical in a technical sense; but he certainly considered his way of life that of a philosopher, defined as 'a temper, a habit of mind . . . a form under which we think our thoughts and live our life'. For his scholarship aimed not at erudition for its own sake (though Pattison may sometimes have given this impression), but at the cultivation of the self through 'an unaffected and unbribed interest in truth'.[72] A life of philosophical

[71] Pattison, 'Philosophy in Oxford', 87.    [72] Pattison, 'Philosophy in Oxford', 83.

learning was one in which each new piece of knowledge was brought to bear upon one's whole system of thought and so made one's own. 'The first principle of philosophical, nay of intellectual, training', he wrote, was 'that all should be educed from the pupil's own mind.'[73]

The other strand in the explanation of the stagnation of Oxford philosophy was equally Pattisonian: it focused on the stranglehold exerted by the examination system and by *elementary* teaching over the intellectual life of the University. Here Pattison has something valuable to say to our present-day concerns about the relationship between 'teaching' and 'research'. Does an academic's teaching feed his or her research, or is it a simple diversion? The question has vital implications for the ways in which universities are organized. If the two activities do not effectively complement each other, why should they not become separate, specialized activities – and why, indeed, should research be carried out in universities at all, rather than in academies or research institutes?

Autobiographically, Pattison was convinced that his career as an undergraduate teacher in the period 1842–55 had had a decisive and beneficial influence upon his intellectual awakening. So he could not accept that teaching must always be prejudicial to the intellectual life of the teacher. Indeed, it might be necessary: 'Every thinker desires to communicate his thoughts; and how much closer and more encouraging is the sympathy of disciples to whom you can speak than that of a public for whom you can only write!'[74] In spite of his contempt for the run-of-the-mill undergraduate, Pattison never shared Scaliger's disgust for university teaching.[75]

Everything depended on what kind of teaching was involved. Was it elementary teaching, the simple communication of the elements of knowledge, in which the teacher must always dwell on 'the alphabet of the science'? Or was it, rather, 'inspired by progressive knowledge'? According to Pattison, Oxford tutors had a 'zeal' for teaching, but it was a zeal inspired not by 'progressive knowledge', but by the hope of helping their pupils to prizes and honours. The tutor thus

finds himself at once the slave of a great teaching engine, which drives him day by day in a round of mechanical work. There is no stepping aside; if you fall out of the ranks, you perish. Study, or research, or self-improvement, is out of the question ... The teacher must not lose a moment in teaching a subject, in searching out its foundations, in inspiring his pupils with a love for it, with a desire to pursue it in a spirit of thoroughness.[76]

---

[73] Pattison, 'Philosophy in Oxford', 93.    [74] Pattison, 'Philosophy in Oxford', 88.
[75] Pattison, *Isaac Casaubon*, p. 53.    [76] Pattison, 'Philosophy in Oxford', 88–9.

The essence of his work was 'training for the race': 'Training, be it observed, not intellectual discipline, not training in investigation, in research, in scientific procedure, but in the art of producing a clever answer to a question on a subject of which you have no real knowledge.'[77]

Pattison's idea of the university, then, was rooted in a conception of the life of learning for its own sake as a noble calling; and that ideal of learning was itself shaped by a broader ethical vision which systematically preferred inner freedom to actions determined by external motivations. I have argued that from one point of view this conception of learning, with its strongly ascetic flavour, could be seen as a secularized form of the Tractarian ideal of holiness. At the same time it cannot be denied that there are deep affinities between Pattison's outlook and the 'German idea' of the university formulated in the French revolutionary and Napoleonic eras by thinkers associated with the idealist, neo-humanist, and romantic movements. Philosophically, the idea that morality depends less on the outward face of actions than on their inner motivation found its most trenchant exposition in the writings of Kant; while the definition of freedom as obedience to laws one has prescribed for oneself was another central tenet of the founder of German idealism, who here followed Rousseau. Kant applied these notions to education. He recognized – as Rousseau did not – that the child has to be educated in 'the concepts of duty and laws'. This schooling should continue 'until the time that nature itself has determined that people should rule themselves': that is, until the age of seventeen or thereabouts. Education beyond that age – university education – should instead draw on the Socratic method to challenge students to use their reason.[78] Pattison endorsed this sharp distinction between the elementary and disciplinary character of school education and the aims of university education, the purpose of which was to develop the student's intellectual autonomy.

The neohumanists and the romantics were alternative – and not altogether distinct – sources for ideas of this kind. The idea of *Bildung* – of the self-formation and self-cultivation of the person – was, famously, the central theme of Goethe's *Wilhelm Meister's Apprenticeship* (1778–96), and had an important influence on thinkers such as Schiller. Rather like Kant, Schiller was contemptuous of the *Brotgelehrten* ('Bread Scholars'), students whose devotion to their studies stretched only as far as their career

---

[77] Pattison, 'Philosophy in Oxford', 89.
[78] Michael J. Hofstetter, *The Romantic Idea of a University: England and Germany, 1770–1850* (Basingstoke: Palgrave, 2001), p. 27.

prospects demanded. These careerists had the souls of slaves. The 'philosophical head', by contrast, was a servant of the spirit and sought not to
train himself for a career but to educate himself as a human being. He
sought breadth – and Schiller presented the study of world history as an
appropriate instrument for the achievement of this breadth.[79] For the
theologian Schleiermacher, every individual has within him the idea of
*Wissenschaft*, and the task of the university was to awaken and nurture this
idea so that it becomes second nature for the student 'to consider everything from the point of view of science, to view individual phenomena not
for themselves ... but in constant reference to the unity and totality of
knowledge'.[80]

The direct influence of Kant and Schiller on Pattison is quite difficult to
trace, and the curious thing about Pattison's intellectual stance is that he
was always deaf to the appeal of philosophical idealism. He dismissed 'the
gratuitous hypotheses and *a priori* constructions of Kant and the other
German schools'.[81] The one German idealist whose influence can be
tracked was Fichte. Following his appointment to the chair of philosophy
at Jena in 1794, Fichte gave a series of public lectures on *The Vocation of the
Scholar*, and a decade or so later he gave another series of lectures at
Erlangen on *The Nature of the Scholar*.[82] His central argument was that
man's goal was to subdue the irrational and to live freely in accordance
with his own laws; and that universities had a decisive role to play in
fostering this objective and hence contributing to the moral regeneration of
mankind. True scholars constituted the elite of humanity, for they quintessentially identified their own existence with the perfection of reason.
One can see why Pattison's Tractarian formation would have prepared him
to be influenced by Fichte's work: Fichte spoke repeatedly of the 'sacred-
ness' and indeed of the 'holiness' of the scholar's vocation: 'The true-
minded Scholar looks upon his vocation – to become a partaker of the
Divine thought of the universe – as the purpose of God in him; and
therefore both his person and his calling become to him, before all other
things, honourable and holy; and this holiness shows itself in all his outward

[79] Hofstetter, *The Romantic Idea of a University*, pp. 36–7.
[80] R. Steven Turner, 'The Prussian universities and the concept of research', *Internationales Archiv für
Sozialgeschichte der deutschen Literatur* 5 (1980), 78.
[81] Pattison, *Memoirs*, p. 129. See also p. 167.
[82] In the German, these publications were entitled, respectively, *Einige Vorlesungen über die Bestimmung
des Gelehrten* and *Über des Wesen des Gelehrten, und seine Erscheinungen im Gebiete der Freiheit*. Both
were translated into English by William Smith in the 1840s, and published by John Chapman: *The
Vocation of the Scholar* in 1847 and *The Nature of the Scholar and its Manifestations* in 1845.

manifestations.'[83] Indeed, the scholar must be '*morally* the *best* man of his age'.[84] Pattison read Fichte's second set of lectures when preparing a university sermon in 1865, and the first when writing his introduction to Appleton's edited volume of *Essays on the Endowment of Research* in 1876.[85] He was already acquainted with Fichte's work, at least through his exposition of his ideas on the philosophy of history, *The Characteristics of the Present Age*. Pattison read this in 1847, and noted in his commonplace book the outlines of its fivefold division of the course of human history.[86] Fichte saw his own age as an age of liberation from instinct and external authority, and held that it would be succeeded by man's learning to live in accordance with the rule of reason. Pattison would return to this book in July 1877, when preparing the lecture he gave to the Teachers' Association in Birmingham that autumn on the question 'What do we mean by education?'[87] There, and still more in another address apparently prepared two or three years later, Pattison portrayed the distinctive function of a university education as the liberation of 'the true man in us from those shackles of prejudice in which untrained minds are hidebound all their lives'. It was not the scholar, he argued, but the uneducated man who was 'the stunted or deformed or crippled being'. The man who had received the benefits of a liberal education was alone capable of realizing 'the true human type of civilised man'.[88]

### THE VOCATION OF THE SCHOLAR

So far we have explored Pattison's deployment of the concepts of self-formation and self-improvement chiefly in the context of the educational life of the university. But Pattison understood the devotion to the culture of the mind as a lifelong commitment. Universities could only perform their educational work satisfactorily if the teachers were themselves committed to scholarship. That was the insight that underpinned his contempt for those dons whom he thought unable to rise above the idea of 'school-keeping'. He deplored the election of George Brodrick to the

---

[83] J. G. Fichte, 'On the Nature of the Scholar and its Manifestations', in Johann Gottlieb Fichte *Popular Works: The Nature of the Scholar, the Vocation of Man, the Doctrine of Religion, with a Memoir by William Smith* (London: Trübner, 1873), p. 195. See also pp. 173, 175, 185, 191, 192, 196, 197, 201, 204, etc.

[84] J. G. Fichte, *The Vocation of the Scholar*, quoted by Turner, 'Prussian universities', 79.

[85] Bodleian MS Pattison 130, f. 129.      [86] Bodleian MS Pattison 7*, pp. 115–6.

[87] The manuscript draft of the lecture is at Bodleian MS Pattison 112, ff. 121–34; the references to reading Fichte at Bodleian MS Pattison 130, ff. 179–80.

[88] Bodleian MS Pattison 112, ff. 148–50.

wardenship of Merton in 1881, for Brodrick was 'wholly on the side of the schoolmasters, & hates learning'.[89] This did not mean that Pattison despised or undervalued the educational side of a university's work. He simply thought it worthless without a sense of the nobility of the academic life. He was famously contemptuous of academics whose work was not infused with a 'real' commitment to learning. Just as the uneducated clergyman disgusted him, so too did the academic who lacked a decent personal library, for the possession of a scholarly library was, to Pattison, the touchstone of a commitment to learning. His father had instilled high expectations of him in this respect, writing to him in his first term at Oxford: 'The library of a Fellow of Oriel should be the best in the universe. Even a commoner of that distinguished society should be surrounded by no mean materials for study; and when your rooms are ready, and you wish for a supply, the Stockton steamer shall be put in requisition.'[90] Pattison took these words seriously, and proceeded to accumulate a library of about fourteen thousand books, the largest private library in Oxford in its day, and one of the largest in the country accumulated by one man rather than by several generations of a family. The collection was, wrote Christie, 'extraordinarily complete for the history of learning and philosophy of the sixteenth, seventeenth, and eighteenth centuries'.[91] Sold by Sotheby's over a period of nine days in July and August 1885 in nearly four thousand lots, the library must have raised a four figure sum, but probably less than two thousand pounds. This is a remarkably small sum given the rarity of many of the volumes, but it was a library assembled for use rather than for storage of value. Pattison cherished his books dearly: 'they have been more to me than my friends', he said, with characteristically self-mockery and exaggeration.[92] 'Few in this busy, energetic island in which we live can say, what I have to confess of myself, that my whole life has been passed in handling books.'[93] It was shameful, he thought, that a middle-class man earning a thousand pounds a year would not spend just fifty pounds a year on books. To plead lack of space was not good enough, for 'a set of shelves, thirteen feet by ten feet, and six inches deep, placed against a wall, will accommodate nearly one thousand volumes 8vo.'[94]

Pattison explored the nature of the scholarly or academic life in many of his mature writings. His fullest exploration of this theme occurred in his life

[89] Bodleian MS Pattison 120, ff. 146–7. [90] Quoted in Pattison, *Memoirs*, p. 109.
[91] R. C. C[hristie], 'Pattison, Mark', *Dictionary of National Biography* (London: Oxford University Press, 1917), 508.
[92] Tollemache, 'Recollections of Pattison', pp. 123–4.
[93] Pattison, 'Books and critics', 659. [94] Pattison, 'Books and critics', 673.

of Isaac Casaubon. By 1850 Pattison had loosened his ties to the Tractarians, and was building a glowing reputation for himself as one of the foremost tutors in Oxford. In that year a canon of Canterbury, John Russell, published an edition of the journal, the *Ephemerides*, of Isaac Casaubon, the great French classical scholar of the late sixteenth and early seventeenth centuries. Casaubon had ended his career as a prebendary of Canterbury, and the manuscript of the journal had been deposited in the chapter library: hence Russell's interest. Shortly afterwards, in 1852, a Frenchman, Charles Nisard, published a study of Casaubon alongside the two other pre-eminent classical scholars of his time, Joseph Scaliger and Justus Lipsius. Pattison reviewed the two books in the *Quarterly Review* in 1853.

This was an epoch-making event in Pattison's life, and not primarily because the most famous of the supposed literary representations of him would also bear the name Casaubon. The importance of the review in Pattison's literary and intellectual career is obscured by Henry Nettleship's decision to exclude it from his edition of Pattison's *Essays*, a decision taken, presumably, on the ground of the review's supersession by Pattison's full-length study of Casaubon published in 1875. But this was the first time – at the age of nearly 40 – that Pattison had published in one of the great literary reviews: indeed, it was the first time he had published anything outside Tractarian organs such as the *British Critic*, the *Christian Remembrancer*, and some collective projects of Newman's prior to his secession. It was also the first time Pattison had touched on what was to become his life's focus, the modern history of classical learning, or even, more broadly, on the intellectual history of modern Europe. His previous publications had been diverse, but they had clustered around two poles: early medieval history and historiography (articles on Gregory of Tours and on Bede, for instance) and recent history, politics and political economy (slavery, for instance, and Mill's *Principles of Political Economy*). These were not themes to which he would return, except incidentally. It was with his review of Casaubon's diary that Pattison, for the first time, truly found his voice as a scholar.[95]

Unlike many of Pattison's later reviews, this one was not commissioned by an editor, but was written out of passion for the subject. It is not clear

[95] A number of Pattison's more important essays flowed directly from his interest in Casaubon. In 1858 he wrote on Calvin's Geneva for the *Westminster Review*. Casaubon spent his formative years in Geneva teaching at the Academy Calvin had founded. In 1865 he contributed to the *Quarterly* a notable essay on the Estiennes, a distinguished family of Parisian and Genevan printers of the sixteenth and seventeenth centuries. Casaubon's second wife, Florence, was the daughter of the second Henri Estienne, c. 1531–98.

precisely when he encountered the *Ephemerides*, but he recalled that '[t]his curious book immediately riveted my attention'.[96] We do know that he read Nisard's sketch of Casaubon in October 1852, and that this gave him the idea of writing an article for the *Edinburgh Review*.[97] He worked on the article between then and January 1853, when he appears to have completed it. In the event, the *Edinburgh*'s editor turned it down because he had already offered the *Ephemerides* to an established reviewer; although ironically it was not reviewed in the *Edinburgh* until 1876, alongside Pattison's own book on Casaubon.[98] The article was instead taken by the *Quarterly*.

So what was it about Isaac Casaubon that fired Pattison's enthusiasm? Perhaps the reader will be able to guess: it was Casaubon the diarist who captured his interest. Or, rather, it was the survival of the diary as a point of access to the mind and character of the scholar. It was with the diary, and not with the broader significance of Casaubon's oeuvre, that Pattison's review began:

On his thirty-eighth birthday and the first year of his Professorate at Montpellier, Casaubon commenced a private Diary. He continued to keep it with a punctuality probably without parallel in the history of journalism, and which of itself indicates the man, till within a fortnight of his death in 1614. It is literally 'Nulla dies sine linea.'[99]

In his biography of Casaubon, Pattison would amplify the point. The nearest parallel, he now believed, was Joseph Priestley, who kept a diary of his studies from the age of twenty two to a few days before his death at the age of seventy one. But Priestley's diary 'shared the fate of all his collections, and became the victim of the savages of one of our great cities', whereas Casaubon's was preserved through the piety of his widow and son. Pattison commends the editor for resisting the temptation to produce only a selection of the most interesting extracts; for the fascination of the diary lay in 'the regularity of the entries'. A scholar's life, he notes, is 'seldom one of incident'; and Casaubon's diary is essentially a record of what he read and what he wrote. Reflections on that reading were reserved for other manuscript volumes. Public events rarely make an appearance. Pattison here describes Casaubon's diary; but he describes also his own. What matters about the scholar's life is not its public face but its private and internal aspect, and the lasting value of a scholar's diary lies in the glimpse it gives us into the interior life. 'We can read anywhere of the battle-field and the council-chamber – show us, if you

---

[96] Pattison, *Memoirs*, p. 318.  [97] Bodleian MS Pattison 129, ff. 77–9.
[98] *Edinburgh Review* 143 (Jan 1876), 189–222.
[99] [Mark Pattison], 'Diary of Casaubon', *Quarterly Review* 93 (Sept 1853), 462. 'No day without a line.'

can, the domestic interior. We are sated with state apartments, let us have a peep into the kitchen or the housekeeper's room.'[100]

But are we not here in danger of confusing two distinct senses of 'interior'? Granted, a glimpse into the soul of the scholar is precious to the historian; but can the same be said of his laundry bills? But for Pattison there is no confusion: for him, the pursuit of the life of the mind was quintessentially a test of character; and the character of the scholar was moulded through the acquisition of *habits* of learning. This is true, he thinks, of any scholar; it is pre-eminently true of Casaubon, 'our journalist', as he calls him. Whereas Scaliger stands for brilliance and Lipsius for wit, Casaubon represents 'laborious industry'. 'Having nothing excentric (sic) about him, he will for this very reason be a better representative man, and furnish a juster idea of the ordinary life of a classical scholar about A.D. 1600.'[101] It was precisely because of the importance of the cultivation of habits of intellectual labour that the minute regularity of the diary was so valuable: as he would later put it, evocatively, 'of the blood and sweat, the groans and sighs, which enter into the composition of a folio volume of learned research, no more faithful record has ever been written than Casaubon's "Ephemerides" '.[102] Pattison saw those habits tested most of all in the preparation of a critical edition. 'From Casaubon's commentaries', he wrote, 'we see that the style of his work demanded nothing less than a complete collection of the classical remains. He wants to found his remarks, not on this or that passage, but on a complete induction.'[103] These qualities were exhibited above all in his edition of *Athenæus*, a task whose 'arduous nature' could hardly be overstated:

Those who suppose that to edit a classic is among the easiest of literary toils, and only a fit occupation for laborious dulness, can form no conception of what Casaubon accomplished. Those only who know that a perfectly good edition of a classic is among the rarest of the triumphs which the literary Fasti have to record; that for the last three centuries we have been incessantly labouring at the Greek and Latin remains, and yet that the number which have been satisfactorily edited is fewer than some of the most popular of ancient authors who have been attempted the oftenest, as *e.g.*, Horace, still awaits a competent expositor – those only can measure what a giant's strength was required to cope with Athenæus, in the state in which his remains existed in the time of Casaubon.[104]

That intellectual labour was a pre-eminent test of character was one of Pattison's most deeply held convictions, and one on which he meditated

---

[100] Pattison, 'Diary of Casaubon', 463.    [101] Pattison, 'Diary of Casaubon', 463.
[102] Pattison, *Isaac Casaubon*, p. 123.    [103] Pattison, *Isaac Casaubon*, p. 38.
[104] Pattison, 'Diary of Casaubon', 479.

throughout his career. He would speak out, as we shall see, against the cult of business, or busy-ness, that he saw as the enemy of the life of the mind, but that should not lead us to think that there was anything of the dilettante in his conception of learning. The literary life was by no means 'a lazy profession' or 'an easy-chair and slipper business', but demanded 'time, industry, arduous endeavour'.[105] The 'bustle and stir', the 'unwholesome feverish pulse' that scarred Pattison's Oxford were inimical to intellectual endeavour, for that required not outward activity but 'true inward energy of philosophical pursuit'.[106] That learning was arduous and required deep reserves of character was a conviction that would stand at the centre of his biography of Isaac Casaubon, published more than two decades after he first encountered Casaubon's journal. 'If anyone thinks that to write and read books is a life of idleness', he there enjoined, 'let him look at Casaubon's diary'.[107] The highlight of the biography, and the section that made most impact on its readers, was undoubtedly the final chapter, which appraises Casaubon's significance. It is there that Pattison provided a much-quoted definition of learning:

Learning is a peculiar compound of memory, imagination, scientific habit, accurate observation, all concentrated, through a prolonged period, on the analysis of the remains of literature. The result of this sustained mental endeavour is not a book, but a man.[108]

What Pattison was doing, through his biography of Casaubon, was to vindicate the manliness of the scholar's life.[109]

Ultimately Casaubon's importance went far beyond the books he wrote. 'The many thousand pages which Isaac Casaubon wrote may be all merged in the undistinguished mass of classical commentary, and yet there would remain to us as a cherished inheritance, the record of a life devoted to learning.'[110] That example did not consist in genius, but in unremitting labour. Casaubon sacrificed his health, and sacrificed himself, for the cause of scholarship:

It is well that we should be alive to the price at which knowledge must be purchased. Day by day, night by night, from the age of twenty upwards, Casaubon is at his books. He realised Boeckh's ideal who has told us that in classical learning

---

[105] Pattison, 'Books and critics', 670.  [106] Pattison, 'Oxford Studies', p. 493.
[107] Pattison, *Isaac Casaubon*, p. 123.  [108] Pattison, *Isaac Casaubon*, p. 489.
[109] See Antonia Ward, 'Men at work: masculinity and late-Victorian literary labour', in Martin Hewitt (ed.), *Scholarship in Victorian Britain*, Leeds Working Papers in Victorian Studies volume 1 (Leeds: Leeds Centre for Victorian Studies, 1998), pp. 78–89.
[110] Pattison, *Isaac Casaubon*, p. 490.

'dies diem docet, ut perdideris quam sine linea transmiseris'. When he is not at his books, his mind is in them. Reading is not an amusement, filling the languid pauses between the hours of action; it is the one pursuit engrossing all the hours and the whole mind. The day, with part of the night added, is not long enough.'[111]

Not only was the scholar's life a laborious one, but it also yielded few rewards. One of Casaubon's mental habits was a tendency to depreciate his own achievements. Much the same could be said of Pattison, who attributed this characteristic of Casaubon's to 'the disparagement of secular knowledge in comparison of [sic] piety, which was the intellectual atmosphere he had to breathe'. But it could also be attributed to 'that oppression of mind, which the infinity of knowledge lays upon its votaries'. For Casaubon was oppressed 'not by hours of teaching, but by his own studies'. Here Pattison was unmistakeably autobiographical. The man of learning, he wrote, 'may joy in pursuit, but can never exult in possession', and more than the scientist he is subject to 'periods of darkness and gloom'. 'Research is infinite', Pattison concluded; it can never be finished.' That was why Casaubon, in his preface, in his commentaries, and in his letters, would constantly complain of lack of time, and it was why Pattison, in his diary, would do the same.'[112]

In his own *Memoirs*, Pattison depicted his own devotion to the life of learning as the product of a slow growth to self-consciousness. It owed little to his circumstances, and in fact was achieved in spite of the remoteness of his upbringing in Wensleydale, the indifference of his undergraduate contemporaries at Oriel, and the mediocrity of the teaching he received. He said much the same of Casaubon:

If it is the general law of nature that genius is evoked and nourished by its environment, Casaubon is a singular exception. Neither in Geneva, nor among his wider circle of correspondents, if we except Scaliger, whom he only came to know in 1594, had he rivalry, example, or encouragement. In Geneva nothing that could be called literary interest existed. A poor and starved seminary for pious training; a trading printing press for the sale of school-books, and sermons; a theology not formal, but infused through every day's life and thinking. An armed enemy crouched at their gates, watching his opportunity for the death spring; each day bringing news of some fresh outrage on their coreligionists, in the countries where the catholic reaction was in its full tide. On this ungenial soil, Casaubon developed out of his own instincts the true idea of classical learning. Not an idea of

---

[111] Pattison, *Isaac Casaubon*, p. 491. The Latin could be translated as 'each day informs the next, so that a day spent without reading a line is wasted'. I am grateful to Dr Ruth Morello for advice here.

[112] Pattison, *Isaac Casaubon*, pp. 59–60.

scientific philology as we conceive it, but that of a complete mastery of the ancient world by exhaustive reading; a reconstruction of Greek and Roman antiquity out of the extant remains of the literature. Instead of wondering that he allowed this ideal to be obscured to him by the clouds of party polemics, what is surprising is that he should ever have been able, an untaught and unfriended man, struggling himself with chill penury, to rise to it.[113]

Pattison's biography of Casaubon made an impact that is difficult to explain today. It was not that it sold well: indeed, when his tax inspector reminded him that his literary profits were subject to income tax, Pattison was evidently offended and complained that he had actually made a loss on the book. But the fact that a tax inspector, even in Oxford, should have been aware of the reception accorded to a biography of a Renaissance philologist is striking. 'I could not of course fail to know of the publication of the book', he wrote, 'and of the hearty reception accorded to it by the journals whose opinions I am most accustomed to respect'.[114] This reaction is less surprising when we realise that the *Times* accorded the book a three-column review, amounting to some five thousand words; and this at a time when the newspapers reviewed far less than they do now (it was one of just seven books to be reviewed in March 1875). It was a remarkably enthusiastic review. It began with the warning that 'the present age, it is to be feared, takes but a languid interest in the history of learning and scholarship.' Yet 'even the unlearned reader will find that [this] is a work replete with interest and instruction'. 'His [Pattison's] erudition is that patient and conscientious kind which is content to efface itself, and, disdaining a cumbrous accumulation of ill-digested material, to re-appear without ostentation in a pregnant sentence or a judicious epithet.' This was 'a work of literary art and skill, organic and complete, patiently thought out, and conscientiously executed, not like too many products of the hasty literary temper of the present age, a mere collection of ephemeral sketches on the one hand, or an amorphous heap of Dryasdust materials on the other.' 'We are confident that few serious readers, whatever their special interests, will take up "Isaac Casaubon" without reading it through'.[115] The reception accorded to the book by *The Times* was by no means untypical. In fact the book was almost universally hailed as a masterpiece. 'Every review great & small has reviewed and praised it and it has already taken a permanent place in English literature', wrote Richard Christie, who

---

[113] Pattison, *Isaac Casaubon*, pp. 58–9.
[114] William Whitwell to Pattison, 3 December and 4 December 1875, Bodleian MS Pattison 57, ff. 166–8.
[115] *The Times*, 8 March 1875, p. 4.

consoled Pattison for the disappointing sales of the book. The dean of Manchester, Christie reported, was 'delighted' with it.[116] Goldwin Smith told Pattison he had read the book with 'admiration and envy', while the social reformer James Kay-Shuttleworth mentioned that he was 'deep in the Life of Casaubon, & exceedingly interested by it'.[117] G. O. Trevelyan, who was completing his life of Macaulay at the time, later told Pattison he was reading *Casaubon* 'exactly at the time when I had still before me the whole task of portraying Macaulay's methods and habits as a writer and reader'. Without it, he said, 'I do not think that I should ever have had the courage deliberately, and at length, to dwell for so long on Macaulay's ways as a scholar'.[118] That comment is revealing, for it suggests that what was so striking about Pattison's book was that it evoked the working methods of the scholar with such power. Gladstone, as we have seen, was enthralled by this 'remarkable' book. A French reviewer considered this 'excellent' volume to be 'without doubt one of the most notable works recently published on the other side of the Channel', and regretted that it was not written by one of his fellow countrymen.[119] A rare exception to this almost universal acclaim was the Master of Balliol. He deplored what he diagnosed as Pattison's dependence on Bernays, 'a man of no real eminence', and saw that the book was no straightforward biography, but the exposition of the author's own values. 'The book is written', wrote Jowett, 'with an undercurrent of allusion to his own contemporaries which impairs its value as a biography.'[120] He must have known Pattison's opinions well enough to identify himself as the target of a barbed depiction of the decay of the Sorbonne in Casaubon's time:

The university of Paris, once the symbol and centre of European intelligence, was sunk into a corporation of trading teachers, whose highest ambition was to compete with the jesuits in a lucrative profession. It was become a school, of which the professors were the masters. They shrank from contact with real knowledge, such as Casaubon possessed, and carried it loftily towards him on the ground of their superior orthodoxy. They shut themselves up with their pupils, before whose wondering eyes they paraded their crude reading.[121]

[116] Richard Christie to Pattison, 12 & 17 November 1875, Bodleian MS Pattison 57, ff. 145–8.
[117] Goldwin Smith to Pattison, 25 November 1875 and James Kay-Shuttleworth to Pattison, 21 March 1875, Bodleian MS Pattison 57, ff. 157–8 & 54–5.
[118] G. O. Trevelyan to Pattison, 25 May 1876, Bodleian MS Pattison 57, ff. 260–1.
[119] Gustave Masson, 'Bibliographie, *Bulletin Historique et Littéraire de la Société de l'Histoire du Protestantisme Français* 24 (1875), 281, 285.
[120] Balliol College: Jowett Papers I.H 27 f. 77, diary 28 Aug. 1875.
[121] Pattison, *Isaac Casaubon*, p. 188.

Jowett – who had been for many years Regius professor of Greek at Oxford – may well have seen himself also in the depiction of Theodorus Marcilius, professor of Eloquence at the Collège Royal, the predecessor of the College de France. Indeed Pattison pointedly refers to Marcilius as 'the regius professor'. He quotes Casaubon as complaining to Scaliger of this 'Parisian schoolmaster, the most arrogant of all living two-legged creatures', a 'buffoon', whose 'ignorance' and 'asinity' were 'beyond anything I had conceived'.[122]

What did Pattison's contemporaries think was so 'remarkable' about his biography of Casaubon? It is certainly a very accomplished book, which like many of his writings has lasted well; but that is not quite enough to explain the nature of its reception. I think its reception is to be explained in three ways. The first point is an obvious one: the Victorian educated public was a *classically* educated public: classical philology, as practised by Casaubon, therefore possessed a cultural centrality of a kind that it lacks today. Next, the book was, as many commentators have observed, a biography in which an autobiography is concealed.[123] Pattison spoke from the heart, especially in his characterization of the life of learning in the final chapter. That gave the book powerful human interest. But, thirdly, it also appealed to readers because of its counter-cultural quality: that is, it set out an ideal of a life devoted to learning that stood out in opposition to much that was characteristic of Victorian society. Of course the emphasis on learning as a work of hard graft and sustained labour would have appealed to the Victorians' work ethic. Similarly, a Victorian public would have found much that was resonant in Pattison's portrayal of the scholarly life as a test of character. But all this challenged conventional assumptions about the nature of the intellectual existence – assumptions which were rooted in the traditional concept of the 'man of letters':

The public of a busy age and an industrial community has quite other notions of a literary life. It is conceived to be a life of ease; it is the resource of the indolent, who would escape from the penalty of labour. An arm chair and slippers before a good fire, and nothing to do but to read books. This is the epicurean existence, the 'nova Atlantis of mediocrity à l'engrais', which we call academic life. Of the self-denial, the unremitting effort, the incessant mental tension, the strain to touch the ever-receding horizon of knowledge, the fortitude which

---

[122] Pattison, *Isaac Casaubon*, pp. 189, 91.
[123] For example, Lloyd-Jones, *Blood for the Ghosts*, p. 17, and Nuttall, *Dead from the Waist Down*, pp. 2, 146.

'Through enduring pain,
Links month to month, with long-drawn chain
Of knitted purport,'
of the devotion of a life, the modern world of letters knows nothing. Our literature
is the expression of the life from which it emanates. It bears the stamp of half
knowledge. It is the dogmatism of the smatterer. It has no groundwork of science.
Its employment is to enforce the chance opinion of the day by epigram and
sarcasm. It hates and ridicules science. It disbelieves in it. Why is it that the
modern man of science stands on a higher level, moral and intellectual, than the
modern man of letters? It is not owing to any superior value in the object of
knowledge, but because the physicist is penetrated by the spirit of thorough
research, from which our literature is entirely divorced.[124]

What Pattison did, then, was to vindicate 'the sweetness that is found in
learning' by emphasizing that it is a sweetness tasted only as the fruit of
exhaustive labour.[125] That was a vindication that was destined to appeal to
the Victorian temper.

He elaborated this contrast between fundamental learning and the
literary productions of the moment in a review published just a year after
*Casaubon*. Commending Alexander Bain for having the courage and
strength of character to produce a thorough reworking of his *Emotions
and the Will* for its third edition, Pattison lamented how rare it was for
authors to subject themselves to the essential discipline of redrafting,
whether for a first or a subsequent edition. 'Our books are now thrown
off, as the daily paper is thrown off, written from the inspiration of the
moment, without correction or reconsideration.' As a compulsive redrafter
who had undergone this challenge so recently, Pattison was sure he knew
the reason. 'The operation of recasting thoughts is not merely laborious, it
has attached to it a mental pain of a peculiar kind. It implies a control of the
will over the intellectual processes, of a more severe kind than the spontaneous attention which easily follows the natural flow of the habitual
thoughts. Reproduction, reconstruction, revision, improvement, are far
more difficult operations than production and extempore gush.' The
danger was that the mental drudgery entailed by the process of revision
would stifle the originality of spirit that gives a book its interest.[126]

*Casaubon* was the fruit of over twenty years' intermittent work, and
much reworking. Yet it had not lost its 'originality . . . of mental spring' in

[124] Pattison, *Isaac Casaubon*, pp. 492–3.    [125] Pattison, *Isaac Casaubon*, p. 495.
[126] [Pattison], Review of Bain's *The Emotions and the Will*, 3rd edn, *Saturday Review* 41 (11 March 1876),
    335–6.

the process.[127] On the contrary, what was so powerful about the book was that Pattison was able to express himself, and his own conception of the life of learning, so evocatively through the portrait of Casaubon. This was what so vexed Jowett, who was notoriously unsympathetic to learning as Pattison understood it. It has often been said that the book was a disguised autobiography. We have seen that Pattison had been preoccupied, since undergraduate days, with the interior life of the scholar. But he had not yet formed any idea of writing his own life. There was something he found repugnant about the prospect: he called it egotistical when Meta Bradley first suggested it, but what he probably meant was that his whole being shied at the thought of exposing itself to the world.[128] Undoubtedly he found it easier to say what he wanted to say about himself through his study of Casaubon. When it was known that he had written a volume of memoirs, those who knew him expected him to appear before the world in disguise: behind a literary mask.[129] For that was what he had done in the life of Casaubon. Yet, contrary to these expectations, that was precisely what he did not do in the *Memoirs*.

There is a final observation to make. Pattison was intellectually drawn to the ascetic dimension of the life of the scholar, and he articulated this vision of the scholarly life both in his sermons and in the life of Casaubon. Evidently there was something in his personality that was attracted to asceticism; but to say that he was ascetic in character would be far from the truth. His was certainly not a life of personal sacrifice for the sake of learning. Had he followed Newman in 1845, or had he been prepared to follow through the logic of his break with orthodoxy in the last decade or so of his life, he would have had to make such a sacrifice; but he was not prepared to do so. His wife thought that, like all the Pattison family except Dora, he simply lacked any capacity for self-sacrifice. He was 'a creature intellectually greedy of satisfaction'.[130] His lack of altruism, she thought, 'shortened his arm among men': he was an icon of the intellectual life, but the deficiencies of his own character weakened his ability to act as an advocate for an ideal of life in which he sincerely believed.

---

[127] [Pattison], Review of Bain's *The Emotions and the Will*, 336, for 'originality . . . of mental spring'.
[128] Pattison to Meta Bradley, 20 Aug. 1881, Bodleian MS Pattison 122, ff. 1–4.
[129] R. S. Osler to T. F. Althaus, 3 Jan. 1885, Lincoln College MS/PAT/1/C.
[130] E. F. S. Pattison to Eleanor Smith, 22 Jan. 1880, Bodleian MS Pattison 118, f. 36.

# CHAPTER 5

# The endowment of learning

Pattison made his imprint on public controversy chiefly in the debates on university reform; and that meant, above all, the reform of the universities of Oxford and Cambridge. Oxford was his home from the age of eighteen to his death, but this was no merely parochial concern. His thinking about the reform of Oxford was informed by a profound knowledge of the history and present state of European universities. Moreover, although he loathed the Victorian passion for being busy, he willingly lent his support to newer universities, and university colleges, in England and Wales: he examined for University College London, served on the Council of University College Aberystwyth, and chaired the Committee of Management and subsequently the Council of Bedford College. He was a good friend to Owens College, Manchester, and became a member of the Court of the Victoria University at its inauguration in 1880.[1] As we have noticed, he was also an active supporter of the higher education of women.

There is a further point: the reform of the universities of Oxford and Cambridge was a hugely important issue in Victorian politics and public life. This was partly because at the beginning of the nineteenth century they were Anglican monopolies, and the principal route to ordination in the established church.[2] Steps to remove confessional restrictions, or to secularize the universities, inevitably awoke the passions of denomination and churchmanship that were the motors of so much of Victorian politics. Moreover, the colleges, viewed collectively, had huge endowments at their disposal, and even if their fellows were inclined towards reform, ancient statutes restricted the ways in which they could deploy their endowment

---

[1] 'Petitions from Yorkshire and Owens Colleges, praying for a Charter for the Creation of a University, to be called the Victoria University', House of Commons Papers 1880, vol. LIV, 368; also *Manchester Guardian*, 15 July 1880, pp. 5–6.

[2] At the time of Pattison's ordination, for example, more than 80 per cent of Anglican clergy were recruited from Oxford and Cambridge: Virgin, *The Church in an Age of Negligence*, p. 134.

income. As Pattison well understood, at a time when the resources of
central government were tiny by modern standards, and there were no
grants either to universities or to their students, the disposal of historic
endowments was a major issue on the agenda of Victorian reformers, and
affected not just universities, but cathedral chapters, public schools, and a
range of other august institutions. So to say that Pattison was one of the
foremost contributors to the debates on the reform of Oxford and
Cambridge, and that he had surely the most original and distinctive
voice in those debates, is to say something significant about his place in
public life.

Oxford and Cambridge were subjected to a barrage of criticism from the
late eighteenth century onwards.[3] In the *Wealth of Nations* Adam Smith
famously denounced the idleness of the professors, which he ascribed to
their being paid salaries out of endowments rather than being reliant on
fees from the students who chose to attend their lectures; and Gibbon's
autobiography, first published in 1796, mounted a no less famous assault
on the tutorial neglect he suffered at Magdalen in the era of 'port and
prejudice'. Utilitarians and Whigs lamented the 'uselessness' of Oxford's
classical curriculum, and argued that universities should be made to serve
the public interest by teaching 'useful knowledge' and preparing students
for the professions. But the decisive intervention came from the Scottish
philosopher Sir William Hamilton in a series of articles on Oxford published in the *Edinburgh Review* beginning in 1831. Hamilton was a Balliol
graduate, and like Smith he had a strong sense of the inadequacy of the
teaching he had received there; but the importance of his articles was due
chiefly to their dialectical astuteness and the deep and wide knowledge of
the history of European universities on which he based his argument.
Conservatives resisted reform by taking their stand on prescriptive rights
and the sanctity of the intentions of the founders of colleges; but Hamilton
studied the Laudian statutes of 1636 under which the university was
notionally still governed, and observed that those statutes provided for a
professorial system of specialized instruction across all the faculties: theology, civil law and medicine, as well as arts. This was what he called the
'authorized system'. The tutorial system run by the colleges, which was
originally an institutionalization of the historic right of all graduates to
teach, and to raise fees from their pupils, might have played a useful role in
supplementing the gratuitous instruction provided by the salaried professoriate, but instead the colleges had, over the centuries, usurped the

[3] See, notably, Briggs, 'Oxford and its critics', pp. 134–45.

university's role altogether. As a result professorial lectures were rarely given, and when given were rarely attended; instruction provided by the higher faculties withered; and elementary tuition for the arts course was the only form of teaching that survived.

It should be noted – for this was a point on which Pattison's thinking would diverge sharply from Hamilton's – that Hamilton's starting point was that the University and the colleges had fundamentally different functions. They were, as he put it, 'neither identical, nor vicarious of each other'. It could not be argued that the University had legitimately chosen to perform its statutory teaching functions through the agency of the colleges, for whereas the University was a national institution, founded solely for education, and run 'for the advantage of the nation', the colleges were private institutions established 'for the interest of certain favoured individuals'. Their existence was 'accessory and contingent' to the operation of the University, and their purpose was essentially to provide 'aliment and habitation'.[4] Pattison would certainly learn from Hamilton's insight that the colleges were not essentially educational bodies: what he saw, as Hamilton did not, was that whereas they had a tendency to degenerate into 'boarding-houses', their statutes conceived their purposes in grander terms concerned with the promotion of learning.

Hamilton's articles had a formative impact on the shape taken by the movement for university reform. His influence on the 1850 Royal Commission was patent: the Commissioners shared his view that the improvement of Oxford's teaching must depend chiefly on the restoration of the University as a teaching body. Since Pattison was later inclined to speak slightingly of the work of the Commission, it should be said that its proposals were far more radical than the Act of 1854, and that in some ways they anticipated Pattison's own ideas, notably in envisaging a hierarchical academic profession incorporating professors, sub-professors and tutors, and in acknowledging (under the influence of reformers such as Bonamy Price and Henry Vaughan) that professors were not simply university teaching officers but must themselves be learned authorities on their subjects.

***

---

[4] [Sir William Hamilton], 'On the state of the English universities, with more especial reference to Oxford', *Edinburgh Review* June 1831, reprinted in Sir William Hamilton, *Discussions on Philosophy and Literature, Education and University Reform* (London: Longman, Brown, Green and Longmans, 1852), p. 389.

Pattison's position in the debates on university reform has been much misunderstood. It is commonly asserted that he performed something of a volte face between his first intervention in these debates, in his evidence to the 1850 Royal Commission on Oxford University, and the mature statements of his position in his *Suggestions on Academical Organisation* (1868) and his evidence to the Royal Commission on Scientific Instruction (1870) and the Selborne Commission (1877).[5] The mature Pattisonian position has been caricatured, even by authorities such as John Sparrow. In these accounts he comes across as a revolutionary who wanted to abolish or emasculate the colleges and to reorganize Oxford as a university on the German model.[6] Not surprisingly, historians who have understood Pattison's proposals in this way have found that they were hopelessly ineffective and had little influence on the practice of university reform. But if we look anew at his classic statements we can see that his position was a much more complex and much more interesting one. He did not wish to import the German university to England, but instead to graft one central feature of the German university – the 'research ethic', or the obligation of the teachers to be themselves lifelong learners – onto an indigenous academic tradition. He argued that this would not be an alien implant, for the research ethic was a more faithful modern translation of the intentions of the medieval founders of colleges than was the practice of the academic life in early Victorian Oxford.

Pattison's first public statement on questions of university organization came with his evidence to the 1850 Royal Commission. On that occasion he spoke as one of the most notable of college tutors, and he explicitly and deliberately chose to restrict his evidence to the consideration of 'the University as a place of education', excluding 'all topics in which the constitution of that body as an academical corporation for the encouragement and maintenance of science and letters is involved'.[7] By 1850 he had definitively broken with Tractarianism and was clearly associated with the liberal reformers in university affairs; but Pattison was never simply a party man, and, at a time when liberals almost uniformly looked to the professorial system as a remedy for the defects of Oxford's teaching, he caused something of a stir by making a principled case from a liberal point of view in favour of the tutorial system against the professorial mode of

---

[5] For example, Heyck, *Transformation of Intellectual Life*, p. 176: 'Mark Pattison ... had done an about-face on the relative merits of colleges and universities, tutors and professors.'

[6] For references, see n. 74 below.

[7] University of Oxford Royal Commission, Minutes of Evidence:1852 Cmd 1482, vol. XXII, 41.

instruction. His case rested on the belief, which he never abandoned, that the 'insensible action of the teacher's character on the pupil's is the most valuable part of any education'. He opposed the admission of non-collegiate students, for they would be dependent on the public instruction offered by the university, and that would entail a 'mischievous' revolution, the substitution of the professorial for the tutorial system.[8] The professorial system, based on the *ex cathedra* lecture, was appropriate for communicating 'current information' to the masses'; but it required no greater mental effort than passive 'lecture-hearing' from the student. It was therefore an inferior mode of instruction to the tutorial system, especially if the aim were to produce 'a cultivated clerisy'. For the tutorial system, which he took to be defined not by the one-to-one tutorial but by the catechetical college lecture, typically put the burden of work on the student, and that was a more wholesome approach, for 'the best part of all education is that which a man does for himself'. It was, in fact, the closest approximation in the modern world to the Socratic principle of education at work.[9]

Pattison is commonly thought to have fundamentally changed his position on university reform between 1850 and 1877, and it is therefore important to combat potential misrepresentations of his position in 1852. In no way did he speak slightingly of the idea that universities should nurture advanced learning, and neither was he against professorships. He simply held that the role of a professor, at least in a university devoted to a liberal education, was to promote science and not to play a leading role in teaching.

The Professor *then* is not the organ of instruction; he is the man of greatest attainment in his branch, rewarded and withdrawn from instruction to enable him to devote himself to the cultivation of the more abstruse parts of his science. The Professor, as lecturer, has to deal with the superficies of his subject, and has his function in the superficial or popular system of education. The Professor, in our higher education, has his function in sustaining and advancing science, and representing its actual condition.[10]

Pattison at this stage did not deny the conception of the university as 'an academical corporation for the encouragement and maintenance of science and letters'; he simply did not regard it as his role to focus on that

---

[8] Royal Commission 1852 Cmd 1482, vol. XXII, 43–4.
[9] Royal Commission 1852 Cmd 1482, vol. XXII, 45, 48–9.
[10] Royal Commission 1852 Cmd 1482, vol. XXII, 46.

dimension.[11] In his mature statements, that was the idea of the university that he would make distinctively his own.

It was from the mid-sixties that Pattison came to occupy a central position in the public discussion of the role and organization of universities. He would give evidence to the Devonshire Commission on Scientific Instruction and the Selborne Commission on Oxford, as well as to the Schools Inquiry Commission (the Taunton Commission) in 1866. But he articulated his conception of the university at greatest length, and with most force, in a volume published in 1868 under the unpromising title, *Suggestions on Academical Organisation with especial reference to Oxford*. This book was by far the most important Victorian statement of the view that universities existed not simply for the sake of undergraduate education, but for the sake of the higher culture. 'It is the clearest, finest thing any of us people [that is, university liberals] had put forth', wrote James Bryce to Henry Sidgwick in January 1868; while Henry Nettleship told Bryce he found the book 'really masterly: thoroughly thought out & articulated from beginning to end'.[12] Even its opponents recognized it as a formidably systematic statement of a cogent conception of the university: it was a 'very able book', wrote Montagu Burrows, Chichele Professor of Modern History.[13] It immediately placed Pattison at the head of the campaign for what would become known, in the 1870s, as the 'endowment of research'. It attracted some notable allies, including Sidgwick and Seeley in Cambridge. The group's chief organizer, Charles Appleton, launched a periodical, *The Academy*, in 1869, which served in part as the mouthpiece of the campaign; and in 1876 he brought out a volume of *Essays on the Endowment of Research*, to which Pattison contributed an introductory essay. That campaign was by no means united in its objectives; it aroused a good deal of antagonism; and Oxford, like other British universities, remained chiefly focused on the education of undergraduates until well after 1945.[14] Nevertheless the research party was important in articulating an alternative view of the idea of a university, and gained some significant victories in the second wave of externally induced reform of Oxford in the 1870s.

[11] Royal Commission 1852 Cmd 1482, vol. XXII, 41.

[12] Bryce papers, Bryce to Sidgwick 4 Jan. 1868, quoted in Harvie, *Lights of Liberalism*, p. 94; MS Bryce 9 ff. 58–9, H. Nettleship to Bryce 6 Jan. 1868, MS Bryce 110, f. 46.

[13] [Burrows], 'University reform', *Quarterly Review* 124 (1868), 394.

[14] For the last point, see Brian Harrison (ed.), *The Twentieth Century* (Volume VIII of *The History of the University of Oxford*) (Oxford: Oxford University Press, 1994), and especially the chapter by Jose Harris, 'The arts and social sciences, 1939–1970', pp. 217–19.

There was a renewed interest in questions of university reform in the 1860s, largely stimulated by the growth of a powerful body of academic liberals. The reforms of the 1850s had, in retrospect, been quite limited: they were largely concerned with the introduction of open competition into the universities by the abolition of 'closed' fellowships, or fellowships restricted typically to natives of a particular county. They had not touched the Anglican monopoly on fellowships and other academic posts, but that was an issue which could no longer be ignored, and the tests were indeed to be abolished by Gladstone's first government in 1871. The prospect of the secularization of the university raised the question of what the university's purpose was, once it was shorn of most of its ecclesiastical functions. Whereas liberals were agreed that the secularization of the university was to be welcomed, the more fundamental question of the university's purpose divided them. There was a growing awareness of the need for some kind of public provision for science, and increasing recognition that German universities performed a larger intellectual function than did Oxford and Cambridge. At the same time, the advent of a mass suffrage in 1867 made it imperative to address the question of access to the university, which was restricted by the excessive costs of residence rather than by the intensity of competition for places.

## SUGGESTIONS ON ACADEMICAL ORGANISATION

Pattison's book should be understood as springing from two sources. On the one hand, it formed part of his lifelong reflection on intellectual culture. From this point of view, he was concerned to find institutional means of nurturing the possibility of a life devoted to disinterested study. The critic might say that it was self-indulgent of Pattison to seek to divert endowments to the support of the kind of existence to which he had devoted his life. This was, indeed, a standard line of attack on the 'endowment of research' party: as the High Church Tory MP for Cambridge, Beresford Hope, put it in the House of Commons in 1876, if research were to be endowed directly, 'the endowment of Research would soon become the research of endowment on the part of speculative philosophers'.[15] But it was Pattison's subjective experience of living a life devoted to learning that made him such a powerful voice for the articulation of the research ethic.

[15] *Parliamentary Debates* ccxxx, column 1087 (Second Reading of the University of Cambridge Bill, 6 July 1876).

On the other hand the book also sprang from his close involvement with university liberals in the 1860s. At the outset Pattison traces its origins to a meeting of 'a few members of Convocation' (that is, Oxford MAs) in May 1866, at the chambers of a Lincoln's Inn barrister, Osborne Morgan. The meeting expressed a wish, Pattison says, for 'fuller information and sug-gestions', and because no one else would undertake the task, Pattison himself drew up 'the following notes and hints'.[16] Frederic Harrison, coordinating the work of the London-based university reformers with that of their counterparts in Oxford, played a key role in convening the meeting, and his initial proposal was that Pattison, with two other resident dons, Goldwin Smith and Sir Benjamin Brodie, should 'draw up a report to be considered at a conference'.[17] That 'report' turned into Pattison's book. No conference of the kind envisaged appears to have taken place, unless the meeting at the Freemasons' Tavern in November 1872 served as such.

Pattison was more closely involved with the university liberals in the 1860s than at any other time in his career. His engagement diaries show him dining regularly with such prominent liberals as Brodie, Goldwin Smith, Bryce, Jowett and Grant Duff. His integration into this party was probably at its zenith in the early 1860s, no doubt in part because of his new-found eminence as a college head, which led his fellow liberals to expect great things of him – expectations which would be disappointed, at least as far as practical action was concerned. By the mid-sixties there were signs that his links were loosening: certainly he was more inclined than previously to decline invitations to liberal dining clubs in Oxford. But they were still strong enough for him to write the *Suggestions* at this group's prompting. This would have been inconceivable a decade later, when Charles Appleton had to cajole Pattison, much against his will, into contributing a short introductory chapter to the collective volume, *Essays on the Endowment of Research*.[18]

That Pattison, though never a party man, acquired a position of ascend-ancy among university reformers was not due solely to his seniority as a head. He had also acquired something of a reputation as an expert on the history of universities, and this enabled him to write with more authority and scholarly depth than his rivals could command on questions of

---

[16] Pattison, *Suggestions*, p. 1.
[17] Frederic Harrison to Pattison, 14 April 1866, Bodleian MS Pattison 56, ff. 212–3.
[18] Charles Appleton to Pattison, 16 December 1875 and 24 February 1876, Bodleian MS Pattison 57, ff. 172–3 and 212–3; also Pattison's diary, MS Pattison 130, f. 129, where he refers to Appleton's 'importunity'.

university organization. University history was an interest of Pattison's that stretched back at least as far as the early 1840s, when his diary would note isolated nuggets such as that 'The first College built in the University of Paris was the College of Navarre, built 1304 by Joan of Navarre.'[19] His status as an authority in this field no doubt owed much to his essay on 'Oxford Studies' (1855). Colleagues within the university and elsewhere would come to him with recondite queries about university history: in November 1856 a Cambridge don consulted him about the reform of his college statutes, explaining that he turned to Pattison because of his admiration of his contribution to *Oxford Essays*.[20]

The fact that Pattison's book was nurtured by his involvement with university liberalism should not detract from his large personal contribution to shaping the objectives of academic liberals towards provision for research, and so to the formation of the 'endowment of research' party. This was by no means the reason for which the meeting in Morgan's rooms in May 1866 was called: indeed, the positivist Harrison shared Comte's disdain for scientific specialization and on that basis was suspicious of the endowment of research.[21] Goldwin Smith, whom Harrison proposed as a collaborator for Pattison, would turn out to be no friend to the cause of the endowment of learning, and wrote a riposte to Pattison's book.[22] And Morgan himself, now Liberal MP for Denbighshire, spoke against the cause in the Commons in 1876.[23] The calling of the meeting seems to have had at least as much to do with the campaign for university extension, to judge from other correspondence of Pattison's in the preceding weeks.[24] This was a cause with which Pattison sympathized warmly, and its place in the genesis of the *Suggestions* helps explain why he went as far as he did in proposing the drastic reduction in the cost of an Oxford education by the elimination of residence in college as the norm for undergraduates. On the other hand he did not want to use endowment income to subsidize poor students: 'Instead of subsidising the poor student

[19] Bodleian MS Pattison 6, f. 127.
[20] H. J. Roby to Pattison, 17 Nov 1856, MS Pattison 51, ff. 293–4. For another instance, A. P. Stanley to Pattison, n.d. [1860], MS Pattison 53, f. 497.
[21] Martha S. Vogeler, *Frederic Harrison: The Vocations of a Positivist* (Oxford: Oxford University Press, 1984), p. 27.
[22] Goldwin Smith, *The Reorganization of the University of Oxford* (Oxford and London: Parker, 1868), pp. 1–2; Engel, *From Clergyman to Don*, pp. 131–3.
[23] *Parliamentary Debates* ccxxix, cols. 1726, 1729–30, Second Reading of the University of Oxford Bill, 12 June 1876.
[24] A. O. Rutson to Pattison, 17 March, 20 March, and 30 March 1866: Bodleian MS Pattison 56, ff. 160–3, 166–7, 179–80.

up to the level of our expenses', he proposed, having criticized schemes of means-tested exhibitions, 'we ought to bring down the expenses to the level of the poor.'[25]

The book was in some respects framed as a technical report rather than as either a literary dissertation or as a polemic. In making, at the outset, the case for the propriety of legislative intervention in the affairs of the university, Pattison almost immediately set before the reader a lengthy disquisition by his former pupil, the Chancery barrister William Stebbing.[26] It is clear from the ensuing pages, however, that Pattison's principal purpose was to make the case for the endowment of research from a liberal point of view. Liberal reform in the early and mid-Victorian period characteristically set out to 'nationalize' historic (and endowed) institutions: to make them serve the needs of the nation, broadly conceived, rather than sectional interests. Pattison's rhetoric appealed to that aim. He held (whereas many Tories did not) that the endowments of the colleges, like the monastic lands at the Henrician Reformation, were not private property, but national property, and the university and its constituent colleges were not 'a private enterprise, existing for their own purposes', but 'endowed corporations, through the medium of which the social body performs one of its vital functions'.[27] He characterized his proposals as 'but a very imperfect contribution towards a scheme for making Oxford fully adequate to the wants of the nation'.[28]

Casual acquaintance might lead the reader to suppose that Pattison's objective was to divert endowments from teaching to research; but this would be to mistake both his purpose and his tactics. He never implied that the teaching of undergraduates was tangential to the academic life, and both in 1852 and in 1877 the evidence he gave to university commissions focused explicitly on the educational side of the University's work. Moreover, from a tactical point of view it would have been a mistake for the endowment of research party to allow itself to be portrayed as undervaluing the activity of teaching.

Pattison instead depicted research and teaching as complementary activities, and set out 'to erect teaching and learning, inseparably united,

---

[25] Pattison, *Suggestions*, p. 76.
[26] Pattison wrote to Stebbing in April 1866 (that is, prior to the meeting at Morgan's chambers) to ask him his legal opinion on the status of the property of colleges: Lincoln College MS/PAT/I, Pattison to Stebbing, 20 April 1866.
[27] Pattison, *Suggestions*, pp. 20–1. For a Tory denial that university and college endowments were national property, see Parliamentary Debates ccxxx, col. 1080, Beresford Hope in the debate on the Second Reading of the University of Cambridge Bill, 6 July 1876.
[28] Pattison, *Suggestions*, 1.

into a life-profession'.[29] The interdependence of teaching and research, one of the principles articulated by Humboldt at the foundation of the University of Berlin in 1810, has become – as W. R. Ward could already write in 1965 – one of 'the familiar clichés of the modern universities';[30] but Pattison had a distinctive, trenchantly articulated and passionately held point of view which is still worth listening to, alien though it may be in some respects to the academic world of today. It is sometimes thought that Pattison favoured the separation of the two activities, because some members of the research party, such as Appleton, adopted that position in the 1870s, and Pattison's critics, when they asserted (inaccurately) that his own scholarly productivity had been at its peak in the days when he was an active tutor rather than an inactive head, assumed that he shared Appleton's position.[31] This is the reverse of the truth, on two counts. First, it is a curious fact about Pattison's academic career that his tutorial career and his literary career were chronologically almost wholly separate. As a tutor, he published only in High Church organs, and on a disparate range of subjects prompted, apparently, simply by the books he was asked to review. It was in 1853 – when his interest in teaching was clearly waning, and just a couple of years before he resigned the tutorship – that his article on Casaubon's diary really launched his literary career: it was his first piece in one of the heavyweight periodicals (the *Quarterly*), and it was his first and decisive step towards academic specialization.

The second reason why this line of criticism of Pattison is incorrect is that, far from wanting to establish an institutional separation of the activities of teaching and research, he in fact urged that university teaching properly understood could only be undertaken by people who were 'researchers', in the special sense in which he used the term: that is, who were themselves actively engaged in a continuing process of learning and improving their minds, as opposed to simply reading ahead of their pupils. That is why he proposed, in the *Suggestions*, a career hierarchy stretching from the tutor to the professor and the senior fellow. This was intended to emphasize and institutionalize the interdependence, rather than the

---

[29] Pattison, *Suggestions*, p. 204. The complementarity of teaching and research in Pattison's thought is discussed by D. B. Nimmo, 'Mark Pattison and the dilemma of university examinations', in Roy MacLeod (ed.), *Days of Judgement: Science, Examinations and the Organization of Knowledge in late Victorian England* (Driffield: Nafferton Books, 1982), especially pp. 162–4.

[30] W. R. Ward, *Victorian Oxford* (London & Edinburgh: Cass, 1965), p. 293.

[31] Goldwin Smith, *Reminiscences*, p. 85, who explicitly states that Pattison held that the holders of University positions should be 'left perfectly free from fixed duties', says that Pattison produced his life of Casaubon while a college tutor. In fact it appeared two decades after he had relinquished the tutorship, and almost fifteen years into his rectorship.

separation, of teaching and research. It was evidently a position many found difficult to grasp. When he gave evidence to the Selborne Commission in 1877 he set out to explore the fundamental question, 'what is the general nature of the education that we intend the university to convey', and asserted a high concept of the office of a university teacher as one of 'spiritual ministration'. This was a lifelong conviction of his, but it was not what the Commissioners expected him to say. So when he had completed his evidence, the Conservative MP Sir Matthew Ridley commented, 'You are viewing the university in the main as a place for learned study in the remarks which you have made to us, leaving almost altogether out of sight the educational view of the university'. Pattison, evidently feeling that the questioner had missed the whole point of his evidence, responded tetchily: 'I beg your pardon, I was viewing the university entirely as an educational body, and directing my remarks to the effect of the arrangement of the colleges as to scholarship and fellowships upon the character of the education given.'[32] For Pattison, Oxford's teaching had certainly become more energetic and industrious since the reforms of 1854, but it would not attain the highest quality until its teachers took seriously their mission as men of learning.

But how could research, or higher learning, be funded by the universities, if not at the expense of teaching? Pattison answered that this could be achieved by the diversion of endowments currently used to fund fellowships. This was not in itself an original approach to university reform: the 1854 Act had attempted to release funds (though not for research) by the suppression of fellowships. But it was rhetorically and tactically important for Pattison to be able to show that fellowships as currently constituted were not an endowment of teaching. On the contrary, they were awarded as prizes, or 'pensions', conferred 'in recompense or acknowledgment of meritorious exertions in the past', and entailed no duties.[33] A fellow might choose to teach; but his stipend was his whether he taught or not, and whether he resided in Oxford or not. Fellowships, as prizes, were no different in kind from undergraduate scholarships and exhibitions: the only difference was that a scholarship rewarded the undergraduate for his achievements as a schoolboy, whereas a fellowship rewarded the young graduate for his achievements as an undergraduate.

---

[32] University of Oxford Royal Commission, Minutes of Evidence: Parliamentary Papers 1881, Cmd 2868, lvi, 255, 257. Ridley was a former fellow of All Souls and a future Home Secretary.
[33] Pattison, *Suggestions*, p. 87.

Granted that a fellowship imposed no obligation to teach, and granted also that fellows who taught were paid additional emoluments for their tutorial work out of the fees paid by the undergraduates; nevertheless, it might be objected, could not a fellowship be construed as a subsidy to the educational work of the college? In the absence of endowed fellowships, would colleges not have had to raise their tutors' pay? Pattison denied this. He argued that the typical pay of a tutor, without his fellowship, was higher than he might expect in an alternative occupation for a young graduate, as a curate or a junior barrister.[34] Economic logic seems to be on Pattison's side here. Given that the fellowship was his for life, on condition only of celibacy, if the college wished him to teach it would have to pay him a fee comparable to what he would earn in other occupations readily open to him. On the other hand, Pattison came to concede that the emoluments of college headships, insofar as they were sinecures rather than onerous administrative posts, and the purchase of advowsons out of the endowment fund could both be considered indirect subsidies to tuition, in the form of 'retiring pensions to college tutors'. This was because an important incentive for a fellow to take on a college tutorship, as opposed to entering another profession, such as the bar, was the prospect of succeeding in time either to a college living or to a headship.[35]

On this basis, and setting aside this concession, Pattison was able to add expenditure on fellowships to that on scholarships and exhibitions, and so to calculate that by far the greater part of endowment income was spent on prize-money.[36] Only a negligible fraction was devoted to science and learning. If prize-money were diverted to the salaries of professional academics, devoted to the pursuit of advanced learning and the specialist teaching of their subject, then teaching, far from suffering, would in fact benefit from the endowment of research.

The centrepiece of Pattison's scheme was the proposal to reallocate college endowments to the support of faculties. College fellowships would be reassigned to form a graduated professoriate which would rise from the post of tutor, through that of lecturer, to that of professor, with a small number of senior fellowships or headships to crown the careers of the leading professors. Any Master of Arts would be entitled to register himself as a tutor in his faculty, and would live off the fees he was able to earn from

---

[34] Pattison, *Suggestions*, p. 93.
[35] Pattison, 'What measures are required for the further improvement of the universities of Oxford and Cambridge?', *Transactions of the National Association for the Promotion of Social Science* 12 (1868), 389.
[36] Pattison, *Suggestions*, p. 119.

his pupils; he would then be eligible to stand as a candidate for a salaried lectureship. Professorships would be filled by open competition.

Much of this looks like a far-sighted plan for a modern academic profession and career structure, and in many ways that is what it was.[37] Today's readers will nevertheless notice some curiosities, such as Pattison's reluctance to deploy endowment income to support young graduates: instead, they would have to make their way in the world of science or humane learning while supporting themselves by the fees earned from teaching. And, as we shall see, Pattison's sense of the centrality of science and higher learning to the life of the university fell short of a championship of original research. The professoriate's function was, he thought, 'to maintain, cultivate, and diffuse extant knowledge'. He understood this as an 'everyday function', quite distinct from the 'very exceptional pursuit of prosecuting researches or conducting experiments with a view to new discoveries'. The promotion of 'original research' in this special sense was, he thought, the responsibility not of universities but of academies such as the Royal Society.[38] It was certainly not that he thought scientific discovery beyond the scope of the university. But it was learning and intellectual depth, rather than original research, that was the distinctive vocation of the academic as he understood it.

Pattison has acquired a reputation for incapacity in the conduct of business, and the endowment of research party has on the whole had a bad press from university historians, who have seen it as ineffective in putting forward workable proposals capable of winning support beyond its own tiny coterie of members.[39] But Pattison can scarcely have thought that he was putting forward a set of proposals likely to be adopted by the university: rather, his aim was to articulate a clear alternative vision of a university's purpose. Controversial though the book was, it was largely to its credit, and testimony to the cogency and depth of the case he propounded, that the interests of science and learning came to be at the heart of the debate on university reform in the 1870s. He was cited personally in parliamentary debates by M. E. Grant Duff, a warm friend of the cause of the endowment of research, as well as by Lyon Playfair, who, though a

---

[37] The 'sharply modern' character of Pattison's argument is emphasized by Christopher Harvie, 'Reform and expansion, 1854–1871', in Brock and Curthoys, *Nineteenth-Century Oxford*, Part 1, p. 719. See also Calder and Kramer, *Introductory Bibliography*, p. 260, who consider it a 'brilliant book, far ahead of its time, that failed to influence contemporaries'.

[38] Pattison, *Suggestions*, pp. 171–2. On this point see also Nimmo, 'Mark Pattison and the dilemma of university examinations', pp. 153–67.

[39] Engel, *From Clergyman to Don*, pp. 188–9.

professor of chemistry, was more of a sceptic.[40] Pattison's case was bolstered by the Devonshire Commission on Scientific Instruction, to which he had given evidence. Its report criticized the low level of endowment for science in Oxford. And, while the movement for the endowment of research was by no means a homogeneous and well-organized campaign, it put its case effectively enough to persuade the 1877 commissioners to establish a Common University Fund, financed by compulsory contributions from the colleges, out of which the creation of new professorships, readerships and lectureships could be supported. It is striking, but often overlooked, that the most vociferous opponents of the endowment of research regarded the 1877 Act, and the subsequent work of the Commissioners, as a defeat.[41]

Pattison also looked to other institutions within the university to promote learning. The University Museum, established in the 1850s, was regarded as a conspicuously successful instance of the endowment of science in Oxford, and Pattison used what influence he had to create comparable institutions to promote learning in the humanities. He served for many years as curator of the Bodleian Library and of the Taylorian Institute, which had been founded in 1845 for the promotion of the study of modern European languages, and he used his position to encourage these institutions to realise that their role was to nurture advanced learning in the humanities. He did much the same as a delegate to the Clarendon Press. It was at his instigation, in the first place, that the Press established what became known as its 'learned fund', the purpose of which was to facilitate 'the publication by the Delegates of Learned and unremunerative Works'.[42] Pattison's influence is also visible – alongside that of Max Müller – in the decision of the delegates in 1878 to write to the University Commissioners urging them to make available resources released by the suppression of prize fellowships to reinforce the learned fund, and so to 'enable scholars, particularly members of the University, to collect materials for the edition of works considered desirable in the interests of scholarship and science'. The letter they wrote gave a characteristically Pattisonian historical context for the decision. The delegates had always undertaken the publication of

---

[40] *Parliamentary Debates* ccxxx, cols. 1104 (Grant Duff) and 1069 (Playfair), Second Reading of the University of Cambridge Bill, 6 July 1876. Playfair declined to give his adhesion to 'the movement for diverting its funds to the endowment of research unconnected with teaching duties'.

[41] Hon. George Charles Brodrick, *Memories and Impressions 1831–1900* (London: Nisbet, 1900), p. 169.

[42] Archives of the Oxford University Press, Orders of the Delegates of the Clarendon Press 1853–81, minutes of 23 Feb., 10 March, 27 Oct. 1871.

unremunerative works 'in the interests of Science and Learning', and this, it was asserted, was one reason why Laud had secured for the University the inestimable privilege of printing Bibles and Prayer Books. They were now eager that the Press should enhance its contribution to the University's efforts in the direction of 'the increase of knowledge and the advancement of science'.[43]

## ENDOWMENTS

It was largely due to Pattison's influence that the campaign for the public funding of research or advanced learning framed its objectives in terms of the *endowment* of research: others insisted on 'research', whereas Pattison might have preferred 'learning', but 'endowment' was very much Pattison's term. The use of this word deserves comment. No doubt there were local reasons for its use: in Oxford and Cambridge, the colleges possessed substantial endowments, and reformers urged that these should be used to support higher learning rather than to subsidize the teaching of under-graduates. In other contexts the word 'endowment' was used much more loosely to indicate any kind of financial provision – just as towards the end of the century campaigners would speak of their aim as the 'endowment of old age' and in the twentieth century campaigners for family allowances the 'endowment of motherhood'.[44] This was presumably what Herbert Spencer had in mind when he identified the endowment of research as one aspect of the reversion, in late-Victorian England, from an 'industrial' type of voluntary cooperation to a 'militant' mode of social organization founded on compulsory cooperation. He evidently interpreted the term 'endowment' to mean 'public funding'.[45] But the use of the term is rhetorically and ideologically interesting.

Much reforming effort in nineteenth-century Britain was directed at the dissolution or diversion of historic endowments. Whereas conservatives regarded founders' intentions as sacrosanct, the reformers insisted that

---

[43] Archives of the Oxford University Press, Orders of the Delegates of the Clarendon Press 1853–81, minutes of 29 Nov. 1878. Pattison's allies on the Board of Delegates would have included Stubbs and Max Müller.

[44] Charles Booth, *Pauperism; a picture: and Endowment of old age; an argument* (London: Macmillan, 1892); Montagu David Eder, *The Endowment of Motherhood* (London: New Age Press, 1908); Eleanor F. Rathbone, *The Disinherited Family: A Plea for the Endowment of the Family* (London: Arnold, 1924).

[45] Herbert Spencer, *The Principles of Sociology* (London: Williams and Norgate, 1882), vol. II, p. 591; Herbert Spencer, 'The Man versus the State', in his *Social Statics, abridged and revised; together with The Man versus the State* (London: Williams and Norgate, 1892), p. 289.

ancient foundations must be made to serve the interests and purposes of the living. John Morley called this one of the burning questions of the age, and Lawrence Goldman has shown how Gladstone's first government's sponsorship of the reorganization of educational endowments was a key factor in the flight of the metropolitan middle class to the Tories in the 1874 election.[46] Perhaps the most famous example of a campaign of this kind is a fictional one from Anthony Trollope's Barchester. There the reformer John Bold launches an attack on the misuse of the revenues from Hiram's charity. These revenues had grown, over the centuries, to such an extent that, while provision for the poor had been continued on the modest scale envisaged by the fifteenth-century founder, the wardenship had become a plum sinecure in the hands of the precentor of the cathedral. The letter of the founder's intention had not been violated, but the changed circumstances meant that the spirit of the endowment certainly had been.

Reformers' and liberals' suspicion of endowments was rooted in the ideas of the classical economists: endowments, like entails, allowed a former owner to dictate from the grave the uses to which property could be put, and this was manifestly contrary to the interests of economic efficiency and the maximization of utility. Adam Smith was particularly trenchant: in the *Wealth of Nations* he bluntly maintained that 'The endowments of schools and colleges have necessarily diminished more or less the necessity of application in the teachers.'[47] This was the context in which he famously asserted that 'In the university of Oxford, the greater part of the publick professors have, for these many years, given up altogether even the pretence of teaching.'[48] Goldwin Smith, one of the leaders of academic liberalism in Oxford, endorsed this line of argument in a riposte to Pattison. 'Intellectual labour is not so different from all other kinds of labour', he wrote, 'as to be stimulated by that by which any other kind of labour would be paralysed.'[49]

In the early Victorian period it was the accepted view among reformers that the tendency of endowments was to set founders' intentions in

---

[46] John Morley, *The Life of William Ewart Gladstone* (London: Macmillan, 1905) vol. II, p. 946; Lawrence Goldman, 'The defection of the middle class: the Endowed Schools Act, the Liberal Party, and the 1874 election', in Peter Ghosh and Lawrence Goldman (eds.), *Politics and Culture in Victorian Britain: Essays in Memory of Colin Matthew* (Oxford: Oxford University Press, 2006), pp. 118–35.

[47] Adam Smith, *An Inquiry into the Nature and Causes of the Wealth of Nations*, R. H. Campbell, A. S. Skinner, & W. B. Todd (eds.) (Oxford: Oxford University Press, 1976), p. 760.

[48] Smith, *Wealth of Nations*, p. 761.

[49] Goldwin Smith, *Reorganization of the University of Oxford*, p. 2.

stone and so to obstruct the progressive movement of society. From time to time endowed corporations such as colleges would have to be remodelled by Act of Parliament, which is what happened, in Oxford's case, in the Oxford University Act of 1854 as a result of the findings of the 1850 Royal Commission. In the 1860s the Taunton Commission inquired into the state of the endowed schools, and found many of them wanting: one of its assistant commissioners, the schools inspector J. G. (later Sir Joshua) Fitch, denounced 'that reverential regard for the rights, and even for the whims of testators, which has become a sort of social superstition in England'. This superstition, he argued, allowed what was effectively government by a 'parliament of dead men – self-constituted, heterogeneous, and wholly incompetent'. Fitch looked enviously to France, where the Napoleonic civil code stipulated that a private individual wishing to bequeath his property for public purposes must leave the property to a body recognized as a 'civil person', rather than, as in England, nominating a body of private trustees.[50]

But by the time Fitch wrote, and the campaign for the endowment of research was launched, opinion was becoming a little more complex. John Stuart Mill's article on 'Endowments', in the radical *Fortnightly Review* in April 1869, contested Fitch's arguments and marked something of a turning point. Mill began with the assertion that the reformers of the last generation had won the argument, so that 'with the bulk of the nation the indefeasibility of endowments is a chimera of the past'.[51] He then set out to counter the extreme position that 'endowments, or certain great classes of them at least, even when their purposes have not ceased to be useful, are altogether an evil, as the purposes would be better attained without them'; and the proposal that new endowments should be allowed only with the express approval of public authority. Here Mill saw the spectre of the dead hand of centralized government, and against it he asserted the principle that 'what the improvement of mankind and of all their works most imperatively demands is variety, not uniformity'.[52] So long as a limit were set on their inviolability – fifty or a hundred years might be appropriate – endowments helped sustain that pluralism of social institutions which would foster the innovations and experience without which there would be no progress.

---

[50] Joshua Girling Fitch, 'Educational endowments', *Fraser's Magazine* 79 (1869), 10–11.
[51] John Stuart Mill, 'Endowments', in *Essays on Economics and Society* II (*Collected Works of John Stuart Mill* vol V), p. 615.
[52] Mill, 'Endowments', 617.

Pattison, like Mill, had an interesting and subtle perspective on the role of endowments. Broadly speaking, those liberals who opposed endowments on principle, seeing them as a cover for privilege, tended to consider society as a rather simple mechanism: to see its simplicity we needed sharp analytical tools, such as classical political economy and utilitarian ethics and jurisprudence, which would help us cut through the obfuscations of traditionalists. Robert Lowe, Gladstone's first Chancellor of the Exchequer, may be taken as representative of this outlook. 'An endowment takes no note of competition', Lowe observed. 'It relies not on the interest of those who are to work, but on formal rules and statutes; and expects men without the stimulus of hope and fear, without competition, to do their duty when it is directly opposed to their interest. Not being founded on the principles of human nature it fails, and in my view, must fail.'[53] Those who saw society as a complex organism, especially if they were receptive to historicist insights, were more inclined to apprehend the social utility of endowments, even though they accepted the liberal reformist principle that the test of the proper use of endowments was not founders' intentions but the national interest. Pattison belonged to the latter class. He declined to give a definite opinion on 'the abstract question of endowed establishments', noting that it was 'one of those points which the progress of political expediency is considered to have still left undecided'. He was aware that an important current of public opinion opposed endowments on principle, and he did not wish to weaken his case by taking the principle of endowment for granted. Indeed, he conceded that in a society 'organised for permanence', endowments would not be needed, since all that the nation wanted to provide collectively it would be prepared to pay for out of general taxation. But he had to deal with 'a transitional period of society', and 'an imperfect stage of national life requires other aids' than those needed in a perfectly organized society.[54]

What did Pattison mean by this? We should not infer that he was a perfectibilist who considered imperfect social organization a merely transitional phenomenon. The contrast he draws between transitional periods and periods in which society is 'organised for permanence' was a familiar positivist trope: the Comtists spoke of 'critical' and 'organic' periods. Pattison was deeply interested in positivism, in much the way Mill was: both men thought it posed vital questions, especially about the laws of historical development. But like Mill he baulked at some of the answers

---

[53] Robert Lowe, *Middle Class Education. Endowment or Free Trade* (London: Bush, 1868), p. 15.
[54] Pattison, *Suggestions*, pp. 49–50.

the positivists offered, and especially he baulked at their intellectual authoritarianism. That authoritarianism underpinned the concept of an organic phase of social development, the key structural characteristic of which was that society came to acknowledge a settled authority in intellectual, moral and spiritual matters, an authority comparable to that of the clergy of pre-Reformation Christendom. Pattison always deplored the positivist tendency to look to science to act as an authority of this kind: for him, the critical spirit was essential to science, and indeed to the university properly understood. So it is highly unlikely that he seriously envisaged the arrival of a state of society in which endowments would be unnecessary. Instead, he set out to disarm anti-endowment fundamentalists by making it clear that, whatever might be appropriate in an ideal society, he was dealing with actual social needs in an increasingly complex society.

Because Pattison was well aware that endowments must be considered national property, he appreciated that endowed institutions such as colleges and universities could not escape public scrutiny. In his *Suggestions* he showed himself acutely conscious of public perceptions of universities and the need to change those perceptions. At the same time, in comparison with reliance on either the taxpayer or the free market, endowments provided some degree of protection from the transient whims of the public. For that protection to be strengthened it was important that the nation should understand that academic endowments existed for a purpose, indeed 'a great national purpose'. Pattison saw the feverish activity – to his mind, an essentially purposeless activity – of the dons of reformed Oxford as a response to a lack of public confidence in the legitimacy of their endowments: 'no great or noble purpose can be answered by endowments when the national grantor allows them to subsist with a half suspicion that they are an abuse, and the grantee is compelled to vindicate his right to live by convulsive efforts to do something or other, merely as evidence of activity'.[55] This is a very Pattisonian remark, which recalls his observation in the *Memoirs* that the university had become like 'a lively municipal borough'.[56] 'Oxford is a very busy place', he said elsewhere. It was not a compliment. For what was the reason? 'We are in the perpetual bustle of preparing for examinations.'[57] In the face of the onward march of the scientific movement, not just in

---

[55] Pattison, *Suggestions*, p. 51.   [56] Pattison, *Memoirs*, pp. 89–90.
[57] Pattison, 'Address on Education', *Transactions of the National Association for the Promotion of Social Science* 21 (1876), 66.

the natural sciences but in philology and history too, 'we have been busy in correcting exercises and awarding prizes'.[58]

This critique of Oxford's convulsive activity rested on Pattison's conception of the life of learning as a life of retirement. This did not mean idleness, and as we have seen Pattison took pains to represent the scholarly life as a laborious life. But it did mean that a life devoted to science and to the pursuit of truth was a life which was fundamentally incompatible with the impulse to be active in the world. He did not believe that academics were called to be Left Bank public intellectuals, nor that they should compensate for the lightness of their official duties by offering themselves for acts of service to the state on royal commissions and the like. London University, he thought, had been 'crushed under the superior weight of metropolitan life': a provincial location was on the whole preferable, because a university, like the poet's garden, should be situated 'Not wholly in the busy world, nor quite beyond it.'[59] This helps us to see why he regarded endowments as such an appropriate way of making provision – a national provision – for academic pursuits.

Pattison's position here may be compared to Tocqueville's analysis of the fate of science and learning in democratic society. Tocqueville, it should be remembered, did not define 'democracy' in narrowly political terms, but saw it as denoting a type of social structure in which status and rank were supplanted by the growth of equality of conditions. He did not think that democratic society – which, at least in the American case, meant a society geared to commerce – would necessarily be antagonistic to science: on the contrary, it would as a rule be zealously interested in the practical uses of scientific discovery. But democracies were typically characterized by restlessness, and this was difficult to reconcile with disinterested learning and pure science, which demanded a certain degree of space for 'meditation' and a certain distance from the world of business and the pressing concerns of the moment:

Everyone is on the move, some in quest of power, others of gain. In the midst of this universal tumult, this incessant conflict of jarring interests, this endless chase for wealth, where is one to find the calm for the profound researches of the intellect? How can the mind dwell on any single subject when all around is on the move and when one is oneself swept and buffetted along by the whirling current which carries all before it?[60]

---

[58] Pattison, 'What is a college?', 72.    [59] Pattison, 'Oxford Studies', p. 420.
[60] Alexis de Tocqueville, *Democracy in America*, edited by J. P. Mayer and translated by George Lawrence (London: Fontana, 1994), p. 460. This is from the volume first published in 1840. I have modified the translation very slightly.

Pattison could have echoed all this. He would certainly have echoed Tocqueville's disdain for the many who show 'a selfish, commercial, and banal taste for the discoveries of the mind', in contrast to 'the disinterested passion [for learning] which burns in the hearts of the few'.[61] It was the distinctive role of the university to nurture that disinterested passion for knowledge: its practical applications needed no special protection.

Yet universities were being distracted from their proper purpose by the urge to be busy. The same, according to Pattison, was increasingly true of the church. The Church of England had once been distinguished by its learned clergy, and cathedral canonries, in particular, had been used to nurture theological and historical learning. But the cathedral endowments had now been dispersed. 'This wanton havoc', Pattison wrote, 'has been committed, not by confiscating statesmen, but by the hands of the bishops, and the consent of the Church herself, which has come to believe that more churches and more services were what were wanted, and that if she got them, she would do well enough without learning.' Prestige now attached to the 'active clergyman' devoted to parochial 'work', and distinguished by 'energy, without development of either mind or character'. This was the type of incumbent who 'builds new schools, and looks in upon the school-master daily', who 'substitutes open seats for pews . . . and works the fabric of the old church, inside and out, up to the mark of the established fashion of the day in decoration'. The active clergyman 'is not "idle", as he can truly boast; for indeed he has not spent an hour a day in solitary and studious retirement since he was ordained.' He was therefore 'as different from the easy-going divine and scholar of the eighteenth century as he is from the Hookers and Herberts of the seventeenth'. The result was that the church was 'fast losing even the lowest form of the tradition of learning'.[62]

Pattison's critique of Oxford on the one hand and the Church of England on the other as sites of convulsive activity which acted in opposition to the true purpose of university and church was a bold and perceptive critique which took issue with the dominant values of Victorian England, where energy and vitality of will were cherished. It is at this point, therefore, that it is appropriate to address Pattison's role as a cultural critic.

So many Victorian writers set themselves up in opposition to the hegemonic values of their time that it is sometimes difficult to find an archetypal Victorian. 'Victorian values' have proved remarkably diverse,

[61] Tocqueville, *Democracy in America*, p. 461.
[62] Pattison, 'Learning in the Church of England', pp. 299, 275–6.

and they defy easy invocation by those who would use them for partisan purposes today. Pattison, however, had a distinctive and perhaps unique line in cultural criticism which has never received any attention from students of Victorian cultural debates. As we have already seen, he made extensive use of the concept of character, and endorsed his contemporaries' inclination to see it as a pivotal ethical concept. But in attaching it, some-what counter-intuitively, to scholarship and mental cultivation, he impli-citly took issue with the gospel of work and especially with the cult of activity. In fact he acknowledged that character and the philosophical life were not natural partners: the public was not wrong to see '[t]he tendency of abstract thought and various knowledge to enervate the will' as 'one of the real dangers of the highest education', and the scholarly temper was often accompanied by 'an Oriental lassitude of habit'.[63] Pattison's critics would have remarked that he himself amply exemplified these dangers; and some reviewers said precisely that when his *Memoirs* were published. But he held that they were dangers rather than necessities, and he thought the important task was to challenge the tendency of energetic activity to smother more reflective pursuits and the recognition of the intrinsic value of self-cultivation.

Some of Pattison's peers vindicated a university education with reference to its usefulness for the active life: the race for prizes and honours was a bracing competition, and the fact that so many who had succeeded in that race had also triumphed in their subsequent careers demonstrated what an invaluable training for life it offered. Given Pattison's deeply rooted antagonism towards 'pot-hunting' as something that demeaned academic life, we should not be surprised to find him recoiling from this defence of higher education. 'The energy of a secular success is only one of the conditions of moral life, and not the whole of it. Refinement, if not actually a subtraction from public energy, is not a basis for it. Education is a preparation for life. Be it so. But then life is not all fighting.' How much better, and more honest, it would be to appeal instead to 'culture for culture's sake' as the justification for a university education. How much better to hold up the ideal of an education which, while it certainly 'fits for the struggle', also, and more importantly, 'leads up to a view of life which is above the struggle'.[64]

One final aspect of Pattison's argument about endowments should be noticed, because it was a characteristic and recurring feature of his writings about university reform, although its logical status in his argument is not

---

[63] Pattison, *Suggestions*, pp. 148–9.    [64] Pattison, *Suggestions*, pp. 145–6.

easy to pin down. This is his insistence that the collegiate foundations of the Middle Ages and the Renaissance were originally designed to provide for the support of mature scholars engaged in advanced study, and not for undergraduates or the subsidy of the tuition of undergraduates. Although Pattison says that 'an historical inquiry into what Oxford was is beyond the scope of this memoir', he embarks on a lengthy digression on this subject.[65] Dicey, a notable and sympathetic reviewer, regretted that 'so much care has been devoted to an historical vindication of the proposed reforms', displaying 'some interesting results of historical investigation', but at the same time concealing from his readers 'the true grounds of present expediency on which his proposals can be defended'.[66] From Pattison's point of view, the purpose of this digression was to enable the reader to apprehend, in concrete terms, the difference between 'an endowment for science' and 'an endowment for education'. In the university of the middle ages and Renaissance, two cycles of studies were distinguished. The first seven years' apprenticeship, confined to the arts course and culminating in the MA, was intended as a general education. It was followed by a period of specialized study of up to fourteen years in one of the faculties, culminating in the doctorate. Although the foundations of some colleges, notably New College and Magdalen, provided support during both cycles, in most cases fellowships were confined, either by statute or by convention, to MAs: in other words, the foundations supported those engaged in advanced work for a doctorate. So the colleges were originally 'endowments not for the elements of a general liberal education, but for the prolonged study of special and professional faculties by men of a riper age'. Although they might incidentally aid the elementary education of the university, they were 'specially devoted to the highest learning'. Their incidental aid to elementary education took two forms: in some cases the foundations, in addition to fellowships for mature scholars, provided for lesser awards (demyships, or half-fellowships, at Magdalen, for instance) for those studying for a BA or an MA; and the MA might, at the same time as holding a fellowship which enabled him to work towards a doctorate, also act as a regent, or teacher, in the schools. But Pattison adds the crucial qualification:

so far from it being the intention of a fellowship to support the Master of Arts as a *teacher*, it was rather its purpose to relieve him from the drudgery of teaching for a maintenance, and to set him free to give his whole time to the studies and

[65] Pattison, *Suggestions*, pp. 121–7.
[66] [A. V. Dicey], 'Suggestions on Academical Organisation', *Fraser's Magazine* 80 (1869), 425.

exercises of his faculty. The arts course was sufficiently in request to support itself; the higher faculties demanded the aid of endowment.[67]

This argument was to be taken up and elaborated by other members of the endowment of research party, and would be denounced as an 'antiquarian' argument by that party's opponents in Parliament.[68] But it was very much Pattison's in conception.

I say that the logical status of this proposition in Pattison's argument for the endowment of learning is unclear, for Pattison, as we have noticed, recognized that the intentions of founders could not be regarded as sacrosanct. He knew that Newman, at the height of the Oxford Movement, had formed the project of restoring Oriel to the purposes originally assigned to the college by its founder, Adam de Brome, and he did not wish the case for the endowment of research to be identified with the Tractarian reverence for antiquity *per se*.[69] So Pattison did not believe that his demonstration of the original purposes of the colleges clinched the argument, although other advocates of the endowment of research were more inclined to regard it as decisive.[70] But it did provide Pattison with an effective counterblast to two kinds of anti-reforming arguments. As he noted, conservatives in 1854 invoked the founders' designs in support of their resistance to the 'spoliation' of the colleges, 'without reflecting that time had long ago repealed and reversed those designs far more effectually than any Act of Parliament'.[71] Subsequently, in the 1870s, opponents of the endowment of research would declaim against the spoliation of the colleges to the benefit of the university: how could it be justified to take endowment property from the colleges, which performed a valuable educational function, and give it to the university, which did not, simply because the former were rich and the latter relatively poor? Pattison had a ready-made response: his plan did not entail the transfer of resources from the colleges to the university, but merely a reassignment of the uses of those collegiate

---

[67] Pattison, *Suggestions*, p. 126.

[68] James Sutherland Cotton, 'The intentions of the founders of fellowships', in *Essays on the Endowment of Research by Various Writers* (London: King, 1876), pp. 26–63; *Parliamentary Debates* ccxxx, col. 1086, Beresford Hope in the debate on the Second Reading of the University of Cambridge Bill, 6 July 1876.

[69] Pattison, *Memoirs*, p. 98.

[70] Cotton, 'Intentions of founders', p. 29, invokes Lord Derby's dictum: 'Respect the founder's object, but use your own discretion as to the means; if you do not do the first you will have no new endowments; if you neglect the last, those which you have will be of no use.' Cotton concludes, p. 59: 'To recover the fellowships for their original destination ought to be the aim of every academical reformer who is content to proceed upon sound principles.'

[71] Pattison, *Suggestions*, p. 127.

endowments; a reassignment, furthermore, which was much closer than present practice to the original intentions of the founders. Pattison's proposal that the colleges – most of them – should be reconceived as faculties may have been ineffectual, but it was a boldly subversive challenge to the assumptions underlying debates about the reform of Oxford and Cambridge throughout the nineteenth century. His strategy was not to empower the university at the expense of the colleges, but to dissolve the distinction between the two.[72] It was absurd to depict the creation of the Common University Fund, for example, as an instance of the plundering of the colleges for the benefit of 'an alien and extraneous power'; they were simply being required to 'combine their contributions for a public end'.[73]

The account just offered of Pattison's argument in the *Suggestions on Academical Organisation* is significantly new. Standard accounts uncritically accept Sparrow's statement that he proposed 'nothing less than the abolition of the colleges and the fellowships'.[74] These accounts echo the arguments of Pattison's opponents in his own day. Montagu Burrows, for instance, regarded Pattison as a revolutionary whose scheme would sweep away all that was distinctive about the English universities and would reinvent them on the German model. The colleges were therefore doomed: '[t]he independent, self-governing position of these venerable bodies would beyond doubt pass away with all the rest, and the State-governed, departmental German University take its place'.[75] But that is not what Pattison said, and cannot have been what he meant: for if he had meant this, much of his supporting argument would have been irrelevant. Of course his proposals would have transformed the colleges as he knew them, and as we know them. But they did not involve the dissolution of the collegiate corporations. He mentioned the possibility of amalgamations: the specific example he gave was the possibility of amalgamating Merton

---

[72] For an example of these assumptions, see Dilke, 'Memoir', p. 45. Dilke took it for granted that to argue for the endowment of research was to argue for a transfer of resources and power from the colleges to the university.

[73] Pattison, 'Address on Education', 55.

[74] Sparrow, *Pattison*, p. 121. This is echoed by Peter Sutcliffe, *The Oxford University Press: An Informal History* (Oxford: Clarendon, 1978), p. 41: 'By 1870 Mark Pattison was of the opinion that all Oxford colleges and fellowships should be abolished.' Even Momigliano writes: 'He [Pattison] proposed the abolition of the colleges and of the fellowships and the transfer of their endowments to the university.' A. D. Momigliano, 'Jacob Bernays', p. 122. Finally, A. H. Halsey, *Decline of Donnish Dominion*, p. 29: Pattison's submission to the Salisbury [i.e. Selborne] Commission recommended 'the abolition of the colleges and their fellowships. The corporations were to be dissolved and their endowments transferred to the University.' This is directly from Sparrow. But it is wholly untrue: Pattison's evidence to the Selborne Commission said nothing of the sort.

[75] [Burrows], 'University reform', 397.

with its neighbour, Corpus Christi.[76] But this was a passing reference, and by no means the centrepiece of his proposals. He did not speak of the abolition of the colleges, but of their reform; not of the extinction of fellowships, but of 'the conversion, or restoration, of college endowments to the maintenance of a professional class of learned and scientific men'.[77] Contrary to Burrows's reading, Pattison explicitly rebutted the bureaucratic model of the university that prevailed in continental Europe, and identified one of the precious strengths of the English system in the survival of '[i]ndependent colleges, incorporated by charters, and possessing property of their own'.[78] Corporations of this kind would not be tolerated by 'an absolute or bureaucratic government', but they existed in England, and should not be destroyed but be cherished and made to serve useful purposes. The colleges had originally been conceived as 'retreats for study', and to that purpose he hoped to restore them.[79] As he told the Royal Commission on Scientific Instruction in 1870, 'each college already constitutes, for a great variety of purposes, a corporation; and I would only propose to superinduce upon the already existing corporate body a given scientific character.'[80] A. V. Dicey was much the most acute reviewer of Pattison's book. He recognized the essence of the scheme: 'the dedication of college funds to the support of corporations, consisting of men, each devoted to the learning and teaching of a particular branch of knowledge'. The corporate endowments would be reapplied, but certainly not dissolved, and, as Dicey noted, 'the whole work is pervaded by a sentiment in favour of endowments'.[81] Pattison did not want to make Oxford and Cambridge into German universities. Rather, he wished to inspire them with a higher purpose of the kind the German universities possessed.

Viewed in this way, Pattison's stance in the 1860s and 70s seems much more in harmony with the position he expounded to the commissioners of 1850 than has usually been believed. Neither in 1850 nor in 1868 did he propose to shift power or resources from the colleges to the university; and in 1877 as in 1850 his evidence focused on educational issues, rather than on research. What is more, the understanding of the colleges as, in their origins, foundations for the support of advanced learning was one that recurred so frequently in his writings that one cannot but regard it as

---

[76] Pattison, *Suggestions*, p. 157.    [77] Pattison, *Suggestions*, pp. 157, 169.
[78] Pattison, *Suggestions*, p. 175.
[79] Pattison, 'Review of the situation', in *Essays on the Endowment of Research*, p. 10.
[80] Royal Commission on Scientific Instruction and the Advancement of Science, Minutes of Evidence: Parliamentary Papers 1872 Cmd 536, vol. XXV, 244.
[81] [Dicey], 'Suggestions on Academical Organisation', 426.

having been especially close to his heart. Indeed, it is remarkable that he seems to have reached this conception as early as 1839, when he was a fully committed Tractarian, living in Newman's house in St Aldate's. In that year, a few months before his election at Lincoln, he submitted an entry for the Chancellor's Latin prose prize. The designated subject for the year was the function of universities: in the Latin, 'Quaenam sint erga Rempublicam Academiae officia'. It was won by A. P. Stanley, who had recently been elected fellow of University College in preference to Pattison. In his journal for 22 March Pattison provides a summary of his own essay. He emphasizes the importance to society of the existence of a learned clerisy devoted to the life of the intellect; but he also acknowledges that this kind of single-minded devotion to mental cultivation will be rare, and that '[t]here are lesser degrees of intellectual culture wh[ich] befit all from the statesman down to the "vile mechanick" in proportion to the needs of their several situations'. It was important to recognize that the university's task was not 'a mere gymnastic training of the intellect', but 'the production of a whole character and habit of mind congenial to the spirit of the national institutions'. These were themes that would recur in some of his later writings, and in his sermons. But what is significant is that he goes on to spell out the specific ways in which the modern European university system, though it differs from country to country, always makes distinct provision for the twofold object of a university: 'it provides a liberal education for the youth of the state in its courses of Arts & its Professors [sic] chairs – while it consults the interests of Science in its degrees in the higher Faculties – wh[ich] require long residence and devoted study – and by the institution of Collegiate foundations.'[82] This is an explicit and remarkably early statement that the foundations of the colleges were part of the provision for 'the interests of Science', whereas professorial chairs were part of the provision for the general and liberal education of youth.

Quite how Pattison attained this way of thinking about universities is unclear, for it appears to be wholly original, and potentially far-reaching in its implications, coming just a few years after Sir William Hamilton lambasted the way in which Oxford had betrayed the interests of the advancement of knowledge by allowing the colleges to trespass on the university's proper territory. As far as I know Pattison's remarks have not been noticed before. But they are a revelation, for they disclose a fascinating continuity in Pattison's thinking which connects his early adhesion

---

[82] Bodleian MS Pattison 6, ff. 74–6.

to Tractarianism with his subsequent promotion of the endowment of research. In the 1830s Newman had conceived an interest in reviving Adam de Brome's medieval conception of Oriel as a community of scholars engaged in advanced learning, and while Pattison in his *Memoirs* was somewhat dismissive of this notion, it had an enduring effect on the way he understood the original purpose of the colleges.[83] In one of his final pronouncements, two years before his death, he returned to this theme: in the middle ages, he wrote, 'the University of Oxford was a school or place of education, with boys and their masters, as schools are now, lodged in their Halls or Hostels; the College was an association for the endowment and encouragement of learning.'[84]

## CULTURE AND DEMOCRACY

Pattison's book appeared shortly after the second Reform Act was passed, and some comment is needed on the place of the book, and the campaign for the endowment of research, in Victorian debates about the relationship between culture and democracy.[85] This debate was at its most lively in the 1860s and 70s, when a range of thinkers in Britain and overseas sought ways of shoring up cultural and intellectual authority in the face of what was perceived as the inexorable onset of democracy. The most important of these cultural critics was Matthew Arnold, who, like French contemporaries such as Taine, Renan and Flaubert, identified democracy with the hegemony of unstable, unpredictable, animal instincts, and in works such as *Culture and Anarchy* (1867–9) asserted the role of the intellectual elite as a guardian of culture to counterbalance the sway of democratic public opinion. Arnold thought that the cultural and intellectual elite needed an institutional home, and in an essay of 1864 he proposed the creation of academies, on the model of the Académie Française, to perform this function. The French Academy acted as 'a sort of centre and rallying-point' for educated opinion; and, furthermore, as 'a sovereign organ of the highest literary opinion, a recognised authority in matters of intellectual tone and taste'.[86]

Arnold's essay certainly influenced Charles Appleton, the animator of the campaign for the endowment of research, as well as other intellectual

---

[83] Culler, *Imperial Intellect*, pp. 89–91; Pattison, *Memoirs*, p. 98.     [84] Pattison, 'What is a college?', 70.
[85] See H. S. Jones, *Victorian Political Thought* (Basingstone: Macmillan, 2000), pp. 63–73.
[86] Matthew Arnold, 'The literary influence of academies', Cornhill Magazine August 1864, reprinted in his *Lectures and Essays in Criticism*, vol. III of *The Complete Prose Works of Matthew Arnold* (Ann Arbor: University of Michigan Press, 1962), pp. 241, 244–5.

entrepreneurs of the period, such as James Knowles, the founder of the Metaphysical Society.[87] And at the meeting at the Freemasons' Tavern in London at which the campaign for the endowment of research was launched, we find Henry Sidgwick, in the opening speech, summoning the aid of scientific authority against the ignorant opinion of 'half-instructed persons'.[88] Perhaps it is not surprising to find the research party identified with the Arnoldians. When the Oxford zoologist Edwin Lankester sought John Stuart Mill's backing for the campaign for the endowment of research, Mill refused in terms that indicate that he identified the campaign with Arnold's advocacy of academies: 'Experience shows that Academies whether of literature or science generally prefer inoffensive mediocrities to men of original genius.'[89]

It is less clear whether Arnold's analysis of the relationship between culture and democracy had any impact on Pattison. The two men were certainly acquainted as a result of their complementary roles as assistant commissioners for the Newcastle Commission on Popular Education in 1859, when Pattison reported on schools in Germany and Arnold on those in France. Their relations were evidently cordial, and Arnold wrote to congratulate Pattison on his election as rector in 1861.[90] About this time Pattison and his wife became close to Arnold's brother, Thomas Arnold the younger, and his niece, Mary Arnold (later Mrs Humphry Ward). But Pattison was contemptuous of Arnold's admiration of the French educational system, and for his neglect of science. 'Arnold', he wrote in his diary in September 1862, 'rather than having science "the principal thing in my son's mind", would gladly have him think that the sun went round the earth, & that the stars were so many spangles set in the bright blue firmament.' Pattison made no comment, but none was needed.[91]

Like many intellectuals of his generation, Pattison was fatalistic about democracy. He cannot be counted an enthusiast for it, given that he

[87] Diderick Roll-Hansen, *The Academy, 1869–1879: Victorian Intellectuals in Revolt* (Copenhagen: Rosenkilde and Bagger, 1957), p. 105.

[88] Stefan Collini, 'The ordinary experience of civilized life: Sidgwick's politics and the method of reflective analysis', in Bart Schultz (ed.), *Essays on Henry Sidgwick* (Cambridge: Cambridge University Press, 1992), pp. 334–5.

[89] J. S. Mill to Edwin Ray Lankester, 8 February 1873, in Francis E. Mineka and Dwight N. Lindley (eds.), *The Later Letters of John Stuart Mill 1849–1873* vol. IV (*Collected Works of John Stuart Mill* vol. XVII) (Toronto & London: University of Toronto Press and Routledge & Kegan Paul, 1972), p. 1937.

[90] Arnold to Pattison, 28 Jan. 1861: Bodleian MS Pattison 54, f. 155.

[91] 26 September 1862: Bodleian MS Pattison 130, f. 33. On the French educational system see, e.g., Pattison, 'Philological Congress at Kiel', *Academy* 1 (1869), pp. 58–9.

supposed that Renan – certainly no populist – held 'the most flattering view of democracy'.[92] But he saw no prospect of averting it. He certainly thought it endangered the survival of a respect for the intrinsic value of culture. The year before Arnold wrote on academies Pattison could warn that 'the instincts of a democratic majority not only lead it to hate culture which it believes to be real, they compel it to disbelieve the existence of such culture'.[93] Probably Pattison understood democracy in a Tocquevillean sense: he was less interested in the advent of a working-class electorate than in a state of society in which 'public opinion' was sovereign. In Victorian England that was essentially a *middle-class* public opinion, and like Tocqueville and Mill, Pattison was inclined to view that as a threat to high culture. Arnold famously thought the commercial middle classes of Victorian England inclined to philistinism, and Pattison endorsed much of the Arnoldian critique: he praised the exposé of 'the dismal blank of the domestic interior of the English middle-class family', and he enumerated their chief defects as 'the prevailing want of refinement, the selfish and material interests, the worship of wealth, the weakness of ideas, and the denominational habits of judging which still enthral them'.[94] In his evidence to the Taunton Commission he lamented the middle-class man's 'want of culture', which led him, typically, to prefer a less intelligent to a more intelligent woman, and commented that '[t]he middle class has been raised many degrees in point of wealth, but its culture, as I think one must see, has not kept pace with the development of its means; that is, it is raised in means and not raised in intelligence'.[95] It should be observed here that like Arnold and like most mid-Victorian social and educational commentators, Pattison understood the term 'middle class' to refer chiefly to the commercial as opposed to the professional classes: this was, for instance, how the term was used in expressions such as 'middle-class schools' and 'middle-class examinations'.[96] With the passage of time Pattison became still more damning in his characterization of the alienation of these middle classes from cultural life and the life of the mind: he told the Social Science Congress that

the outer darkness in which their self-complacent existence is passed, while the inexhaustible riches of the several worlds of science, of literature, poetry, and art

[92] Pattison, *Suggestions*, p. 140.     [93] Pattison, 'Learning in the Church of England', p. 303.
[94] Pattison, Review of Matthew Arnold, *Mixed Essays*, 426; Pattison, *Suggestions*, p. 145.
[95] Schools Inquiry Commission [Taunton Commission] House of Commons Parliamentary Papers 1867–8 vol. XXVIII pt 4, 945.
[96] Honey and Curthoys, 'Oxford and schooling', pp. 559–60.

are unopened to them, is a modern phenomenon which has now attained the proportions of a social blot.[97]

But Pattison always insisted on the intrinsic importance of culture, and it was alien to his whole cast of mind to defend science and learning with reference to their usefulness in combatting the effects of democracy. While the relationship between culture and democracy certainly engaged his attention, this was rather because he saw democracy as a potential threat to culture than because he saw culture as a counterweight to democracy or a potential remedy for it. His trust in endowments was distinct from Arnold's Francophile faith in the state; and there is little to suggest that he, or indeed other members of the endowment of research party, looked to research universities as cultural authorities in Arnold's sense. Pattison cited Arnold's study of the French secondary schooling, but he also insisted on the distinction between universities and academies.[98] As we have seen, he was sceptical of Ruskin's claim to exercise a general cultural authority on the basis of his expertise in one field, art; and there is no reason to think that he was any more sympathetic to the scientist's authority beyond his immediate specialism.[99]

## LEARNING AND LIBERAL EDUCATION

Pattison was always convinced that the only form of education with which a university could properly concern itself was a liberal education. This was something which his opponents in the debates on university reform commonly misunderstood, whether wilfully or not.[100] But Pattison was quite clear on the matter. 'It is no part of the proper business of a University to be a professional school', he told the Congress of the Social Science Association in 1876, speaking as president of its education section. 'Universities are not to fit men for some special mode of gaining a livelihood; their object is not to teach law or divinity, banking or engineering, but to cultivate the mind and form the intelligence.'[101] But is there not a difficulty here? The idea of a liberal education surely embraces the education of the whole person, and prizes balance and breadth. That was what it meant when deployed at the beginning of the century by Edward

---

[97] Pattison, 'Address on education', 45.     [98] Pattison, *Suggestions*, pp. 21, 172.

[99] Pattison, Review of John Ruskin, *Arrows of the Chace*, *The Academy* 19 (12 Feb. 1881), 110; cited in Chapter 1, above.

[100] [Burrows], 'University reform', 391; [Henry Craik], 'The universities and their critics', *Quarterly Review* 150 (July 1880), 190.

[101] Pattison, 'Address on Education', 61–2.

Copleston to defend Oxford against the criticisms formulated by the *Edinburgh Review*. He argued that the purpose of a university education should be to cultivate breadth of outlook, and so to combat the narrowness of a mechanistic age. He defended Oxford's undifferentiated classical and mathematical curriculum on the basis of the mental training it afforded.[102] Pattison, by contrast, was a vocal advocate of the cause of academic special-ization and, indeed, of the differentiation of the curriculum. Furthermore, while there was certainly a case to be made that Victorian universities had to embrace the cause of research and the advancement of knowledge, could it seriously be maintained that the researcher was the person best equip-ped to provide a liberal education, as opposed to a specialist professional training? There was, after all, an important current of reforming thought in the Victorian period which sought to reorientate the universities towards education for the professions. Why did Pattison reject this position?

The concept of a liberal education seems originally to have been inven-ted for defensive purposes: to provide an *ex post facto* justification for the existing curriculum in the face of demands for its modernization.[103] The fact that the English university curriculum at the beginning of the nine-teenth century was dominated by classics and mathematics was due to historical accident rather than to a conviction that they were superior to other subjects in their ability to impart mental breadth or discipline; but once their hegemony was threatened, academic conservatives discovered that these were, after all, the subjects best positioned to equip students with a liberal education. The ideal of a liberal education is therefore sometimes represented by its opponents as an essentially conservative piece of obfus-cation designed to prop up the status quo. But in fact some of the most heated of Victorian cultural debates turned on the continued relevance of the idea of 'liberal education', and on its meaning: they were not so much between proponents and antagonists of liberal education, as between different kinds of proponents. For instance, did modern industrial society's demand for a population trained in the natural sciences and in modern foreign languages pose a threat to the very hegemony of a liberal under-standing of education; or did it simply require a broader understanding of the meaning of a liberal education? Pattison favoured the latter answer.

---

[102] Peter R. H. Slee, *Liberal and a Liberal Education. The Study of Modern History in the Universities of Oxford, Cambridge and Manchester 1800–1914* (Manchester: Manchester University Press, 1986), pp. 10–11.

[103] Slee, *Liberal and a Liberal Education*, p. 10; Peter Slee, 'The Oxford idea of a liberal education 1800–1860: the invention of tradition and the manufacture of practice', *History of Universities* 7 (1988), 65.

In this he echoed John Stuart Mill, who set out the most famous Victorian vindication of the ideal of a liberal education in his inaugural address as rector of St Andrews University in 1867.

Mill had no personal interest in shoring up the major cultural and educational institutions of Victorian Britain: famously, he was himself educated neither at school nor university. He was, however, profoundly Hellenistic in his outlook: he prized the idea of wholeness, and placed this at the centre of his understanding of liberal education. 'Universities', he insisted, 'are not intended to teach the knowledge required to fit men for some special mode of gaining their livelihood. Their object is not to make skilful lawyers, or physicians, or engineers, but capable and cultivated human beings.'[104] But in confronting the 'great controversy' which 'most broadly divides educational reformers and conservatives', Mill was unambiguously in favour of the teaching of the sciences, which he defended in terms of their capacity to complement literary subjects in furnishing a fully rounded liberal education.

If there were no more to be said than that scientific education teaches us to think, and literary education to express our thoughts, do we not require both? and is not any one a poor, maimed, lopsided fragment of humanity who is deficient in either?[105]

The origins of the idea of liberal education lie in classical antiquity: in the idea of educating the whole person and of forming a character and not just a mind. It was rooted in classical, and especially Greek ideas of wholeness and balance as elements of the good life. Human nature was regarded as indivisible, and education should therefore seek to educate the whole person. As Mill put it, 'it is a very imperfect education which trains the intelligence only, but not the will'.[106] The characteristically English model of liberal education sought to realise the education of the whole person through residential institutions: the public (i.e. endowed) schools and the colleges of Oxford and Cambridge. It was taken for granted that the curriculum alone was insufficient to effect the goal of forming the character, and in the Victorian period it came to be recognized that extracurricular activities, such as team games, had a vital role to play. So Sheldon Rothblatt argues:

[104] John Stuart Mill, 'Inaugural Address Delivered to the University of St. Andrews', in Mill, *Essays on Equality, Law, and Education*, ed. John M. Robson (*Collected Works of John Stuart Mill* vol. XXI) (Toronto and London: University of Toronto Press/Routledge & Kegan Paul, 1984), p. 218.
[105] Mill, 'Inaugural Address', pp. 220–1. [106] Mill, 'Inaugural Address', p. 247.

For the nineteenth century I would even suggest that there is a dialectical relationship between the spread of an intellectual ideal of liberal education and the revival of the college as a model institution . . . the ideal of the whole person is kept alive by the idea of the college.[107]

Pattison had an important and distinctive place in the debates on liberal education. As Rothblatt has observed, 'No one of his era was more sophisticated or original in comprehending the social or intellectual assumptions behind the several forms of learning.'[108] But two plausible but misleading assumptions need to be dispelled if we are to make sense of Pattison's place in these debates.

First, the research ethic is commonly supposed to be antithetical to the idea of a liberal education.[109] It replaces the idea of the transmission of a canon or tradition with an emphasis on the sovereign importance of discovery. It abandons breadth for specialization; for only the specialized mind can penetrate deep enough to make real discoveries. It replaces the education of the whole person with the focused training of the mind; and then replaces the training of the whole mind with a narrow training of a part of the mind. In the institutional context of the collegiate universities of Oxford and Cambridge, the research ethic sees the college system as a diversion, and prefers an organization based on faculties or departments, which group academics according to their specialism. For a physicist to have lunch in college with an historian or an economist may make him or her a more rounded person; but it is unlikely to produce a better research scientist.

Second, it has become fashionable to suppose that the cult of 'character' which stood at the heart of the conception of liberal education served an anti-intellectual purpose. Education was supposed to be about the formation of the character rather than simply of the mind; and non-intellectual activities, such as sport, were seen as the most effective instruments for the formation of character, which is why some influential graduate employers, such as the colonial civil service, developed a reputation for preferring 'blues' to first-class degrees.[110]

---

[107] Sheldon Rothblatt, 'The limbs of Osiris: liberal education in the English-speaking world', in Sheldon Rothblatt and Björn Wittrock (eds.), *The European and American University since 1800: Historical and Sociological Essays* (1993), pp. 45–6.

[108] Rothblatt, 'Limbs of Osiris', p. 52.     [109] Rothblatt, 'Limbs of Osiris', p. 52.

[110] For this argument, see the many works of J. A. Mangan, e.g. his ' "Oars and the Man": pleasure and purpose in Victorian and Edwardian Cambridge', *British Journal of Sports History* 1 (1984), 263–71. For a more nuanced understanding of the late-Victorian concept of character, see Nathan Roberts, 'Character in the mind: citizenship, education and psychology in Britain, 1880–1914', *History of Education* 33 (2004), 177–197.

As Rothblatt has noticed, Pattison's place in this narrative is more complex than we might imagine. The stance he came to adopt needs to be explored in depth if we are to grasp the originality of his position in Victorian debates about culture. We know that he was a leading advocate of the movement for the 'endowment of research', and of academic specialization, and that he came to see the college system in its existing form as an obstacle to these objectives. He wanted to see the colleges specialize in particular disciplines, and so be transformed, in effect, into faculties. We know that he despised the intimate relationships with political and civil service elites which Jowett's Oxford forged, and we know also that he was deeply antagonistic towards the games cult that took hold of Oxford, especially during the period of his rectorship of Lincoln College from 1861 to 1884. Yet he was a staunch defender of the idea of liberal education. In an address at Birmingham in 1877 he deplored the fact that this idea of education had more or less ceased to be understood. Properly grasped, it meant that the boy was not taught what would be useful to him in later life, but rather 'was moulded into a man and a citizen'. Education aimed to confer 'faculty' rather than knowledge: the boy was trained in the 'virtuous employment' of his faculties'.[111]

It is clear from the evidence he gave to the Devonshire Commission on Scientific Instruction in 1870 that Pattison espoused the research ethic as a means towards liberal education and culture, not as an alternative to that idea of education and culture. He thought specialization and research offered a more effective way of achieving the goals of rounded character-formation. 'All real culture', he crucially insisted,

must be founded upon specialisation; that the system of general information, knowing a little of the surface of half a dozen things, has its value, but that on the whole, the result of such an education is an inferior result to the result of a deep and thorough investigation of some one great branch of knowledge.[112]

It might be useful to compare Pattison's position with Mill's here. Mill's aim was to combat the assumption that the introduction of scientific education must be at the expense of classical and literary subjects: no one could adequately embrace both. This 'strangely limited estimate of what it is possible for human beings to learn' alarmed Mill, who looked to education to preserve an integrated humanity in the face of the disintegrating tendencies of a modern industrial economy founded on the division of

---

[111] Bodleian MS Pattison 112, ff. 121–34.
[112] Royal Commission 1872 Cmd 536, vol. XXV, 248 (15 November 1870).

labour. '[I]f in order to know that little completely, it is necessary to remain wholly ignorant of all the rest, what will soon be the worth of a man, for any human purpose except his own infinitesimal fraction of human wants and requirements?' Any study or pursuit, practised to the exclusion of all the others, would tend, he believed, to 'narrow and pervert the mind'. But he did not believe that this principle must obstruct any kind of specialization. 'It is not the utmost limit of human acquirement to know only one thing, but to combine a minute knowledge of one or a few things with a general knowledge of many things.' Indeed, it was necessary to have studied one subject in depth in order to appreciate 'what real knowledge is'.[113] This was Pattison's belief too. No one could be an effective university teacher whose interests did not extend beyond his narrow specialism. But, equally, no one could be an effective university teacher who did not have a specialism, because without a specialism one cannot grasp what it means to be an investigator, as opposed to one who merely knows what he has to teach.

The second misapprehension is the assumption that the idea of character served anti-intellectual purposes. It is easy to see where this assumption springs from: the point was, after all, that it was not enough for an educational system to form the mind alone; it should concern itself with the whole person. But we get a fresh insight into the uses of the concept of character when we see the central importance it had for Pattison, devoted as he was to the cultivation of the mind as the highest form of human existence. For Pattison, education properly understood must act on the character: that was, indeed, the liberal concept of education. 'Everything is educative which modifies the nature or character, the habits or powers of the person. What does not do this is not education.' But notice how he continues, in this address given towards the end of his life.

That, and that only, is education, which moulds, forms, modifies the soul or mind. Out of a piece of cold metal you can fashion nothing. Iron must be heated before it can be bent & shaped to our purposes. Nothing is educative which does not raise the mental powers at least to a red heat. It is more efficacious still if it can raise them to a white heat, or still more, if it can fuse them.[114]

For Pattison the mind was integral to the character, and character formation entailed an action upon the mind. So education as character training was not something distinct from education as intellectual formation:

---

[113] Mill, 'Inaugural Address', pp. 222–3.
[114] Bodleian MS Pattison 112, f. 140. This is the manuscript text of an address on education given at some point in 1879 or after.

rather, the point of insisting that education entailed a modification of the character was to dispel the crude notion that it was simply about the communication of knowledge.

\*\*\*

A final point of comparison suggests itself. If we ask how Pattison came to believe that the University's distinctive product was a man of philosophical temper, the most plausible answer is that he absorbed this belief through the influence and example of Newman. It was in Newman that he first encountered a high and noble conception of the purpose of a university, something that was so lamentably lacking in the Oxford he encountered as an undergraduate.

But is this explanation not perverse? Surely Pattison insisted that the intellectual life was the highest form of existence, whereas Newman held that it was as nothing beside the life devoted to service of God. Did he not cite Newman as the foremost exponent of the Catholic conception of education, a conception, like the positivist conception, wholly concerned with 'the inculcation of truth', with indoctrination, as opposed to the humanist conception of the cultivation of the mind for its own sake?[115] Moreover, did not Newman see the university essentially as an educational institution, whereas for Pattison it was about learning? The two men have often been taken as occupying opposite ends of the spectrum of Victorian conceptions of the university. They were 'antithetical figures', writes Halsey, Newman advocating the 'tutorial model' of the university, and Pattison expounding 'the prototype of the research university'.[116] But that account, though often repeated, is misleading, and leans too heavily on Pattison's tendency, in public though not always in private, to distance himself from Newman and his legacy.

The Tractarian movement that Newman headed was not simply a religious movement. It was also a movement for academic renewal. That was probably what Pattison found most appealing in it. What is more, the movement gave birth to the most important Victorian elucidation of the purposes of a university. Newman's *Idea of a University* originated in a series of lectures he gave in Dublin in 1852 at the request of the Archbishop of Armagh, who asked him to assist in the establishment of (and then to head) a new Catholic university for Ireland. But the conception of the university he expounded there was profoundly rooted in his Oxford (and Anglican)

---

[115] Pattison, *Sermons*, pp. 122–5.    [116] Halsey, *Decline of Donnish Dominion*, pp. 26–7.

experience. Like Edward Copleston, who had been provost of Oriel when Newman was elected fellow, he defended the idea of a liberal education against the proponents of useful knowledge, but he also deployed it against those who pressed for a more specifically Catholic higher education.

Newman held firm to the Coplestonian doctrine that a university education should have as its chief purpose to train the mind 'to have a connected view or grasp of things'.[117] If a university sought to teach its students to think for themselves, it should not, however, aim to nurture the leader-writer's facility for having a ready opinion on any subject under the sun. A university education must be grounded in a 'habit of method', and its beneficiary will be able to distinguish 'what he knows from what he does not know'. On this basis, Newman believed, 'I conceive he will be gradually initiated into the largest and truest philosophical views, and will feel nothing but impatience and disgust at the random theories and imposing sophistries and dashing paradoxes, which carry away half-formed and superficial intellects'.[118] The university's purpose was to nurture the philosophical habit: that is, 'the power of viewing many things at once as one whole, of referring them severally to their true place in the universal system, of understanding their respective values, and determining their mutual dependence'.[119]

The aim of the university was to convey a general culture, and not to provide a mere professional training. Newman deplored the way in which the onward march of the division of labour tended towards the fragmentation of the human person. He looked to general culture to combat this tendency. Generality did not, however, imply a mere smattering of knowledge of all fields – such as might be acquired, presumably, from the university as conceived by the utilitarians – 'a sort of bazaar, or pantechnicon, in which wares of all kinds are heaped together for sale in stalls independent of each other'.[120] It was a mistake to suppose that the proliferation of disciplines contributed to the fulfilment of the university's mission. He denounced 'the error of distracting and enfeebling the mind by an unmeaning profusion of subjects ... All things now are to be learned at once, not first one thing, then another, not one well, but many badly.'[121] Not learning alone, but 'culture of mind' was Newman's ideal.[122]

---

[117] Newman, *Idea of a University*, p. 11.    [118] Newman, *Idea of a University*, p. 13.
[119] Newman quoted by Culler, *Imperial Intellect*, p. 190.    [120] Culler, *Imperial Intellect*, p. 174.
[121] Culler, *Imperial Intellect*, p. 193.    [122] Culler, *Imperial Intellect*, p. 194.

Pattison was in many ways the most important legatee of the Copleston – Newman conception of the university, and could have endorsed practically the whole of Newman's teaching as just summarized. He fully shared Newman's disdain for superficiality, and his belief that what the university distinctively produced was not knowledge, but thinking men. With Newman he held that the 'product' of the university was not 'knowledge', but a philosophical mind. Pattison's formulation of his ideas was sometimes misleading on this point. He concluded his *Suggestions* with the proposition that the university is not 'a class-school, nor mainly a school for youth at all'; rather, it is 'a national institute for the preservation and tradition of useful knowledge'.[123] Copleston and Newman would both have deprecated the invocation of 'useful knowledge', which was the old mantra of Scottish Whigs and utilitarians. Pattison was evidently willing to use this term, especially when he was working closely with the university liberals, but in fact the adjective 'useful' sits uneasily beside his more customary insistence that the kind of knowledge with which universities had to concern itself was *disinterested* knowledge, or knowledge shorn of any immediate practical purpose.[124] There was one occasion when Pattison publicly took issue with Newman on the idea of the university. This was in a university sermon he preached in 1865. But he did not advocate useful knowledge against Newman, and neither did he advocate a research university against him. His point was that the Catholic and Newmanite conception, like the Comtean, held that education had to do with the 'inculcation of truth' rather than the culture of the mind for its own sake.[125] Most readers of Newman have thought that the culture of the mind for its own sake was at the heart of his understanding of the idea of the university. So Pattison could distance himself from Newman only by misrepresenting him. He probably knew he was misrepresenting him. Certainly, the fact that he would re-read parts of Newman's *Idea of the University* when in the final stages of composing his life of Casaubon was a tribute to his appreciation of his mentor.[126]

What then did Pattison add to the conception of the university developed by Copleston and Newman? The crucial point is that he thought that the idea of the university he had inherited from his Oxford predecessors, although it encapsulated a part of the truth, was one-sided. It understood

---

[123]  Pattison, *Suggestions*, p. 327.
[124]  Pattison, 'Review of the situation', pp. 23–5; also his 'Note on Evolution and Positivism', *Fortnightly Review* 28 O.S. (1877), 285–6.
[125]  Pattison, *Sermons*, pp. 122–5.    [126]  Bodleian MS Pattison 130, ff. 75, 80.

the nature of a university education, but it failed to see what this implied for the vocation of the academic, and hence gave an incomplete account of the mission of the university. What Pattison came to lament about Newman was that he was unable to give the commitment to truth the priority it demanded. He deplored the *Apologia pro vita sua* as a 'most pathetic story! of a soul wholly detached from worldly interests, and seeking only its future interests – *not* truth. . . . it has not the interest of a search for speculative truth, as in the Confessions of Augustine, or the Diary of Blanco White'.[127] The university teacher's role, as Pattison understood it, was to produce men of philosophical habit; and only a man who had himself acquired that habit and who had committed his life to its practice could do this.

---

[127] Bodleian MS Pattison 130, f. 46.

CHAPTER 6

# *The history of ideas as self-culture*

## THE DISCOVERY OF INTELLECTUAL HISTORY

It is not easy to classify Pattison in terms of modern academic disciplines. He might be defined as a classicist, an historian, a philosopher, or a theologian, but none of these definitions quite captures the nature of his intellectual endeavours. His central preoccupation was what we now call intellectual history. This was largely a nineteenth-century invention: 'to most persons', wrote Jowett, 'the very notion that ideas have a history is a new one'.[1] It was new, but it rapidly became pervasive. 'In the last century', wrote Morley in 1874, 'men asked of a belief or a story, Is it true? We now ask, How did men come to take it for true?'[2] Enlightenment historians had included ideas and culture within their category of the history of 'manners', but this also embraced what we would call social and economic history, and the history of ideas did not exist as a separate pursuit.[3] Donald Kelley has sought to persuade us that the history of ideas emerged in France from the work of Victor Cousin and the Eclectics, but its genealogy can equally plausibly be traced to the German idealists and historicists.[4] In any case it would be a mistake to tie it to one particular intellectual tradition. The conviction that ideas ultimately drove history was a widespread belief – sometimes almost a commonplace – in the nineteenth century, and by no means only within the idealist tradition: Auguste Comte and John Stuart Mill, for example, both articulated this belief. No doubt that strengthened interest in the history of ideas. But the subject was largely eschewed by the emergent class of professional historians, whose focus was chiefly on constitutional and diplomatic history. Instead, the history of ideas was chiefly practised on the one hand by generalist

---

[1] Quoted in Basil Willey, *More Nineteenth Century Studies. A Group of Honest Doubters* (London: Chatto & Windus, 1963), p. 151.

[2] Morley, *On Compromise*, p. 31.

[3] P. R. Ghosh, 'Macaulay and the heritage of the Enlightenment', *English Historical Review* 112 (1997), 358–9.

[4] Donald R. Kelley, *The Descent of Ideas: The History of Intellectual History* (Aldershot: Ashgate, 2002).

men of letters (John Morley, for example), and on the other hand by philosophers or by philosophic historians: those who inquired into the long-term laws of historical development. Some pioneers of the genre, such as Leslie Stephen, could make some claim to belong to both groups.

Mill was the most important single authority in Victorian discussions of the laws of progress and the science of history. He wrote no history himself – except, in his *Autobiography*, a history of his own mind – but in his periodical reviews he produced extensive commentaries on the intellectual significance of historians of his own day, especially those of the French school such as Guizot and Michelet. And in the final book of his *System of Logic* (1843) he provided an important, though qualified, account of the necessarily historical character of the social or moral sciences: in the words of one commentator, 'an intriguing mixture of continental historicism and English scepticism'.[5] Like the historicists, he had a strong sense of the interconnectedness of the diverse social phenomena in a given state of society, and an equally strong sense that the predominant agent of social progress was 'the state of the speculative faculties of mankind', from which he concluded that the key to the law of human progress must lie in 'the law of the successive transformations of human opinions'.[6] Eldon Eisenach has argued recently that Mill's whole intellectual outlook rested fundamentally on an engagement with the history of ideas. His liberalism, on this account, should not be thought of as 'a philosophy of timeless and logically coercive principles', but as 'a tradition and hermeneutic' requiring 'a critical reflexivity towards the ideas that we inherit'.[7] Eisenach sees Pattison, along with Lewes, Harrison, Morley and the Stephen brothers, as a leading exponent of this Millite cultural liberalism. He certainly shared one of Mill's central convictions about intellectual self-culture: that it crucially required an engagement with the traditions passed on to us and an ability to place ourselves within the larger framework of the history of ideas. If we read past thinkers in a spirit of irreverent debunking, we are unlikely to penetrate beneath the surface of their thought, and hence our own ideas will be 'reared [on] nothing but an edifice of sand'.[8] For Pattison, intellectual

[5] Alan Ryan, *J. S. Mill* (London: Routledge and Kegan Paul, 1974), p. 92.

[6] John Stuart Mill, *A System of Logic Ratiocinative and Inductive* vol. II (volume VIII of the *Collected Works of John Stuart Mill* (Toronto: University of Toronto Press, 1974), pp. 926–7. The 1843 and 1846 editions read 'the law of the successive transformations of religion and science'.

[7] Eldon Eisenach, 'Mill's reform liberalism as tradition and culture', *Political Science Reviewer* 24 (1995), 73.

[8] Mill, 'Use and abuse of political terms' [1832], in *Essays on Politics and Society* vol. I (volume XVIII of the *Collected Works of John Stuart Mill*) (Toronto: University of Toronto Press, 1977), p. 7, quoted by Eisenach, 'Mill's reform liberalism', 74.

history mattered because it was an indispensable instrument in the project of self-culture which was his lifetime's endeavour.

There is no positive evidence that Pattison ever met Mill, although it seems likely that they would have encountered each other at the Athenaeum. A reference to Pattison in a letter of Mill's from 1865 suggests that if they had met, their acquaintance was at best superficial: Mill was 'surprised' at the positive tone of Pattison's review of his book on Sir William Hamilton's philosophy, and of his review of Grote's book on Plato.[9] Mill, who moved most easily in freethinking or dissenting circles, probably identified Pattison as a clerical don who was therefore likely to be unsympathetic to his philosophy. In fact Pattison had reviewed a number of Mill's earlier works, notably the *Principles of Political Economy* in 1848 and the fourth edition of the *Logic* in 1856. His reaction to them was strongly favourable: he recognized the authoritative standing of Mill's works, and his main criticism was that this quality might be undermined by a certain wordiness and – in the latter work – a tendency to conduct polemics arising out of responses to earlier editions.[10] It is difficult to see Pattison as a disciple of Mill, but Mill's works certainly formed part of his mental furniture, as they did of so many educated Englishmen: 'from 1860 to 1865 or thereabouts', wrote Sidgwick on Mill's death, 'he ruled England in the region of thought as very few men ever did'.[11] In particular, Mill's work was one of the principal resources on which Pattison drew when he addressed the problem of the history of ideas.

Pattison shared the Victorian fascination with laws of historical change, although he tended to eschew grand theories of progress. His interest in the history of ideas can be detected as early as 1838, before Mill's *Logic* had appeared and probably before he had any acquaintance with Mill's work. Here we find him identifying 'the history of opinion' and the philosophy of history as two of his particular subjects of study.[12] At the same time he speculated that 'an account of the alternate influence of Platonism and Aristotelianism' would practically suffice to constitute 'a past history of human opinion'.[13] But this interest crystallized, as he recalled in his *Memoirs*, in the years following his resignation of his tutorship at the end

[9]  Mill to George Grote, 18 June 1865, in Francis E. Mineka and Dwight N. Lindley, *The Later Letters of John Stuart Mill 1849–1873*, vol. III (volume XVII of the *Collected Works of John Stuart Mill*) (Toronto, University of Toronto Press, 1972), p. 1068.

[10]  [Pattison], 'Mill's Political Economy', 315–44; [Pattison], Review of J. S. Mill, *System of Logic*, 4th edn, *Saturday Review* 2 (1856), 735–6.

[11]  Quoted in Schultz, *Henry Sidgwick*, p. 141.

[12]  Diary for July 1838, Bodleian MS Pattison 6, ff. 4–5.

[13]  Bodleian MS Pattison 6, f. 6. He returned to the theme later in the year: MS Pattison 6, f. 36.

of 1855, when he sought to define a subject area to make his own. He identified the 'larger form of investigation which constituted the framework within which my thoughts habitually moved – viz. the laws of the progress of thought in modern Europe'.[14] Broadly, this was to be his main intellectual interest for the rest of his life, although he soon came to appreciate that it had to be broken down into more manageable projects. When he read Lecky's history of rationalism in 1865, his response was that it was 'a very suggestive book and on my own subject': specifically, it was 'full of original views on the laws of Progress'.[15] As a reviewer he tended to be critical of straightforwardly empirical historians who displayed no interest in the philosophy of history: 'Neither the events, nor the opinions, treated of, are brought within the scope of the great European progress', he wrote of one ecclesiastical historian. 'No law of development is discernible in his pages.'[16]

We sometimes think of the Victorians as intellectually cautious empiricists, in contrast to their systematizing contemporaries in France and Germany.[17] But this is probably not even a half-truth. Certainly British thinkers zealously entered the quest for laws of historical development. Why were they drawn so strongly to the search for the laws of progress? The first thing to say is that it was by no means the symptom of a facile optimism. On the contrary, many of the most important contributors to the investigation of the laws of development were obsessed with a sense of the fragility of progress: Walter Bagehot and Sir Henry Maine, for example, identified and tried to explain the progressiveness of western civilization because they wished to ensure the transmission of this precarious inheritance.

One kind of interpretation holds that developmentalism appealed to Victorian thinkers because it enabled them to reconcile liberal reformism with the historicist sensibility that was such a distinctive mark of the nineteenth-century mind. The awareness of living through a period of unprecedented change attuned thinkers to the need to understand people and institutions as products of time and place. The problem was that this historicist understanding seemed to imply a relativism that would blunt the cutting edge of reformism and radicalism. Did it not imply that what is, has to be? Mill was particularly concerned with this dilemma. He had been brought up a Benthamite; and though some revisionists have questioned it,

[14] Pattison, *Memoirs*, pp. 310–11.
[15] Bodleian MS Pattison 130, f. 58, diary 17 and 26 May 1865.
[16] Pattison, Review of John Stoughton, *Ecclesiastical History of England: the Church of the Restoration*, 2 vols., in *Academy* 2 (1870), 10.
[17] For example, Perry Anderson, 'Components of the national culture', *New Left Review* no. 50 (July–Aug. 1968), 3–57.

Benthamite utilitarianism was characterized by an insensitivity to cultural and historical difference.[18] That was certainly how Mill saw the matter, which was why he was so profoundly impressed by his encounter with romanticism in the 1820s and 30s. As he made clear in his essays on Bentham and Coleridge, he wanted to assimilate the romantics' sophisticated understanding of society without acquiescing in their conservatism. Mill was not himself a practitioner of philosophic history, but in Book Six of his *System of Logic* he tried to sketch out its logical foundation. His projected science of ethology was an attempt to demonstrate the relevance of a dynamic philosophic history to a reformist social science.

Perhaps the most important Victorian investigation of the laws of progress was itself undertaken by a follower of Mill: H. T. Buckle's *History of Civilization*, published incompletely in two volumes in 1857 and 1861. Buckle set out to construct a science of history from an advanced liberal and secularist point of view. This science was intellectualist, because Buckle wanted to identify the struggle between scientific knowledge and theological dogma as the central conflict in history. It was also determinist, because he had to demonstrate the inevitability of the victory of science in this conflict. The progress of knowledge, and not that of morals, was, he argued, the engine of historical change.

Buckle's work had an enormous impact on the educated reading public, not just in Britain but also in Germany, France and especially (and curiously) in Russia.[19] That impact is hard to recover, since Buckle has been neglected by intellectual historians of the period, perhaps because he died so young. It is difficult to base a full-length study on one incomplete book, although an indefatigable German has recently made the effort.[20] In his own day Buckle was much criticized: the young Lord Acton, for instance, baulked at what he saw as Buckle's monocausal approach to history, which ignored on the one hand the influence of individuals, and on the other hand the influence of race. Others attacked the pretensions of a work of such ambitious scale being undertaken by a man who lacked formal education: Ruskin thought the work exemplified 'the impudence of the modern cockney mind'.[21] But then, retorted Henry Sidgwick, 'Abuse

---

[18] For one revisionist account, see Jennifer Pitts, 'Legislator of the world? A rereading of Bentham on colonies', *Political Theory* 31 (2003), 200–34.
[19] Bernard Semmel, 'H. T. Buckle: the liberal faith and the science of history', *British Journal of Sociology* 27 (1976), 373.
[20] Eckhardt Fuchs, *Henry Thomas Buckle: Geschichtschreibung und Positivismus in England und Deutschland* (Leipzig: Leipziger Universitätsverlag, 1994).
[21] Quoted by Giles St Aubyn, *A Victorian Eminence: The Life and Work of Henry Thomas Buckle* (London: Barrie, 1958), p. 166.

him as you like, he is the first Englishman who has attempted to write scientific history.'[22]

Pattison reviewed the first volume for the *Westminster Review*, and his review is still worth reading as one of the fairest and deepest appreciations of the importance of Buckle's work.[23] Certainly it exhibits none of Ruskin's disparagement of the author for his lack of formal education; and this is not surprising, for Pattison himself had been educated at home and had a low view of the typical Oxford education provided in his undergraduate days. By this time Pattison was coming to share Buckle's view of Oxford as 'refuge of superstition'.[24] The review also provides as much insight as any of his writings into Pattison's own approach to the philosophy of history.

Pattison began by saluting the scale of Buckle's achievement. His book was 'perhaps the most comprehensive contribution to philosophical history that has ever been attempted in the English language'. He admired it for characteristically Pattisonian reasons: 'It is learned in the only true sense of the word.' The book was certainly 'full of thought and original observation', but it was 'no speculative creation of a brilliant theorist'. He meant that Buckle was not the kind of thinker who sought to dazzle his readers with a few flashes of insight. On the contrary, the book had a solidity about it beneath its intellectual originality: Pattison marvelled at 'the labour and reading which it has cost to quarry the materials'.[25] Buckle, who as a young man inherited a substantial fortune, was careful with his money but lavish in his spending on books, and by the time of his death in his early 40s had built up a library of over twenty thousand books. Pattison was inclined to judge scholars by the size of their libraries, and, as Gibbon might have said, the richness of Buckle's footnotes showed that the library was no mere ornament.

Pattison characterized the nature of Buckle's intellectual project by deploying the familiar contrast, inherited from the eighteenth century, between the 'general' or 'philosophic' historian on the one hand and the 'special' historian on the other. Buckle belonged to the former category.

---

[22] Semmel, 'H. T. Buckle', 373.

[23] Curiously Semmel, who quotes Pattison's review, does not identify Pattison as the author, although the review was reprinted in Pattison's posthumous *Essays* and was discussed at some length by J. M. Robertson in his *Buckle and his Critics: A Study in Sociology* (London: Swan Sonnenschein, 1895), the book Semmel recognizes as the best treatment of Buckle's ideas: Semmel, 'H. T. Buckle', 380 & 384 n.2.

[24] Ian Small, *Conditions for Criticism: Authority, Knowledge, and Literature in the Late Nineteenth Century* (Oxford: Clarendon Press, 1991), pp. 49–50.

[25] Pattison, 'History of civilization in England', *Westminster Review* 68 o.s. (1857), reprinted in *Essays* II, p. 396.

But the reason why the philosophic historian could not get by on showy intellectualism alone was that 'special' or empirical historians had not done their work effectively. Whereas the general historian ought to be able to work on the basis of the findings of the special historian, in practice 'the work of [special] history-writing has been mostly performed by inferior men, who have not known what was worth recording and what was not'. As a result the philosophic historian had to do much of the drudgery himself. That reinforced the magnitude of Buckle's achievement.[26]

While Pattison approved of Buckle's philosophic history, he did not think he had succeeded in creating a science of society. Instead he thought he had done no more than formulate empirical generalizations – or what Mill, in his *System of Logic*, misleadingly termed empirical laws. After all, Buckle's principle that 'the totality of human actions is governed by the totality of human knowledge' was, on his own account, true only of European civilization: in tropical civilizations, 'external nature' is all. Pattison accepted Mill's principle that laws of historical development, to count as scientific, must be grounded in 'the laws of the human mind'; and hence it seemed to follow that Buckle had presented 'no law of society as such, but an empirical generalization from the course of affairs in a particular region'.[27]

Pattison was much more of a pessimist than Buckle. In particular, he did not share Buckle's confidence in the inevitable victory of knowledge over ignorance. He thought Buckle underestimated the role of human passions, and indeed of force, in history. Of course he agreed that intellectual progress was 'an element of national history', but he could not see that Buckle had demonstrated that it must be the determinant element. Is intellectual advance an inevitable process, he asked? 'Will society be regenerated by its intellect in spite of its passions?' Pattison wished he could believe it, but all societies hitherto had been characterized by a tension between a small educated minority and 'an overwhelming unen-lightened mass'. Usually the role of the educated minority had been a leavening role, rather than a directive one. For Pattison the position of knowledge and learning in society was always a precarious one, always vulnerable to an eruption of 'the sleeping volcano of passion'.[28] In his commonplace book Pattison continued to reflect on the problem of the role of ideas and knowledge in shaping history, citing instances that he thought disproved Buckle's intellectualism. Free trade, he considered, did

---

[26] Pattison, 'History of civilization', p. 397.     [27] Pattison, 'History of civilization', pp. 410, 424–5.
[28] Pattison, 'History of civilization', p. 430.

not triumph due to the diffusion of the abstract teachings of Adam Smith, but rather because of manufacturers' resentment at obstacles protection placed in the way of their own business. 'Prevailing systems of thought', he pronounced, 'are theories of that which is seen to succeed.'[29]

Pattison's position was unreservedly a liberal one: he insisted that knowledge was not a stationary possession to be defended against the barbarians, but was real only if it continued to press forward. 'The vitality of knowledge consists in its advance', he proclaimed, from which he inferred that 'We cannot suppress liberty to save civilization. The condition of true knowledge is freedom of speech and opinion.'[30]

There is an obvious echo here of Mill's *On Liberty*, which had been drafted but not yet published when Pattison reviewed Buckle. Pattison and Mill both took the view that knowledge had value only when it was 'real', and that it was real only when liable to be tested at the bar of free and open debate. We also have an echo of the conception of 'real' knowledge that Pattison deployed in his *Sermons* and in his various contributions to the debates on university reform. Pattison was deeply imbued with the characteristically nineteenth-century conviction that that which does not move forward stagnates and dies. We can speculate on possible sources of this notion: romanticism was one, and the emergent life sciences were another. Mill and Bagehot believed it as firmly as Pattison did. But in Pattison's case Newman is another possible source. 'Growth the only evidence of life' was one of Newman's cherished maxims, derived, he tells us, from the evangelical Thomas Scott.[31]

Pattison, then, was powerfully drawn towards the quintessentially nineteenth-century pursuit of the laws of intellectual development. But this captures only one side of his engagement with the history of ideas. To see the other side, we should turn to his review of John Veitch's *Memoir of Sir William Hamilton* in 1869.[32] This anonymous review, which has not previously been attributed to Pattison, provides such a deep insight into his fundamental convictions about intellectual culture that it deserves extended treatment.

---

[29] Bodleian MS Pattison 7*, pp. 602–3.   [30] Pattison, 'History of civilization', p. 430.
[31] Newman, *Apologia*, 26.
[32] [Pattison], Review of John Veitch, *Memoir of Sir William Hamilton, Bart, Saturday Review* 27 (1869), 683–4 (22 May) and 778–80 (12 June). This can be positively attributed to Pattison on the basis of a letter that Francis Pattison wrote to her sister, Rose Tuckwell, on 7 August 1869: 'I daresay William [Tuckwell] noticed 2 notices of Mark's on Veitch's Life of Sir W. Hamilton', Bodleian MS Pattison 140 f. 13.

We have already encountered the Scottish baronet Sir William Hamilton as a critic of *ancien régime* Oxford, and in that capacity he attracted Pattison's admiration. Professor first of Civil History and then of Logic and Metaphysics at Edinburgh, Hamilton was best known as a neo-Kantian philosopher, though nowadays he is encountered, if at all, by way of J. S. Mill's famous assault in his *Examination of Sir William Hamilton's Philosophy*. Pattison was no more friendly than Mill towards Kantian philosophy, which like Mill he thought potentially a prop for tradition and prejudice, and he reviewed Mill's book positively in 1865. In his notice of Veitch's life of Hamilton, however, he was much warmer towards Hamilton, who, he said, deserved to recover from his currently low reputation and to be restored to 'a noble niche in the temple of fame'. But the ground on which Pattison claimed such a niche for Hamilton is significant: he deserved to be remembered, Pattison wrote, not as an intellectual innovator or as the founder of a system, but as 'a transmitter of what has been thought and said'.[33] Whatever his purely philosophical standing, as a scholar and a man of learning Hamilton was unequalled in his time. He held in harness what Pattison elsewhere identified as 'the so often severed qualities – laborious industry and philosophical view'.[34] The remainder of the review develops this theme at some length: it is a very long review, amounting in all to some eight thousand words. It is worth dwelling on this piece, because Pattison can hardly have failed to be aware, at some level, that in appraising Hamilton's intellectual standing he was also appraising himself. Given his lifelong fascination with the scholar's journal, Pattison was evidently drawn to Hamilton in part by his commonplace book, a folio of twelve hundred pages which, he wrote, 'bears witness to a course of reading as varied, inquisitive, and resolute as was ever accomplished by man'.[35]

Pattison draws a contrast between philosophers and scholars. Scholars tend to have a horror of metaphysics, whereas metaphysicians generally have limited knowledge of what has been written before them on their subject. From this point of view Erasmus was the quintessential scholar, whereas Hobbes, Locke, Reid and Whately all had the characteristic vice of the metaphysician. What set Hamilton apart was that he combined the gifts of the philosopher with those of the scholar:

[33] [Pattison], Review of Veitch, *Memoir of Hamilton*, 683.
[34] [Pattison], 'Theology and philosophy', *Westminster Review* 63 o.s. (Jan. 1855), 227.
[35] [Pattison], Review of Veitch, *Memoir of Hamilton*, 779.

The characteristic distinction of Sir W. Hamilton's mind is the equilibrium in which the acquisitive and inventive faculties held each other. No professed metaphysician in our time has known so much of past philosophical opinion. No one so deeply read in philosophical literature has retained so much vigour of judgment and ingenuity of original thought.[36]

In short, his claim to distinction rested not on his contribution of new truths to philosophy, but rather on what Pattison terms his 'philosophical learning'. It is illuminating to find Pattison, who was no unthinking traditionalist, commending Hamilton for standing out against the modern cult of originality, to which he objected because it was often accompanied by a disdain for and ignorance of the past:

Instead of that superficial knowledge of the past, and that disdainful attitude towards it, which is the characteristic of 'modern thought,' he stood up to show that it is only in the light of the past that a true apprehension of the present is possible. For the narrow world of contemporary impression, dignified by the name experience, which bounds the horizon of our 'thinkers,' Hamilton aimed to substitute the experience of the race, as recorded in books. The conceited neglect of the historical aspect of philosophical questions throws away the only data for a solution of the questions themselves, as the very terms in which the questions must of necessity be stated depend for their meaning on their history. Hamilton may be justly stated in this respect to have restored and vindicated the true method of philosophical inquiry. The unlaborious interrogation of consciousness which had constituted the method of the Scottish philosophy of the last century sank at once on Hamilton's appearance. For the first time in the history of British speculation an encyclopaedic enumeration of the departments of intellectual philosophy, a statement of their mutual relations, and of the questions appropriate to each, was brought forward. This habit of mind has not yet become, as it has in Germany, a law rigorously incumbent on all who undertake to write, but that the existence of such a requirement is no longer unknown among us, even in the walks of speculation, is in great measure due to the precept and example of Hamilton.[37]

This passage gives us abundant insight into the criteria by which Pattison judged other thinkers. For him intellectual endeavour was a laborious activity which was not to be accomplished by flashy genius alone. As a reviewer, his favourite kind of commendation was to describe a book as 'a scholar's book'.[38] Next to that was to say that it rested on real labour: 'There is altogether a solid, hardworking character about the book

---

[36] [Pattison], Review of Veitch, *Memoir of Hamilton*, 778. Cf. Pattison, 'Present state of theology in Germany', pp. 229–30, where he commends the theologian F. C. Baur for his 'rare union of opposite qualifications – viz. the most extensive reading, with the most elastic vigour of original speculation. He has Mosheim's colossal capacity for details, with Schleiermacher's inventive genius'.

[37] [Pattison], Review of Veitch, *Memoir of Hamilton*, 779.

[38] For example, [Pattison], Review of Edward Poste, *Aristotle on Fallacies, or the Sophistici Elenchi; with a Translation and Notes*, *Saturday Review* 25 (1868), 21–2.

which distinguishes it very favourably among the shoals of showy and flimsy productions with which we are daily inundated.'[39] While he admired Michelet's 'artistic skill', what made his history of France 'magnificent' was the 'labour of research' on which it rested, and which that artistic skill tended to conceal.[40] Pattison had no great respect for the virtue of wearing one's learning lightly. He regarded it rather as a badge to be worn with pride. To be a truly learned thinker was to approach one's subject from a position of full and deep familiarity with its history. Some might hear the voice of Dryasdust speaking here, but that would be to underestimate the importance of what Pattison was saying. He was fundamentally right to say that the intellectual problems we encounter, at least in the humanities, are problems that can only be understood – indeed, only make sense – historically; that is, in the light of an awareness of how these problems have been formulated and 'solved' in different intellectual traditions:

In short, whatever might have been the case in the days of Lamech and Methuselah, it is vain to attempt to write now independent of extant philosophies. It is not in our power, either in philosophy or in poetry, to begin the world anew. Every word we use has a history, and its history modifies its signification.[41]

Pattison, then, had a powerful sense of being the trustee of an intellectual inheritance which he could not escape or renounce, and which it was his duty to help pass on to the next generation of scholars. This standpoint shaped his understanding of universities: far from conceiving 'research' chiefly in terms of the discovery of new knowledge, he understood it in terms of the transmission of an intellectual inheritance that was constitutive of civilization. Intellectual history was important to him not as a specialist pursuit but as an essential aspect of the duty of mental cultivation. As he wrote of Hamilton, conceding all his faults and areas of ignorance, 'what remains constitutes a vast possession of learning, understanding by that term not mere acquisition, but acquisition impregnated by a living mind, and subordinated to a rational judgment'.[42] It was not learning itself that was the highest value for Pattison: it was that 'living mind', that 'rational judgment', that ever-developing intellect which, in his *Memoirs*, he found in himself.

---

[39] [Pattison], Review of Thomas Lewin, *Fasti Sacri; or, a Key to the Chronology of the New Testament* (1865), *Saturday Review* 21 (1866), 172–3.
[40] [Pattison], 'History, biography, voyages and travels', *Westminster Review* 68 o.s. (Oct. 1857), 576–7.
[41] [Pattison], 'Theology and philosophy', *Westminster Review* 63 o.s. (Jan. 1855), 224.
[42] [Pattison], Review of Veitch, 779.

There are two passages in the *Memoirs* which echo remarkably closely these themes from his review of Hamilton. The first occurs in his discussion of the principles applied in elections to Oriel fellowships in the era of the Noetics. Oriel was notable for being willing to overlook the verdict of the public examiners, most famously in electing Newman in spite of his mediocre degree. This was because the college designed its own fellowship examination with the aim of detecting originality as opposed to solidity of achievement. Pattison, who was nearly a beneficiary of this policy, accepts it was by no means ideal:

There was doubtless a serious defect in this system. The men thus picked out as men of original minds were apt to have too little respect for the past because they were ignorant of it. A man who does not know what has been thought by those who have gone before him is sure to set an undue value upon his own ideas – ideas which have perhaps been tried and found wanting. As accumulated learning stifles the mental powers, so original thinking has been known to bring about a puffy, unsubstantial mental condition. It was only in the then condition of the University, hidebound in the traditions of narrow clerical prejudice, that the new Oriel school of the Noetics, as they came to be called, could be welcomed as a wholesome invasion of a scurfy pond, stagnant with sameness and custom. The Noetics knew nothing of the philosophical movement which was taking place on the continent; they were imbued neither with Kant nor with Rousseau, yet this knot of Oriel men was distinctly the product of the French Revolution. They called everything in question; they appealed to first principles, and disallowed authority as a judge in intellectual matters.[43]

Pattison thought the cult of originality for its own sake had resurfaced in Oxford in the effluence of the liberal revival that followed Newman's secession. 'The sudden withdrawal of all reverence for the past has generated a type of intellect which is not only offensive to taste but is unsound as training.'[44] He deplored this mental one-sidedness, which made men vulnerable to intellectual fashion, something that was just as contemptible as the prejudice of the past. He even thought the 'reactionary wave' which he expected to flow from the idealist revival might have a salutary effect on Oxford, in undermining 'the egoism and the ignorant adoption of fashionable freethinking, which now characterises young Oxford', and in their place restoring 'the lost virtues of humility, reverence, and the recognition of a power beyond ourselves'. If the discovery of Kantianism led to 'a

---

[43] Pattison, *Memoirs*, pp. 78–9. This passage was noted with approval by Gladstone: British Library Add MS 44792 f. 53. It echoed an analysis of the Noetics which Pattison had previously offered in 'Philosophy at Oxford', 84.

[44] Pattison, *Memoirs*, p. 240.

reexamination of the old problem of thought', Pattison was confident that the progressive party would benefit from the challenge, and 'a reasoned conviction may arise to take the place of a lazy and thoughtless acquiescence in the opinions of the fashionable periodicals'.[45]

The synthesis of history and philosophy which he found in Hamilton was at the heart of intellectual culture as Pattison understood it. He detested the supreme confidence of the man who was familiar only with the latest body of ideas, and as a reviewer was severe on the thinker who wrote with little reference to previous systems, and who 'elaborates a familiar thought with the proud march of a traveller who is disclosing an undiscovered region'.[46] He would have agreed with Mill that 'originality, in any high sense of the word, is now scarcely ever attained but by minds which have undergone elaborate discipline', and with F. D. Maurice that the most profoundly original thinkers of the present are those who know most thoroughly what their predecessors thought.[47] For Pattison, philosophical wisdom depended upon an historically informed perspective on the ideas and opinions of the present. In one of his university sermons he maintained that public opinion governed the world, and that the notion that we shape our ideas for ourselves is an illusion:

It is only the philosophic observer who has risen to take a survey of human history as a whole who can trace the genesis of opinion, who can see that the individual is a molecular unit, that what society thinks and does is determined by a law from which there is no escape.[48]

To be learned in the history of ideas, then, was an essential step on the road to philosophic freedom, an indispensable technique in the pursuit of the philosophical life. Only on that basis could one hope to liberate oneself on the one hand from bondage to the past, and on the other hand from enslavement to the latest fashion.

RELIGION AND THE AGE OF REASON

Pattison's most enduring contribution to the history of ideas was his study of 'Tendencies of Religious Thought in England, 1688–1750', published in *Essays and Reviews* in 1860. This was a substantial piece of work, stretching to about 25,000 words; and it inspired one of the most distinguished of Victorian studies in intellectual history, Leslie Stephen's *History of English*

---

[45] Pattison, *Memoirs*, p. 243.
[46] [Pattison], 'Theology and philosophy', *Westminster Review* 63 o.s. (Jan. 1855), 224.
[47] Quoted in Capaldi, *John Stuart Mill*, p. 282.    [48] Pattison, *Sermons*, p. 129.

*Thought in the Eighteenth Century.* Stephen acknowledged his debt in the preface, and said that he wished to 'give a more detailed and systematic account of the movement so admirably characterised in that essay'.[49] This is something Pattison himself had planned to do, and he was distressed to find that Stephen had beaten him, although there is no evidence that Pattison had seriously embarked on writing such a book. Stephen's debt to Pattison is quite well known. Less well known is the influence the essay exerted on Pattison's old pupil, the jurist A. V. Dicey. He wrote that it was Pattison's contribution to *Essays and Reviews* that 'originally kindled' his interest in the history of public opinion, which bore fruit in another famous Victorian contribution to the history of ideas, his *Lectures on the Relation between Law and Public Opinion in England during the Nineteenth Century.*[50] Indeed, Dicey's argument bore a striking structural similarity to the argument Pattison developed in his pioneering essay.

Pattison's essay was set apart from the other contributions to *Essays and Reviews* by its purely historical character, and for that reason it was exempt from much (but not all) of the controversy. It has also lasted better than the other essays: for Josef Altholz it was 'the one truly original and enduring contribution to *Essays and Reviews*', for Owen Chadwick 'the best single study in the book', and for Basil Willey it was 'in a class apart from all the other essays'.[51] Its focus is on the deistical controversy in English religious thought in the first half of the eighteenth century. The essay certainly has something strikingly modern about it. It was partly that it eschewed theological partisanship, and partly that it developed a strong historical thesis around which its material was economically organized. Centrally, it argued that the rationalistic principle – the appeal to reason as the ultimate judge in matters of religion – was not the property of one party to the theological polemics of the age, but was a shared assumption that linked all parties.

This argument was presented as the main finding of Pattison's essay, but it could be considered the basic postulate of his method as an intellectual historian. Here too Pattison's work is illuminated by reference to Mill. In the *Logic*, Mill had followed Coleridge in emphasizing the high degree of consensus, or interdependence, existing among the different social

[49] Leslie Stephen, *History of English Thought in the Eighteenth Century* (London: Smith, Elder & Co., 1876), vol. I, p. v.
[50] Robert S. Raitt (ed.), *Memorials of Albert Venn Dicey* (London: Macmillan, 1925), pp. 1–2. Dicey's book was first published in 1905, but originated in a series of lectures he gave at Harvard in 1898.
[51] Josef L. Altholz, *Anatomy of a Controversy*, pp. 26–7 (for the Chadwick quotation as well as Altholz's own); Basil Willey, *More Nineteenth-Century Studies*, p. 150.

phenomena in a given society at a particular time. For that reason, in attempting to develop social dynamics – that is, a sociology setting out to determine the laws of social change – it was impossible to proceed incrementally by isolating particular social phenomena: 'in the filiation of one generation and another, it is the whole which produces the whole, rather than any part a part'.[52] Likewise, Pattison's method as an intellectual historian was to posit the common assumptions that underpinned the different branches of thought. The sciences might constitute a partial exception to this, he conceded, insofar as they proceeded progressively as one generation of scientists built on the findings of the preceding generation. But the starting point for the intellectual historian, or historian of thought, was that the 'thought' of an age possessed a unity, a common thread of assumptions that joined the different branches of thought. In an undated manuscript probably dating from 1865 he depicted 'European progress as one homogeneous growth', and inquired into the 'general causes which simultaneously affect all branches of knowledge'.[53]

In his contribution to *Essays and Reviews* Pattison was obviously concerned with just one branch of thought, but he was clear that to speak of 'religious thought' as opposed to 'theology' was already to highlight the permeability of the frontier between this area of thought and the rest of the intellectual world. The omnipresence of the rationalist principle was the organizing principle that allowed him to depict the period as a whole. A study of the entire religious thought of the period 1688–1750 was a very different undertaking from a study of, for example, the high church tradition or evangelicalism over a longer period. Pattison's essay could be seen as taking up Mill's invitation to explore 'the filiation of one generation and other'. Indeed, he wrote of 'tracing the filiation of consecutive systems'.[54] Thus he argued that the next coherent period in English religious thought, stretching from the middle of the eighteenth century to the advent of Tractarianism, was chiefly concerned with the 'external' rather than the 'internal' vindication of Christianity. Whereas in the earlier period controversialists aimed to show 'that there was nothing in the contents of the revelation which was not agreeable to reason', in the later period attention switched to 'the historical proof of the genuineness and

---

[52] Mill, *System of Logic* vol. II, p. 924.
[53] Bodleian MS Pattison 103, f. 3. On the previous folio of this notebook, Pattison refers to Lecky's history of rationalism, which was published in 1865 and which we know (MS Pattison 130, f. 58) that Pattison read in May of that year; and later on f. 3 he cites an article by Hillebrand in the *Revue Moderne* of May 1865.
[54] Pattison, 'Tendencies of religious thought', p. 256.

authenticity of the Christian records'.[55] The religious thought of the later period was shaped by the evidential school, whose most famous representative was William Paley. Importantly, Pattison did not treat the rise of the evidential school as an accidental occurrence or the product of mere conjuncture: rather, it was 'the natural sequel and supplement of that which had preceded it, which dealt with the intrinsic credibility of the Christian revelation'. The history of ideas proceeded according to the workings of the laws of mind: 'This historical succession of the schools is the logical order of the argument. For when we have first shown that the facts of Christianity are not incredible, the whole burden of proof is shifted to the evidence that the facts did really occur.'[56]

There are two ways in which Pattison's essay might be read. On the one hand, it may be seen as an exercise in 'scientific' theology or non-partisan history of religious thought of the kind he had studied in Germany. 'We have not yet learnt, in this country [unlike in Germany], to write our ecclesiastical history on any better footing than that of praising up the party, in or out of the Church, to which we happen to belong.'[57] This was how he represented the essay in his *Memoirs*, where he concluded bitterly that the response to the volume showed that this kind of scientific theology remained impossible in England. On the other hand it may be read as an attempt to vindicate his own growing rationalism by uncovering its roots in an authentically Christian tradition of religious thought:

Rationalism was not an anti-Christian sect outside the Church making war against religion. It was a habit of thought ruling all minds, under the conditions of which all alike tried to make good the peculiar opinions they might happen to cherish. The Churchman differed from the Socinian, and the Socinian from the Deist, as to the number of articles in his creed; but all alike consented to test their belief by the rational evidence for it.

So rationalism was not, as the Puseyites thought, 'a system opposed to revealed religion, and imported into this country from Germany at the beginning of the present century'.[58]

Probably Pattison would not have recognized the distinction between the two ways of reading his essay. Indeed he said as much in a university sermon he preached a decade later. There he covered much of the same ground as in the essay of 1860, but now he traced the German roots of

[55] Pattison, 'Tendencies of religious thought', p. 260.
[56] Pattison, 'Tendencies of religious thought', pp. 260–1.
[57] Pattison, 'Tendencies of religious thought', p. 255.
[58] Pattison, 'Tendencies of religious thought', p. 257.

eighteenth-century English theological rationalism, before going on to
chart the demise of natural theology in the middle of the nineteenth
century. The eighteenth-century rationalists, he argued, followed
Leibnitz in the belief that truth was unitary. Our observation of God's
dealings with the natural world enabled us rationally to infer his moral
attributes. This was, for Pattison, 'the only footing on which a sound
theology can rest, if it is to rank as co-ordinate with other branches of
knowledge, and to command the assent of an instructed society'.[59] So in
exploring the eighteenth-century rationalists, Pattison was on the one hand
undertaking a scientific investigation in the history of religious thought,
and on the other hand he was uncovering the ancestry of the kind of
scientific theology to which he was committed.

But it is appropriate also to comment on the significance of the idea of a
history of ideas for Pattison's essay. Basil Willey thought it 'an early –
indeed, in England, a pioneering – effort in a genre since become familiar,
I mean the "history of ideas"'.[60] And Pattison framed his line of investigation in terms that remind one of his review of Buckle: it was an attempt
to do something that had not hitherto been attempted, namely 'to apply
the laws of thought, and of the succession of opinion, to the course of
English theology'.[61] Quite what Pattison meant by the 'laws of thought' is
elusive, but it was an expression that recurred in his works: in his *Memoirs*,
he describes the development of his interest in 'the laws of the progress of
thought in modern Europe', while in his essay on German theology he
identifies as 'the historical law of the progress of the human Mind' that '[i]n
each wave of its advance, in each epoch-making conquest, some one nation
has taken the lead, and done the work, while all have shared in the
profits'.[62] The expression makes his ambitions seem rather grander than
what he actually set out to do. In practice Pattison's investigations into the
'laws of the progress of thought' aimed, more modestly, to understand
ideas historically. That was an integral part of what he understood by
learning. An essential step in the creation of a scientific theology was to
understand religious ideas as products of time and place, and not to read
the theological writers, preachers and religious polemicists of the past as if
they were participants in the battle of church parties in the present.

The idea of development – the notion that any phenomenon is to be
understood in the light of what went before – was an important feature of

[59] Pattison, *Sermons*, pp. 205–7.    [60] Willey, *More Nineteenth-Century Studies*, p. 151.
[61] Pattison, 'Tendencies of religious thought', p. 255.
[62] Pattison, *Memoirs*, pp. 310–11; 'Present state of theology in Germany', p. 217.

Pattison's intellectual outlook. This is how he articulated the idea in *Essays and Reviews*:

There is a law of continuity in the progress of theology which, whatever we may wish, is never broken off. In tracing the filiation of consecutive systems, we cannot afford to overlook any link in the chain, any age, except one in which religious opinion did not exist. Certainly we, in this our time, if we would understand our own position in the Church, and that of the Church in the age, if we would hold any clue through the maze of religious pretension which surrounds us, cannot neglect those immediate agencies in the production of the present, which had their origin towards the beginning of the eighteenth century.[63]

In a review of a German study of Epicharmus and the origins of comedy, he provides a brief survey of interpretations of the genesis of modern drama, and observes that 'There are "convulsionists" in literary history as in geology, who like epochs without antecedents. To others nothing begins to be; all is progress and development.'[64] Pattison belonged squarely with the developmentalists. Ideas had to be located in time and place. 'The one generalisation which is of any value in a history of opinions, theological or philosophical' was, he thought, 'to detect the hidden thread of connection which binds together the opinions of any generation with those of the generation which preceded and the generation which followed it.'[65] Ideas were not what people simply happened to be thinking: rather, they must be disclosed as emerging from a social and intellectual context. Each generation built on the work of the generation that went before, even if in some respects it reacted against it. Otherwise there was no reason to believe in a progressive interpretation of history. As he put it in his review of Buckle, intellectual truth, unlike moral sentiment, is 'in its very essence traditive and progressive'.[66]

This insistence on the importance of showing how each generation depends on the immediately preceding one is liable to strike Pattison's readers as odd. Is it not something of a platitude to the historian? If so, why did Pattison, whose aversion to platitude was well known, repeat the point so often? Why did he represent it as a fundamental dictum of the philosophy of history and the history of ideas?

The clearest answer may be found in a lecture he gave at the London Institution early in 1881 and published in an American periodical shortly

---

[63] Pattison, 'Tendencies of religious thought', p. 256.
[64] Pattison, Review of Aug. O. Fr. Lorenz, *Leben und Schriften des Koers Epicharmos, nebst seiner Fragmentensammlung*, *Saturday Review* 18 (29 Oct. 1864), 541–2.
[65] Pattison, Review of Stoughton, *Ecclesiastical History*, 10.
[66] Pattison, 'History of civilization', p. 410.

afterwards. There he depicted the engine of the historical process as a dialectic in which the conservative's championship of stability confronted the reformer's drive for innovation: a dialectic, in short, between 'the thing that is' and 'the thing that might be'.[67] Because when young we tend to be impatient for change, but as we get older we develop a stronger attachment to existing institutions and tried and tested ways, the thesis and the antithesis are held in check by nature, and on that foundation 'the equilibrium of a political community is maintained'.[68] But this equilibrium is a progressive equilibrium which ensures stability in change, and change in stability. 'The progress of human society, from the lowest type of animal aggregation toward the most highly organized state which we can conceive, is being conducted all the while by means of the perpetual struggle between what is and what might be.'[69]

It was obvious, Pattison remarked, that conservatism, or 'persistence in the old', could not on its own generate progress; but neither, he argued, could 'the spirit of improvement'. Each required the other. The reason he gave is illuminating:

A little reflection, however, will show us that no improvement whatever in art, in science, in government, in manufacture, or in any process of any kind, can be made except by one who is in complete and practical possession of the old method which is to be improved upon.[70]

At one level Pattison's argument reads as a straightforwardly Burkean vindication of gradual change against radicalism, a vindication of evolution against revolution. His remarks on the French Revolution are fully in line with the standard criticisms levelled at it by nineteenth-century Whiggery. It sprang from a philosophy – that of the Encyclopédie – which 'conceived of man as of a being everywhere and at all times one and the same', and sought to design a system of law 'not by the cumbrous process of codifying and correcting existing customary law', but instead by deriving it 'directly from the dictates of right reason'. The French mind was too logical to deal with 'the friction of personal interests', and their temper was 'too impatient to await the natural growths of time', and so they 'dreamed of constitutions

---

[67] In a university sermon preached two decades previously, Pattison made a similar point, speaking of a dialectic between 'the tendency to perpetuate type, and the tendency to deviate from it': Pattison, *Sermons*, pp. 48–9. In an address given a few months before his lecture to the London Institution he spoke of 'the force of custom' and 'the force of the reason of the thing': Pattison, 'Industrial shortcomings: an address', *Fortnightly Review* 34 o.s. (1880), 738.

[68] Pattison, 'The thing that might be', *North American Review* 132 (1881), 320. A manuscript draft of this paper, mostly in Meta Bradley's hand, is to be found in Bodleian MS Pattison 117, ff. 1–31.

[69] Pattison, 'The thing that might be', 321.   [70] Pattison, 'The thing that might be', 322.

framed according to an abstract idea of the state'. What was the result? 'The history of France for the last hundred years is a comment on the impossibility of superseding the natural agencies of progress by artificial legislation; it is an exhibition, on a vast scale, of the fallacy of imposing by authority the what might be, instead of ingrafting it with scrupulous care upon what is.'[71] The French, in short, simply misconceived the nature of social progress:

Institutions, like minds, only grow by enlargement and assimilation, not by abrupt change. It has been said of our commerce, by the present premier, that it advances by leaps and bounds. Not so with progress toward the social ideal. The march of civilization, like the march of nature, is one of imperceptible transformation.[72]

However, it is worth noting also that Pattison's conception of evolutionary progress has a direct bearing on why he was so drawn to the history of ideas. For the dictum that successful innovation rests on a firm grasp of 'the thing that is' applies not just to practical but also to theoretical innovation. Consider what he had to say about the Copernican revolution, for example:

One of the most radical revolutions on the record of science is that which substituted the Copernican conception of our system for the Ptolemaic conception, according to which the earth was stationary and placed at the center of solar space. This is an extreme case of novelty, inasmuch as the whole of the old idea had to be thrown away, and a new conception, the direct contradictory of the old, had to be taken up in its place. But the new conception could not have been arrived at, and was not in fact reached by Copernicus, without a thorough possession of, and habitual meditation upon, the Ptolemaic hypothesis, and the mathematical tradition of the Greeks.[73]

Similarly, Arkwright could not have invented the water-frame if he had not had a prior familiarity with the mechanics of the spindle. Indeed, in general '[i]t is the man who can most deftly and expeditiously use the received method who is most likely to strike out an easier way of doing the same thing'.[74] Michael Oakeshott could not have put it better.[75] Improvement depends upon immersion in an established technique rather than upon abstract reasoning from first principles about the best way of doing something. Pattison made the same point in his presidential address to the Salt Schools at Shipley in October 1880. There he warned against the simplistic

[71] Pattison, 'The thing that might be', 323.    [72] Pattison, 'The thing that might be', 324.
[73] Pattison, 'The thing that might be', 323.    [74] Pattison, 'The thing that might be', 327.
[75] Michael Oakeshott, 'Rationalism in politics', in his *Rationalism in Politics and Other Essays* (London: Methuen, 1967), pp. 1–36.

view that custom was 'a dead weight, a useless burden, from which it is a gain in the race of life to be able to free ourselves'. Tradition was an evil only when regarded as sacred. Properly considered, it had to be our starting point in any enterprise, practical or theoretical:

Tradition is the wisdom of our ancestors, the form in which the world-experience has been preserved for us. We cannot afford to throw our inheritance away, and to begin the world anew with each generation as it is born. We begin with the tradition, but conscious that it is ours to add to it, to improve it where it is defective, to amend it where it is erroneous. Custom must work *with* life and not *against* it.[76]

This was why a long-range account of the progress of humanity should not confine itself to a general depiction of the abstract forces at work – the conflict between science and faith, for instance – but must consider particular progressive movements in the context of their time and place. But we can also see why the study of the history of ideas was so integral to Pattison's intellectual project. He thought of himself as a philosopher; as one interested in the exploration of general ideas. But he came to the realization that any progress in solving intellectual problems must begin with a full historical exploration of how they came to be seen as problems, and solutions must be framed against the background of previous attempts to solve them.

Pattison's fullest analysis of the progressive theory of history came in his extended review of Leslie Stephen's history of eighteenth-century English thought, published in the radical *Fortnightly Review* in March 1877.[77] This was commissioned by John Morley, who had a high esteem for Pattison as a philosopher of history, and who evidently urged him to use this opportunity to address this large topic.[78] Certainly the article cost Pattison more effort than most: he complained in his diary about 'this tiresome art[icle] for Morley', and vowed 'never will I write again upon a thesis set by an editor'.[79] He was unhappy with having to deliver an article he deemed 'in a very crude state' after some six weeks' work.[80] As we have noted, Pattison felt that Stephen's book was one he himself could and should have written,

---

[76] Pattison, 'Industrial shortcomings', 738–9. In some notes for his autobiography written soon after this, Pattison quoted A. P. Stanley: "The choice is between absolute individual separation from every conceivable outward form of organisation, & continuance in one or other of those wh[ich] exist, in the hope of modifying or improving it.' Bodleian MS Pattison 138, f. 32.
[77] Pattison, 'The Age of Reason', *Fortnightly Review* 27 o.s. (1877), 343–61. It is curious that Nettleship did not reprint this in the posthumous edition of Pattison's *Essays*.
[78] Morley, *Recollections*, vol. I, pp. 71–2.
[79] Bodleian MS Pattison 130, f. 164, 18–19 Jan. 1877.
[80] Bodleian MS Pattison 130, f. 169, 17 Feb. 1877.

and its appearance discouraged him from developing his contribution to
*Essays and Reviews* into a full-length study, as many people, including
Matthew Arnold, had urged him to do.[81] But, perhaps realizing that this
was a book he aspired to write rather than one he was seriously planning to
bring to fruition, he recognized the quality of Stephen's book and did not
vent his annoyance at a rival. Instead – having already published a notice of
the book in the *Academy* – he took the opportunity to survey the rise of
progressive at the expense of cyclical conceptions of history, and to consider their significance. He seems to have engaged particularly closely with
a study of French and German philosophies of history published a few
years before by a St Andrews philosopher, Robert Flint.[82] Pattison seems
not to have drawn the distinction which Mill drew in the *System of Logic*
between the idea of progress as linear development and the idea of progress
as improvement, which is why he was able to identify the cyclical conception (or the 'theory of the decay of nations as the inevitable law of
history') with 'Calvinistic pessimism' and the developmental conception
('the theory of the progress of humanity') with philosophical optimism. He
put forward some interesting speculations on the reasons for the demise of
the former and the rise of the latter: the theory of decay was the 'natural
expression' of an era in which religious wars had wrought 'misery and
desolation', whereas the optimistic conception was equally naturally 'the
expression of the desire to live and enjoy which gradually diffused itself
over the West, dating from 1648'.[83] Herder and Kant were the key figures in
the promulgation of this 'gospel of progress'; though Pattison, who always
thought philosophical idealism a form of obfuscation, regretted that in
Germany 'the theory was sublimated into an obscure metaphysic, useless
but harmless'. Darwinism, in which many have detected an underlying
pessimism, was for Pattison the English application of this gospel of
progress.[84]

The other important theme in his review of Stephen was his identification of the novelty and distinctiveness of the 'history of thought' as an
intellectual pursuit. He observed that to speak of 'thought' as an abstract
noun was something of a nineteenth-century innovation: in the eighteenth
century it might have been possible to speak of 'chaos of thought and
reason, all confus'd', but not of 'modern thought', or 'Greek thought', or

[81] Matthew Arnold to Pattison, 20 Jan. 1876: Bodleian MS Pattison 57, ff. 191–2.
[82] Robert Flint, *The Philosophy of History in France and Germany* (Edinburgh and London: Blackwood, 1874). Pattison records reading this on 2, 5, 6, 8 and 10 January 1877: Bodleian MS Pattison 130, ff. 162–3.
[83] Pattison, 'Age of Reason', 349.    [84] Pattison, 'Age of Reason', 349.

'English thought'. These expressions were characteristic of the nineteenth century; and what was characteristic about them was that they implied an underlying interdependence of the different kinds of intellectual pursuits coexisting in a given society at a given time. On this assumption rested the logic of a history of thought. Indeed, Pattison went further. What was at issue here was not simply the interdependence of different intellectual pursuits, but the interdependence of all aspects of social life: the idea 'that all the branches of human activity are allied developments of some few governing thoughts'. Without that organic conception of society, 'a philosophy of history is not possible'. Why has Pattison – echoing Stephen – slipped from intellectual history to general history here? And why has he slipped from 'a history of thought' to 'a philosophy of history'? His process of reasoning, I think, went like this. A philosophy of history depends on a law of progress; progress is a necessary feature of the history of ideas, whereas it is not a necessary feature of other kinds of history; and hence the idea that general history is a story of progress must depend on an intellectualist account of history, in which 'all the varied doings and sayings of any generation [are] an efflux of its leading ideas'.[85]

Pattison was certainly not simply describing or analysing Stephen's approach here. We can find the same core ideas in a manuscript draft for his projected history of European learning which he appears to have written in 1865 or soon after. 'It has been gradually becoming more evident that the history of Literature, Science, the Arts, Philosophy, cannot be treated apart from each other, or from that of general progress. These were not so many independent developments, but all alike due to the same general causes.' Whereas history had formerly been written in terms of 'the efforts of individual genius', it was now coming to be understood that 'European progress' constitutes 'one homogeneous growth', and consequently that the individual is to be seen as 'the exemplification instead of the cause'. The premise that would underpin Pattison's projected history of learning, then, was that '[t]he doctrines or theories prevailing at any given epoch, are the efflorescence of all the mental conditions then extant'.[86]

Pattison does not appear to have explored the possible tension between two ideas which he tended to run together. One was the conception of society as an organic whole, in which a few leading ideas shaped developments in all branches of intellectual activity: art and literature, science and philosophy, history and political theory. The other was the idea that progress was pre-eminently a characteristic of the history of ideas, because

---

[85] Pattison, 'Age of Reason', 344–6.    [86] Bodleian MS Pattison 103, f. 3.

in the intellectual world, unlike (he thought) other spheres of social activity, each generation built on the discoveries of the generation that went before. But this conception of incremental progress surely works better for a single branch of intellectual activity considered in isolation than for mentalities. After all, in his review of Stephen, Pattison dwelt at some length on the romantic 'reaction against the eighteenth century' which he took to be a decisive feature of the intellectual history of the nineteenth century. While he acknowledged that there was something inevitable about this reaction against the 'arrogant self-satisfaction' of eighteenth-century rationalism, nevertheless it was a *mere* reaction which had contributed little of lasting value: 'In many departments of mind, in the discipline of character, in the loftiest manifestations of feeling, such as religion, philosophy, art, architecture, it has been fifty years lost. But the rights of the legitimate monarch – the sovereign reason – have only been in abeyance the while; they are inalienable.' In the course of time the heritage of the eighteenth century would have to be recovered.[87]

Moreover, Pattison seems to have been less than convinced that the theory of the interdependence of intellectual activities applied equally well to all branches of mental activity. His justification for a biographical approach to his history of classical learning seems to have been that in the sciences, both physical and historical, the influence of individuals counted for more, and the influence of the *Zeitgeist* for less, than the 'school of spontaneous development' allowed. While the test of time, and the assent of the community of scientists and scholars, was necessary to establish truths, it was important not to overlook 'the influence of individual reasons in putting in a true light these proved truths'.[88] In another draft he declared: 'The progress of Philology in modern Europe from the Revival to the present time should be treated in a separate History. Like the Physical Sciences, the subject is too special to be properly included in the General Histories of Literature.'[89] While the postulate that the more specialized and technical academic pursuits are harder to incorporate into a general history of thought than other branches of literature might be readily accepted, the reason Pattison offered – that the influence of great individuals is more important in the sciences – seems paradoxical. He was sensitive to the social context of intellectual activity, and it may be that he simply meant that public opinion did more to shape general literature than it did to influence more specialist work.

---

[87] Pattison, 'Age of Reason', especially 350–1, 356.
[88] Bodleian MS Pattison 103, f. 3.    [89] Bodleian MS Pattison 112, f. 111.

We cannot leave the subject of Pattison's interest in developmental theories of history without considering the question of the influence of Newman, whose *Essay on the Development of Christian Doctrine* was published in November 1845, just weeks after his reception into the Roman church. It constituted an important justification for his conversion. The Oxford Movement had defended the essential catholicity of the Church of England by means of an appeal to antiquity: Rome had added doctrines that were unknown to the early church; the Protestant denominations had tended to jettison even some practices and doctrines that were present in the primitive church; the Church of England was the closest to authentic antiquity. As Pattison noted in his diary just at the point he was entering the Tractarian fold, 'The study of the Fathers is important to the Christian Divine of every Church, but necessary to the Divine of the Ch[urch] of England, whose doctrines and institutions rest on the basis of primitive usage.'[90] The starting point of Newman's *Essay* was a growing recognition that the appeal to the authority of primitive usage was insufficient. If growth was the only evidence of life, as Newman believed, then surely the living church must develop also, in doctrine as well as in practice. But did that mean that the Church had changed, and that what the Church had once been it was no longer? No, according to Newman: it was not that the Church now held doctrines which it had once rejected; rather, it now defined truths of which it had once been unconscious.[91]

Since Pattison was often at Littlemore when Newman was working on the *Essay* this direction of thought must have impressed itself on his mind. Indeed, it may be that he anticipated Newman: whereas Newman was preoccupied with the theory of development from late 1842, the diary shows Pattison articulating the outline of the concept of the development of doctrine as early as 1838, in his discussion of Hampden's Bampton Lectures of 1832.[92] One of Newman's predecessors in working out the idea of development and its implications was the German Catholic theologian, J. A. Möhler. It is unclear whether Newman read him: he might have done, since his key work, *Die Einheit in der Kirche* (*Unity in the Church*) (1825) had been translated into French, and this translation was to be found in the library at Littlemore. Whether or not Newman read it,

---

[90] Bodleian MS Pattison 5, ff. 8–9.
[91] Owen Chadwick, *From Bossuet to Newman: The Idea of Doctrinal Development* (Cambridge: Cambridge University Press, 1957), p. 154.
[92] Duncan Nimmo, 'Towards and away from Newman's theory of doctrinal development: pointers from Mark Pattison in 1838 and 1846', *Journal of Theological Studies* N. S. 29 (1978), 160–1.

Pattison certainly did, along with another of his works, the *Symbolik*.[93] In short, Pattison was probably much more than a passive recipient of Newman's interest in the theory of development.

THE CRITIQUE OF POSITIVISM

A final major influence on nineteenth-century theories of history was Comtean positivism. As Pattison put it, positivism pointed 'triumphantly to the past history of humanity as the record of its inevitable march to conquest'.[94] Pattison's prolonged encounter with this movement deserves extended treatment.

Auguste Comte (1798–1857) was one of the seminal minds of the nineteenth century. Although he drew on the ideas of a number of predecessors, especially his mentor Henri de Saint-Simon, there can be no real doubt that the system of ideas that made such a deep impact on the intellectual world of the nineteenth century bore Comte's own distinctive stamp, not least in its encyclopaedic range and in its dogmatic articulation.[95]

Positivism sprang, in the first place, from the conflict of political ideas in the era of the French Revolution and Restoration. Coming to intellectual maturity under the Restoration, Comte diagnosed the political crisis of the time as, at root, an intellectual and spiritual crisis which arose from the absence of any settled spiritual authority following the demise of medieval Christendom. This might seem too long-range a diagnosis: what kind of crisis is it that lasts three centuries? But for Comte this crisis may have begun with the Reformation, but it came to a head with the questioning of Christian belief in the Enlightenment.

This diagnosis was underpinned by a metahistorical narrative which does much to explain the appeal of positivism to an age which thirsted for system. Comte thought that ideas drove history, and he divided history into three stages according to the reigning cast of mind. These were the theological, the metaphysical and the positive stages. What characterized the modern mind was that it limited itself to an inquiry into the relations among observable phenomena, whereas formerly human beings had sought some ultimate explanation of those phenomena in terms of

---

[93] Chadwick, *From Bossuet to Newman*, p. 118. Pattison mentions reading *Unity*, in the French, in a diary entry for 3 October 1843 which is quoted in the *Memoirs*, although Pattison, or his widow, or the printer, wrongly rendered the author's name as 'Mœhrer': Pattison, *Memoirs*, p. 193.

[94] Pattison, *Sermons*, p. 130.

[95] The paragraphs that follow draw chiefly on the introduction to H. S. Jones (ed.), *Comte: Early Political Writings* (Cambridge: Cambridge University Press, 1998), pp. vii–xxviii.

supernatural agency (God or gods) or some abstract force such as 'nature'. Most sciences had made the transition to the positive state: astronomy had supplanted astrology, and chemistry had replaced alchemy. Sociology, however, dealt with the most concrete and complex subject matter and was the last to make the transition: hence the prevalence of notions of divine right, which belonged to the theological state, and natural rights, which belonged to the metaphysical. But it too was destined to become a positive science, and once it had done so the reconstruction of social order on a positive basis would become possible.

Positivism repudiated theism and theology; but it embraced religion, which Comte considered a necessary part of any cohesive social order. Comte found in medieval Europe the prototype of a stable social order: in particular, he highlighted the separation of the temporal power from the spiritual, and the organization of the latter on an international basis under the control of the papacy. Any social order must exhibit these structural characteristics. But the clergy could no longer supply the spiritual power, for their authority rested on a doctrinal system that was intellectually obsolete. Since all knowledge must henceforth be positive, the spiritual power must pass accordingly to a positivist clerisy: not the scientists themselves, since they were specialists who lacked an overview, but the positive philosophers. Their role would be to formulate authoritative teachings on the basis of the positive sciences. And since Comte came to believe that man was as much a creature of emotion as of reason – indeed, more so – the trappings of religion would be needed to support the social order, and a 'religion of humanity' would be instituted. People would now worship not some supernatural being, but humanity itself considered collectively.

Comte's impact on the world of ideas was both deep and broad in the decades after his death. It was by no means confined to France, but extended as far as Latin America, where his influence was especially important and prolonged. His followers played formative roles in shaping new republics in France, Portugal, Brazil and Czechoslovakia. While positivism cannot be said to have had much of an impact on British politics, its intellectual significance was by no means negligible.

Victorian Comtism is often depicted as a small-scale and rather ineffective movement. Narrowly defined, it was. There were few strict disciples of Comte, and many of these, curiously enough, came from one rather obscure Oxford college, Wadham. But considered more loosely it was an almost omnipresent feature of the intellectual landscape for a quarter of a century – the period roughly coinciding with Pattison's rectorship. The idea of a 'religion of humanity' had a powerful appeal to many intellectual figures who sought a way to sustain moral earnestness in the face of an erosion of Christian belief. Most of the leading intellectual figures of the period engaged with the claims of the religion of humanity, whether they came out in favour of it or against it. These included J. S. Mill, Gladstone, Seeley, Sidgwick, Sir James Fitzjames Stephen, Leslie Stephen and Mallock. Such was its place in the intellectual life of the period that in October 1888 Arthur Balfour took time off from his commitments as Chief Secretary for Ireland to address the Church Congress on precisely the topic of the religion of humanity. He understood the term to embrace 'attempts to find in the "worship of humanity", or, as some more soberly phrase it, in the "service of man", a form of religion unpolluted by any element of the supernatural'.[96]

The reader might expect to find Pattison among these positivist fellow-travellers. He had abandoned Christian orthodoxy for essentially intellectual reasons. As we have seen he was interested in grand philosophies of history, and wrote sympathetically about Buckle, whom many commentators took for a Comtist. He evidently re-read Comte in writing his article on 'The Age of Reason' for John Morley.[97] He was deeply interested in the role that a clerisy, or intellectual elite, might have to play in modern society. And he took for granted the characteristically positivist dictum that social cohesion and solidarity must depend on 'benevolence', since 'interest is ever a dissociating and disorganising force'.[98] Moreover, many in Pattison's own circle were drawn in this direction, not least George Eliot, Mrs Humphry Ward, and, for a time, Francis Pattison; and in general there were curious points of contact between liberal Anglicans and positivists.[99] The topic of positivism recurred in Pattison's correspondence with his various women friends, including the American Mary Carroll, who told him that she had always meant to read Comte and had expected to find in him 'a good deal that was germane to my own mental tendencies'.[100] And the freethinking Meta Bradley, wanting to know 'what "religion" really means', reported that she had attended a positivist service in Liverpool in October 1880, although she was not impressed.[101]

Yet in fact Pattison came down firmly against the positivists. We can trace his antagonism towards positivism at least as far back as 1865, when in

---

[96] Arthur J. Balfour, *The Religion of Humanity. An Address delivered at the Church Congress, Manchester, October 1888* (Edinburgh: David Douglas, 1888), p. 2.
[97] Bodleian MS Pattison 130, f. 168, 10–11 Feb. 1877.
[98] Pattison, 'Age of Reason', 361.
[99] Christopher Kent, *Brains and Numbers: Elitism, Comtism, and Democracy in Mid-Victorian England* (Toronto, Buffalo & London: University of Toronto Press, 1978), p. 63; Dilke, 'Memoir', pp. 10, 21.
[100] Mary P. Carroll to Pattison, 12 July 1876: Bodleian MS Pattison 57, ff. 280–3.
[101] Meta Bradley to Pattison, 5 October 1880: Bodleian MS Pattison 119, ff. 180–2.

a university sermon he coupled together Catholicism and positivism as doctrines which identified education with 'the inculcation of truth', or 'indoctrination', and he contrasted them with '[t]he idea of the culture of mind for its own sake' which he advocated. The positivist did not value science properly so called, but rather 'the possession for use of truths which have been established as the result of the various moral and physical sciences'.[102] These themes were elaborated at greater length in 1876 in Pattison's most explicit engagement with positivism, his polemic with the leading positivist publicist Frederic Harrison.

Harrison, who had been a fellow of Wadham in the 1850s before settling in London and establishing himself in the law and journalism, was well known to Pattison. He had already played an important role in two key episodes in Pattison's career. He was the anonymous reviewer who, by highlighting the contributors' heterodoxy, had drawn the eyes of orthodoxy upon *Essays and Reviews* and thus unleashed the most famous religious controversy of the century. Some years later he had been instrumental in convening the meeting of university reformers in April 1866 out of which Pattison's *Suggestions on Academical Organisation* emerged. The two men also encountered each other at meetings of the Metaphysical Society. They were on amicable terms, though they were never intimate.

Harrison had met Comte in 1855, before he had been in any sense 'converted' to the positivist creed, and in the course of the next decade drew gradually closer to mainstream British positivism. By the 1870s he had emerged as Comte's most vocal and influential British disciple. In 1875 he contributed a pair of articles on positivism to the *Contemporary Review*. This journal was edited by James Knowles, the founder of the Metaphysical Society, and it reflected its editor's interest in projects of intellectual reconstruction which would help transcend the polarities of the time and resolve its perplexities and doubts.

This was very much the agenda addressed by Harrison in his articles on 'The religious and conservative aspects of positivism'. It was an age, he wrote, when 'all men are reconstructing their belief along with their armies and their navies'.[103] He set out to enhance the appeal of positivism by presenting its conservative credentials. The fact that positivists sought to subvert Christianity did not mean that they also aimed to subvert social

---

[102] Pattison, *Sermons*, pp. 122–5, sermon delivered 30 April 1865.
[103] Frederic Harrison, 'The religious and conservative aspects of positivism' (Part 1), *Contemporary Review* 26 (1875), 993.

order. On the contrary, they realized that, because Christianity was intellectually indefensible, a social order that took Christianity for its foundation was doomed to collapse. Positivists agreed with conservatives that there could be no social order without religion. What was needed, therefore, was religious reconstruction: the formation of a religion which, because it made no theological or metaphysical claims, could be reconciled with intellectual honesty and integrity.

Harrison was dismissive of mystical and theosophical offshoots of Christianity which sought to track the source of human knowledge of the divine to some innate or intuitive quality rather than to revelation.[104] In confining itself to 'the relation of man's soul to the unseen', religion was in danger of turning its back on its social function.[105] Yet that social function was precisely what Harrison valued in religion.

Pattison's reply constituted an incisive critique of positivism, and casts important light on his understanding of the relationship between religion and the progress of knowledge. He began with a warning against the resurgence of Catholicism, and especially of Ultramontanism, which he characterized as 'the organisation of the clerical power against modern society'. At the time he wrote, the reactionary pontificate of Pius IX was in full swing, and Pattison warned that Catholicism was no longer dormant, but had become 'an aggressive and menacing force' backed by 'millions of hereditary believers'.[106] In one sense positivism was the direct opposite of Catholicism: whereas Catholicism belonged to the past and set its face against reason, positivism was progressive and even revolutionary, since 'it would organise society on knowledge, instead of on usage and tradition as at present'.[107]

Pattison distinguished between the spirit and the doctrine of positivism. He was unreservedly in favour of the former, to which he thought the future must belong, provided that 'the conditions of peace and progressiveness are continued to the human race'; in other words, provided that political power did not align itself with the enemies of knowledge.[108] Pattison had, indeed, long held, with George Henry Lewes and others, that the spirit of positivism indicated the direction in which philosophy now had to proceed, since

---

[104] The Theosophical Society was founded in New York in 1875. It was thus a topical reference for Harrison to make, and for Pattison to take up. It aimed at the reconciliation of religious sects on the basis of a common system of ethics.

[105] Harrison, 'The religious and conservative aspects of positivism' (Part 1), 1000.

[106] Mark Pattison, 'The Religion of Positivism. By a "Theosophist"', *Contemporary Review* 27 (1875–6), 594.

[107] Pattison, 'Religion of Positivism', 595.     [108] Pattison, 'Religion of Positivism', 599.

metaphysics had fallen into discredit.[109] The *doctrine* of positivism was another matter altogether: it was 'one more impediment in the way of progress'. Indeed, the fundamental error of the positivists had been to reduce science into a doctrine. Pattison was quite right to see this as central to Comte's system: science was to yield a series of authoritative teachings. As Pattison realized, this notion betrayed a misunderstanding of the very spirit of modern science, which depended on conditions of intellectual liberty. 'Scientific method', he wrote, ' is not of importance to us only as intellectual training, it is of the essence of science.'[110]

For Pattison it was Comte's very zeal for systematization that led him astray. 'No one human intellect is capable of embracing and codifying all truth. It is not to be denied that truth is uniform and consistent. But it is at the same time so complex, and has so many sides to it, that as soon as it is systematised it is marred. All systems of philosophy are, as systems, false, because they are inadequate.'[111]

He went on to characterize the nature of Comte's enterprise in ways that make it seem practically the polar opposite of Pattison's own lifetime endeavour, as we have defined it. Comte, he maintained, was interested only in practical thought, and not in pure intellectual activity:

Of the vast regions over which the pure intellect can range, the larger part lies under a spiritual anathema. Of the pursuit of knowledge for its own sake as a good per se, as the most exalted form of human existence, of the contemplative life, he will not hear. Intellect presents itself to him as a disturbing force, as a breaking up the dead uniformity of habit and tradition which is to reign in his state.[112]

Pattison's whole life was devoted to 'the pursuit of knowledge for its own sake', and rested on the premise that this 'contemplative life' was indeed 'the most exalted form of human existence'. Yet he found in Comte a root-and-branch opponent of this ideal.

Pattison was no great admirer of France and the French, and this antagonism towards the contemplative life was, he thought, a distinctive characteristic of the French mind: in France, such is the influence of society over the individual intelligence that the mind is impelled to seek practical outlets, to act upon society. Intellectuals were thus led astray into devising utopian schemes, as Comte was.[113]

---

[109] Pattison, Review of George Henry Lewes, *The History of Philosophy from Thales to Comte*, 3rd edn, *Saturday Review* 23 (1867), 790–2.
[110] Pattison, 'Religion of Positivism', 599–600.     [111] Pattison, 'Religion of Positivism', 598–9.
[112] Pattison, 'Religion of Positivism', 602.     [113] Pattison, 'Religion of Positivism', 600–1.

In short, Pattison thought that Harrison was right to see positivism as a conservative system of thought, and that was precisely why he regarded it with such disapproval. Indeed, positivist doctrine was a betrayal of the positive spirit, for the essence of that spirit was the constant desire to press forward, to question, and to criticize. Comte, by contrast, wanted to freeze the findings of science at a given moment to enable them to serve his conservative purposes:

Comte indeed professes in words to provide for future progress. But the real assumption which underlies his polity, is that humanity has reached the terminus, and that knowledge can now be summed. Yet even in the thirty years which have elapsed since Comte wrote, this assumption has been belied, and his crude idea of the three stages has been enveloped in a much more comprehensive conception of the Evolution of the Species.[114]

Here Pattison anticipates the argument that Comte mis-characterized the nature of scientific knowledge and discovery in his attempt to use science as the foundation for a new and stable social order. Whereas Comte thought that ongoing change was abnormal, a symptom of a transitional and inorganic social state, Pattison saw change as normal: 'The mutability of human affairs', he pronounced in a university sermon, 'is not a contingent instability, but an inexorable law of change.' It was pointless, therefore, to seek to establish institutions designed to last for ever.[115]

Conversely, whereas Harrison regarded religion as an integral element in Comte's system, Pattison retorted that Comte was not really interested in religion at all, but only in 'the incidental uses to which religion may be turned, viz.: that of organising society'.[116] Harrison cited Comte's definition of religion as 'complete harmony in human life, whether social or individual, when all the parts of life are ordered in their natural relation to each other'. This, for Pattison, was an extraordinarily paradoxical definition, for 'none of the nations of the West, since literature began, have ever applied the term religion, or its equivalents, in this sense'. The idea of religion was inseparable, he argued, from '[t]he imagination . . . of a power above us, the intelligent and conscious arbiter of our destinies'.[117] The religious part of positivism was 'a mere fiction – an afterthought, an arbitrary creation of Comte's individual fancy'.[118]

In his last decade or so Pattison rarely wrote about religion, except to express his contempt for clericalism and, more particularly, for

[114] Pattison, 'Religion of Positivism', 613.     [115] Pattison, *Sermons*, p. 51.
[116] Pattison, 'Religion of Positivism', 604.     [117] Pattison, 'Religion of Positivism', 606.
[118] Pattison, 'Religion of Positivism', 608.

Catholicism. Harrison told him he was looking forward to reading his critique of the religion of humanity, because 'you will have to indicate the point of view, Christian or Deist, from which your objections to Positivism are directed. Hitherto our religion has only been attacked by men who avow no religion.'[119] In fact in his discussion of Comte and religion Pattison spoke as a liberal Anglican, or at least a liberal Christian. In contrast to Comte, who he thought borrowed all that was worst in Catholicism without capturing any of its religious spirit, Pattison represented religion less as a set of dogmas than as an ongoing quest. The entire history of religious thought – including the evolution from fetishism to theism as traced by Comte – was

determined by one mental effort – the effort to bring the conception of this unseen power more into conformity with our constantly improving knowledge of natural law. From the dawn of thought till the present moment, the human intelligence has laboured to fashion its idea of God to a consistency with its knowledge of nature.

That labour could only be brought to a halt by the intervention of physical force and the suppression of intellectual freedom.[120]

Prior to the publication of Pattison's articles, Harrison warned that 'I am inclined to think that some of those whom you regard as making churches square with reason, I should consider to be propping up a system in which they disbelieve';[121] and Pattison certainly detected that the ulterior purpose of Harrison's paper was 'an assault upon rational Christianity', or 'neo-Christianity'. Harrison admired Catholicism, and would have liked all Christians to be Ultramontane followers of Pius IX. Neo-Christians and Theosophists – those groups later labelled 'Modernists' – were altogether too slippery. 'Protestantism in general, but in any especial manner philosophical Protestantism, or Rationalism, is the steady object of his general denunciation.'[122] Pattison evidently continued to identify himself with these philosophical Protestants, or with 'those who, from Clement of Alexandria downwards, have endeavoured to harmonise Christian faith with philosophical speculation'. But whereas fifteen or twenty years earlier he had been active in promoting the cause of a rational Christianity and proud of the Church of England's standing as a learned church, now he was profoundly pessimistic about its prospects. The 'liberal clergyman' who

[119] Harrison to Pattison, 23 January [1876], Bodleian MS Pattison 57, ff. 193–4.
[120] Pattison, 'Religion of Positivism', 606–7.
[121] Harrison to Pattison, 25 January 1876, Bodleian MS Pattison 57, ff. 210–11.
[122] Pattison, 'Religion of Positivism', 612–3.

was the target of Harrison's animus was 'a phantom of his imagination'. With the deaths of such men as F. D. Maurice, F. W. Robertson and Charles Kingsley, philosophical Christianity no longer had any representatives in England, and 'with them that Broad Church which a quarter of a century ago formed a third party within the Establishment, has melted into vapour'. Any survivors who could be found lurking in 'some out-of-the-way corner of the Church' were merely 'lurking fugitives of a dispersed and defeated army'.[123]

Pattison's friend, the Oxford professor of Chemistry Sir Benjamin Brodie, wrote to congratulate him on the article, 'a truly admirable bit of criticism' which set out 'the case against Harrison & Co' effectively for the first time. 'The cry about the <u>religion</u> of positivism', wrote Brodie, 'I have always felt to be truly contemptible the object being to falsely identify their convictions with those of the rest of the world and enable their old aunts conscientiously to leave them legacies.'[124] Nevertheless Harrison himself complimented Pattison on the article, which he thought 'serious, weighty, & full', and he described it as the most 'important & suggestive' judgement on Comte since Mill's *Auguste Comte and Positivism* eleven years earlier. He was pleased to find that it was not a merely negative criticism, but made Pattison's own position clear. Its criticisms of Comte were in many ways just, but the criticisms of Harrison himself less so: indeed, Harrison thought Pattison's paper at times recalled the *Essays and Reviews* controversy. 'Perhaps you were really replying to Neo-Christianity after so many years.'[125] He went on to write a reply, framed as a dialogue on humanity between 'a critic' and 'a positivist'. The former lamented Oxford's 'Niagara of everlasting examinations, our prize-hunting, our cub-grinding, and the general millennium of cram', and Pattison may not have been persuaded by Harrison's protestation that he was not the prototype.[126] The nub of the argument was that that the critic objected to 'all connecting knowledge together', and insisted that intellect must be 'ever untrammelled, ever soaring free through boundless space', whereas the positivist urged instead that 'the highest ideal of the intellect is to be social, systematic, practical, useful, sympathetic, and synthetic'.[127]

[123]  Pattison, 'Religion of Positivism', 613.
[124]  B. C. Brodie to Pattison, 26 March 1876, Bodleian MS Pattison 57, ff. 241–2.
[125]  Harrison to Pattison, 6 March 1876, Bodleian MS Pattison 57, ff. 224–5.
[126]  Harrison to Pattison, 26 April 1876, Bodleian MS Pattison 57, ff. 245–6. The article was Frederic Harrison, 'Humanity: a dialogue', *Contemporary Review* 27 (1876), 862–85, and the quotation is on p. 862.
[127]  Harrison, 'Humanity: a dialogue', 885.

Other positivists were less complimentary than Harrison. J. H. Bridges, one of Comte's leading English acolytes, accused Pattison of superficiality in his treatment of Comte, especially in his remarks about Comte's hatred of intellect. Pattison defended himself in print, and significantly he cited in support of the accusation that the Comtists detested intellect 'the epithets applied by a distinguished Comtist to all those who have endeavoured to give a rational exposition of religion'. This was, presumably, Harrison. And he again asserted that Comte valued science only for its practical utility, whereas for Pattison true science was disinterested, 'the self-prompted effort of intelligence to ascertain the positive qualities and relations of the parts of which the universe is made up'.[128]

What do Pattison's encounters with positivism tell us? They certainly reveal his deep antipathy for fixed intellectual systems, which he regarded as a betrayal of the true vocation of the scholar, the scientist and the philosopher. That vocation must be critical: scholars are called to regard all their beliefs as provisional and to subject them to a ceaseless process of questioning and investigation. In his review of the essays of John Morley, who had as a young man been drawn to secular systems such as positivism, he extolled him for his ongoing mental development:

With Mr Morley there has been steady growth, not of power and intelligence, but of intellectual comprehensiveness ... We have watched Mr Morley emerge from the narrow scheme of Comtism, or Benthamism, or what not, some form of the half-true which crushes the growth of many valuable but less vigorous minds, and step out upon the broad platform which is above all sect and all doctrine, where the only appeal is to world experience.[129]

Morley's intellectual growth contrasted with the more dogmatic cast of his contemporary, Frederic Harrison. Just six months before he died Pattison wrote to Mrs W. D. Hertz, one of his most intimate correspondents in the final years of his life. He refers to an address by Harrison that he had just read. He admired the vigour of Harrison's writing, but Pattison's antipathy towards positivism remained as strong as ever. 'Positivism condemns itself by the fact of its being an "ism"', he wrote.

No sect or denomination with a ready made creed or cut & dried set of dogmas can ever be adequate to maintain the ever fluctuating equilibrium between the human mind & its environment in the universe. This has to be re-adjusted almost from year to year to year.[130]

---

[128] Pattison, 'A note on evolution and positivism', 285–6. This was a reply to a footnote in J. H. Bridges, 'Evolution and positivism', *Fortnightly Review* 27 o.s. (1877), 858.
[129] Pattison, Review of Morley, *Critical Miscellanies*, 353.
[130] Pattison to Mrs W. D. Hertz, 6 January 1884: Bodleian MS Pattison 144, f. 66.

In addition, these encounters with the claims of positivism bring two of his most enduring concerns into sharp focus. One was the idea of the disinterested pursuit of knowledge, and the other was the idea of a rational theology. The former, as we have seen, was a lifelong passion to which he became, if anything, even more attached with age, whereas he became increasingly pessimistic about the prospects of the latter. He perceived positivism as the enemy of both. In his contribution to Appleton's volume on the endowment of research he depicted the Comtists as the most vocal enemies of disinterested knowledge or 'research', and thought their work valuable chiefly in clarifying the ideal they opposed. He took positivism to be a system which was oriented towards practice, and which was therefore uninterested in or even suspicious of purely theoretical investigations. Pattison, like Julien Benda in the twentieth century, saw this practical orientation as a betrayal of the duty of the intellectual: 'la trahison des clercs'.[131]

The antithesis Pattison saw between positivism and rational theology is harder to explain, although it certainly reinforces the fact that Pattison, for all his equivocation on matters of religious doctrine, remained committed in principle to the idea of a rational theology, even though he had given up pursuing it himself in the aftermath of *Essays and Reviews*. Perhaps the matter is best put like this. The essence of the liberal Anglican project, to which the 1860 essayists were committed, was the reconciliation of reason and religion. 'Truth is one', as Pattison was fond of saying.[132] For different reasons, *Origin of Species* and *Essays and Reviews* both made the pursuit of this project within the Church of England problematical: Darwin seemed to push a wedge between science on the one hand and scriptural revelation on the other, which undermined the possibility of a natural theology which would reinforce the essence of Christian orthodoxy; on the other hand, the response to *Essays and Reviews* seemed to make it clear that the Church was not interested in the insights of modern biblical, historical and theological scholarship. All this was highly discouraging for Pattison. But it simply had the effect of releasing him from the moorings of Christian orthodoxy. Or, to put it another way, henceforth he adhered to a project of a rational theology rather than a rational Christianity.

The alternative response to the nineteenth-century crisis of belief consisted in a frank acceptance that the claims of science and the claims of

---

[131] Julien Benda, *La Trahison des clercs* (Paris: Grasset, 1927).
[132] Pattison, *Sermons*, p. 144.

religion simply occupied separate spheres. To suppose that science had refuted Christianity, or could do so, was to commit a category mistake. Today this approach commends itself to many liberal Christians. But Pattison was repelled by this strategy, which he thought led to an ultra-montane and reactionary Catholicism. So in 1865 he concluded a review of a study of Coleridge's thought with these words:

> To deny that Christianity is capable of a philosophical exposition is suicidal in Protestants, as it would drive all Christians upon the only other alternative – the authority of an infallible Church, concrete in a human head. But it is a task reserved for the future as, notwithstanding the numerous attempts from the time of the Gnostics and St. Clement of Alexandria downwards, there is not one which has attained any great reputation. In our own country, especially, every attempt is valuable, however imperfect, to rescue the treatment of religious subjects from the routine repetition of stereotyped conventionalities which congregations, Sunday after Sunday, expect without curiosity and listen to without edification.[133]

Pattison saw positivism as the obverse of this reactionary Catholicism and unthinking Christianity more generally. It fed on the sense that Christianity and all forms of theism were intellectually out of date, which is why positivists were particularly contemptuous of rationalist theologians. Significantly, Pattison was curiously lacking in that ethical enthusiasm – that 'enthusiasm of humanity', to use a pregnant phrase which was much in use at the time – that impelled many of his contemporaries towards secular religions of one form or another.[134] At the lowest point in their relationship Francis thought this was because his calculating mind always stifled any 'truly generous impulse'.[135] Religion possessed value, he thought, only when grounded on a rational theology. The geological and biological sciences – the sciences of development – had mined the foundations of the old natural theology of the eighteenth century. But the Anglican Church had 'never yet broken with reason or proscribed education'. Its proper response must be to reconstruct a natural theology in harmony with the latest scientific thinking. The task was 'to re-establish the synthesis of science and faith'.[136]

---

[133] Pattison, Review of J. H. Green, *Spiritual Philosophy; founded on the Teaching of the late Samuel Taylor Coleridge*, in *Saturday Review* 20 (9 December 1865), 742.

[134] On Pattison's lack of the 'enthusiasm of humanity', see Tollemache, 'Recollections', pp. 145, 164.

[135] E. F. S. Pattison to Eleanor Smith, 22 Jan. 1880, Bodleian MS Pattison 118, f. 36.

[136] Pattison, *Sermons*, p. 214.

# Epilogue. The don as intellectual?

Pattison's importance rests in the fact that, at a time of upheaval in British and European universities and the reinvention of the academic profession, he stood for a distinctive conception of the nature of the academic life. If that conception has to be summed up in a phrase, we could say that Pattison held that the don had an obligation to be an intellectual. But the term 'intellectual', which was just coming into usage in Pattison's time, is an ambiguous one which needs some unpacking.

Stefan Collini has recently distinguished three very different senses of the term. It is sometimes used in a sociological sense, to designate the educated class as a whole: 'all those who create, distribute, and apply culture', in Seymour Martin Lipset's words. Academics plainly fall within this socio-professional category, and did so before the nineteenth-century transformation of the university as well as afterwards. In this sense, to say that the academic should be an intellectual is like saying that a miner should be a manual worker. More relevant for our purposes are Collini's other two senses. The term is sometimes used in a 'subjective' sense: here it denotes 'a particular commitment to truth-seeking, rumination, analysis, argument, often pursued as ends in themselves'. More commonly, the term has a cultural sense, in which it highlights the authority which intellectuals enjoy, or aspire to. This is the sense that Collini foregrounds. His book considers, and criticizes, the widespread belief that British society has been peculiarly resistant to intellectuals' assertion of the right to exercise this kind of general cultural authority.[1]

Pattison was quintessentially an intellectual in the second, 'subjective' sense. He felt a calling to devote himself to the life of the mind, and was contemptuous of academics who showed no sign of having ever felt such a calling. They had no business in universities at all. By contrast, he never

---

[1] Stefan Collini, *Absent Minds: Intellectuals in Britain* (Oxford: Oxford University Press, 2006), pp. 46–8.

voiced any particular disapproval of academics who failed to speak out on matters of public concern. He himself came to possess a public standing which he certainly found gratifying, and from time to time in later life he engaged in the manifesto-drafting and petition-signing activities we have come to associate with the public intellectual. But these were incidental to his sense of identity. It was certain inner qualities, he believed, and not any kind of external recognition he might attract, that made him a 'real' academic.

Collini points out that this 'subjective' definition of the intellectual does not lend itself easily to historical analysis, because 'it is difficult to isolate any external markers of membership of this category'.[2] It is impossible to say whether more people felt an intellectual vocation in nineteenth-century England than in nineteenth-century France or Renaissance Italy. That is why the idea of the intellectual vocation is better studied biographically than sociologically. Nevertheless, Pattison's intellectual subjectivity would be of limited interest if his mental life had been lived wholly in the private realm. He had a broader significance because his contemporaries recognized in him the personification of a distinctive and compelling conception of the academic's calling to be an intellectual. For that reason it is possible to conclude with some reflections on his place in the evolution of intellectual life in modern Britain.

Two familiar and intertwined narratives stand at our disposal as we consider these questions. One highlights a 'secularization of the European mind' in the nineteenth century: religious concerns were pushed from the centre to the margins of the intellectual world, and a formerly hegemonic Christian world view became fragmented and contested.[3] The other identifies a shift from an intellectual world dominated by the 'man of letters' to one dominated by the alienated intellectual. In this latter narrative, the man of letters is portrayed as culturally well integrated and existing in a close relationship with his reading public, over which he exercises the authority of a sage. The alienated intellectual, by contrast, sees intellectual life as counter-cultural: it exists in opposition to the mainstream culture of the society in which he lives. Most accounts see the man of letters as an unusually durable social type in England, whereas the alienated intellectual is thought to have flourished in continental European societies, especially Russia. But even in England the rise of the alienated intellectual has been recognized as a striking feature of twentieth-century cultural life. The

[2] Collini, *Absent Minds*, 47.
[3] The classic study is Owen Chadwick, *The Secularization of the European Mind in the Nineteenth Century* (Cambridge: Cambridge University Press, 1975)

growth of disciplinary specialization in universities has been identified as one of the drivers of the alienation of the intellectual, who has been deprived of the possibility of exercising a sagacious authority over the whole intellectual field.[4] It would be possible to connect these two narratives, since the possibility of a general authority exercised by men of letters might be thought to depend upon the salience of an integrated view of the world, and Christianity was the last system of belief to offer that in the west. It is significant that self-consciously Christian intellectual figures such as A. D. Lindsay and Sir Walter Moberly were prominent critics of the disciplinary fragmentation of the university curriculum in twentieth-century Britain.[5] For them, a university education must offer something more coherent than a cacophony of unconnected disciplines.

Pattison was critical of those of his contemporaries who apparently aspired to exercise the authority of a sage: John Ruskin, for example, whom he otherwise admired. He insisted that there could be no such thing as a general intellectual authority, but only a specialized authority founded on expertise. He saw the growth of disciplinary specialism as necessary and desirable, and he realised that in future expertise would be the basis of the university's legitimacy. To that extent he stood on the side of the modernizers. The reader of his *Memoirs* might easily form the impression that, having abandoned his youthful enthusiasm for Tractarian reaction, he became a radical secularizer, for whom the modernization of the university along the lines of disciplinary specialization was the natural corollary of the secularization of the European mind. But this would be a misleading conclusion.

The Princeton historian Anthony Grafton has written a massive study of Scaliger of the kind that Pattison projected, but could not complete. In an interesting set of reflections on his predecessor, Grafton has depicted Pattison as a man torn between two worlds, powerfully drawn to the German idea of learning, but unwilling or unable to detach himself from the English conception of the man of letters.

He admired German learning from a great distance in space and Renaissance erudition from a great distance in time. He appreciated both and wrote vividly about them. But he lacked the courage to practice the Spartan intellectual virtues

⁴ See, for example, the conclusion to Noel Annan, *Leslie Stephen: The Godless Victorian* (London: Weidenfeld and Nicolson, 1984), pp. 339–40. This kind of narrative is now challenged by Collini, *Absent Minds*.

⁵ Matthew Grimley, 'Civil society and the clerisy: Christian élites and national culture, c. 1930–1950', in Jose Harris (ed.), *Civil Society in British History: Ideas, Identities, Institutions* (Oxford: Oxford University Press, 2003), p. 245.

that he loved to praise, when there was no English public to applaud or pay him for doing so.[6]

Grafton is right to emphasize Pattison's liminal standing at the threshold that led from the generalist world of the Victorian periodical to the specialist world of the academic who writes for fellow academics. But he is surely wrong to say that only a want of courage stopped Pattison from whole-heartedly endorsing the onward march of specialization. As we have seen, Pattison used the German ideal as a foil against which he could set off the failings of English culture, and in particular of Oxford's academic life. But that is not to say that he was vouchsafed with a vision of modern academic life which he simply failed to practise. He was an even more complex figure than that. His propensity to overstate his case has led others, not surprisingly, to oversimplify his position and to caricature it. In fact he did not believe that universities were for 'research' as opposed to 'teaching'. In Oxford he was not for the University against the colleges, nor even for the professors against the tutors. Neither was he for academic specialism against literary generalism. His end was a *general* intellectual culture whose practitioner would not merely work away at his own little special-ism, but would be able to grasp his own place in the history of thought. But he saw that specialization of a sort was a necessary means to that general culture. No one can grasp the relations between all the different branches of knowledge unless he has a detailed grasp of one in particular. Minute research in ancient history, for example, does not separate one from, say, the research chemist, but creates a closer sympathy.

Pattison was a staunch opponent of what in his day was the incipient idea of the 'two cultures': he spoke of 'the separation between the literary and the scientific class', and thought it more developed in Germany than in Britain.[7] He was a proponent of the introduction of the natural sciences into the Oxford curriculum and of the public funding of scientific research. Unlike Jowett, who professed no knowledge of science, Pattison had in some ways a good grasp of the scientific mind. He repudiated Comtean positivism, as we have seen, because it represented science as a body of conclusions rather than an ongoing process of critical investigation. But the reason why he disapproved of the divorce between the two cultures was that he conceived of science as an integral part of the philosophical life in the modern world. He continued to think of science as an essentially individual

---

[6] Anthony Grafton, 'Mark Pattison', *American Scholar* 52 (Spring 1983), 236.
[7] Royal Commission on Scientific Instruction and the Advancement of Science, Minutes of Evidence: Parliamentary Papers 1872 Cmd 536, vol. XXV, 248.

pursuit, as it was still possible to do before the advent of large-scale funding of collective research projects in the twentieth century. Today the humanities have begun to ape the natural sciences in their methods of operation, but the result is an intellectual endeavour that is a world away from anything that Pattison could have envisaged. For him, research in the humanities was only incidentally about new discoveries. Fundamentally, it was about bringing the insights of today's currents of thought to bear upon the age-old but historically defined problems of philosophy. Pattison was the most lucid of Victorian proponents of the high conception of learning (*Wissenschaft*) and the academic vocation that emerged from Germany in the Humboldtian era; and the Humboldtian model of the university was undoubtedly the most powerful model for academic reformers in England as elsewhere in the nineteenth century. The 'endowment of research' movement which he inspired won the support of advocates of the kind of public funding of academic science that would transform the university landscape in the twentieth century. Today's commentators on university politics, if they search for historical roots of contemporary dilemmas, tend to contrast Humboldt's idea of the university with Newman's, and to see an enduring and creative tension between them.[8] But Pattison was led to the German idea of the university by a tortuous process in which his engagement with Newman personally and Tractarian asceticism played a key role. He never abandoned the High Church conception of the university as a place of learned retreat, nor Newman's insistence that a university education must depend crucially on the personal influence of mind on mind. The idea that the university exists for the production of research papers or PhDs would have seemed as much a betrayal as the idea that it exists for the generation of firsts or Platonic guardians or hearty men of character. For Pattison, what mattered about the idea of *Wissenschaft* was not its ability to transform the world but its capacity to nurture the spiritual development of the self.

[8] See *supra*, p. 9.

# Bibliography

PRIMARY SOURCES

## 1. Principal Manuscript Sources

*All Souls College, Oxford*
    Sparrow papers
*Balliol College, Oxford*
    Jowett papers
*Bodleian Library, Oxford*
    Bryce papers
    Bywater papers
    Pattison papers
*British Library*
    Gladstone papers
*John Rylands University Library, Manchester*
    Alexander papers
*Lincoln College, Oxford*
    College archives
    Pattison papers
*Oxford University Press*
    Orders of the Delegates of the Clarendon Press
*Pusey House, Oxford*
    Ffoulkes papers
    Mrs Humphry Ward papers
*University of Texas at Austin, Harry Ransom Center*
    The Times Collection (Pattison–Stebbing correspondence)

## 2. Parliamentary Papers

*Report of Her Majesty's Commissioners Appointed to Inquire into the State, Discipline, Studies and Revenues of the University and Colleges of Oxford* XXII, 41–50 [1482], 1852, 'Answers from the Rev. Mark Pattison, M.A., Subrector and Tutor of Lincoln College'.

*Royal Commission to inquire into State of Popular Education in England: Reports of Assistant Commissioners (Continental Europe, and Educational Charities in England and Wales)* XXI Pt. 4, 161–266 [2794-IV], 1861, 'Report of Mark Pattison, B. D.'.

*Royal Commission to inquire into Education in Schools in England and Wales*: Volume V. *Minutes of Evidence, Part II*, xxviii pt.IV, 943–54 [3966-IV], 1867–8, 'The Rev. Mark Pattison, D. D. [sic], examined'.

*Royal Commission on Scientific Instruction and Advancement of Science: First (Supplementary) and Second Report, Minutes of Evidence, Appendices.* xxv, 240–50 [C. 536], 1872, 'The Rev. Mark Pattison, B. D., examined'.

*University of Oxford Commission 1877: Part 1: Minutes of Evidence taken by the Commissioners*, lvi, 255–9 [C. 2868], 1881, 'The Rev. Mark Pattison, B. D. (Rector of Lincoln College), examined'.

### 3. Works published by Pattison in his lifetime and posthumously

Pattison's work was dispersed across a wide range of periodicals, and much of it was published anonymously. It is therefore impossible to claim that the bibliography below is absolutely comprehensive, but it is as full and accurate as possible.

### Books

[Anon], Stephen Langton, in *Lives of the English Saints, A. D. 51–1250* [ed. John Henry Newman] (London: James Toovey, 1845).

[Anon], The Life of S. Edmund, in *Lives of the English Saints, A. D. 51–1250* [ed. John Henry Newman] (London: James Toovey, 1845).

*Suggestions on Academical Organisation with especial reference to Oxford* (Edinburgh: Edmonston and Douglas, 1868).

(Ed., with notes) Pope's *Essay on Man* (Oxford: Clarendon Press, 1869).

(Ed.) Pope's *Satires and Epistles* (Oxford: Clarendon Press, 1872).

*Isaac Casaubon* (London: Longmans, Green, 1875). A second edition was published by the Clarendon Press in 1892.

*Milton* (London: Macmillan, 1879).

(Ed.) *The Sonnets of John Milton* (London: Kegan Paul, Trench, 1883).

### (Posthumous)

*Memoirs* (London: Macmillan, 1885).

*Sermons* (London: Macmillan, 1885).

*Essays by the late Mark Pattison, sometime Rector of Lincoln College* (Oxford: Clarendon, 1889), ed. Henry Nettleship, 2 volumes. A second edition, smaller in scale, was published in the New Universal Library in 1908. Essays reprinted in the 1889 edition are marked * below.

## Articles, Reviews and Contributions to Books

1842    Translation of Aquinas on St Matthew in *Catena Aurea: Commentary on the Four Gospels, collected out of the Works of the Fathers by S. Thomas Aquinas* [ed. J. H. Newman] (Oxford: J. H. Parker, 1842), vol. I parts 1–3, including a preface in volume 1.1, pp. i–xii.

1842    'Earliest English poetry', *British Critic* 21: 1–36.

1844    'Miss Bremer's novels', *Christian Remembrancer* 8: 13–25.

1845    'Gregory of Tours', *Christian Remembrancer* 9: 66–85.*
      'Thiers's Consulate and Empire', *Christian Remembrancer* 10: 105–32.
      'Wordsworth's diary in France', *Christian Remembrancer* 10: 356–76.

1846    'Church poetry', *Christian Remembrancer* 11: 96–112.
      'The Oxford Bede', *Christian Remembrancer* 11: 331–46.
      'Slave-grown sugar', *Christian Remembrancer* 12: 325–76.

1847    'Hugh Miller's first impressions of England', *Christian Remembrancer* 14: 290–313.

1848    'Mill's Political Economy' *Christian Remembrancer* 16: 315–44.

1851    'Lord Holland's Foreign Reminiscences', *Christian Remembrancer* 21: 465–74.

1853    'Thomas Moore's Life and Poems', *Christian Remembrancer* 25: 289–327.
      'Diary of Casaubon', *Quarterly Review* 93: 462–500.

1854    'English letter-writers of the eighteenth century', *Fraser's Magazine* 50: 629–40.

1855    'Theology and Philosophy', *Westminster Review* 63 O. S.: 206–27.
      'Theology and Philosophy', *Westminster Review* 64 O. S.: 224–5.
      'Oxford Studies', in *Oxford Essays* (London: Parker, 1855), pp. 251–310.*
      'Peter Daniel Huet – Life and Opinions', *Quarterly Review* 97: 290–335.*
      'Review of James F. Ferrier', *Institutes of Metaphysic: The Theory of Knowing and Being*, *Saturday Review* 1: 54.
      'University reform in Austria', *Saturday Review* 1: 97.

1856    'New Biographies of Montaigne', *Quarterly Review* 99: 396–415.*
      Review of W. E. Jelf (ed.), *Aristotle's Ethics*, *Saturday Review* 1: 378–9.
      Review of J. S. Mill, *System of Logic*, 4th edn, *Saturday Review* 2: 735–6.

1857    'Theology and Philosophy' (as above), *Westminster Review* 67 O. S.: 246–62.
      'The present state of theology in Germany', *Westminster Review* 67 O. S.: 327–63.*
      'Buckle's Civilisation in England', *Westminster Review* 68 O. S.: 375–99.*
      'History, Biography, Voyages and Travels', *Westminster Review* 68 O. S.: 568–85.
      'The Birmingham Congress', *Fraser's Magazine* 56: 619–26.

1858    'History, Biography, Voyages and Travels', *Westminster Review* 69 O. S.: 272–90.
      'History and Biography', *Westminster Review* 69 O. S.: 603–21.
      'Calvin at Geneva', *Westminster Review* 70 O. S.: 1–29.*

'The Calas Tragedy', *Westminster Review* 70 O. S.: 465–88.*

'History and Biography', *Westminster Review* 70 O. S.: 587–606.

1859    'Antecedents of the Reformation', *Fraser's Magazine* 59: 114–20.*

1860    'Tendencies of Religious Thought in England, 1688–1750', in *Essays and Reviews* (London: Parker), pp. 254–329.*

'Joseph Scaliger', *Quarterly Review* 108: 34–81.*

'Philanthropic Societies in the Reign of Queen Anne', *Fraser's Magazine* 61: 576–82.*

1861    'Early intercourse of England and Germany', *Westminster Review* 75 O. S.: 403–18.*

1862    'Popular education in Prussia', *Westminster Review* 77 O. S.: 169–200.

'Life of Bishop Warburton', *National Review* 17: 61–102.*

'Learning in the Church of England', *National Review* 16: 187–200.*

'Mackay's Tübingen School', *Westminster Review* 80 O. S.: 510–31.

1864    Review of T. K. Abbott, *Sight and Touch. An Attempt to Disprove the Received, or Berkleian, Theory of Vision*, *Saturday Review* 18: 281–2.

Review of Aug. O. Fr. Lorenz, *Leben und Schriften des Koers Epicharmos, nebst seiner Fragmentensammlung* (1864), *Saturday Review* 18: 541–2.

1865    'Classical learning in France: the great printers Stephens', *Quarterly Review* 117: 323–64.*

'J. S. Mill on Hamilton', *Reader* 5: 562–3.

'F. A. Wolf', *North British Review* 42 OS: 245–99.*

'Grote's Plato', *Reader* 5: 644–5.

Review of J. H. Green, *Spiritual Philosophy; founded on the Teaching of the late Samuel Taylor Coleridge*, *Saturday Review* 20: 675–6 & 741–2.

1866    Review of Thomas Lewin, *Fasti Sacri; or, a Key to the Chronology of the New Testament*, *Saturday Review* 21: 172–3.

Review of Sir Alexander Grant, *The Ethics of Aristotle. Illustrated with Essays and Notes*, *Saturday Review* 21: 563–4.

Review of Simon S. Laurie, *On the Philosophy of Ethics*, *Saturday Review* 21: 785–7.

Review of E. Caro, *La Philosophie de Göthe*, *Saturday Review* 22: 365–6.

Review of Dr Bodichon, *De l'Humanité*, *Saturday Review* 22: 460–2.

Review of M. P. W. Bolton, *Inquisitio Philosophica. An Examination of the Principles of Kant and Hamilton*, *Saturday Review* 22: 552–3.

Review of H. L. Mansel, *The Philosophy of the Conditioned; comprising some Remarks on Sir W Hamilton's Philosophy, and on Mr J. S. Mill's Examination of that Philosophy*, *Saturday Review* 22: 645–7.

Review of Edward A. Bond, *Chronica Monasterii de Melsa* [Chronicle of Meaux], volume I, *Saturday Review* 22: 799–800.

1867    Review of Henry Maudsley, *The Physiology and Pathology of the Mind*, *Saturday Review* 23: 661–2.

Review of *Christian Schools and Scholars, or Sketches of Education from the Christian Era to the Council of Trent*, *Saturday Review* 24: 347–9.

Review of P. Sièrebois, *La Morale fouillée dans ses fondements: essai d'anthropodicée, Saturday Review* 23: 693–4.

Review of George Henry Lewes, *The History of Philosophy from Thales to Comte*, 3rd edition, *Saturday Review* 23: 790–2.

1868 'Theology and Philosophy', *Westminster Review* 90 O. S.: 507–29.

'What measures are required for the further improvement of the Universities of Oxford and Cambridge?', *Transactions of the National Association for the Promotion of Social Science* 12: 385–90.

Review of Edward Poste, *Aristotle on Fallacies, or the Sophistici Elenchi; with a Translation and Notes, Saturday Review* 25: 21–2.

Review of Albert Schwegler, *Handbook of the History of Philosophy*, translated and annotated by J. H. Stirling, *Saturday Review* 25: 52–4.

Review of E. Caro, *Le Matérialisme et la Science, Saturday Review* 25: 455–6.

Review of R. S. Wyld, *The World as Dynamical and Immaterial; and the Nature of Perception, Saturday Review* 26: 163–4.

Review of Alexander Bain, *Mental and Moral Science: A Compendium of Psychology and Ethics, Saturday Review* 26: 593–4.

Review of F. D. Maurice, *The Conscience: Lectures on Casuistry delivered in the University of Cambridge, Saturday Review* 26: 656–7.

1869 Review of *Geschichte der klassischen Philologie in den Niederlanden, The Academy* 1: 25.

'The Philological Congress at Kiel', *The Academy* 1: 58–9.

Review of John Veitch, *Memoir of Sir William Hamilton, Bart, Saturday Review* 27: 683–4 and 778–80.

1870 Review of Dr Jacob Probst, *Geschichte der Universität in Innsbruck seit ihrer Entstehung bis zum Jahre 1860, The Academy* 1: 161–2.

Review of Newman's *Grammar of Assent, The Academy* 1: 228–30.

Review of John Stoughton, *Ecclesiastical History of England: the Church of the Restoration*, 2 vols., *The Academy* 2: 10.

Review of *The Characters of Theophrastus*, trans. and ed. by R. C. Jebb, *The Academy* 2: 52–4.

1871 Review of *The Works of Alexander Pope*, ed. by the Revd W. Elwin, vols. I–II, *The Academy* 2: 125–6.

1872 'Pope and his editors', *British Quarterly Review* 55: 413–46.*

'The arguments for a future life', *Papers for the Metaphysical Society* no. 25.

Review of Rev. John Hunt, *Religious Thought in England from the Reformation to the End of the Last Century*, 2 vols., *The Academy* 3: 210–11.

Review of George Grote, *Aristotle*, A. Bain & G. C. Robertson (eds.), 2 vols., *Saturday Review* 34: 218–20.

1873 Review of G. H. Lewes, *Problems of Life and Mind. 1st Series. The Foundations of a Creed, Saturday Review* 36: 757–8.

1874 Review of Jevons's *Principles of Science: a Treatise on Logic and Scientific Method, Saturday Review* 37: 654–6.

1875    'Milton', *Macmillan's Magazine* 31: 380–7.
        'A Chapter of University History', *Macmillan's Magazine* 32: 237–46 and 308–13.*
        Review of Sidgwick's *Methods of Ethics*, *Saturday Review* 39: 118–20.
1876    'Review of the situation' in C. Appleton (ed.), *Essays on the Endowment of Research* (London: King), pp. 3–25.
        'The Religion of Positivism', *Contemporary Review* 27: 593–614.
        'Philosophy in Oxford', *Mind* 1: 82–97.
        Review of Bain's *The Emotions and the Will*, 3rd edn, *Saturday Review* 41: 335–7.
        'Address on education', *Transactions of the National Association for the Promotion of Social Science* 21: 44–68.
        Review of Leslie Stephen, *English Thought in the Eighteenth Century*, *The Academy* 10: 533–4.
1877    'The Age of Reason', *Fortnightly Review* 27 O. S.: 343–61.
        'A note on evolution and positivism', *Fortnightly Review* 28 O. S.: 285–6.
        'Books and Critics', *Fortnightly Review* 28 O. S.: 659–79.
        Review of John Morley, *Critical Miscellanies*, *The Academy* 12: 353–4.
1878    'Double truth', *Papers of the Metaphysical Society* no. 74.
        Review of James Sime, *Lessing: His Life and Writings*, *The Academy* 13: 45.
        Review of Helen Zimmern, *Gotthold Ephraim Lessing, his Life and Works*, *The Academy* 13: 201–2.
        Review of J. C. Morison, *Gibbon*, *The Academy* 14: 349–50.
1879    Review of Matthew Arnold, *Mixed Essays*, *The Academy* 15: 425–6.
1880    'Middle-class education', *New Quarterly Magazine* 13 O. S.: 737–51.
        'Industrial shortcomings', *Fortnightly Review* 34 O. S.: 737–51.
        'Introduction to John Milton' in T. H. Ward (ed.), *The English Poets* (London: Macmillan, 1880), II, 293–305.
1881    'The thing that might be', *North American Review* 132: 320–31.
        'Etienne Dolet', *Fortnightly Review* 35 O. S.: 35–43.
        Review of John Ruskin, *Arrows of the Chace*, *The Academy* 19: 109–10.
        Review of John de Soyres (ed.), *The Provincial Letters of Pascal*, *The Academy* 19: 1. Review of *Dr Appleton: his life and literary relics*, *The Academy* 19: 127–8.
        Review of Whitwell Elwin & W. J. Courthope (eds.), *The Works of Alexander Pope*, vol. III, *Poetry*, *The Academy* 20: 411–12.
1882    'Courthope's Pope', *The Times* 27 January, p. 3.
        Review of Mozley's *Reminiscences*, *The Academy* 22: 1–3.
        'Muretus', *The Times* 23 August, p. 4.*
        'What is a college?', *Journal of Education* n. s. 4: 69–72.
1883    Review of Henry Craik's *Life of Swift*, *The Guardian* 16 May 1883.
        Review of George Meredith's *Poems and Lyrics of the Joy of Earth*, *The Academy* 24: 36–7.

1875–83  Encyclopaedia Britannica, 9th edition. Eight biographical articles:
  Bentley:          vol. III, 1875, 578–80.
  Casaubon:         vol. V, 1876, 172–4.
  Erasmus:          vol. VIII, 1878, 512–8.
  Grotius:          vol. XI, 1880, 217–21.
  Lilye, William:   vol. XIV, 1882, pp. 643–4 [not signed].
  Lipsius:          vol. XIV, 1882, pp. 685–6.
  Macaulay:         vol. XV, 1883, 125–9.
  More:             vol. XVI, 1883, 815–19.

### 4. Other Printed Primary Sources

[Eliza Lynn Linton], 'Mark Pattison', *Temple Bar* 74 (1885), 221–36.

Althaus, T. F., 'Recollections of Mark Pattison', *Temple Bar* 73 (January 1885), 31–49.

Arnold, Matthew, 'The literary influence of academies', *Cornhill Magazine* August 1864, reprinted in his *Lectures and Essays in Criticism*, vol. III of *The Complete Prose Works of Matthew Arnold* (Ann Arbor: University of Michigan Press, 1962), 241, 244–5.

Balfour, Arthur J., *The Religion of Humanity. An Address delivered at the Church Congress, Manchester*, October 1888 (Edinburgh: David Douglas, 1888).

Benson, Arthur Christopher, *The Life of Edward White Benson, sometime Archbishop of Canterbury* (London: Macmillan, 1900), 2 vols.

[T. B. i.e. Benson, A. C.,] *The Upton Letters* (London: Smith, Elder, 1905).

Briggs, Asa, (ed.), *Gladstone's Boswell. Late Victorian Conversations by Lionel A. Tollemache and Other Documents* (Brighton: Harvester, 1984).

Brodrick, Hon. George Charles, *Memories and Impressions 1831–1900* (London: Nisbet, 1900).

Church, R. W., 'Mark Pattison', *The Guardian*, 6 August 1884, reprinted in R. W. Church, *Occasional Papers Selected from the Guardian, the Times, and the Saturday Review 1846–1890* (London: Macmillan, 1897), vol. II, pp. 351–6.

Church, R. W., 'Pattison's Essays', *The Guardian*, 1 May 1889, reprinted in R. W. Church, *Occasional Papers Selected from the Guardian, the Times, and the Saturday Review 1846–1890* (London: Macmillan, 1897), vol. II, pp. 357–72.

Coghill, Mrs Harry (ed.), *The Autobiography and Letters of Mrs M. O. W. Oliphant* (Edinburgh: Blackwood, 1899).

Cockshut, A. O. J. (ed.), *The Autobiography of John Stuart Mill* (Halifax: Ryburn, 1992).

Davies, Emily, *The Higher Education of Women*, ed. Janet Howarth (London and Ronceverte: Hambledon, 1988).

[Dicey, A. V.,], 'Suggestions on Academical Organisation', *Fraser's Magazine* 80 (1869), 407–30.

Dilke, Sir Charles W., 'Memoir [of the author]', in Lady Dilke, *The Book of the Spiritual Life* (London: Murray, 1905).

*Essays and Reviews* (London: Parker, 1860).

*Essays on the Endowment of Research by Various Writers* (London: King, 1876).

Fichte, Johann Gottlieb, *Popular Works: The Nature of the Scholar, the Vocation of Man, the Doctrine of Religion, with a Memoir by William Smith* (London: Trübner, 1873).

Fitch, Joshua Girling, 'Educational endowments', *Fraser's Magazine* 79 (January 1869), 1–15.

Flint, Robert, *The Philosophy of History in France and Germany* (Edinburgh and London: Blackwood, 1874).

Fowler, William Warde, *Reminiscences* (Oxford: privately printed, 1921).

Freeman, E. A., 'Oxford after forty years', *Contemporary Review* 51 (1887), 609–23 and 814–30.

Gibbon, Edward, *Memoirs of my Life and Writings*, A. O. J. Cockshut and Stephen Constantine (eds.) (n. p., Ryburn, 1994).

Gladstone, W. E., *Studies Subsidiary to the Works of Bishop Butler* (Oxford: Oxford University Press, 1896).

    *The Romanes Lecture, 1892, An Academic Sketch delivered in the Sheldonian Theatre*, October. 24, 1892 (Oxford: Oxford University Press, 1892).

Goodwin, Michael (ed.), *Nineteenth-Century Opinion* (Harmondsworth: Penguin, 1951).

[Hamilton, Sir William], 'On the state of the English universities, with more especial reference to Oxford', *Edinburgh Review* June 1831, reprinted in Sir William Hamilton, *Discussions on Philosophy and Literature, Education and University Reform* (London: Longman, Brown, Green and Longmans, 1852), pp. 386–434.

Harrison, Frederic, *Autobiographic Memoirs*, 2 volumes (London: Macmillan, 1911).

    'Humanity: a dialogue', *Contemporary Review* 27 (1876), 862–85.

    'The religious and conservative aspects of positivism', *Contemporary Review* 26 (1875), 992–1012, and 27 (1875–6), 140–59.

Harrison, Hall, *Was the Revised Constitution of the Diocese Legally Approved? Or is it Null and Void? A Letter to the Right Reverend William Woodruff Niles, D. D., Bishop of New Hampshire* (Boston: Williams, 1879).

Hobhouse, L. T., and Hammond, J. L., *Lord Hobhouse: A Memoir* (London: Arnold, 1905).

Hutton, William Holden (ed.), *Letters of William Stubbs, Bishop of Oxford, 1825–1901* (London: Constable, 1904).

Jones, H. S., (ed.), *Comte: Early Political Writings* (Cambridge: Cambridge University Press, 1998).

Kenny, Anthony (ed.), *The Oxford Diaries of Arthur Hugh Clough* (Oxford: Clarendon, 1990).

Lowe, Robert, *Middle Class Education. Endowment or Free Trade?* (London: Bush, 1868).

Matheson, P. E., *The Life of Hastings Rashdall D. D.* (London: Oxford University Press, 1928).

Matthew, H. C. G. (ed.), *The Gladstone Diaries*, vols. VIII and IX (Oxford: Oxford University Press, 1982–6).

Meyrick, Frederick, *Memories of Life at Oxford, and Experiences in Italy, Greece, Turkey, Germany, Spain, and Elsewhere* (London: Murray, 1905).

Mill, John Stuart, 'Endowments', in *Essays on Economics and Society*, ed.
J. M. Robson, vol. II (vol. V of the Collected Works of John Stuart Mill),
(London: Routledge & Kegan Paul, 1967), 613–29.

'Inaugural Address Delivered to the University of St. Andrews', in Mill, *Essays
on Equality, Law, and Education*, ed. John M. Robson (vol. XXI of the
*Collected Works of John Stuart Mill* (London: Routledge & Kegan Paul,
1984), 217–57.

*A System of Logic Ratiocinative and Inductive*, 2 vols. (vols. VII & VIII of the
*Collected Works of John Stuart Mill* (Toronto: University of Toronto Press,
1974).

Mineka, Francis E., and Lindley, Dwight N. (eds.), *The Later Letters of John Stuart
Mill 1849–1873*, 4 vols. (vols. XIV–XVII of the *Collected Works of John Stuart
Mill*) (London: Routledge & Kegan Paul, 1972).

Morison, James Cotter, 'Mark Pattison. In Memoriam', *Macmillan's Magazine* 50
(October 1884), 401–8.

Morley, John, *On Compromise* (London: Macmillan, 1888).

'On Pattison's *Memoirs*', *Macmillan's Magazine*, April 1885, reprinted in his
*Critical Miscellanies* (London: Macmillan, 1908–9) vol. III, 133–73.

*Recollections*, 2 vols. (London: Macmillan, 1917).

Newman, John Henry, *Apologia pro vita sua*, ed. Ian Ker (Harmondsworth:
Penguin, 1994).

*The Idea of a University Defined and Illustrated*, ed. I. T. Ker (Oxford:
Clarendon, 1976).

Oliphant, Mrs, *A Memoir of the Life of John Tulloch, DD, LLD.* (Edinburgh &
London: Blackwood, 1888).

Perry, Walter C., *German University Education*, 2nd edn (London: Longmans,
1846).

Raitt, Robert S. (ed.), *Memorials of Albert Venn Dicey* (London: Macmillan, 1925).

Rousseau, Jean-Jacques, *Confessions*, trans. J. M. Cohen (London: Penguin, 1953).

Sayce, A. H., *Reminiscences* (London: Macmillan, 1923).

Sidgwick, Henry, *The Ethics of Conformity and Subscription* (London: Williams
and Norgate, 1870).

*Miscellaneous Essays and Addresses* (London: Macmillan, 1904).

Smith, Adam, *An Inquiry into the Nature and Causes of the Wealth of Nations*,
R. H. Campbell, A. S. Skinner & W. B. Todd (eds.) (Oxford: Oxford
University Press, 1976).

Smith, Goldwin, *Reminiscences*, ed. Arnold Haultain (New York: Macmillan, 1910).

*The Reorganization of the University of Oxford* (Oxford and London:
Parker, 1868).

Spencer, Herbert, 'The Man versus the State', in his *Social Statics, abridged and
revised; together with The Man versus the State* (London: Williams and
Norgate, 1892).

*The Principles of Sociology* (London: Williams and Norgate, 1882), vol. II.

Stephen, Leslie, *History of English Thought in the Eighteenth Century*, 2 vols.
(London: Smith, Elder & Co., 1876).

Taine, Hippolyte, *H. Taine. Sa Vie et sa Correspondance*, vol. III 3rd edn (Paris: Hachette, 1908).

Thom, John Hamilton, (ed.), *The Life of the Rev Joseph Blanco White written by himself with Portions of his Correspondence* (London: John Chapman, 1845).

Tocqueville, Alexis de, *Democracy in America*, edited by J. P. Mayer and translated by George Lawrence (London: Fontana, 1994).

Tollemache, L. A., 'Recollections of Pattison', in Tollemache, *Stones of Stumbling*, 2nd edn (London: William Rice, 1885), 119–203.

Tuckwell, William, *Reminiscences of Oxford* (London & New York: Cassell, 1900).

Ward, Mrs Humphry (ed.), *Amiel's Journal. The Journal Intime of Henri-Frédéric Amiel* (London: Macmillan, 1885).

Ward, Mrs Humphry, *A Writer's Recollections (1856–1900)* (London: Collins, 1918).
*Robert Elsmere* (Edinburgh: Nelson, 1952).

SECONDARY SOURCES

Allen, Peter, 'The meanings of "an intellectual": nineteenth- and twentieth-century English usage', *University of Toronto Quarterly* 55 (1986), 342–58.

Altholz, Josef L., *Anatomy of a Controversy: the debate over 'Essays and Reviews', 1860–1864* (Aldershot: Scolar 1994).
'Periodical origins & implications of *Essays and Reviews*', *Victorian Periodicals Newsletter* 10 (1977), 140–54.

Altick, Richard D., *The English Common Reader. A Social History of the Mass Reading Public 1800–1900* (Chicago & London: University of Chicago Press, 1957).
'The sociology of authorship: the social origins, education and occupations of 1,100 British writers, 1800–1935', *Bulletin of the New York Public Library* 66 (1962), 389–404.

Anderson, Perry, 'Components of the national culture', *New Left Review* no. 50 (July–August 1968), 3–57.

Anderson, R. D., *European Universities from the Enlightenment to 1914* (Oxford: Oxford University Press, 2004).

Annan, Noel, *The Dons: Mentors, Eccentrics and Geniuses* (London: HarperCollins, 1999).
*Leslie Stephen: The Godless Victorian* (London: Weidenfeld and Nicolson, 1984).

Askwith, Betty, *Lady Dilke: A Biography* (London: Chatto & Windus, 1969).

Bebbington, David, *Holiness in Nineteenth-Century England* (Carlisle: Paternoster, 2000).

Benda, Julien, *La Trahison des clercs* (Paris: Grasset, 1927).

Betjeman, John, *Summoned by Bells: A Verse Autobiography* (London: Murray, 2001).

Bevington, Merle Mowbray, *The Saturday Review 1855–1868: Representative Educated Opinion in Victorian England* (New York: Columbia University Press, 1941).

Bill, E. G. W., *University Reform in Nineteenth-Century Oxford: A Study of Henry Halford Vaughan 1811–1885* (Oxford: Clarendon, 1973).

Brilioth, *The Anglican Revival. Studies in the Oxford Movement* (London, New York & Toronto: Longmans, Green, 1933).

Brink, C. O., *English Classical Scholarship: Historical Reflections on Bentley, Porson, and Housman* (Cambridge: Clarke, 1985).

Brock, M. G., and Curthoys, M. C., (eds.), *Nineteenth-Century Oxford*, Parts 1 and 2 (Volumes VI–VII of *The History of the University of Oxford*) (Oxford: Oxford University Press, 1997–2000).

Calder, William M. III, and Kramer, Daniel J., *An Introductory Bibliography to the History of Classical Scholarship Chiefly the XIXth and XXth Centuries* (Hildesheim, Zurich and New York: Georg Olms, 1992).

Capaldi, Nicholas, *John Stuart Mill: A Biography* (Cambridge: Cambridge University Press, 2004).

Chadwick, Owen, *From Bossuet to Newman: The Idea of Doctrinal Development* (Cambridge: Cambridge University Press, 1957).

*The Secularization of the European Mind in the Nineteenth Century* (Cambridge: Cambridge University Press, 1975).

*The Victorian Church*, 2 vols. (London: Black, 1966–70).

Church, R. W., *The Oxford Movement: Twelve Years 1833–1845* (London: Macmillan, 1904).

Clayton, Ruth, 'W. E. Gladstone: an annotation key', *Notes and Queries* 246 (N. S. 48) (June 2001), 140–3.

Cockshut, A. O. J., *The Art of Autobiography in 19th and 20th Century England* (New Haven & London: Yale University Press, 1984).

Collini, Stefan, 'The idea of "character" in Victorian political thought', *Transactions of the Royal Historical Society* 5th series 35 (1985), 29–50.

*Arnold* (Oxford: Oxford University Press, 1988).

*Public Moralists: Political Thought and Intellectual Life in Britain 1850–1930* (Oxford: Oxford University Press, 1991).

'The ordinary experience of civilized life: Sidgwick's politics and the method of reflective analysis', in Bart Schultz (ed.), *Essays on Henry Sidgwick* (Cambridge: Cambridge University Press, 1992), pp. 333–67.

*Absent Minds: Intellectuals in Britain* (Oxford: Oxford University Press, 2006).

Cowling, Maurice, *Religion and Public Doctrine in Modern England.* Volume III: *Accommodations* (Cambridge: Cambridge University Press, 2001).

Culler, A. Dwight, *The Imperial Intellect: A Study of Newman's Educational Ideal* (New Haven: Yale University Press, 1955).

Daunton, Martin (ed.), *The Organisation of Knowledge in Victorian Britain* (Oxford: Oxford University Press, 2005).

Delafons, John, *Politics and Preservation: A Policy History of the Built Heritage 1882–1996* (London: Spon, 1997).

Dessain, C. S., *John Henry Newman*, 3rd edn. (Oxford: Oxford University Press, 1980).

Dockhorn, Klaus, *Der deutsche Historismus in England* (Göttingen: Vandenhoeck and Ruprecht, 1950).

Dowling, Linda, *Hellenism and Homosexuality in Victorian Oxford* (London: Cornell University Press, 1994).

Duxbury, Neil, *Frederick Pollock and the English Juristic Tradition* (Oxford: Oxford University Press, 2004).

Eisenach, Eldon, 'Mill's reform liberalism as tradition and culture', *Political Science Reviewer* 24 (1995), 71–146.

Ellis, Ieuan, *Seven Against Christ: a study of 'Essays and Reviews'* (Leiden: Brill, 1980).

Engel, A. J., *From Clergyman to Don: The Rise of an Academic Profession in Nineteenth-Century Oxford* (Oxford: Oxford University Press, 1983).

Faber, Geoffrey, *Oxford Apostles: A Character Study of the Oxford Movement* (London: Faber and Faber, 1933).

Forbes, Duncan, *The Liberal Anglican Idea of History* (Cambridge: Cambridge University Press, 1952).

Francis, Mark, 'The origins of *Essays and Reviews*: an interpretation of Mark Pattison in the 1850s', *Historical Journal* 17 (1974), 797–812.

Fuchs, Eckhardt, *Henry Thomas Buckle: Geschichtschreibung und Positivismus in England und Deutschland* (Leipzig: Leipziger Universitätsverlag, 1994).

Ghosh, P. R., 'Macaulay and the heritage of the Enlightenment', *English Historical Review* 112 (1997), 358–95.

Goldman, Lawrence, 'The defection of the middle class: the Endowed Schools Act, the Liberal Party, and the 1874 election', in Peter Ghosh and Lawrence Goldman (eds.), *Politics and Culture in Victorian Britain: Essays in Memory of Colin Matthew* (Oxford: Oxford University Press, 2006), pp. 118–35.

Grafton, Anthony, 'Mark Pattison', *American Scholar* 52 (Spring 1983), 229–36.

Green, V. H. H., *Oxford Common Room: A Study of Lincoln College and Mark Pattison* (London: Arnold, 1957).

  *The Commonwealth of Lincoln College* (Oxford: Oxford University Press, 1979).

  *Love in a Cool Climate: The Letters of Mark Pattison and Meta Bradley 1879–1884* (Oxford: Oxford University Press, 1985).

Grimley, Matthew, 'Civil society and the clerisy: Christian elites and national culture, c. 1930–1950', in Jose Harris (ed.), *Civil Society in British History: Ideas, Identities, Institutions* (Oxford: Oxford University Press, 2003), pp. 231–47.

Gross, John, *The Rise and Fall of the Man of Letters: Aspects of English Literary Life since 1800* (London: Weidenfeld, 1969).

Gwynn, Stephen, *Saints and Scholars* (London: Thornton Butterworth, 1929), pp. 81–114.

Haig, A. G. L., 'The church, the universities and learning in later Victorian England', *Historical Journal* 29 (1986), 187–201.

Halsey, A. H., *Decline of Donnish Dominion: The British Academic Professions in the Twentieth Century* (Oxford: Oxford University Press, 1992).

  'Pattison: a prophet in need of rediscovery', *Times Higher Education Supplement* 18 January 1974, p. 2.

Harrison, Brian, (ed.), *The Twentieth Century* (Volume VIII of *The History of the University of Oxford*) (Oxford: Oxford University Press, 1994).

Harvie, Christopher, *The Lights of Liberalism. University Liberals and the Challenge of Democracy 1860–86* (London: Allen Lane, 1976).

Hayek, F. A., *John Stuart Mill and Harriet Taylor: Their Friendship and Subsequent Marriage* (London: Routledge & Kegan Paul, 1951).

Hewitt, Martin (ed.), *Scholarship in Victorian Britain*, Leeds Working Papers in Victorian Studies volume I (Leeds: Leeds Centre for Victorian Studies, 1998).

Heyck, T. W., *The Transformation of Intellectual Life in Victorian England* (London: Croom Helm, 1982).

Hilton, Boyd, 'Manliness, masculinity and the mid-Victorian temperament', in Lawrence Goldman (ed.), *The Blind Victorian: Henry Fawcett and British Liberalism* (Cambridge: Cambridge University Press, 1989), pp. 60–70.

Hirst, F. W., *Early Life and Letters of John Morley* (London: Macmillan, 1927).

Hoare, Joyce, 'Mark Pattison 1813–1884: a bibliography of his published works', University of London Dip. Lib. thesis, 1953.

Hofstetter, Michael J., *The Romantic Idea of a University: England and Germany, 1770–1850* (Basingstoke: Palgrave, 2001).

Holt, Richard, *Sport and the British: A Modern History* (Oxford: Oxford University Press, 1989).

Houghton, Walter E., 'Periodical literature and the articulate classes', in Joanne Shattock and Michael Wolff (eds.), *The Victorian Periodical Press: Samplings and Soundings* (Leicester: Leicester University Press, 1982), 3–27.

Israel, Kali, *Names and Stories: Emilia Dilke and Victorian Culture* (Oxford: Oxford University Press, 1999).

Jackson, W. W., 'Ingram Bywater 1840–1914', *Proceedings of the British Academy* 7 (1915–16), 521–32.

Jocelyn, H. D., 'C. O. Brink and Liverpool,' *Liverpool Classical Monthly* 19 (1994), 37–55.

Jones, H. S., *Victorian Political Thought* (Basingstone: Macmillan, 2000).

Kelley, Donald R., *The Descent of Ideas: The History of Intellectual History* (Aldershot: Ashgate, 2002).

Kenny, Anthony, *Arthur Hugh Clough: A Poet's Life* (London: Continuum, 2005).

Kent, Christopher, *Brains and Numbers: Elitism, Comtism, and Democracy in Mid-Victorian England* (Toronto, Buffalo & London: University of Toronto Press, 1978).

Ker, Ian, *John Henry Newman: A Biography* (Oxford: Oxford University Press, 1988).

Kijinski, John L., 'John Morley's "English Men of Letters" series and the politics of reading', *Victorian Studies* 34 (1991), 205–25.

'Professionalism, authority, and the late-Victorian man of letters: a view from the Macmillan archive', *Victorian Literature and Culture* 24 (1996), 229–47.

Levine, Philippa, ' "So few prizes and so many blanks": marriage and feminism in later nineteenth-century Britain', *Journal of British Studies* 28 (1989), 150–74.

Lloyd-Jones, Hugh, *Blood for the Ghosts: Classical Influences in the Nineteenth and Twentieth Centuries* (London: Duckworth, 1982).

*Classical Survivals. The Classics in the Modern World* (London: Duckworth, 1982).

Lowe, John, *The Warden: A Portrait of John Sparrow* (London: HarperCollins, 1998).

Mangan, J. A., ' "Oars and the Man": pleasure and purpose in Victorian and Edwardian Cambridge', *British Journal of Sports History* 1 (1984), 263–71.

Matthew, H. C. G., *Gladstone 1809–1874* (Oxford: Oxford University Press, 1988).

Momigliano, Arnaldo, 'Jacob Bernays', *Koninklijke Nederlandse Akademie van Wetenschappen*, n. s. 32, no. 5 (1969), 151–78, reprinted in A. D. Momigliano, *Studies on Modern Scholarship*, eds. G. W. Bowersock and T. J. Cornell (London: University of California Press, 1994), pp. 121–46.

Montague, Francis Charles, 'Some early letters of Mark Pattison', *Bulletin of the John Rylands Library* 18 (1934), 156–76.

Morley, John, *The Life of William Ewart Gladstone* (London: Macmillan, 1905) vol. II.

Murphy, G. Martin, 'White, Joseph Blanco (1775–1841)', *Oxford Dictionary of National Biography* (Oxford: Oxford University Press, 2004).

Newsome, David, *Godliness & Good Learning: Four Studies on a Victorian Ideal* (London: John Murray, 1961).

Nimmo, Duncan B., 'Mark Pattison and the dilemma of university examinations', in Roy MacLeod (ed.), *Days of Judgement: Science, Examinations and the Organization of Knowledge in late Victorian England* (Driffield: Nafferton Books, 1982), pp. 153–67.

'Learning against religion, learning as religion: Mark Pattison and the "Victorian crisis of faith" ', in Keith Robbins (ed.), *Religion and Humanism*: *Studies in Church History* 17 (1981), pp. 311–24.

'Towards and away from Newman's theory of doctrinal development: pointers from Mark Pattison in 1838 and 1846', *Journal of Theological Studies* N. S. 29 (1978), pp. 160–2.

Nockles, Peter Benedict, *The Oxford Movement in Context. Anglican High Churchmanship, 1760–1857* (Cambridge: Cambridge University Press, 1994).

'An academic counter-revolution: Newman and Tractarian Oxford's idea of a university', *History of Universities* 10 (1991), pp. 137–97.

Nolan, F., 'A study of Mark Pattison's religious experience 1813–1850', Oxford University D. Phil thesis, 1978.

Nuttall, A. D., *Dead from the Waist Down: Scholars and Scholarship in Literature and the Popular Imagination* (New Haven & London: Yale University Press, 2003).

Oakeshott, Michael, 'Rationalism in politics', in his *Rationalism in Politics and Other Essays* (London: Methuen, 1967), pp. 1–36.

O'Donnell, James J., *Augustine, Sinner and Saint: A New Biography* (London: Profile, 2005).

Peterson, William S., 'Gladstone's review of *Robert Elsmere*: some unpublished correspondence', *Review of English Studies* n. s. 21 (1970), 442–61.

*Victorian Heretic: Mrs Humphry Ward's Robert Elsmere* (Leicester: Leicester University Press, 1976).

Pfeiffer, Rudolf, *History of Classical Scholarship: from the beginnings to the end of the Hellenistic Age* (Oxford: Clarendon, 1968).

*History of Classical Scholarship from 1300 to 1850* (Oxford: Clarendon, 1976).

Pitts, Jennifer, 'Legislator of the world? A rereading of Bentham on colonies', *Political Theory* 31 (2003), 200–34.

Roberts, Nathan, 'Character in the mind: citizenship, education and psychology in Britain, 1880–1914', *History of Education* 33 (2004), 177–97.

Robertson, J. M., *Buckle and his Critics: A Study in Sociology* (London: Swan Sonnenschein, 1895).

Roll-Hansen, Diderick, *The Academy, 1869–1879: Victorian Intellectuals in Revolt* (Copenhagen: Rosenkilde and Bagger 1957).

Roper, Michael, and Tosh, John (eds.), *Manful Assertions: Masculinities in Britain since 1800* (London: Routledge, 1991).

Rose, Phyllis, *Parallel Lives: Five Victorian Marriages* (Harmondsworth: Penguin, 1983).

Rothblatt, Sheldon, 'The limbs of Osiris: liberal education in the English-speaking world', in Sheldon Rothblatt and Björn Wittrock (eds.), *The European and American University since 1800: Historical and Sociological Essays* (Cambridge: Cambridge University Press, 1993), pp. 19–73.

*The Revolution of the Dons: Cambridge and Society in Victorian England* (London: Faber and Faber, 1968).

*Tradition and Change in English Liberal Education: An Essay in History and Culture* (London: Faber and Faber, 1976).

Rothblatt, Sheldon, and Trow, Martin, 'Government policies and higher education: a comparison of Britain and the United States, 1630–1860', in Colin Crouch and Anthony Heath (eds.), *Social Research and Social Reform: Essays in Honour of A. H. Halsey* (Oxford: Clarendon, 1992), pp. 173–215.

Rowell, Geoffrey, Stevenson, Kenneth, and Williams, Rowan, (eds.), *Love's Redeeming Work. The Anglican Quest for Holiness* (Oxford: Oxford University Press, 2001).

Rüegg, Walter (ed.), *Universities in the Nineteenth and Early Twentieth Centuries* (Volume III of *A History of the University in Europe* (Cambridge: Cambridge University Press, 2004).

Ryan, Alan, *J. S. Mill* (London: Routledge and Kegan Paul, 1974).

Sadleir, Michael, *Michael Ernest Sadler (Sir Michael Sadler K. C. S. I.) 1861–1943. A Memoir by his Son* (London: Constable, 1949).

St Aubyn, Giles, *A Victorian Eminence: The Life and Work of Henry Thomas Buckle* (London: Barrie, 1958).

Schalenberg, Marc, *Humboldt auf Reisen? Die Rezeption des 'deutschen Universitätsmodells' in den französischen und britischen Reformdiskursen (1810–1870)* (Basel: Schwabe, 2002).

'Die Rezeption des deutschen Universitätsmodells in Oxford 1850–1914', in Rudolf Muhs, Johannes Paulmann and Willibald Steinmetz (eds.), *Aneignung und Abwehr. Interkultureller Transfer zwischen Deutschland und Großbritannien* (Bodenheim: Philo, 1998), pp. 198–22.

Schmidt, James, 'Inventing the Enlightenment: Anti-Jacobins, British Hegelians, and the *Oxford English Dictionary*', *Journal of the History of Ideas* 64 (2003), 421–43.

Schmidt, James (ed.), *What is Enlightenment? Eighteenth-Century Answers and Twentieth-Century Questions* (Berkeley and Los Angeles: University of California Press, 1996).

Schultz, Bart, *Henry Sidgwick: Eye of the Universe* (Cambridge: Cambridge University Press, 2004).

Semmel, Bernard, 'H. T. Buckle: the liberal faith and the science of history', *British Journal of Sociology* 27 (1976), 370–86.

Shannon, Richard, *Gladstone and the Bulgarian Agitation* (London: Nelson, 1963).

Shea, Victor, and Whitla, William (eds.), *Essays and Reviews. The 1860 Text and its Reading* (Charlottesville and London: University Press of Virginia, 2000).

Slee, Peter R. H., *Liberal and a Liberal Education. The Study of Modern History in the Universities of Oxford, Cambridge and Manchester 1800–1914* (Manchester: Manchester University Press, 1986).

'The Oxford idea of a liberal education 1800–1860: the invention of tradition and the manufacture of practice', *History of Universities* 7 (1988), 61–87.

Small, Ian, *Conditions for Criticism: Authority, Knowledge, and Literature in the Late Nineteenth Century* (Oxford: Clarendon Press, 1991).

Sparrow, John, *Mark Pattison and the Idea of a University* (Cambridge: Cambridge University Press, 1967).

Stelzig, Eugene L., *The Romantic Subject in Autobiography: Rousseau and Goethe* (Charlottesville and London: University Press of Virginia, 2000).

Stone, Lawrence, 'The size and composition of the Oxford student body 1580–1910', in Lawrence Stone (ed.), *The University in Society* (Princeton and London: Princeton University Press, 1974), vol. I, pp. 3–110.

Stray, Christopher, 'From one museum to another: the *Museum Criticum* (1813–26) and the *Philological Museum* (1831–33)', *Victorian Periodicals Review* 37 (2004), 289–314.

'From oral to written examinations: Cambridge, Oxford and Dublin, 1700–1914', *History of Universities* 20/2 (2005), 76–130.

Stuchtey, Benedikt, and Wende, Peter (eds.), *British and German Historiography 1750–1950: Traditions, Perceptions, and Transfers* (Oxford: Oxford University Press, 2000).

Sturrock, John, *The Language of Autobiography. Studies in the First Person Singular* (Cambridge: Cambridge University Press, 1993).

Sutcliffe, Peter, *The Oxford University Press: An Informal History* (Oxford: Clarendon, 1978).

Sutherland, John, *Mrs Humphry Ward: Eminent Victorian, Pre-eminent Edwardian* (Oxford: Oxford University Press, 1990).

Tosh, John, 'Gentlemanly politeness and manly simplicity in Victorian England', *Transactions of the Royal Historical Society* 6th series 12 (2002), 455–72.

*A Man's Place: Masculinity and the Middle-Class Home in Victorian England* (London: Yale University Press, 1999).

Tuke, Margaret J., *A History of Bedford College for Women 1849–1937* (London: Oxford University Press, 1939).

Turner, Frank M., *Contesting Cultural Authority: Essays in Victorian Intellectual Life* (Cambridge: Cambridge University Press, 1993).

*John Henry Newman: The Challenge to Evangelical Religion* (New Haven and London: Yale University Press, 2002).

Turner, R. Steven, 'The Prussian universities and the concept of research', *Internationales Archiv für Sozialgeschichte der deutschen Literatur* 5 (1980), 68–93.

Varouxakis, Georgios, *Victorian Political Thought on France and the French* (Basingstoke: Palgrave, 2002).

Virgin, Peter, *The Church in an Age of Negligence: Ecclesiastical Structure and Problems of Church Reform 1700–1840* (Cambridge: James Clarke, 1989).

Vogeler, Martha S., *Frederic Harrison: The Vocations of a Positivist* (Oxford: Oxford University Press, 1984).

'More light on *Essays & Reviews*: the rôle of Frederic Harrison', *Victorian Periodicals Review* 12 (1979), 105–16.

Wach, Howard M., 'A "still, small voice" from the pulpit: religion and the creation of social morality in Manchester, 1820–1850', *Journal of Modern History* 63 (1991), 425–56.

Walcott, F. G., *The Origins of "Culture and Anarchy": Matthew Arnold and Popular Education* (Toronto: University of Toronto Press, 1970).

Ward, W. R., *Victorian Oxford* (London & Edinburgh: Frank Cass, 1965).

Watters, Tamie, 'An Oxford provocation and caricature: Rhoda Broughton and Mark Pattison', *Encounter* 36.4 (April 1971), 34–42.

Weisz, George, *The Emergence of Modern Universities in France, 1863–1914* (Princeton: Princeton University Press, 1983).

Wheatcroft, Geoffrey, 'A lazy life lived grandly', *New Statesman*, 25 September 1998.

Whyte, William, 'The intellectual aristocracy revisited', *Journal of Victorian Culture* 10 (2005), 15–45.

Willey, Basil, *More Nineteenth Century Studies. A Group of Honest Doubters* (London: Chatto & Windus, 1963).

Wilson, A. N., *God's Funeral* (London: Murray, 1999).

Woodfield, Malcolm, 'Victorian weekly reviews and reviewing after 1860: R. H. Hutton and the *Spectator*', *Yearbook of English Studies* 16 (1986), 74–91.

Young, B. W., 'Knock-kneed giants: Victorian representations of eighteenth-century thought', in Jane Garnett and Colin Matthew (eds.), *Revival and Religion since 1700: Essays for John Walsh*, (London: Hambledon, 1993), pp. 79–93.

Young, G. M., *Victorian England: Portrait of an Age* (London: Oxford University Press, 1936).

# Index